ALL ABOUT BRAISING

Color Photographs by Gentl & Hyers / Edge

Black-and-White Illustrations by Yevgeniy Solovyev

Wine Notes and Selections by Tim Gaiser

ALL ABOUT BRAISING

The Art of Uncomplicated Cooking

MOLLY STEVENS

W. W. NORTON & COMPANY | NEW YORK LONDON

For information about permission to reproduce selections from this book, write to
Permissions, W. W. Norton & Company, Inc., 500 Fifth Avenue, New York, NY 10110

Manufacturing by Maple-Vail Book Manufacturing Group
Book design by Barbara M. Bachman
Production managers: Andrew Marasia and Julia Druskin

Library of Congress Cataloging-in-Publication Data

Stevens, Molly.
All about braising : the art of uncomplicated cooking / Molly Stevens ; color
photographs by Gentl & Hyers/Edge ; black-and-white illustrations by Yevgeniy
Solovyev ; wine notes and selections by Tim Gaiser.— 1st ed.
p. cm.
Includes bibliographical references and index.
ISBN 0-393-05230-3 (hardcover)
1. Braising (Cookery) I. Title.
    TX686.S74 2004
    641.7'7—dc22

                                                    2004017907

W. W. Norton & Company, Inc., 500 Fifth Avenue, New York, N.Y. 10110
                www.wwnorton.com

W. W. Norton & Company Ltd., Castle House, 75/76 Wells Street, London W1T 3QT

1 2 3 4 5 6 7 8 9 0

This book is dedicated to Chef Chambrette

who taught me so much more than I ever dreamed—

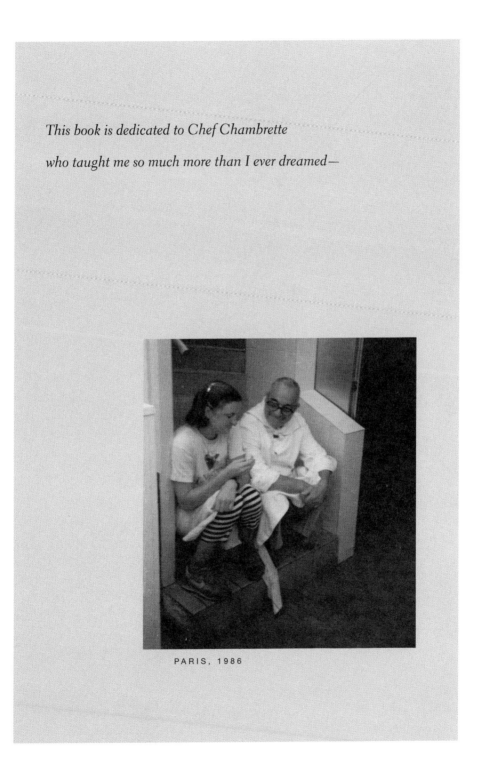

PARIS, 1986

CONTENTS

A C K N O W L E D G M E N T S

I would like to raise a glass to the many generous and extraordinary people who helped bring this book to the table. I feel incredibly fortunate to count you as friends, colleagues, and advisers. Here's to you!

First, I offer my sincere thanks to all of you who shared recipes, answered questions, tasted, tested, and generally cheered me on. In particular, I am grateful to Amy Albert, Jennifer Armentrout, Steve Bogart, Annie Copps, Abby Dodge, Maryellen Driscoll, Doralece Dullaghan, Cynthia Cromwell Fallen, Sarah Jay, Barbara Haber, Martha Holmberg, Fran McCullough, Susie Middleton, Randall Price, Gérard Rubaud, Robin Schempp, Steve Schimoler, Ari Weinzweig, Anne Willan, and Daphne Zepos.

A big debt of gratitude goes to Judy Rodgers and Sam Hayward, who so generously welcomed me into their kitchens (Zuni Café and Fore Street Grill, respectively) when I was floundering and just needed to cook. Thanks also to Debbie Funkhouser for digging through old texts at the Schlesinger Library on my behalf. And to Nancy Harmon Jenkins for taking the time to set me straight on a few details of Italian cooking. A special thanks to my brother, Reed, and his wife, Carolyn, for being my braising sleuths in western New York and for falling head-over-heels for the Caribbean Pork Shoulder. And to Ron Savenor at Savenor's Market in Boston for his help unraveling the mysteries of meat.

To my recipe testers: the incomparable Didi Davis who bailed me out of more than a few tough spots and solved many of my biggest recipe riddles; to Mariana Velasquez, whose company I enjoyed in the kitchen on many long Saturday afternoons; to Kate Hays, whom I admire for the calm and confident way she approaches cooking; and to Charlie Hays, who jumped in at the end for several last-minute run-throughs. Thank you all for making sure that my recipes deliver.

One of my greatest pleasures in the process was observing the making of the beautiful photographs in the sure hands of the talented food-stylist Michael Pederson, and the equally gifted and amiable photography team of Andrea Gentl and Marty Hyers. Greatest thanks to all of you along with your fabulous team, including Tracey Harlor, Yill Ruchala, Sabine Tucker (for those gorgeous props), Alethia Weingarten, and Kate Sears.

In addition to the great-looking photos, I feel so lucky to include the work of two first-rate contributors. Thank you to Tim Gaiser for the enlightened and thoughtful wine notes. And to Yevgeniy Solovyev for the beautiful illustrations.

Huge thanks go to the entire team at Norton for doing such a wonderful job at every step of the way. They include Julia Druskin, Andy Marasia, Debra Morton Hoyt, Nancy Palmquist, Don Rifkin, Susan Sanfrey, Louise Brockett, Bill Rusin, and Jeannie Luciano. Extra special thanks to Erik Johnson, whom I pestered with endless loose ends and last minute fixes. Never once did he falter or lose patience. And to Judith Sutton for her careful and astute copyediting. And to Barbara Bachman for the elegant design that brings it all together so perfectly.

This book would probably not exist if it weren't for the determination and dedication of my editor, Maria Guarnaschelli, who decided long before I did that I was up to the task. In addition to her encouragement, I am profoundly grateful to Maria for her thorough and intelligent editing and for truly caring about every detail at every pass.

Heartfelt thanks to Marian Young, my agent, counselor, and friend, who so gracefully looked after me during the making of this book. And to my dear friend Roy Finamore, who is always there when I most need help. There is no one I would rather share a kitchen with.

Finally, I am forever grateful to my entire family for their undying support and sincere interest, to Elizabeth for remaining my best friend for so long, and to Mark, for, well, everything.

WHY I COOK

A few years ago, my sister called and asked me to retrieve several storage boxes I had left in her attic and forgotten about. They had been sealed since 1982, when we moved out of our family house sometime after I graduated from college. Most of the boxes contained childhood memorabilia—baby book, report cards, class pictures—but there was one item that uncannily prophesized what I would do with my future. It was a cassette with no label and no case. When I plugged it into my tape player, a world of memories flooded back.

I recorded the tape when I was about nine years old. At the time, I was completely obsessed with Harriet the Spy, the feisty heroine of a 1960s children's book. In my role as Harriet, I would go around the house recording conversations, and on this particular occasion, I had taped the entirety of my father's birthday dinner. As I listened to the recording more than thirty years later, I heard the young voices of all six members of my family—my parents, my two brothers, my sister, and myself—engaged in animated discussion about the day, our lives, and whatever else each of us wanted to share. There was some teasing, some scolding, and requests for seconds, but most of the hour-long recording is taken up with a lively exchange of thoughts and feelings among the six of us around the table. My father tells about an incident at his office that day, my older brother goes on about wanting to get his driver's license, my sister recites the words to a new cheer she learned, my mother tells us how someone we know is adopting a baby, and my little brother asks why anyone would give away their baby. There's also an off-key but spirited rendition of "Happy Birthday," but what is remarkable about the conversation is not the fact that it was my father's birthday, but that it represented what occurred at our house most every night of every week.

As far back as I can remember, my entire family sat down together for dinner. My parents believed strongly in the sanctity of the dinner hour, and they decided early on to commit to bringing us all around the table, no matter how busy our lives became. It's the way they'd both been raised, and they were convinced that it was key to building a strong family. To this day, I have no doubt that this is why all of us remain close in spite of geography, careers, and families of our own. It's also why we still end up congregating around the table whenever we get together, and why we rarely get up from one meal until we've decided on where and when the next will occur. It's where we connect.

Ours was a traditional household, with my father working hard as a lawyer to support a big family and my mother assuming the care of the children and the house, as well as many volunteer activities. There were only six years age difference between the oldest and youngest of us four kids, so things were hectic—school, homework, sports, music lessons, Boy Scouts, friends, and chores, as well as a dog, a cat or two, and a neighborhood full of other families. Yet somehow, in the midst of all this coming and going, my mother managed to put a hot meal on the table every night and gracefully wrangle us all to sit down together to eat.

In addition to the six of us, there were frequent guests—friends from school, foreign students from the university, colleagues of my father's, a stray cousin or neighborhood kid. My father always sat at the head of the table and served the main course, which often meant carving. Then we passed the plates to my mother at the other end of the table, who served up the vegetables. Once everyone was served, my father would call on one of us to say a quick grace, and then the eating and conversation would begin. Everyone was expected to contribute to the discourse, even if it was as simple as sharing something that happened that day.

I think now that pursuing a career in cooking has always been the means to get back to the feeling of closeness and sharing that I experienced around the dining room table of my childhood. For instance, when I first lived in Paris in my twenties after college, my friends and I would gather for a meal and end up sitting at the table for hours, eating, drinking wine, telling stories, debating, laughing, and carrying on. I remember thinking, "This is it. This is how I want to live my life. This is where I am at home."

By cooking, I know that the dining table is never far from the kitchen, and there is always the chance to invite others to share in a meal and conversation. In spite of the many rewarding years I've spent cooking in professional kitchens, I'm happiest at home (mine or someone else's) when everyone takes the time to sit down to eat together and to engage in some kind of discourse. I'm also happiest when the food that we sit down to share is tasty and satisfying, which is why I took the time to learn how to really cook in the first place and why I devote myself to teaching others today. Knowing how to cook gives you the means to bring people together.

After years of cooking everything from burgers and pizza to bouillabaisse and *tournedos Rossini*, I've learned that the technique of braising produces food that draws people together like no other. Sharing a meal from one pot, as you often do with a braise, creates a feeling of communality that leads to sharing a congenial meal. The warmth of the pot from the oven, the concentrated aromas of slow-cooked meat (or poultry or fish or vegetables), the tender textures, and the deep flavors all contribute to set people at ease. Plus, the uncomplicated nature of braising is easy on the cook. Once you master a few basic techniques, there's little that can go wrong. Everyone feels more at home than they would if you were to fuss with a fancy, individually plated meal. It's the kind of food that makes us remember the comfort of childhood, whether we ate braised foods or not.

In writing this cookbook, I've looked for inspiration in all corners of the world, from near and far, from humble to elaborate, and from the classic to the exotic. Some of the ingredients and recipes may not be ones you've seen before, but the satisfaction of the finished dishes will be as familiar as your mother's pot roast. I invite you to cook your way through my book, to improvise as inspiration strikes, and to gather your friends and family around your table to share the results.

ALL ABOUT BRAISING

THE PRINCIPLES OF BRAISING

Braise tr. v.   To cook (meat or vegetables) by browning in fat, then simmering in a small quantity of liquid in a covered container [French *braiser*, from *braise*, hot charcoal, from Old French *brese*, from Germanic *bhreu*: to boil, bubble, effervesce, burn; with derivatives referring to cooking and brewing].

—*The American Heritage Dictionary*

Braising   A method of cooking food in a closed vessel with very little liquid at a low temperature and for a long time.

—*Larousse Gastronmique*

Mention braising to a member of the general public and you might draw a blank. But go on to name some classic braised dishes (osso buco, short ribs, coq au vin, lamb shanks) and chances are you'll draw an expression of pleasure. The term *braising* may be somewhat less familiar than other cooking techniques, such as grilling, baking, or roasting, but braised dishes are among the most beloved recipes in any cook's repertoire.

At its most basic, braising refers to tucking a few ingredients into a heavy pot with a bit of liquid, covering the pot tightly, and letting everything simmer peacefully until tender and intensely flavored. The technique reaches back to the earliest days of cooking, when the braising pot would be buried in the embers of an open hearth or slid into the community bread oven after the day's baking and left to simmer slowly for hours. The miracle of braising lies in the fact that the process demands so little from the cook yet what actually occurs is quite complex and wonderful.

What Really Happens Under the Lid
of a Braising Pot

The best way to understand braising is to picture the exchange between the moisture in the food you're braising and the liquid in the pot. Whenever you cook fresh ingredients (such as meat, poultry, seafood, or vegetables), they release moisture. In sautéing and grilling, this produces the sizzle you hear. In braising, these juices are trapped in the sealed pot, so that they mingle with the braising liquid. The enriched braising liquid, in turn, bathes the food. It's a delicious cycle of flavor give-and-take between the braising liquid and the other ingredients inside the closed pot. Braising brings out a depth of flavor impossible in any other form of cooking. All this also yields a sauce rich with the essence of every ingredient you added to the pot.

For example, imagine placing a pot roast in a heavy braising pot, arranging a few chopped carrots, onions, and celery around it, adding a sprig or two of parsley, a bay leaf, and some salt and pepper, and then pouring over a little bit of red wine. Place the lid on the pot so you have a very tight seal, and slide the pot into a slow oven. As the liquid around the beef begins to simmer, it vaporizes into steam that swirls around the pot and begins to cook the beef and vegetables. As the beef and vegetables heat through, they release flavorful juices that combine with the wine. Soon the wine takes on the aromas of a beef-vegetable-herb broth. And this broth continues to simmer and steam to further cook the beef and vegetables. The beef takes on the flavor of the wine-based broth, the

Inside a Braising Pot

vegetables become infused with the flavor of beef and wine, and the braising liquid—which began as a few simple ounces of red wine—evolves into a complex sauce with nuances of beef, wine, carrots, onions, celery, and herbs. In the end, all the distinct flavoring characteristics meld and emerge as something truly greater than the sum of their parts.

Why Braised Meats and Vegetables Are So Remarkably Tender

Any discussion of the qualities of braised meats and vegetables invariably turns to the subject of the indescribable tenderness of these dishes. The reason for this is simple: moist, gentle heat melts the protein in meat known as *collagen*. Collagen is a strong, pliant tissue that connects muscle groups and provides flexibility. Certain cuts of meat (those from the well-worked areas of the shoulder, neck, breast, and leg) and young animals (primarily veal) contain high amounts of collagen. When cuts of meat are cooked to rare or even medium-rare (internal temperatures in the range of 125 to 140 degrees), the collagen remains elastic and fairly tough. Collagen doesn't begin to melt and give way until the meat reaches an internal temperature of around 200 degrees. Ordinarily this challenges a cook, because meat heated to internal temperatures in excess of 200 degrees will be quite overdone, stringy, and unpalatable. That is where braising comes in. By simmering meat gently in the moist environment of the braising pot, you are ensuring that the meat cooks slowly and is constantly bathed in flavorful juices. The meat will emerge well-done, but it will be tender and succulent throughout and surrounded by a velvety sauce. In addition, when collagen melts away, it turns to gelatin, a very soft protein that contributes a rich silky texture and thickness to the braising sauce.

Unlike roasting, grilling, and sautéing, where the window for doneness is a very narrow one—a few minutes too many, and the meat can be ruined—braising allows a much more forgiving time line. Foods cook slowly in a braising pot, and therefore they overcook slowly too. Because braising is gentle and slow, you are much less likely to race by the moment of perfect doneness. The temperature inside a braising pot is limited by the temperature of the simmering liquid (in the range of 185 to 200 degrees), so you can never achieve those high temperatures used for roasting and grilling (upward of 375 degrees). Certainly these high-heat methods of cooking have their place, but not when it comes to tough cuts of meat rich in collagen. The low temperature inside the braising pot is essential. That is why in the recipes in this book I remind you to check inside the pot to see that the liquid is not simmering too vigorously. If you find that it is, lower the oven heat to reduce the simmer to a peaceful one.

Mastering the Art of Braising

Braising is a building process. The cook adds layer upon layer of flavor, nuance, and character to a dish at each stage of the game. The basic technique can be broken down into a series of simple steps. If you are new to braising, follow the recipes in the book closely and pay attention to the headings in the procedures: "*browning the meat*," "*the aromatics*," "*the braising liquid*," "*the finish*," *etc.* They act as signposts to identify each stage. They provide first-hand knowledge of the process and the choices available as you go. What differentiates one braised recipe from the next are the ways in which the cook handles each and every stage. The more you braise, the more familiar you will become with the process. You will see how braising is a matter of making choices as you move through the stages. For instance, do you want to brown the meat before braising? Will you brown it in olive oil or butter? Will you add wine and stock to the pan for the braising liquid, or perhaps just wine? Do you include garlic or shallots? Or a few sprigs of rosemary? All of these little decisions add up to create unique and wonderful dishes. In the end, you'll learn that one of the greatest attributes of braising is that it is infinitely flexible and open to adaptation at every stage.

I invite you to read the following detailed explanation of each stage of braising. Armed with this knowledge, a world of braising awaits you.

Stage One

THE MAIN INGREDIENT

Selecting the main ingredient for a braise has everything to do with deciding what method you intend to use. *Long braising* is the more traditional approach: a tougher cut of meat (like short ribs, lamb shanks, or pork shoulder) simmers quietly for anywhere from 1 1/2 to 4 hours or more, until falling-apart tender. *Short braising* takes less than an hour and is reserved for more tender foods like cut-up chicken, seafood, and vegetables. Since these ingredients are not naturally tough, they don't rely on braising to tenderize them. But the process of short braising delivers the same complexity of flavor produced by the traditional long braise.

The Best Foods for Long Braising

The great advantage of long braising is its ability to tenderize even the toughest cuts of meat. Using this knowledge to your advantage in the kitchen, however, requires a quick lesson in anatomy. Food scientist Harold McGee summarizes what you need to know when he says, "the further away from hoof or horn, . . . the more tender the meat." This means that the hard-working shoulder, neck, breast, and leg muscles (those close to the hoof and horn) are going to be tough and gristly, while the less-exercised rib, loin, and saddle area will be tender. But what every good cook and food lover also knows is that tenderness and flavor have an inverse relationship. The more tender the cut, the less flavor it offers. Super-tender cuts such as tenderloin and loin steaks possess nowhere near the robust flavor of chuck roast, shoulder chops, or brisket. The other advantage of these tough cuts is that they typically cost less than the prized tender cuts. But these more rugged cuts must be handled properly by the cook, and this is where braising comes in. A long, gentle braise is the secret to revealing the true goodness of a tough cut of meat.

Understanding Why a Certain Cut of Meat Is Tough or Tender

There are two factors that affect the meat's texture. The first is the grain. Finely grained meat is tender, coarsely grained meat is tough. Meat is muscle, and as the muscles of a young animal develop and strengthen, they become larger and more coarsely grained. The stronger muscles, the ones an animal uses for moving about and chewing (those near the hoof and horn), contain the thickest fibers as a result. The next time you're at the meat case at the supermarket, hold a package of filet mignon in one hand and a chuck steak in the other. The filet will be smooth, very finely textured, and uninterrupted by any fat or gristle. The chuck steak, on the other hand, will be coarsely grained and mottled with bits of fat and probably some gristle.

The second factor contributing to meat's texture is collagen, a resilient protein that holds muscles together. All muscles contain some amount of collagen, often referred to as connective tissue, because collagen is what binds muscles to one another. The amount of collagen varies from cut to cut. It exists in highest concentration in the coarsely grained cuts from the shoulder, arm, neck, breast, and leg areas. Because tough cuts of meat contain a lot of collagen, they are excessively chewy if not properly cooked. When braised in a covered pot at a low temperature, however, the collagen dissolves and melts into gelatin, so the meat emerges fork-tender and the sauce possesses a remarkably smooth richness.

The best cuts for long braising, then, whether beef, veal, lamb, or pork, are the tougher, coarser-grained ones from the shoulder, breast, neck, and legs. Unfortunately, decoding the labels in the meat case often poses a few challenges since the system is neither straightforward nor consistent, differing from market to market and state to state. For instance, what some markets label as the *flat half* of a beef brisket other markets call *thin cut*. To help you sort through this maze, I've gone into more detail on specific cuts in the corresponding chapters.

In addition to meat, many heartier vegetables need the slow, steady heat of a long braise to emerge tender. Cabbage, celery, fennel, and root vegetables are a few prime examples.

The Best Foods for Short Braising

Determining what ingredients are best suited to short braising is not as clear-cut as with long braising. For instance, the indisputably best technique for cooking breast of veal or lamb shank is long braising. But what about chicken? Certainly if you roast, grill, or sauté chicken, and do so correctly, you will produce delectable results. Yet chicken—whole cut or cut into parts—also makes a great braise. This is where short braising comes in. The role of short braising is not to tenderize tough cuts of meat, but to bring out a depth of flavor not attainable through any other technique.

Short braising employs the same technique as a traditional long braise with one big difference: the amount of time the food braises. Since we're not relying on the braise to melt the collagen out of tough meat, a short braise takes only as long as needed to cook the food through—much like a roast—and to meld the flavor of the braising liquid with the other ingredients. Because the size and nature of the ingredients vary, a short braise can take as little as ten minutes for scallops or radishes, for example, and as long as an hour for a cut-up chicken. Generally, the foods best suited to short braising are poultry, seafood, and many vegetables.

I find short braising especially handy during the week, when I need to put dinner on the table and don't have the time to wait around. Many of the chicken recipes and almost all of the seafood recipes take under an hour to braise and make a deeply satisfying evening meal.

Stage Two

CHOOSING THE RIGHT BRAISING POT

The characteristics of a good braising pot, for either long or short braising, are that it is heavy (both the base and sides), that it holds the food snugly, that the sides are high enough to contain the liquid, and that the lid fits securely in place. (This last detail, the lid, is less critical than the others, as you can always fashion a lid out of foil.) Since many braising recipes involve browning the ingredients on the top of the stove and then transferring them to the oven, an ideal braising pot is both flameproof and ovenproof. If you cook at all, chances are you already own one or two pots that will fill the bill for the recipes in this book.

The Importance of the Weight of a Braising Pot

A braising pot needs to be heavy so that it conducts heat slowly and gently. The best braising pots are made of cast iron (some coated, some not). This very dense, very heavy metal is a slow conductor of heat. It does take a while to heat up, but once hot, it holds a gentle even heat, which is ideal for keeping foods at a consistent gentle simmer. Certain other materials, such as stainless steel–clad aluminum and earthenware, also work well. Steer clear of thin steel or aluminum pots that can heat up and cool down too quickly and therefore not give you the consistent heat you're after.

The Importance of the Size of a Braising Pot

In choosing which pot to use for which recipe, the deciding factor should be the size of the pot. The food should fit without a lot of extra space in the bottom of the pot or headroom above. The better the fit, the closer the sauce is to the main ingredient, and the better the flavor in the end. Since the success of braising depends on the cycle of steam from the braising liquid rising up, condensing on the underside of the lid, and dripping back down onto the main ingredient, the smaller the pot, the tighter this cycle, and the more concentrated the juices will become. If the braising pot is too big for the ingredients being braised, the vapors and steam will swirl around the sides without coming in close contact with the food at all. Another drawback of choosing too large a pot is that the braising liquid will spread over too wide a surface and risk evaporating and drying up— even in the confines of a closed pot. And if you add more liquid to avoid this possibility, you will be left with an overly dilute sauce. The ideal pot will mimic the shape and size of the food you're braising. For instance, if you were braising a loaf-shaped pot roast or a whole chicken, the best pot would be a deep oval Dutch oven in which the pot roast or chicken fits without a lot of wiggle room. The rounded shape of a pork shoulder or rolled lamb shoulder will fit nicely in a deep round pot. For a flatter brisket or chicken thighs, choose a shallower pot that won't leave too much headroom. Below I have listed my favorite braising pots.

DUTCH OVENS

These sturdy pots with tight-fitting lids take their name from the Pennsylvania Dutch who crafted them in the late eighteenth century. They remain the favored workhorses in American kitchens. Fashioned out of cast iron, the original Dutch oven featured either a swinging handle or tripod feet (or both) so the cook could suspend it above or settle it into an open hearth. Today Dutch ovens have flat bottoms so you can sear food on the top of the stove before sliding the pot into the oven. Most have two sturdy ear-like handles to make hoisting them in and out of the oven easier—the larger of these pots can weigh a lot. The most popular Dutch ovens are constructed of enameled cast iron, which requires none of the preseasoning and special care of ordinary cast iron but maintains the same gentle, even heat. Best of all, enameled cast iron is remarkably easy to clean. Good-quality Dutch ovens are expensive, but they last a lifetime. A good all-purpose size for the recipes in this book is one with a 5- to 6-quart capacity. Most Dutch ovens are round or oval, but some novelty shapes (such as heart-shaped and square) are now appearing. The round shape is generally more useful. The oval is designed for braising elongated roasts and whole poultry. If you do a lot of braising, acquiring both a round and an oval Dutch oven makes good sense. The other shapes are more cute than practical.

My favorite brand of Dutch oven has long been the colorful line of enamel-coated cast-iron from Le Creuset. I still use a 3-quart oval that I lugged back from France in 1984, and it's every bit as beautiful and useful today as it was when I bought it. Le Creuset also offers the most diverse selection of sizes and colors of any company.

Another excellent maker of top-quality enameled cast-iron Dutch ovens is Staub. Also from France, Alsace to be precise, Staub pots come in round and oval shapes, some-

Round Dutch Oven (or Cocotte)

times called *cocottes*. Although the company is well established in Europe and favored by many chefs, these durable and handsome pots have only recently come available to home cooks through Sur La Table (see Sources, page 458).

Oval Dutch Oven

Finally, I still rely on my old-fashioned cast-iron Lodge Dutch oven. Lodge is a family-run company based in Tennessee that has been making sturdy and inexpensive cast-irons pots and skillets for more than a hundred years. Their heavy 7-quart Dutch oven makes a great braising vessel for large cuts, like a whole pork Boston butt. The only draw-backs of uncoated cast iron are that you need to season the surface so that it won't rust and then take care to keep it seasoned. You may also notice that acidic foods, like tomato sauces or vinegary dishes, may discolor slightly if left to sit for too long in a cast-iron pot. There's nothing unsafe about this, but to avoid it, remove foods soon after braising. I know some cooks who complain about the sheer heft of uncoated cast-iron pots. Since they are made from a heavier gauge of cast iron than the coated ones, plain cast-iron pots do take some muscle to lift. If this is a concern for you, stick with the lighter enameled cast iron.

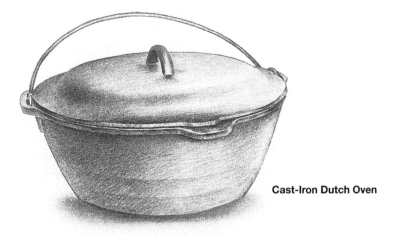

Cast-Iron Dutch Oven

To braise ingredients that are less than a few inches high (chicken legs, beef steaks, fish fillets or steaks, and most vegetables), I often use a large deep skillet, frying pan, or sauté pan with a tight-fitting lid. These three terms are interchangeable for describing a round cooking pan with 2- to 4-inch sides and a long handle. *Skillet* and *frying pan* are American terms, and *sauté pan* comes from the French. What term you use probably depends on where you learned to cook. In this book, I use the term *skillet*.

For braising, I recommend a heavy-gauge 12- or 13-inch skillet lined with stainless steel. It should also have an ovenproof handle and lid. Stainless steel is a poor conductor of heat, so the best-quality stainless skillets are made with a core of aluminum or copper. Because aluminum and copper are efficient conductors of heat, the pan will heat up quickly. Once heated, the steel retains the heat well. The reason to avoid aluminum or copper on the surface of pans is that both are highly reactive and can cause problems when in direct contact with food. Aluminum and copper are also soft, so they scratch, dent, and warp easily. Stainless steel, on the other hand, may be an inefficient conductor of heat but it won't react with the food and is wonderfully easy to clean and durable. Sandwiching a layer of aluminum or copper between layers of stainless steel provides the best of both worlds. The pan heats quickly and holds the heat. Most top-quality brands (All-Clad, Cuisinart, and KitchenAid, to name a few) offer an extensive line of stainless-clad pots and pans. When shopping for a good skillet, bear in mind that high-end manufacturers tend to refer to them as *sauté pans*.

Whichever skillet you choose, be sure the sides are high enough to come above the

Large Skillet with Lid

ingredients and hold the braising liquid. Whether the sides are sloped or straight makes little difference for braising. A slope-sided skillet is technically a sauté pan (or *sauteuse*), as the sloping sides make it easier (and less messy) to toss food and catch it back in the pan the way you may have seen chefs do on TV or in a class. I also find that an old-fashioned "chicken fryer" (a deep straight-sided cast-iron skillet) works well, as long as you keep the pan well seasoned and don't leave acidic foods sitting in it for too long.

In the category of skillets, a favorite of restaurant chefs is the wide, deep, two-handled stainless steel casserole that looks something like a squat-shaped stockpot. These rugged pots are used by chefs for all manner of cooking—everything from braising veal shanks to making stock and roasting meats. The French call this pot a *rondeau,* but I've also heard them referred to as braziers and even roasters. Usually constructed with a layer of aluminum or copper sandwiched between stainless steel, its heavy bottom provides excellent heat retention, making it a good choice for a braising pot. Having learned to cook in restaurant kitchens, I developed a real fondness for *rondeaux,* since they are virtually indestructible and endlessly useful. Two reliable brands are Centurion by Lincoln Wearever and Duraware by Carlisle. The best place to find these serious (and expensive) pots is at a restaurant supply store, or through mail-order (see Sources, page 458). You may have to search to find a 7-quart model convenient for home use, but these can be found.

Rondeau

These are old-fashioned French braising casseroles, traditionally hammered out of copper. They are wide and deep with straight sides and handles on both sides. If you've never seen one of these majestic vessels, picture a very heavy, slightly shallow Dutch oven made from copper with brass handles. Some of the older *braisières* have sunken lids designed to hold hot coals when the pot was tucked into the embers of an open hearth. This sunken lid provided the added benefit of reducing the space above the food being braised. The steam has nowhere to go, so it immediately condenses and drips back down onto the food. With or without the sunken lid to hold coals, these pots are still ideal for braising because they are so heavy that they conduct the heat gently and evenly—which is exactly what you're after. Being shallower than a standard Dutch oven, *braisières* are especially good for shorter foods, such as a flat-cut brisket or chuck roast, since the reduced headroom means a more concentrated sauce.

A modern-day version of the *braisière* is called a *doufeu*, which translates literally as "gentle fire." Made by Le Creuset of enameled cast iron, this Dutch oven also has a sunken lid, but the sides are a bit taller than a *braisière*—more in line with the standard Dutch oven. Interestingly, the recessed lid of the *doufeu* is designed to hold ice to create condensation under the lid that then falls back down and bastes the braising foods. When I first purchased a *doufeu*, I dutifully filled the top with ice, and it certainly melted in the oven. What I didn't notice, however, was any change in the quality or character of the braise or the braising liquid. I no longer bother with the ice, but I do love the design of the *doufeu* because it keeps the lid closer to the food the same way a *braisière* does. I highly recommend these pots for long braising, especially for shorter foods such as thin-cut brisket or a flat pot roast, because the shallower sides offer a more snug fit.

Doufeu

If you're an avid braiser and want to fully outfit your kitchen, consider buying one of the smart-looking shallow braising pans bearing names like *braiser pan* (made by All-Clad) or *bistro pan* and *buffet casserole* (both made by Le Creuset). These round, slope-sided pans are designed with 2 1/2- to 3-inch sides and well-fitting, often dome-shaped lids to create the ideal, snug environment for braising low profile ingredients, such as chicken parts, vegetables, fish fillets, pork chops, and stuffed beef rolls. Made of either heavy-duty stainless-clad aluminum or enameled cast-iron, these pans provide the slow, even heat required for a braise with a fraction of the headspace of a Dutch oven. I use mine for everything from Quick Lemony Chicken with Prunes & Green Olives (page 131) to End-of-Summer Green Beans Braised with Tomatoes (page 43) The other reason to love these shallow pans is their versatility. They work equally well as a gratin dish, a baking dish, a casserole, and even a roasting pan. The most useful size holds 3 1/2 to 4 1/2 quarts and is 12 to 13 inches in diameter. (See Sources, page 458.)

Braiser Pan

Bistro Pan

Buffet Casserole

GRATIN DISHES, ROASTING PANS, OR BAKING DISHES

These 2- to 3-inch-deep baking dishes and pans designed for baking or roasting are also useful for braising foods that don't stand too high, such as vegetables (endive, celery, or scallions, for instance), fish fillets, and steaks. Since most of these dishes aren't designed for heating on top of the stove, you'll need to first brown the food in a skillet and then transfer it to the pan. The gratins and roasting pans that I use most often for braising are oval or rectangular and of 2 1/2- to 3-quart capacity (about 13 inches long). There are a few occasions when I call my largest roasting pan (16-by-14-inches) into use. For instance, since I don't own a proper braising pot large enough to accommodate an entire bone-in leg of lamb, I use a roasting pan to make the Seven-Hour Leg of Lamb (page 426).

Gratin Dish

Baking Dish

EARTHENWARE CASSEROLES

Glazed clay or terra-cotta vessels are good braising dishes because they are thick walled and conduct a gentle even heat. Their one drawback is that they are not flameproof, so you need to brown the food in a separate skillet and then transfer it to the casserole. Also, few come with secure lids, but that's easily remedied with a sheet of heavy-duty foil. What I also appreciate about braising in earthenware is that it is handsome enough to carry to the table to serve family-style.

Glazed Terra-Cotta Casserole

SLOW-COOKERS OR CROCK-POTS

I should begin by saying that I don't own a slow-cooker—and the reason is simple: I like cooking on the stove and in the oven. When I set a pot to simmer or slide a dish into the oven, I know the intricacies of how the heat will transfer from its source to the food, and I have an ingrained sense of how to control the outcome. I find pleasure in checking on a dish as it cooks—turning it, stirring it, and anticipating its progress. Having said all that, I know many good cooks who love their slow-cookers, and in talking with them and cooking alongside them, I have learned that you can indeed produce some very good meals in a slow-cooker.

Designed to cook food slowly while you're elsewhere, slow-cookers (also called Crock-Pots) generally have two settings: the difference being the time it takes for the food to reach a slow simmer. The notion is simple: you fill the pot with raw ingredients, set the cover in place, plug it in, and go off to work or wherever you need to be. When you return—ta-da!—dinner. In the moist, gentle heat of the slow-cooker, the ingredients become tender while their flavors meld—much like what happens in a braising pot.

In my trials, however, I discovered some drawbacks to braising in a slow-cooker. The biggest is the inconvenience of not being able to sear food in the pot before braising. To solve this, you need to sear the ingredients in a skillet and then transfer them to the slow-cooker, being certain to deglaze the skillet to dissolve the drippings and add these to the slow-cooker as well. The other negative aspect of this type of braising is that it can be awkward to finish the sauce. For instance, if you want to reduce the sauce to thicken it or concentrate its flavor, you need to transfer the liquid to a saucepan on top of the stove.

In the end, I did surmise that you can successfully braise in a slow-cooker, but it would never be my first choice. In addition to the nuisance of having to sear and finish in separate pans, there is a subtle, but definite, lack of richness in the flavor of braises prepared in a slow-cooker. However, if the efficiency of the slow-cooker outweighs this loss, and if it's a matter of slow-cooker braising or no braising, then by all means, plug the thing in and braise away. Unfortunately, I cannot offer a specific conversion chart for adapting my recipes to a slow-cooker. In my research and trials, I've found you need to double or triple the braising time when using the high setting, and triple or quadruple the time with the low setting. Then it's a matter of using your senses and the guidelines provided in each recipe to judge doneness.

Lids and Parchment Paper

Since much of the success of braising depends on trapping moisture in the pot so it can meld together with the natural juices of the food you're braising, a secure lid is important. Even with a well-fitting lid, I like to reinforce the seal by laying a sheet of parchment paper over the ingredients, pressing down so the paper just touches the food and extending the edges of the paper over the rim of the pot, and then setting the lid in place. This also reduces the headroom in the braising pot, which helps to concentrate the braising juices. If you visualized the inside of a pot during braising, you would see vapor rising up from the food, hitting the lid, condensing there, and dripping back down. The further these vapors have to travel, the more dilute they become. With parchment directly above the food, you create a tight little cycle of evaporation and condensation. Also with an ordinary dome-shaped lid, most of the drips run down the sides of the pot. By covering the food with parchment, you've changed that concave lid to a convex one, so that most of the dripping will happen in the center of the pot, basting the food directly.

Some pots made specifically for braising come equipped with downward pointing stalactite-like "spikes" or bumps on the underside of the lid. These are designed to collect the moisture as the steam condenses and then coax the condensed moisture into dripping back down, basting the food being braised. Since I usually cover the pot with parchment, the spikes become ineffective. Many companies use these spikes as a selling point, and if you were to braise without parchment, they would be of benefit. If, like me, you almost always place a sheet of parchment under the lid, whether or not a lid has spikes shouldn't affect your buying decision. The spikes are not a disadvantage, but don't buy a pot solely because of the spikes.

If the pot you've chosen doesn't have a matching lid, heavy-duty foil will work fine. When I use foil, I often leave off the parchment, since it can be awkward getting the parchment and foil to form a tight seal together around the rim of the pot. If, however, the braise contains many acidic ingredients, such as tomatoes or vinegar, it is a good practice to protect the food from the reactivity of foil with a sheet of parchment. The only thing to watch with a foil "lid" is that you don't scorch yourself peeling it back when you check on the simmering braise. Somehow a foil lid seems to release steam in a more malevolent fashion than a regular lid.

**Sealing a Braising Pot
with Parchment Paper**

BROWNING, THE FIRST STEP TOWARD A MEMORABLE BRAISE

Browning, also called searing, refers to cooking the exterior of food at a moderately high temperature to caramelize it. No discussion of braising is complete without looking closely at why and how to accomplish browning. Many chefs and food authorities insist that food must *always* be browned before being braised. In truth, I have found recipes that don't rely on searing (most notably red-cooked braises from China, see page 385, as well as a few delicately flavored dishes like Monkfish Braised with Cherry Tomatoes & Basil, page 104). But these are exceptions to the rule. Most braising recipes rely on browning for much of their character and flavor.

The reason that browning is usually the first step in making a great braise comes down to simple chemistry: Moist-heat cooking methods (braising, simmering, and boiling) will never rise above the boiling point of water (212 degrees). Food begins to brown only at temperatures in excess of 310 degrees. This means that a piece of brisket, for example, simmered in a braising pot without being browned first will cook through to tenderness but won't develop the gorgeous dark hue and depth of flavor we anticipate in a braise. The meat will take on a light brown, almost gray appearance, and it won't deliver the layers of flavor of a brisket that was browned before being braised.

The appeal of well-browned or caramelized food is in part aesthetic—browned meat just looks more appetizing to us than pale, grayish simmered meat. But it has a scientific basis as well. As the surface of food browns, layers of otherwise unrevealed flavors emerge. More than just bringing out a food's natural flavors, browning actually adds new, more interesting flavors. Think of what happens when you roast a marshmallow over an open flame. The surface of the marshmallow gradually turns golden, then brown, and finally black. If you bite into an untoasted marshmallow, it will taste like pure sugar. As the surface is exposed to heat and becomes darker, the flavor will become more appealing and exciting. Browning adds an interesting and tasty dimension to food, as long as you don't take it too far and burn it.

Technically speaking, there are two types of browning that occur: the straight caramelization of sugar, which is what happens when you turn sugar into caramel, and the somewhat more complicated Maillard reaction (named after the Frenchman who discovered it), which explains why foods such as meats, breads, and nuts turn toasty brown when you heat them above a certain temperature. Although these two reactions differ on a molecular level, they are very much the same to the cook. All browning, whether the caramelization of sugars or the Maillard reaction of proteins and starches, occurs at around 310 degrees, and both types make foods taste immeasurably better.

The flavors that browning brings out establish the first layer of flavor on which the character of the finished braise rests. That's why it's important to take care with this step. The most common method is to brown ingredients in a small amount of fat in the braising pot on top of the stove. Using the same pot for browning and for braising has two advantages. First, when you brown food, the drippings caramelize on the bottom of the pot. These cooked-on drippings are tiny concentrated bombs of flavor that explode into bigger flavors when they dissolve into the braising liquid. So not only do you have the advantage of a browned pot roast, for example, but you also have the extra flavor that the browned drippings offer. The second advantage to browning directly in the braising pot is convenience—you need to clean only one pot.

Tips for Successful Browning

- **The surface of the food must be dry.** Moisture will cause food to steam, not brown. Moisture also tends to cause meats, poultry, and fish to stick to the pan and prevent them from forming an appealing browned crust.
- **Use just enough oil or fat to coat the bottom of the pan.** Fat conducts heat from the surface of the pan to whatever you're searing, and it helps promote an even, brown crust. Too little fat will result in uneven, spotty browning. An excess of fat can make the dish greasy.
- **Give food plenty of space.** All fresh meat, poultry, fish, or vegetables throw off moisture as soon as they come into contact with a hot pan—that's the sizzling sound you hear. If the pan is too crowded with cubes of meat, for example, the released moisture can't escape and will cause the meat to steam, not brown. So it's essential that you leave enough room for the moisture to evaporate, even if this means browning the meat in batches.
- **Be patient.** Heat the pan and whatever fat you're using over medium or medium-high heat before adding the food. Once the pan and fat are hot, add the food and give it time to brown. If you're making a chicken braise, for example, avoid the temptation to nudge and fuss with the pieces when they first hit the pan. If you move the chicken around too much, it won't have time to caramelize and it will tend to stick. Let the chicken sit undisturbed until it develops a handsome sear. The goal is to gradually

achieve a deeply caramelized surface. The same holds true for all other meats, vegetables, and seafood.

- **Don't walk away, and don't set the heat too high.** Either way you risk burning the surface of whatever you're trying to brown. A charred taste can ruin the entire flavor of a carefully prepared dish. Just as the browned surface of a well-caramelized steak will contribute a rich, toasty flavor, a few blackened bits of burnt steak will contribute a bitter charred taste that can overpower all the other flavors. If you do accidentally burn the surface, remove the offending charred bits before continuing. If the edges of a pot roast are blackened, for example, trim them off with a sharp knife. If you've scorched the skin on a chicken thigh, remove the skin and proceed without.

- **After browning, evaluate the drippings and the pan.** Depending on what you've browned, there may or may not be an excess of fat in the pan. Some cuts, such as country-style pork ribs, tend to throw off quite a bit of fat. In that case, pour off all but a thin film before continuing. And if the fat is burnt or flecked with black specks, you should discard it or pick out the black specks with a spoon or with the corner of a paper towel before continuing. The same is true for the drippings. If they are black and charred looking, wipe the pan with damp paper towels before proceeding.

Alternative Methods for Browning

- **Using the broiler.** I particularly like to brown any large, unwieldy cuts of meat, such as a bone-in leg of lamb, under a broiler, because these large cuts are so difficult to maneuver on the top of the stove. I also sometimes broil excessively fatty cuts, such as short ribs, to avoid the grease they splatter on the top of the stove. Set the meat on a broiler pan or half sheet pan, something with a rim high enough to catch the drippings, and slide it under the broiler so the surface is 4 to 6 inches from the heat. Turn the meat a few times, using sturdy tongs, to brown all sides evenly, and don't walk away. Broiling happens quickly, and a brief moment of inattention could ruin all your efforts. After browning, transfer the meat to the braising pot, and degrease and then deglaze the broiling pan or half sheet pan by transferring it to the top of the stove and following the instruction for deglazing on page 27.

- **Using a skillet.** If you will be braising in an earthenware pot, any other nonflameproof vessel, or a slow-cooker, you'll have to brown the ingredients in a separate skillet, then transfer them to the braising pot. Heat a small amount of fat (I generally use extra-virgin olive oil) in a large heavy skillet (12 inches) over medium to medium-high heat, and brown the meat, poultry, or vegetables in batches so you don't crowd the skillet. As the individual pieces become seared on all sides, transfer them to the earthenware pot. Pour off and discard the fat and deglaze the skillet according to the method described on page 27.

- **Using a grill.** Some chefs like to grill foods to create a sear on the exterior before braising. While this method results in remarkable flavor, I've found that the drawbacks outweigh the benefits. My main complaint is the danger of charring. Grills run much hotter than most stove burners, and it's all too easy to create a blackened surface on a piece of meat or poultry. In addition, most of us like to braise in the wintertime when an outdoor grill is inaccessible or at least inconvenient. If you do have an indoor grill top and would like to try your hand at this method, just be vigilant.

- **No browning at all.** There are some braising recipes that do not rely on browning as the first step. Some texts classify these as *white braising* or *blonde braising*, but I find that no one such classification holds true. There are a few reasons for omitting browning as the first step. In some cases, such as Braised Halibut Steaks with Creamy Leeks (page 99), the goal is to produce a delicately flavored dish. In others, such as Honey-Glazed Five-Spice Baby Back Ribs (page 376), the browning is done at the end. In Chinese red-cooked dishes, the soy-based braising liquid renders the pork, beef, or even tofu a deep reddish brown, so no actual searing is necessary.

Browning as a first step is certainly the norm for braising, but there are exceptions that you will discover throughout this book. And that's exactly what makes braising so infinitely adaptable and varied.

Stage Four

THE ROLE OF FAT IN ADDING FLAVOR TO A BRAISE

The role of fat in a braise is to act as a medium in which to brown the main ingredients, a beef pot roast and its accompanying vegetables, for example. This role is much more than mechanical. Fat also enriches the overall flavor of a dish. Here's how: by browning the beef in olive oil, setting it aside, and then sautéing a combination of onion, carrot, celery, and garlic in the same oil, you are not only browning the beef and vegetables, you are infusing the oil with their flavors. When you then add the braising liquid, the flavor-infused olive oil works its way through the entire dish, producing a melding of tasty flavors. One of the reasons low-fat cooking presents such a challenge to a cook aiming for bold-flavored food is that there is no replacement for the way that fat brings together all the flavor elements in a dish. Imagine a simple tomato sauce without first sautéing the garlic in olive oil. All the ingredients may still taste good, but they won't coalesce into the same harmony of tastes. This is the role of fat.

The type of fat used to brown ingredients at the start of a braise varies according to personal taste and what the recipe requires. I tend to reach for a mild extra-virgin olive oil before anything else both for taste and for health reasons. I don't enjoy the flavor of highly processed vegetable oils, such as safflower, soybean, or canola oil. (For more on olive oil, see page 439.) For more flavor than a mild olive oil provides, I use butter, duck fat, bacon drippings, or some combination of these. Since butter has a low smoke point and will typically burn before you've finished searing, I generally specify butter in combination with another fat, such as olive oil, that won't burn as quickly.

Stage Five

THE AROMATICS—THE FOUNDATION OF A BRAISE

Beyond the main ingredient, the browning, and the fat, an essential part of most every braise are what cooks refer to as *aromatics*. Added to the pot at the very beginning of the braising process, aromatics contribute a fullness of flavor that meat or poultry alone cannot provide. Under the heading of aromatics come all sorts of vegetables, notably carrots, celery, onions, leeks, garlic, and shallots; fresh or dried herbs; spices; cured meats (like pancetta and bacon); and any number of other ingredients. The French refer to these enrichments as *les fonds,* or foundations, because they establish a base layer of flavor that defines the character of a braised dish. As the aromatics simmer in the braise, they contribute flavor and aroma to the braising liquid, which in turn bathes and bastes the meat or poultry at the center of the pot. For comparison, imagine a roast chicken with no stuffing and no seasonings beyond salt and pepper. As flavorful as this chicken may be in itself, it lacks the enhancement provided by adding a selection of aromatics.

Your selection of aromatics should be determined by personal taste and compatibility of flavor. For instance, beef and mushrooms make ideal companions, so when I braise short ribs (page 241), I include some dried porcini mushrooms in the aromatic mix. By varying the selection and proportion of the aromatics, you create a world of possibilities with which to develop many fine braises. If you study recipes from around the world, you will notice national and regional trends in the use of aromatics. You will also see that individual cooks will often personalize their own formulas. As a starting point, consider how the following combinations represent the overriding flavors of their respective cuisines:

- **Mirepoix:** The classic French combination of vegetables used as a flavor base. Carrots, celery, and onions are chopped into uniform pieces (small or large, depending on the recipe) and sautéed in butter, or other fat, to create a subtly sweet and herbaceous background to a range of dishes.
- **Battuto:** The classic Italian foundation for braises and soups. Onions, carrot, celery leaves, parsley, and garlic are chopped, and sautéed in olive oil. Useful for meats, poultry, seafood, and vegetables with a Mediterranean accent.
- **Sofrito:** The term *sofrito* appears in both Spanish and Italian kitchens (spelled *soffrito* in Italian) and refers to a combination of aromatics (usually chopped onion, celery, carrots, garlic, parsley, and sometimes tomato) stewed in olive oil and used as a multipurpose flavor base. A Spanish sofrito is often distinguished by the inclusion of paprika. Sofrito is also commonly used to describe a flavor base used throughout the Caribbean and Latin America. A Latino cook makes a sofrito by first infusing pork or other fat with annatto seeds, and then stewing a mix of chopped onions, garlic, bell peppers, and herbs in the infused fat until the mixture is cooked down and flavorful.
- **Chinese flavor base:** Glance through a Chinese cookbook, and you'll see the same four ingredients repeated over and over again: ginger, garlic, chiles, and scallions. Sautéing these together in a bit of oil at the beginning of a recipe lends an unmistakable Chinese accent to any number of braises, soups, and stir-frys.

Readying Aromatics for the Braising Pot

Aromatics can be chopped fine or coarse or, in some cases, left whole. The longer the braising time, the larger the pieces should be. For instance, if a pot roast needs a solid 2 ½ hours to braise, leave the aromatic vegetables in large chunks so they won't disintegrate before the meat is done. For something quick, like chicken thighs, chop the aromatics fine so they will cook (and lend their flavor to the sauce) in the 40 minutes the chicken takes to braise.

In most cases, the aromatic vegetables must be sautéed after the initial browning of the meat. This releases their flavors into the fat used to sauté. Sautéing also browns the vegetables to enhance their flavors.

Depending on the nature of the braise, aromatics may be left in or strained out before serving. For a rustic, chunky sauce to spoon over Country-Style Pork Ribs Braised with Mango, Lime & Coconut (page 363), the aromatics stay in. For a more refined smooth sauce, such as the one for the Zinfandel Pot Roast with Glazed Carrots & Fresh Sage (page 264), you strain out the aromatics and discard them. For long braises, the aromatics often need to be strained out because they've given up all their flavors and retain little taste. After such an extended cooking time, vegetables can become mushy and flavorless. The flavor has not vanished, however—it's been transferred into the braising liquid and therefore into the meat itself.

As an alternative approach, I sometimes recommend adding some aromatics at the start of a long braise and then more about halfway through. As an example, for the Pot-Roasted Brisket with Rhubarb & Honey (page 267), I add 2 cups of chopped rhubarb at the beginning of the braise. As the brisket simmers, the rhubarb collapses completely. Desiring a pronounced rhubarb presence in the finished dish, I add another 2 cups to the pot halfway through the braise. In the end, the sauce has two layers of rhubarb flavor, both fresh and muted. I follow a similar path with Yankee Pot Roast Redux (page 251) by adding the turnips, carrots, and potatoes to the pot halfway through the braise. This way the vegetables contribute an earthy flavor to the dish without sacrificing their texture.

Stage Six

CHOOSING THE BRAISING LIQUID—
DETERMINING THE FLAVOR OF THE SAUCE

The only thing all braising recipes have in common is that they all contain some amount of liquid. The liquid is the conduit for the other flavors. Therefore, the choice of liquid has a great influence on the ultimate character of a braise. In the recipes that follow, you'll find that I recommend a diversity of liquids, the most common being wine and stock. Wine (most often dry red or dry white) contributes a welcome acidity to balance the richness of other flavors. Stock underscores the hearty, caramelized nature of a braise. In general, think of matching the wine and/or stock with the main ingredient: light for light and dark for dark. Beyond wine and stock, many other liquids come into play. Vinegar, dry white vermouth, hard or sweet cider, beer, sake, brandy, sweet wines, sherry, rum, tomato juice, mushroom soaking liquid, and even water all have their place.

A common mistake in assembling a braise is to add too much liquid. The liquid should come less than one third of the way up the sides of the main ingredients. This may look like a scant amount of liquid to start, but keep in mind that all foods release moisture as they simmer, contributing their own juices to the liquid in the pot. If you add too much liquid at the beginning, the resulting sauce will be lacking in body and intensity. With just the right amount of liquid, the final sauce will be deeply flavored and delicious.

DEGLAZING AND REDUCING — TWO KEYS TO MAXIMUM FLAVOR

One of the greatest lessons I learned while cooking in France was how and when to deglaze a pan and to reduce a liquid. Without these two simple techniques, there would be far fewer great sauces.

Deglazing refers to adding liquid after sautéing, in order to capture the drippings left in the pan. For instance, when making Osso Buco alla Milanese (page 321), after browning the veal shanks and aromatic vegetables and removing them from the pan, you add a cup of dry white wine to the pan. As the wine comes to a boil, you stir and scrape the bottom of the pan with a wooden spoon to dislodge the caramelized drippings. These cooked-on drippings (the French call them *sucs*) are little nuggets of flavor. They contain all the richness of the caramelized meat juices, and they contribute enormously to the overall sauce. These cooked-on bits dissolve in the simmering wine and enrich the braising liquid with the flavor of the seared veal. This is deglazing.

Reducing. Once the pan has been deglazed, the next step is *reducing* the liquid. Reducing is a shorthand term for simmering a liquid to evaporate the water and to concentrate the flavor and thicken the body of the liquid. Once you've added the white wine, for example, and deglazed the pan, the wine must be reduced down by about half to concentrate its flavor. In many recipes, I recommend more than one reduction to build an even more complex layering of flavors. After the wine has reduced for about 5 minutes, I add the stock and reduce this down to about half its original volume.

Deglazing the Drippings in a Broiler Pan or on a Baking Sheet

If the meat or poultry has been browned under a broiler, it's still possible to deglaze the pan. Begin by pouring off the grease from the pan, being careful not to discard any meat juices or drippings. Then set the broiler pan or baking sheet over medium-high heat (two burners may be necessary) and pour in 1/4 to 1/3 cup liquid, preferably either the same liquid used in the recipe or water. Bring to a boil, stirring with a wooden spoon to dissolve the drippings. Finally, pour this flavorful liquid over the ingredients in the braising pot.

THE CHOICE BETWEEN BRAISING ON TOP OF THE STOVE
AND BRAISING IN THE OVEN

In French, the word *braise* means glowing-hot embers, and the technique originally referred to burying a covered pot in a bed of hot coals and leaving it there to simmer for hours. Few, if any, of us braise in live embers today, but the image of that gentle, even heat is a reliable guide for how a braise should occur. The objective is to keep the liquid inside the pot at a gently bubbling simmer. When the heat is too high, the braising liquid boils, the meat toughens up, and the aromatics overcook.

I braise both on top of the stove and in a low oven. Each method has its advantages. For long braises, where the meat simmers for hours, the oven is the better choice. The sealed braising pot is surrounded by an even heat, and there is no need to be concerned about hot spots or cool spots. Heated from all sides, the meat or poultry will need turning less frequently, and the pot can be left unattended for longer. When braising in the oven, place the pot on a rack in the lower third of the oven so that the hot air can circulate freely around the pot. The ideal braising temperature is somewhere in the range of 275 to 350 degrees. Since all ovens differ slightly, I suggest peeking under the lid during the first 30 minutes to make sure that the liquid is not simmering too vigorously. If the oven is too hot, lower the temperature by 10 to 15 degrees. In my experience, electric ovens provide more even heat, gas ovens tend to fluctuate more. But both produce wonderful results as long as you pay attention.

Braising on top of the stove works best for shallow braises and for short braises, like Monkfish Braised with Cherry Tomatoes & Basil (page 104) or Sausages & Plums Braised in Red Wine (page 396). This method is also used for Asian braises (such as Beef Rendang, page 291, or Red-Cooked Pork Belly with Bok Choy, page 385) where you need to regularly monitor the pot, often without the lid. The disadvantage of braising on top of the stove is that all the heat comes from below, so you don't have the surrounding heat you have in an oven. This means that you must stay close by and turn the food often so that it braises evenly. The biggest challenge is keeping the heat level low enough without shutting it down altogether. For this, I prefer a gas flame for its superior responsiveness. As soon as I have reduced the liquid, I turn the flame to very low, and the braising liquid immediately settles to a quiet simmer. With an electric stove or no small burners (especially if you have a professional range), you may need to employ a heat diffuser to moderate the heat. Braising on top of the stove requires more vigilance on the part of the cook. You must stay close by and monitor and turn the food often.

One final note about braising on top of the stove: most traditional Italian braising happens this way. Consult any good Italian cookbook (such as Marcela Hazan's *Classic Italian Cookbook*) and you'll find braised recipe after braised recipe simmered on the stove. The reason for this is that traditionally Italian home cooks didn't have their own ovens. The only ovens were community bread ovens, so everyday braising was done at home on the stove. In developing my own versions of Italian classic braises, such as Pork Loin Braised in Milk (page 346) or Duck Ragù with Pasta (page 203), I usually moved the braise into the oven, because it provides more consistently reliable results with less fuss. In a few Italian recipes, though, such as Peperonata (page 45), where I want to monitor the progress of the braise and the ingredients aren't so thick as to require constant turning, I adhere to tradition and simmer them on top of the stove.

The Utility of a Heat Diffuser

The greatest challenge of braising on top of the stove is maintaining a gentle simmer. On many stoves, it seems that the heat vacillates between too high and too low. Fortunately, there's a simple solution: a heat diffuser, often referred to as a flame tamer. This unremarkable kitchen gadget is nothing more than a flameproof disk that you place between the burner and the pot to moderate the heat, resulting in more even, gentler cooking. The best heat diffusers I've found are made of enameled cast iron. They heat up slowly but, once hot, provide the ideal soft, regular heat for a braise. Look for the Italian brand Ilsa at cookware stores (see Sources, page 458). Calphalon also sells a more contemporary-looking half-inch-thick disk of anodized aluminum that works according to the same principle. The more old-fashioned perforated steel heat diffusers also work, although not quite as well. Some manufacturers make small (6-inch) diffusers. These are only useful for very small burners and small pots. For braising, look for an 8- to 11-inch diffuser.

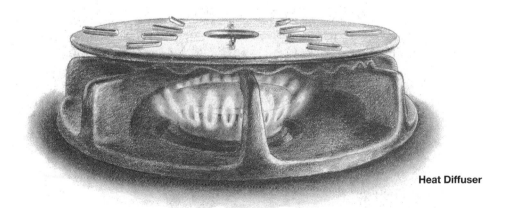

Heat Diffuser

INDIVIDUALIZING A BRAISE, ADDING A FINAL LAYER
OF FLAVOR—ENRICHMENTS

Braising is infinitely variable and full of opportunities for improvisation. "Enrichments" is the broad name that I give to ingredients or extra steps added to a basic braise in order to enhance its texture, flavor, or overall character. In many instances, it's these enrichments that elevate the simple to the sublime. Here I've listed some of the most important and/or useful of these.

Spice Rubs and Herb Pastes

A spice rub is a dry mix of whole, cracked, or ground spices, along with salt and sometimes herbs, fresh or dried. An herb paste is a wet mix of fresh herbs and salt that may contain other ingredients such as citrus zest and juice, spices, or olive oil. These potent mixtures are rubbed onto the surface of meat, poultry, or fish and left to sit for several hours, or longer in the refrigerator, before braising. The seasonings infuse the meat, poultry, or fish deeply so that the flavors become integrated into the food, unlike seasonings simply sprinkled on the surface. Rubs and pastes also enhance the appearance of a dish by creating a savory crust. Consider the Moroccan Spice-Rubbed Lamb Shoulder Chops (page 416): the mixture of fragrant spices adds a Moroccan-inspired flair to the flavor of the dish, but it also gives the surface of the lamb chops a gorgeous brown crust.

Dredging

A common technique for assembling a braise is to roll the main ingredient (typically meat, poultry, or sometimes fish) in flour before browning it. Referred to as dredging, this step serves two purposes. First, food that is lightly floured browns readily and forms an appealing crust on the exterior. Second, the bit of flour clinging to the food will add body to the braising liquid, so that the final sauce develops a coating texture. The few principles to remember when dredging are:

- Food should be dry before dredging. If it's wet (from being rinsed, for instance), the flour will gum up and create a thick, unappetizing coating.

- Season the food with salt and pepper before dredging, and then dredge in plain all-purpose flour. Many recipes direct you to season the flour, but I've found that this can result in uneven seasoning.
- After rolling the food in flour, lift it over the plate and pat it to remove any excess flour. A light, even coating is ideal.
- Do not dredge ingredients until you're ready to add them to the pan. If flour-coated meat, poultry, or fish sits for any amount of time, it will become moist and gummy. If you're browning in batches (so as not to crowd the pan), dredge in batches as well.
- Discard the excess flour after all the food has been dredged.

Meaty Enrichments

This final category is where I group all the wondrous odd bits like pig's feet, fresh pork rind, and chicken wing tips, backs, necks, hearts, and gizzards that I sometimes add to the braising pot. While these don't usually end up on anyone's plate, they will greatly improve your braises. The virtue of these enrichments is that each contains a high percentage of collagen, the protein that melts into gelatin and gives body and viscosity to a sauce. Pig's feet and pork rind contain more gelatin than chicken parts, but it takes a minimum of 2 hours to extract it. It would be a waste to add either one to a short braise. Chicken parts, on the other hand, require relatively little time, anywhere from 20 to 40 minutes, to break down and are therefore useful for most any braise of meat, poultry, or vegetables.

Depending on where you live, you may or may not be able to find pig's feet (also called trotters) or fresh pork rind. If they don't appear in the meat case, it's certainly worth asking. Most butchers will at least have fresh pork rind that they've trimmed off some cut of pork and would otherwise toss away. The rind freezes well, so if you get more than you need, cut it into 3- to 4-ounce squares, wrap each one in waxed paper so they don't stick together, and freeze in a quart-size freezer bag. Pig's feet may be harder to come by, but if you do find them, ask to have them sawed in half lengthwise—most places that carry them do this automatically. I often add only one half to any braise and freeze the other half for another time.

Before adding pork rind to a dish, cut it into 2 or 3 strips. (If it's frozen, leave it overnight in the refrigerator to defrost.) If there is still a thick layer of fat on the rind, trim it to a minimum. Place the rind in a small saucepan filled with cold water and bring to a boil over high heat, then reduce to a gentle boil and blanch the rind for 5 minutes. This removes some of the fat still attached to the rind and mellows the strong pork taste. Drain and set aside.

Chicken wing tips, backs, necks, hearts, and gizzards are the by-products of cutting up a whole chicken for a braise (see page 161). For this reason, they are usually available to add to a chicken braise. If you do, however, cut up a chicken for another use or have a friendly butcher who supplies you with chicken parts, collect them in the freezer to have them ready for any type of braise. It's a good practice to rinse and pat dry chicken parts before using. Trim off and discard the lumps of fat. If the recipe calls for browning the main ingredient, you can brown the chicken parts right alongside—or do so immediately after to avoid crowding the pan. Browning these parts adds more flavor to your braise.

Stage Ten

FINISHING THE BRAISE

Once the main ingredient is tender and the flavor exchange between the braising liquid and the other ingredients has taken place, there are still a number of steps a cook can take to perfect a braised dish.

Straining the Braising Liquid

The decision to strain the braising liquid is based on tradition, practicality, and personal preference. Some recipes, such as the Chengdu Braised Pork with Daikon Radish (page 371), are strained to remove ingredients—here, bits of ground Sichuan peppercorns—that would be unpleasant to eat. For other recipes, the liquid is strained to produce something more elegant and refined, as is the case of Stracotto with Garlic & Pancetta (page 260). In many long braises, the aromatics (carrots, onions, celery, etc.) will have collapsed completely and become tasteless. While many people like the melting texture of these spent vegetables, they do create a decidedly rustic dish. Some recipes also call for retrieving a few inedible bits (bay leaves, whole star anise, pork rind, chicken necks, etc.) without the trouble of straining the entire dish. In the recipes in this book, I have indicated when to strain and when not to strain, but there are no hard-and-fast rules. Feel free to evaluate the sauce and make your own decision.

When you do strain the braising liquid, first use tongs or a slotted spoon to lift out the main ingredient(s). Set aside on a large platter, to capture the juices, and cover loosely with foil to keep warm. Then pour the braising liquid through a fine-mesh strainer into a heatproof container (glass or stainless steel are always better than plastic). Wipe out the pot with damp paper towels to remove any stray bits of herb stems or citrus rind that may have hung on, and return the liquid to it. Discard the strained-out solids or add them to the compost heap.

Degreasing the Braising Liquid

As meats and poultry braise, they contribute more than flavor to the sauce: they also yield some amount of fat. This rendered fat floats to the surface of the braising liquid and can be skimmed off quite neatly. If you are straining the braising liquid, degreasing is most easily done after straining, so you won't be skimming around floating bits of onions, carrots, and other aromatics. Degreasing is best done with a large flat spoon, something like a serving spoon or soupspoon. The more surface fat there is, the larger the spoon should be. If there is a significant layer of surface fat, start skimming the braising liquid as it stands. As the layer becomes thinner and the fat becomes elusive, bring the liquid to a simmer. This will cause the fat to coalesce in pools that are easier to skim off. I offer one strong cautionary note for degreasing: do not feel the need to remove every last droplet of fat. A bit of fat in a dish improves its taste.

If you own a gravy separator—and not all cooks do—there may be instances where it comes in handy as a way to degrease a braising liquid, especially after braising very fatty meats such as duck and lamb. Personally, I tend to forget about using a gravy separator, but this is because I really enjoy the process of skimming braising liquid—it gives me a chance to study the liquid and think about whether it needs reduction or another finishing touch. If you sometimes lack the patience for skimming, though, by all means bring out the gravy separator. It's better than serving a greasy sauce.

And finally, the easiest method of all for degreasing a braise is to let the entire dish sit overnight in the refrigerator. The next day, the fat will have solidified on the surface of the cooled liquid and can be removed effortlessly before reheating. The added advantage of this technique is that most every braised dish tastes better the next day!

Reducing the Braising Liquid

A wide variety of techniques are available for transforming a braising liquid into a sauce. The most common one is reduction: simmering a liquid to reduce the volume and concentrate the flavor. In many of the recipes in this book, I instruct you to "taste and evaluate the braising liquid" before reducing. Because of the variations among ingredients, pots, and techniques, it's nearly impossible to determine the exact outcome of every braise. For instance, fresh aromatics (carrots, onions, celery, etc.) will have more moisture in the summer than in the dead of winter. This means that the resulting sauce will have a higher water content and need more reduction in summertime. Before reducing a braising liquid, transfer the main ingredient(s) to a large plate or tray and cover loosely with foil to keep warm. Set the liquid over medium-high heat and bring to a steady simmer. It should bubble rapidly, but not as aggressively as a full boil. Never abandon a pot when you are reducing a liquid. It's important to stop when the liquid has reached the concentration you seek, and the only way to know this is to watch and taste continually. As water evaporates, the liquid will become thicker. In some cases, it won't get any thicker than a classic vinaigrette—not thick enough to coat a spoon, but with enough body to cling to a leaf of lettuce. Other times it will become as thick as blackstrap molasses. It depends on the original composition of the braise. If the goal is reducing the braising liquid entirely to a glaze, the liquid must be transferred to a smaller pan so that it doesn't evaporate completely in the wide surface of a braising pot. Wait to season a reduced liquid until the end. Seasonings, especially salt, become more concentrated as the water evaporates. It can be all too easy to overpower a sauce.

If you're new to reducing, you may at first have some trouble gauging when a sauce has reduced by the desired amount. A good trick for developing a sense for this is to pour the liquid into a spouted glass measuring cup before you begin reducing. Make a note of how much liquid there is, and then return it to the saucepan to simmer away and reduce. When you think the liquid has reduced by a certain amount—say, one half—pour it back into the measuring cup to check. After monitoring the reduction this way a few times, you'll develop an eye for judging how far you've reduced something—the way the pros do—and soon you'll no longer need to measure.

Other Finishing Touches

I couldn't begin to list all the different ways to finish a braise, but as you read through the recipes that follow, you'll find everything from yogurt to heavy cream to fresh herbs to honey to horseradish and more. You'll also find many recipes that emerge from the oven ready to serve with no final flourish. I encourage you to taste and assess your braises and do what seems right to you. If the sauce seems a little flat, perhaps it needs a squeeze of lemon. If you're in the mood for something rich, stir in a heaping spoonful of créme fraîche. As long as you taste as you go, it's almost impossible to go wrong with a well-made braise. In fact, much of the pleasure comes in adding your own personal finishing touches.

VEGETABLES

(continued on next page)

Braised Potatoes with Garlic & Bay Leaves ✈

I make this simple dish so often, and without thinking, that I really had to scratch my head to come up with an actual recipe. Let me explain: I start by placing as many potatoes as I want to braise in a single layer in any saucepan that accommodates them snugly without crowding. Then I pour in enough water or stock to come halfway up the potatoes and add a generous drizzle of olive oil, a few whole cloves of garlic, bay leaves, salt, and pepper. I pop on the lid, and braise gently until the potatoes are tender. During the last few minutes, I remove the lid, crank up the heat to evaporate the water, and shake the pan back and forth so the potatoes roll around and get coated in the garlicky-olive oil glaze that's forming. The potatoes come out all creamy and delicately infused with the flavors of bay and garlic.

I learned this technique from my close friend Roy Finamore, with whom I wrote an entire cookbook on potatoes. Roy calls these "seethed potatoes." I call them good. Look for small potatoes that you can braise whole. I especially like German Butterball and French fingerlings, but regular supermarket small red potatoes are wonderful too.

Serves 4 to 6 | Braising Time: about 25 minutes

1 1/2 pounds small red or white potatoes, scrubbed

3 tablespoons extra-virgin olive oil

1 cup water or chicken stock, homemade (page 448) or store-bought, or as needed

2 bay leaves, fresh if you can find them

2 to 3 garlic cloves, peeled and bruised

Coarse salt and freshly ground black pepper

1. **Evaluate the potatoes:** If the potatoes are larger than a golf ball, cut them in half. If you are leaving them whole, check to see if they have thick skins by scraping your thumbnail across the skin. If the skin doesn't tear, remove a strip of skin around the circumference of each potato with a vegetable peeler—this will allow the flavors of the braising liquid to penetrate the potato better. If the skins are relatively thin, leave them intact.

2. **The braise:** Place the potatoes in a saucepan large enough to hold them in a snug single layer without crowding. Add the olive oil and pour in enough water or stock to come halfway up the sides of the potatoes. Tear the bay leaves in half and add them along with the garlic. Season with salt and pepper. Cover and bring to a simmer over medium heat. When the water is simmering, lower the heat to medium-low so the liquid simmers gently. Braise, lifting the lid and turning the potatoes with a spoon once halfway through, until the potatoes are just tender when pierced with a thin skewer, about 20 minutes.

3. **The finish:** Remove the lid, increase the heat to high, and boil, gently shaking the pan back and forth, until the water evaporates and you can hear the oil sizzle, about 5 minutes. The braised garlic cloves will break down and coat the potatoes as you shake the pan. Serve hot.

VARIATION: BRAISED POTATOES WITH BUTTER & ROSEMARY

Once you've braised small potatoes a few times, you'll see that the recipe is ripe for improvisation. Feel free to vary the herbs, substitute dry white wine for the chicken stock or water, or use butter in place of olive oil. One of my favorite variations is to use 2 leafy sprigs of rosemary in place of the bay leaves and butter in place of the olive oil. Use chicken stock as the braising liquid and braise as directed. Delicious with Pork Loin Braised in Milk (page 346).

The Simplest Potato & Leek Braise ⇥

This is what I make when I want something luxurious but don't want to do any real work. Other than washing the leeks and cutting up the potatoes, the recipe practically cooks itself. You simply toss everything together in a gratin dish, cover tightly, and braise gently for an hour or so. Then the lid comes off, a little cream goes in, and the braised leeks and potatoes roast until they absorb the cream and turn all bubbly and browned on top. Serve this with Ham Braised in Madeira with Rosemary & Green Peppercorns (page 388) or Herb-Stuffed Leg of Lamb Braised in Red Wine (page 419).

Serves 6 | *Braising Time: about 1 3/4 hours*

3 medium or 2 large leeks (about 1 1/2 pounds trimmed of their leathery dark green tops) (see "Shopping for Leeks," page 88)

1 1/2 pounds yellow-flesh potatoes, such as Yukon Gold

1 1/2 teaspoons chopped fresh thyme

Pinch of freshly grated nutmeg

Coarse salt and freshly ground black pepper

1 1/4 cups chicken stock, homemade (page 448) or store-bought, heated to near boiling

2 tablespoons unsalted butter, cut into 1/2 pieces

1/4 to 1/3 cup heavy cream

1. **Heat the oven to 325 degrees.**

2. **Trimming and washing the leeks:** Trim the root ends and leathery green top parts from the leeks. You want only the whites and tender pale green parts. Slice the trimmed leeks lengthwise in half and then again into quarters. Chop into 3/4-inch pieces. Fill a large bowl with cold water and put the leeks in it. Swish the leeks around with one hand, then lift them from the water, leaving any sand and grit behind, and drain in a colander. Pour out the water, rinse the bowl, and repeat. This second rinse ensures that you won't ruin the dish with gritty leeks. Drain again in the colander.

3. **Peeling and chopping the potatoes:** Peel the potatoes and cut them into 3/4-inch chunks.

4. **The braise:** Place the leeks (it's fine if they are still wet) and potatoes in a buttered, shallow baking dish or gratin dish (a 10-by-14-inch oval works nicely). Add the thyme and nutmeg, and season generously with salt and pepper. (Potatoes tend to need a lot of salt, so don't be timid.) Toss with a rubber spatula to distribute the seasonings evenly, and spread the potatoes out in one layer. Pour over the hot stock. Dot the top with the butter. Cover tightly with heavy-duty foil and slide onto a rack in the middle of the oven. Braise, without disturbing, until the potatoes and leeks are almost tender, about 45 minutes.

Remove the foil, gently stir the potatoes and leeks with a rubber spatula, and check the amount of liquid left in the pan. If there is barely any left, cover again with the foil. If the liquid comes halfway up the sides of the dish—or more, leave the foil off. (The difference in the amount of liquid depends on the season; fall potatoes tend to absorb more liquid, while fresher spring and summer potatoes absorb less.) Continue to braise until the potatoes and leeks are completely tender, another 20-25 minutes. Check by piercing a potato and a piece of leek with the tip of a sharp knife.

5. **Browning the top:** Remove the dish from the oven, and increase the oven temperature to 425 degrees. If you haven't already, remove the foil from the dish. Give the potatoes and leeks a stir, and pour over the cream. Return the dish to the oven, uncovered, and bake until the top is browned and bubbly and the cream is mostly absorbed, another 25 to 30 minutes. Let rest 5 to 10 minutes, and serve directly from the baking dish.

End-of-Summer Green Beans Braised with Tomatoes →→

We've become so accustomed to quick-cooking green beans just until crisp and bright that many of us overlook the pleasure of tender slow-cooked beans. When left to braise for an hour with summer ripe tomatoes, the beans become supple, sweet, and satisfying.

While I've made this with supermarket beans throughout the year, the very best green beans for braising are locally grown ones that appear in the farmers' market toward the end of summer, when the season is winding down. It's a great way to cook beans that are beginning to bulge and show signs of being overly mature. Do not substitute skinny haricot verts.

Serves 4 | *Braising Time: about 1 hour*

3 tablespoons extra-virgin olive oil

3 to 4 garlic cloves, thinly sliced

2 anchovies, minced

Heaping 1/2 teaspoon dried oregano

1 pound green beans, topped and tailed

1 1/4 cup chopped ripe tomatoes or
    one 14 1/2-ounce can whole peeled
    tomatoes, drained and chopped

1/2 cup water

Coarse salt and freshly ground black
    pepper

1. **The aromatics:** Heat the oil in a large lidded skillet (12- to 13-inch) over medium heat. Add the garlic and sauté gently until it releases its fragrance and just begins to show touches of gold on the edges, about 2 minutes. Do not let the garlic brown.

2. **The braising liquid:** Add the anchovies and oregano, smashing the anchovies with a wooden spoon to blend them into the oil, and sauté for a minute longer. Immediately add the green beans, stirring and tossing to coat them with the oil and seasonings. Add the tomatoes and bring to a simmer. Add the water and season with pepper and just a pinch of salt, keeping in mind the saltiness the anchovies add.

3. **The braise:** Cover, lower the heat to a gentle simmer, and braise the beans, stirring

occasionally and checking to make sure that they are not simmering too energetically. If they are, lower the heat a notch or place a heat diffuser beneath the pan. Continue to braise gently until the beans are completely soft and are beginning to wrinkle but not splitting open or falling apart, about 1 hour.

4.   **The finish:** Depending on the beans and the tomatoes you used, there may or may not be a lot of liquid remaining in the pan. If the beans are swimming in sauce, remove the lid, increase the heat, and boil for 3 to 5 minutes, until the sauce is the consistency of a loose tomato sauce that generously coats the beans. Taste for salt and pepper. Serve hot or warm.

Peperonata →→

Make this in the late summer and early fall when the markets are overflowing with local peppers of all sorts. Best described as a sweet pepper stew, peperonata is one of those great rustic Italian dishes that you almost make up as you go along. Sometimes I add a splash of white wine at the start. Other times a bit of garlic makes its way in. Some cooks add ripe tomatoes, but I tend not to, because they mute the taste of the peppers and make the dish soupier than I like. And, of course, every batch of peperonata varies according to the peppers I find at the market. Ideally I look for a multicolor mix of sweet bell peppers and a few Italian Cubanelle or frying peppers. Avoid green bell peppers, since their sharp grassy flavor can overpower the dish. When shopping for peppers, choose ones that feel heavy in your hand, and give them a good sniff—they should smell fresh and, well, peppery.

Peperonata makes a great addition to an antipasto platter. I also like to serve it as a relish alongside grilled meats and fish. Try it on sandwiches (especially meat loaf sandwiches), on warm crostini with a smear of fresh goat cheese, as an omelet or frittata filling, or, perhaps best of all, tossed with pasta along with bits of sautéed spicy sausage. Once you make a batch of peperonata, you'll find a world of delicious uses for it, so don't be afraid of making too much.

Working Ahead

To best appreciate the sweet flavor of peperonata, let it cool to lukewarm or room temperature before serving. It also keeps for a week covered in the refrigerator. After refrigerating, bring to room temperature or warm slightly before serving.

Makes about 1 quart | *Braising Time: about 40 minutes*

2 pounds sweet peppers, preferably a mix
    of sweet Italian and yellow and
    red bell peppers
1/4 cup extra-virgin olive oil
1 large yellow onion (about 8 ounces),
    thickly sliced
3 anchovies, minced

A hefty pinch of crushed red pepper flakes
Coarse salt
2 teaspoons balsamic vinegar
Freshly ground black pepper
Chopped flat-leaf parsley, basil, or chives
    (optional)

1.   **Trimming the peppers:** Cut all the peppers lengthwise in half, and remove the stems, cores, and seeds. Cut the peppers crosswise into 1/2-inch-wide strips. Set aside.

2.   **The aromatics:** Heat the oil in a heavy-based saucepan (4- to 5-quart) over medium heat. Add the onion and cook, stirring occasionally, until just softened and not at all browned, about 6 minutes. Stir in the anchovies, pepper flakes, and a substantial pinch of salt.

3.   **The braise:** Add the peppers and stir to combine, then reduce the heat to medium-low and cover the pan. Simmer gently, stirring and checking every 15 minutes to ensure that the liquid is bubbling quietly and that none of the vegetables are sticking. Reduce the heat if the vegetables appear to be sticking or cooking too quickly, and continue to braise until the peppers are completely tender and silky, about 40 minutes. Stir in the vinegar, and set aside to cool to warm or room temperature. (The peperonata can be stored for up to a week, covered in the refrigerator. Bring to room temperature or warm slightly before serving to appreciate its full flavor.)

4.   **The finish:** Season the peperonata to taste with salt and pepper. If desired, add chopped fresh herbs.

Stuffed Eggplant Braised with Dill & Mint →⊱

Traditionally these herb-and-vegetable-stuffed eggplant fall in the category of meze (small dishes eaten with drinks at the start of a Mediterranean meal), but I've found that they are equally good served as a side dish, on a buffet, or as a light lunch. Once you grasp the technique of scooping out the eggplant, filling them back up with a fresh-tasting stuffing, and braising them in chopped tomato, you'll find there's endless opportunity for improvisation. No dill available? Go for fresh basil. Don't care for cooked celery? Substitute fennel. In other words, don't feel tied to the recipe. I also play around with how I serve these. Sometimes I like them warm and plain, other times I'm in the mood for a little yogurt topping. And when the weather is sultry, they're best lightly chilled, with a lemony vinaigrette. (See below for all these variations.)

Make this in the summer when eggplant are small and tight-skinned and tomatoes are at their peak. If you cannot find truly ripe, local tomatoes, substitute canned. The dish will still be lovely.

wine notes

Crisp, herbal Sauvignon Blanc from New Zealand or South Africa, or a dry rosé from France.

Working Ahead

These can be made up to a day ahead and kept refrigerated. To serve, either warm briefly, covered, in a low oven or let come to room temperature.

Serves 6 | Braising Time: about 1 1/2 hours

6 small eggplant (total 2 pounds),
preferably Italian (see "Shopping for
Eggplant," page 50), each about
6 inches long

Coarse salt

3 ½ tablespoons extra-virgin olive oil

2 large or 3 medium celery stalks, cut into
¼-inch dice

2 garlic cloves, minced

Freshly ground black pepper

2 tablespoons chopped fresh dill, plus
more for serving

2 tablespoons chopped flat-leaf parsley

1 tablespoon chopped fresh mint,
preferably peppermint

2 pounds ripe plum tomatoes, cored,
seeded, and coarsely chopped, or one
28-ounce can whole peeled tomatoes,
seeded and chopped, juice reserved

1. **Heat the oven to 325 degrees.**

2. **Making eggplant shells for stuffing:** Slice lengthwise once down each eggplant to cut off a slice about ½ inch thick. Reserve these slices. With a melon baller, cut out the inside of the eggplant, leaving a good ¼-inch wall to contain the stuffing. (I like to leave the stem ends on the eggplant for a nice rustic look, but you can trim them off if you prefer.) Capture all the scooped-out trimmings, and chop them into small pieces. Place in a large bowl. Chop all the reserved top slices, with skin, into ¼-inch dice. Add to the bowl. Season the inside of the eggplant shells with salt, and arrange them cut side down on paper towels.

3. **The stuffing:** Heat 2 ½ tablespoons of the oil in a large skillet (11- to 12-inch) over medium-high heat. Add the celery and sauté, stirring occasionally, until it begins to soften, about 2 minutes. Stir in the garlic and sauté until it begins to release its aroma, about 30 seconds. Add the chopped eggplant, season with salt and pepper, and sauté, stirring often, until the eggplant softens, about 4 minutes. Add the chopped herbs and remove from the heat.

4. **The aromatics:** Place the chopped tomatoes and their juice in a medium bowl, season lightly with salt and pepper, and drizzle over 2 teaspoons oil. Toss with a large spoon to coat evenly. Spread in the bottom of a large baking dish (9-by-13-inch works well).

5. **Stuffing the eggplant:** Rinse the eggplant shells quickly under cold water, and blot dry with paper towels. Season with pepper. Spoon the stuffing into the shells. Arrange the stuffed eggplant on the bed of tomatoes. Using your fingers or a small pastry brush, dab or brush the remaining 1 teaspoon oil onto the exposed cut surface of the eggplant shells. Drizzle any remaining drops of oil over the stuffing.

6. **The braise:** Cover tightly with foil and braise until the eggplant is tender and the stuffing is hot all the way through, about 1 hour and 15 minutes. Check after 40 minutes and add a little water if the tomatoes have dried out and are starting to brown.

7. **The finish:** Uncover the dish and increase the oven temperature to 400 degrees. Continue to braise until the tomatoes begin to brown around the edges, another 15 minutes or so. Sprinkle with chopped dill and serve hot, warm, at room temperature, or lightly chilled. Spoon some of the cooked tomatoes alongside each eggplant.

VARIATION: YOGURT-TOPPED STUFFED EGGPLANT

Serve the stuffed eggplant warm with a dollop of plain yogurt on top. Or prepare Feta-Dill Yogurt: Combine 3/4 cup plain whole-milk yogurt with 2 tablespoons crumbled feta, 1 minced garlic clove, 1 tablespoon chopped dill, a squeeze of lemon, salt to taste, and plenty of cracked black pepper. Spoon onto the warm eggplant.

VARIATION: VINAIGRETTE-TOPPED STUFFED EGGPLANT

When the weather is steamy, I prefer to serve the eggplant lightly chilled, topped with a lemon vinaigrette. Whisk together 2 tablespoons freshly squeezed lemon juice, 1 teaspoon grated lemon zest, 1 garlic clove, minced, and salt and pepper to taste. Whisk in 5 tablespoons extra-virgin olive oil. Drizzle over the eggplant.

VARIATION: FETA-STUFFED BRAISED EGGPLANT

In Step 3, stir 1/2 cup crumbled feta into the eggplant mixture along with the herbs. Serve the stuffed eggplant warm with either plain yogurt or the Feta-Dill Yogurt spooned on top.

Shopping for Eggplant

There are two principal categories of eggplant: globe-shaped and the more elongated banana-shaped Asian varieties. For stuffing, globe eggplant provide the best shape, and of these, the smaller, more delicately flavored Italian eggplant are my favorite. They are neater to handle and serve, and their flavor best matches the Mediterranean character of the braise here. Shop for smallish globe eggplant that are tight-skinned, shiny, and heavy for their size. The super-sized bulbous ones that you find out of season tend to have large seeds and can be wooly in texture. If you have access to a farmers' market or a produce department that sells local produce, that is the way to go. As eggplants sit around in storage, they deteriorate in quality and often become bitter. Many cooks recommend salting eggplant before cooking to remove bitterness. I have found that if you choose small, fresh, locally grown eggplant, bitterness is never an issue. Salting will, however, draw off some of the moisture from the eggplant, which will help them retain their shape a bit better when stuffed and braised.

World's Best Braised Green Cabbage, page 59

Braised Halibut Steak with
Creamy Leeks, page 101

Escarole Braised with Cannellini Beans, page 53

Endive browned before braising, page 57

Braised Endive with Prosciutto, page 56

Braised Leeks & Bacon in a Tart, page 89

Sausages & Plums Braised in Red Wine,
page 396, with polenta and salad greens

Monkfish Braised with Cherry Tomatoes & Basil, page 104

Peppery Braised Broccoli Rabe with Arugula ⤙⤜

There's no end to the variations on, or my appetite for, greens. Bitter, earthy, tough, sharp, spicy—whatever their character, I love them all. I especially appreciate what happens when they are braised down to something soft and soulful. The idea for treating arugula like an herb and tossing it in toward the end of braising comes from the charmingly inspiring British chef Jamie Oliver. I saw him demonstrate a recipe similar to this on TV once, and thought I'd "give it a bash," as he might say. It's a brilliant little idea. Arugula's sharp bite adds just the right lift to the braised greens.

These greens are just as good at room temperature as they are warm, making them a candidate for any sort of antipasto spread or buffet. Escarole could be substituted for the broccoli rabe, using the same quantities and timing.

Serves 4 | Braising Time: About 30 minutes

1 bunch broccoli rabe (12 to 14 ounces)

1/4 cup extra-virgin olive oil, plus more
for serving

1 small yellow onion (4 ounces),
thinly sliced

3 garlic cloves, thinly sliced

Pinch of crushed red pepper flakes

Coarse salt

1/2 cup chicken stock, homemade (page
448) or storebought, or water

4 to 5 ounces arugula

3 tablespoons pine nuts, lightly toasted
(optional)

1. **Trimming and washing the broccoli rabe:** Trim the bottom 1/4 inch from the broccoli rabe stems (they are generally rather dried out). Chop the remaining stems into 1-inch pieces, and cut the leafier tops into 1-inch-wide strips. Rinse and drain.

2. **Sautéing the broccoli rabe and aromatics:** Heat the oil in a large skillet (11- to 12-inch) over medium-high heat. When the oil shimmers, add the broccoli rabe—it will splat-

ter from the drops of water left on it. Stir the greens with tongs and sauté until wilted down to a flat layer, about 3 minutes. Add the onion, garlic, crushed red pepper, and a generous pinch of salt, stir to combine, and sauté for another minute.

3. **The braise:** Pour in the stock or water, lower the heat to medium-low, and cover the pan. Check the heat after a few minutes to make sure that the liquid is simmering quietly, not ferociously; you may need to turn it down a bit. Continue simmering, stirring every 5 minutes or so, until the greens are tender, about 20 minutes. Check by picking out a stem piece, letting it cool some, and biting into it—it should be completely tender but not mushy.

4. **The finish:** Remove the lid, add the arugula, stir, and increase the heat to medium. Simmer until the liquid is mostly evaporated and the arugula is tender but still retains some bright green, about 10 minutes. Taste for salt and remove from the heat.

5. **Serving:** Transfer to plates or a shallow serving dish. Drizzle a thread of olive oil over the top, and sprinkle with the pine nuts, if using. Serve warm or at room temperature.

VARIATION: PEPPERY BRAISED BROCCOLINI WITH ARUGULA

In place of broccoli rabe, make this with broccolini, the miniature sprouting broccoli that is now available in many produce departments. In Step 2, expect the broccolini to take closer to 5 minutes to wilt down. Braise the broccolini for 30 minutes before adding the arugula.

Escarole Braised with Cannellini Beans

I have a deep fondness for the casual family-run southern Italian restaurants scattered throughout the cities of the Northeast. Just a step up from pizza places, the best of these eateries offer honest food heavily laced with garlic and olive oil, serve pasta only as a first course or side dish, and almost always have escarole and white beans somewhere on the menu. The silky bitterness of escarole braised with tender, meaty cannellini beans tempts me every time.

Serve this in pasta bowls as a first course, either on or accompanied by toasted Italian bread rubbed with garlic. The escarole also makes a fine side dish to meats and poultry.

For a shortcut version, use canned cannellini beans. You sacrifice some depth of flavor, but get a wonderfully quick weeknight dish in return. (See "A Note on Canned Beans," page 55.)

wine notes

Vibrant white with citrus and herbal flavors from Italy, such as Pinot Grigio, Soave, or Vernaccia di San Gimignano.

Working Ahead

The cannellini beans require a bit of advance planning (Step 1). First they need to soak for 8 to 12 hours. Then they simmer for 1 to 1 1/2 hours. Once the beans are tender, you need to let them cool in the cooking water—a step that helps them absorb more flavor. At this point, the beans can be refrigerated for 1 to 2 days, as suits your schedule.

Serves 6 | Braising Time: about 20 minutes, plus 1 1/4 hours bean cooking time

THE BEANS

1 cup (8 ounces) dried cannellini beans,
    picked over and rinsed
1 cup chicken stock, homemade (page 448)
    or store-bought
Water as needed
1 small onion (about 4 ounces), peeled and
    quartered

1 small carrot, peeled and quartered
2 garlic cloves, peeled and bruised
1 bay leaf
1 tablespoon extra-virgin olive oil
Coarse salt

THE BRAISE

1 medium head escarole (about 1 pound)
1/4 cup extra-virgin olive oil
3 garlic cloves, thinly sliced
Pinch of crushed red pepper flakes

Coarse salt and freshly ground black
    pepper
1/2 lemon
Best-quality extra-virgin olive oil
    for drizzling

1. **Soaking the beans—8 to 10 hours in advance:** Place the beans in a medium bowl, cover with cool water, and leave to soak for 8 to 12 hours at room temperature. Drain and rinse.

2. **Cooking the beans:** Place the soaked beans in a medium heavy-based saucepan (2 1/2- to 3-quart). Add the stock and enough water to cover by 1 1/2 inches, then add the onion, carrot, garlic, bay leaf, and oil. Bring to a simmer over medium heat. Once the liquid simmers, partially cover the pot, lower the heat to a gentle simmer, and cook until the beans are tender, 1 to 1 1/2 hours. (The cooking time will vary according to the dryness of the beans.) If at any time the level of the liquid threatens to drop below the level of the beans, add just enough water to cover. Ideally, when the beans are tender, they should have absorbed enough of the cooking liquid so that the pot is moist but not soupy. Season with salt to taste, and set aside to cool in the cooking liquid. (*The beans may be made 1 to 2 days ahead. If they will be sitting for more than 2 hours, transfer the beans and the cooking liquid to a bowl and keep them covered and refrigerated.*)

3. **Washing and trimming the escarole:** Tear the escarole leaves from the head and soak them in a large bowl of cold water for 10 to 15 minutes to loosen any dirt. Rinse and drain, paying special attention to the hollows at the base of the outer leaves, the place where dirt usually collects. You may need to rub any stubborn dirt away with your thumb. Rinse again and drain briefly in a colander. Slice the escarole leaves into 1 1/2-inch-wide strips and return the strips to the colander to drain.

4. **The aromatics:** Combine the oil, garlic, and crushed red pepper in a large lidded skillet

(12- to 13-inch) over medium heat. Warm just until the garlic becomes fragrant and golden around the edges, about 2 minutes. Don't allow the garlic to become dark brown or you'll have to start over.

5. **Wilting the escarole:** Add the escarole a handful at a time, stirring and allowing it to wilt some before adding the next handful. (It's fine if the escarole still has water clinging to it, this will help it begin to braise.) Season with salt and pepper.

6. **The braise:** Pull the carrot and onion pieces and the bay leaf from the pot of beans and discard. But don't be too fussy and try to get every last bit of onion, as some may have disintegrated right into the beans, along with the garlic. When all the escarole has wilted, spoon the beans and cooking liquid into the skillet, season with salt and pepper, gently stir to incorporate the beans. Bring to a gentle simmer. Cover, adjust the heat to maintain a low simmer, and braise until the greens are very tender and the cooking liquid has thickened some from the starch released from the beans, about 20 minutes.

7. **The finish:** I prefer this dish soupy, so I serve as is. If you would like it less soupy, remove the lid and boil to reduce the liquid for about 5 minutes. Season the braise with a generous squeeze of fresh lemon juice and salt and pepper. Serve warm or at room temperature, with a thread of best-quality olive oil drizzled over the top.

A Note on Canned Beans

Many cooks suggest that canned beans can stand for home-cooked beans. I don't always agree. Canned beans don't deliver the same earthy flavor and creamy texture. They taste bland and often become mushy and broken—especially when cooked a second time. When you cook dried beans from scratch, you also end up with a tasty bean broth to add to braises and soups. Although simmering dried beans takes a few hours, they cook largely unattended and can be made a day or two ahead.

If you choose to use canned beans for convenience sake, the brands with the truest bean flavor and nicest texture are Goya and Bush's. Before using, drain and rinse beans thoroughly—the liquid they come packed in can be unpleasantly viscous and salty. If using canned beans for the Escarole Braised with Cannellini Beans (page 53), you'll need about 2 1/2 cups (a little less than two 15-ounce cans). Omit Steps 1 and 2 in the recipe, and add the beans as directed in Step 6, along with 1 cup of chicken stock. Without the starchy bean broth, the liquid won't have much body.

Braised Endive with Prosciutto ✈

If I had to name my favorite vegetable for braising, it would be endive. When it is browned first in butter and then slowly cooked in just a bit of golden chicken stock, endive's inherent bitterness transforms into something marvelously complex and luscious. Some cooks insist on adding a pinch of sugar to endive. I don't. I like the way the edge of bitterness offsets the remarkably soft, silky texture that slow cooking produces. Thin strips of prosciutto lend a welcome salty, meaty edge to the dish. It's also quite nice with other good-tasting ham such as serrano and Smithfield. If you're serving vegetarians, omit the ham altogether. The dish may be a bit less dramatic, but it will still be delectable.

wine notes

Rich, fruity white to offset the bitterness of the endives—Pinot Gris from Alsace or Oregon, or an off-dry Riesling from the Rheingau, Pfalz, or Rheinhessen regions.

Serves 6 | Braising Time: about 45 minutes

6 to 9 Belgian endive (about 1 ¹/₂ pounds; see "Shopping for Belgian Endive," page 58)

3 tablespoons unsalted butter

4 thin slices prosciutto (about 2 ounces), cut crosswise into 1-inch-wide strips (don't trim off the fat)

Coarse salt and freshly ground black pepper

¹/₂ cup chicken stock, homemade (page 448) or store-bought

¹/₄ to ¹/₃ cup heavy cream

1. **Heat the oven to 375 degrees.** Butter a large gratin dish or baking dish (9-by-13-inch).
2. **Trimming the endive:** Remove the outermost leaves from the endive, and trim the bottoms if they appear brown or dried out. Cut each endive lengthwise in half.

3. **Browning the endive:** Melt 2 tablespoons of the butter in a large skillet (12-inch) over medium heat (nonstick or well-seasoned cast iron are good choices since the delicate endive leaves won't stick and tear, but any decent skillet will do). When the butter just stops foaming, add as many endive, cut side down, as will fit in a loose layer and cook until the cut sides are nicely browned, about 4 minutes. Using tongs, turn the endive and brown for a minute or two on the other side. Transfer the browned endive to the gratin dish, arranging them cut side up. Add the remaining tablespoon of butter to the skillet and brown the rest of the endive. The endive should fit in a snug single layer in the gratin dish.

4. **The aromatics and braising liquid:** There should still be a film of butter in the skillet. Still over medium heat, add the prosciutto strips to the skillet and turn to coat them with the butter. Tuck a few strips between the endive and drape the rest over the tops. Season with salt and pepper, keeping in mind that the prosciutto is salty. Add the stock to the skillet and bring to a boil over high heat. Scrape the bottom of the pan with a wooden spoon to loosen any browned bits, and pour the stock over the endive and prosciutto.

5. **The braise:** Cover the dish tightly with foil. Braise until the endive are collapsed and tender when pierced with a sharp knife and have a burnished hue, 30 to 35 minutes.

6. **The finish:** Remove the foil and baste the endive by spooning over any juices from the pan. If the pan is dry, add 2 tablespoons of water. Braise, uncovered, for another 8 to 10 minutes, until the pan juices have turned a caramel color and almost completely evaporated. Pour over the heavy cream—the lesser amount if you want something less rich tasting—and bake until the cream takes on a caramel color and thickens to a sauce-like consistency, another 6 minutes or so. Spoon over any pan drippings, and serve warm or at room temperature.

VARIATION: BRAISED ENDIVE WITH FRIED EGGS

Paired with eggs fried in olive oil, the braised endive makes a fabulous supper. Add an extra slice of prosciutto to the recipe in Step 4. When the endive are done, fry as may eggs as you like in olive oil in a large skillet over medium heat. Slide the fried eggs onto dinner plates, and return the skillet to medium-high heat. Add 1 teaspoon sherry vinegar or balsamic vinegar, and let it boil for about 1 minute. Drizzle the reduced vinegar over the eggs. Place the warm or room-temperature braised endive and prosciutto next to the eggs, and serve immediately.

What Is Belgian Endive?

Belgian endive, a member of the chicory family, is an often overlooked and often misunderstood vegetable. These tightly layered pod-shaped heads are grown in a most unusual way. Chicory roots (which are the source of the roasted and ground chicory sometimes blended with coffee) are harvested and then left in a dark, damp spot, like a cellar, for several months, where they eventually sprout the small very pale shoots we know as endive. The spent roots are discarded, and the cycle begun again the next spring with the sowing of new chicory seeds. The fresh shoots earned their name Belgian endive because a Belgian farmer is credited with "discovering" them in the mid nineteenth century.

Belgian endive may have first gained popularity because it was the only fresh, crisp vegetable available in the dormant winter months (think nineteenth-century Northern Europe). Its continued popularity, however, is due to its alluring combination of bitterness and tenderness. Used fresh in salads, it adds crunch and a delicate bitterness. Its scoop-shaped leaves also make it a festive receptacle for dips.

Shopping for Belgian Endive

Look for regular-shaped, tight heads with leaves that are pale all the way to the tips. If the edges of the leaves have begun to turn a darker green, it is a sign that the endive has been exposed to light for too long, which turns them tough and excessively bitter. Avoid any endive with soft or slimy spots on the outside. I prefer medium to small endive, not more than 4 ounces each. As they get larger, the heads become less compact and the leaves less smooth and a bit less tender.

Because endive heads are so tightly layered and were not grown in dirt, the leaves don't need the same careful washing as other greens. I just pull off and discard the outer leaves and give them a quick rinse.

World's Best Braised Green Cabbage ⇢⇢

We all have certain things we make over and over again, either because they are so easy or because they are so good—or, like this braised cabbage, both. The recipe comes from friends in Richmond, Virginia, who were smitten by a braised cabbage side dish at their favorite Italian restaurant. They talked about it with such enthusiasm that I had to try to re-create it at home. Once you read through the recipe, you'll see that there's not much to it at all. Indeed, after you make the dish once, you won't need a recipe—it's that simple. The cabbage here is plain old green cabbage, and the seasonings are coarse salt, freshly ground black pepper, and crushed red pepper flakes. The extended cooking time renders the cabbage intensely tender and sweet. If you stock *fleur de sel* in your pantry, a sprinkle before serving adds a crunchy counterpoint to the supple cabbage; if not, any coarse sea salt will have a similar effect.

Serve as a wintertime side dish or as an appealing vegetarian supper with beans or mashed potatoes.

wine notes

The rich, aromatic whites of Alsace (Pinot Gris, Pinot Blanc, or a dry Gewürztraminer) make the best possible match for braised cabbage.

Working Ahead

Like many braises, this cabbage tastes even better the next day, either at room temperature or warmed in a moderate oven for about 20 minutes.

Serves 6 | Braising Time: about 2 1/4 hours

1 medium head green cabbage (about
    2 pounds)

1 large yellow onion (about 8 ounces),
    thickly sliced

1 large carrot, cut into $1/4$-inch rounds

$1/4$ cup chicken stock, homemade (page
    448) or store-bought, or water

$1/4$ cup extra-virgin olive oil

Coarse salt and freshly ground black
    pepper

$1/8$ teaspoon crushed red pepper flakes,
    or to taste

Fleur de sel or coarse sea salt

1. **Heat the oven to 325 degrees.** Lightly oil a large gratin dish or baking dish (9-by-13-inch works well).

2. **Trimming the cabbage:** Peel off and discard any bruised or ragged outer leaves from the cabbage. The cabbage should weigh close to 2 pounds (if you don't have a kitchen scale, consult the grocery store receipt). If the cabbage weighs more than 2 pounds, it won't fit in the baking dish and won't braise as beautifully. To remedy this, cut away a wedge of the cabbage to trim it down to size. Save the leftover wedge for salad or coleslaw. Then cut the cabbage into 8 wedges. Arrange the wedges in the baking dish; they may overlap some, but do your best to make a single layer.

3. **The braise:** Scatter in the onion and carrot. Drizzle over the oil and stock or water. Season with salt, pepper, and the pepper flakes. Cover tightly with foil, and slide into the middle of the oven to braise until the vegetables are completely tender, about 2 hours. Turn the cabbage wedges with tongs after an hour. Don't worry if the wedges want to fall apart as you turn them; just do your best to keep them intact. If the dish is drying out at all, add a few tablespoon of water.

4. **The finish:** Once the cabbage is completely tender, remove the foil, increase the oven heat to 400, and roast until the vegetables begin to brown, another 15 minutes or so. Serve warm or at room temperature, sprinkled with *fleur de sel* or other coarse salt.

VARIATION: BRAISED GREEN CABBAGE WITH BALSAMIC VINEGAR

I sometimes add a splash of balsamic vinegar to the cabbage to enhance its sweetness. In Step 4, after you remove the foil, sprinkle on 1 $1/2$ tablespoons balsamic and turn the cabbage with tongs to distribute the vinegar, then roast for another 15 minutes, uncovered, as directed.

Savoy Cabbage Gratin with Saint-Marcellin ✈

This is a deeply satisfying winter dish—braised Savoy cabbage topped with a mild, creamy, soft cheese. The idea came from my friend Daphne Zepos, who takes care of the cheeses at Artisanal Cheese Center in New York City. One bitter February morning, Daphne and I were having coffee together at City Bakery in New York and she described a perfectly ripe Saint-Marcellin cheese she had recently tasted. Her impassioned description led me directly to the cheese store and then to this dish. If you're not familiar with Saint-Marcellin, it's a cow's milk cheese from southeastern France (Dauphine, near Grenoble). The little disks (about 3 inches across and an inch tall) are soft, creamy, and full of nuance. If you can't find Saint-Marcellin, select a triple-cream, like the easily found Explorateur or Brillat-Savarin or Pierre Robert. Not Brie, not Camembert—neither has enough character.

wine notes

Fruity dry white with little or no oak, such as Chenin Blanc from California or Washington State, or Viognier from California.

Serves 6 | Braising Time: 1 1/4 hours

3 tablespoons unsalted butter

1 head Savoy cabbage (about 1 1/2 pounds), quartered, cored, and sliced into 1/2 inch-wide shreds

1 bunch scallions, white and green parts, sliced into 1/2-inch-wide pieces

Coarse salt and freshly ground black pepper

1 3/4 cups chicken stock, homemade (page 448) or store-bought

1 ripe Saint-Marcellin cheese (about 3 ounces)

1. **Heat the oven to 350 degrees.** Butter a large gratin dish (10-by-14-inch).

2. **Wilting the cabbage:** In a large skillet (13-inch works well), melt the butter over medium-high heat. Add the cabbage and scallions, season with salt and pepper, and sauté, stirring often, until the cabbage is just beginning to brown in spots, 10 to 12 minutes. Pour in the stock, bring to a steady simmer, scraping the bottom of the pan, and cook for about 2 minutes.

3. **The braise:** Scrape the cabbage, scallions, and all the juices into the gratin dish. Cover tightly with foil, slide onto the middle rack of the oven, and braise for 45 minutes. Remove the foil and continue to cook until the liquid is mostly evaporated, another 20 minutes.

4. **The finish:** Cut or tear the cheese into small lumps (about 1/2 inch) and scatter them across the gratin. Increase the oven temperature to 375 degrees, and cook until the cheese is thoroughly melted, about 10 minutes. Serve hot or warm as a first course, side dish, or on its own as a light supper.

Red Cabbage Braised with Maple & Ginger ⇥

An old-fashioned dish that appears on my holiday dinner table just as it did on my grandmother's table when I was a child. Braising cabbage this way renders it lusciously silky and aromatic with the flavors of spice and fruit. The enchanting sweet-and-sour taste comes from apple, fresh cider, a shot of maple syrup, and a generous measure of red wine vinegar. I add bacon at the beginning of the braise so it will lend its smoky savor to the dish. If you prefer, hold the bacon back and crumble it over just before serving for a crunchy contrast.

Serves 6 to 8 | *Braising Time: about 1 hour*

1 teaspoon extra-virgin olive oil or
    vegetable oil
2 slices thick-cut bacon (2 ounces),
    cut into 1/2-inch-wide strips
1 1/2 tablespoons unsalted butter
1 medium yellow onion (6 ounces),
    thinly sliced
Coarse salt and freshly ground black
    pepper

1 Granny Smith apple, peeled, cored,
    and thinly sliced
1 teaspoon grated fresh ginger
1 medium head red cabbage (about 1 3/4
    pounds), quartered, cored, and thinly
    sliced
1/4 cup cider vinegar
2 tablespoons pure maple syrup

1. **Heat the oven to 300 degrees.**

2. **Frying the bacon:** Combine the oil and bacon in a large deep ovenproof skillet (12- to 13-inch), set the skillet over medium heat, and fry the bacon until it renders its fat and begins to crisp, 5 minutes. Scoop out the bacon with a slotted spoon and set aside on paper towels to drain.

3. **Sautéing the aromatics and wilting the cabbage:** Add the butter to the bacon fat in the pan and stir in the sliced onion. Season with salt and pepper and sauté, stirring a few times, until the onion turns limp, about 2 minutes. Add the apple and ginger and stir to combine. Increase the heat to medium-high and begin adding the cabbage a few handfuls at a time. Once all the cabbage is in the skillet, sauté, stirring frequently, until the strands begin to wilt and have a moist gleam, about 6 minutes. Add the cider and syrup, and return the bacon to the pan. Stir to incorporate, and let the liquid come to a boil.

4. **The braise:** Cover the pan and slide into the middle of the oven. Braise at a gentle simmer, stirring every 20 minutes, until the cabbage is tender and deeply fragrant, about 1 hour. Serve warm or at room temperature.

Shopping for Maple Syrup

I know that I'm spoiled here in Vermont, where I can buy real maple syrup out of the back of a pickup just down the road, but I would never dream of using an imitation. If you ever come across *Grade B* maple syrup (as opposed to the more commonly available *Grade A fancy*), I encourage you to try it. Grade B has a deeper maple flavor and slightly darker color than A. It's what the Vermont sugar makers use at home, and that's good enough for me.

Creamy Braised Brussels Sprouts ➻

I know that not everyone adores Brussels sprouts, but I'm convinced that it's only because they don't know how to prepare them. When they are left whole and steamed or boiled, the strong taste of the sprouts can be too much for all but the most die-hard cabbage fans. The key to cooking Brussels sprouts is to chop them into small pieces so they release their pungency. Only then does the earthy, sweet essence of these little gems emerge. Using heavy cream as the braising liquid brings out their inherent sweetness even more, and the cream itself reduces into a thick, ivory-colored glaze that coats the sprouts. I've even served this to devout Brussels sprout haters and listened to them rave.

Brussels sprouts appear in the markets in late fall and winter, making this an ideal holiday dish. If you'd like to dress it up a bit, sprinkle on a handful of toasted hazelnuts or crisp bits of crumbled bacon.

Working Ahead

These can be prepared a couple of hours ahead up through Step 3. Just leave the pan covered and out of the way at room temperature. To finish, remove the lid and heat over medium till warm, then add the lemon juice and season to taste. The cream will have thickened up by itself and you won't need to boil it to do so.

Serves 4 to 6 | Braising Time: 30 to 35 minutes

1 pound Brussels sprouts

3 tablespoons unsalted butter

Coarse salt and freshly ground white
   pepper

1 cup heavy cream

1/2 lemon

1. **Trimming the Brussels sprouts:** Trim the very base of each sprout with a sharp paring knife and then peel off any ragged outer leaves. Cut the Brussels sprouts through the core into halves. If the sprouts are large, cut each half into thirds, or, if they are smallish, cut each half again in half to make quarters. Ultimately, you want little wedges that are no more than 1/2 inch across.

2. **Browning the Brussels sprouts:** Melt the butter in a large skillet (12-inch) over medium-high heat. When the foaming stops, add the Brussels sprouts and season with salt and white pepper. Cook, stirring occasionally, until the sprouts begin to brown in spots, about 5 minutes.

3. **The braise:** Pour in the cream, stir, cover, and reduce to a slow simmer. Braise over low heat until the sprouts are tender enough to be pierced easily with the tip of a sharp knife, 30 to 35 minutes. The cream will have reduced some and turned a fawn color.

4. **The finish:** Remove the cover, stir in a generous squeeze of lemon juice, and taste for seasoning. Let simmer, uncovered, for just a few minutes to thicken the cream to a glaze that coats the sprouts. Serve hot or warm.

Fennel Braised with Thyme & Black Olives ⇸

Cooking fennel is akin to cooking onions. Whereas raw fennel is crisp, and almost biting, braised fennel becomes tame and seductively tender. The sharp anise flavor of the raw vegetable mellows into a sweetness that even non–licorice lovers will appreciate. Don't be at all put off by the anchovies in the recipe. They are discernable only as a bass note of flavor to match the higher tones of the sweet fennel. If you're serving these to professed anchovy haters, don't say a word. They'll never guess what makes the dish taste so good.

      Serve the braised fennel warm as a side dish to meat or fish, or serve it room temperature as a salad or part of an antipasto.

Working Ahead

Braised fennel is a natural make-ahead side dish because it tastes just as good at room temperature as it does warm from the oven. I sometimes make it in the morning to serve that evening. You can also braise the fennel a day or two in advance and keep it refrigerated until an hour or so before serving. Just be sure to allow time for it to come to room temperature. The cold will mute its flavor.

Serves 6 | Braising Time: 1 1/4 hours

3 large or 4 medium fennel bulbs (about
    3 pounds total; see "Shopping for
    Fennel," page 69)

3 tablespoons extra-virgin olive oil

Coarse salt and freshly ground black pepper

1/2 cup pitted oil-cured black olives,
    such as Nyons or Moroccan

2 garlic cloves, minced

5 to 6 anchovy fillets, minced

1 teaspoon chopped fresh thyme

1/2 teaspoon fennel seeds, toasted and
    lightly crushed

1/2 teaspoon coriander seeds, toasted and
    lightly crushed

1/3 cup dry white wine or dry white
    vermouth

3/4 cup chicken stock, homemade (page
    448) or store-bought

1. **Heat the oven to 325 degrees.**

2. **Trimming the fennel:** If the fennel came with the feathery green stalks attached, use a large knife to chop these off right down at their base, where the bulb begins. Reserve a few of the brightest and freshest-looking fronds for garnish, and save the rest for stock or discard. If the very base of the fennel bulbs looks brown or at all dried out, slice off a thin sliver. Check the sides of the bulbs as well, and trim off any brown parts with a vegetable peeler. Cut each bulb in half through the core and then halve again, into quarters.

3. **Browning the fennel:** Heat 2 tablespoons of the oil in a large heavy-based skillet (12-inch) over medium-high heat until it ripples. Add as many quarters of fennel as will fit without crowding, one cut side down. Leave the fennel undisturbed for 3 minutes—moving the pieces around will only slow down the browning process. With tongs, lift a few quarters to check to see if they've browned in spots. Because of its uneven surface, the fennel won't brown evenly: you're looking for patches of caramelization. Turn the quarters onto the other cut side and leave again until browned, another 3 to 4 minutes. Remove the quarters from the pan and arrange them browned side up in a large gratin dish or shallow baking dish (9- to 10-by-13- to 14-inches). Add the remaining oil to the skillet and brown the remaining fennel. Add this batch of fennel to the gratin dish, arranging it as best you can so the wedges line up in a single layer. It's okay if the wedges are a bit cramped; they will collapse and shrink some as they braise. Season with salt and pepper. Scatter over the olives.

4. **The aromatics and braising liquid:** Combine the garlic, anchovies, thyme, fennel seeds, and coriander in a small saucepan, and smash the mixture against the bottom of the pan with a wooden spoon to make a rough paste. Add the wine, bring to a boil over high heat, and boil until reduced by about half, about 2 minutes. Add the stock and bring to a simmer.

5. **The braise:** Pour the seasoned liquid over the fennel, cover tightly with foil, and slide onto the middle rack of the oven. Braise until the fennel has collapsed and a small knife penetrates the core of the wedges with no resistance, about 1 hour and 15 minutes.

6. **Serving:** If you reserved the feathery tops, chop them to give you about 2 tablespoons, and sprinkle them over the top of the braise. Serve warm or at room temperature.

Shopping for Fennel

Bulb fennel, known also as Florence fennel, is one of the many exciting additions to our produce departments in the last decade. A vegetable formerly appreciated in the United States only by those lucky enough to have traveled to Europe (Italy and southern France in particular), fennel is no longer considered exotic or even a specialty. It does mystify me some that many markets still wrongly label it as *anise*, but at least they carry it. (Botanically speaking, fennel and anise are two very different plants, although both have a definite anise/licorice taste. Fresh anise is something you'll never see in a standard market. Its seeds are harvested, dried, and packed into small spice jars.)

As with any vegetable, look for fennel bulbs that feel heavy in your hand. If a bulb feels light, it will taste cottony and bland. If the feathery branches are attached, they should be bright green, fresh smelling, and perky. As fennel deteriorates, the branches begin to sag and darken. If they've been lopped off, it may have been done to hide the fact that the fennel is past its prime. The base of the fennel bulb should be white and without cracks or slime.

When you shop for fennel, you may notice that some bulbs are flatter and more elongated, while others are more bulbous and swollen looking. The flatter ones tend to have a stronger, more pronounced licorice flavor, while the round, squat shape ones taste a bit sweeter and more mild. The flatter ones can also be tougher, but for braising that's a nonissue, since they become tender no matter what. Here either type will do, as long as you shop for the freshest, most pristine examples you can find. There are two peak seasons for fennel: fall and spring/early summer.

Roman-Style Artichoke Bottoms ⇥

I grew up eating artichokes only one way, steamed whole, and anytime they were served, it felt like a party. Each of us would get our own artichoke, sitting proudly in the center of a plate, and a teacup of melted butter to share with whomever we were sitting next to. We would each tuck in, pulling leaves, dipping them in butter, scraping them across our front teeth to get all the meat, and then dramatically tossing the spent leaves into a great big bowl in the center of the table and going for the next. It was always a marvel to me how the leaves would grow softer and more bountiful as I neared the heart, and I would race through the outer leaves only to slow myself down when the leaves turned pale and tender. That was the sign that I was close to the prize meat at the base of every artichoke. If only I'd known then what I know now, I might have just carved up the artichoke and gone immediately for that bottom where the leaves attach, which is really what eating artichokes is all about.

Paring the artichokes down to the bottom (the meaty saucer-shaped part of the artichoke, also called a crown) and cutting it into wedges before braising makes serving much less of an ordeal. The technique of braising the wedges in a simple combination of olive oil, white wine, garlic, and lots of fresh herbs comes from Italy. The slow aromatic braise concentrates the unique sweet artichoke flavor and leaves them tenderly irresistible. They taste just as good warm or at room temperature, with grilled meats, or as part of an antipasto. Or you could toss them on a salad or even pasta. Go ahead and double the recipe, leftovers are never a problem.

wine notes

Bone-dry white with a touch of mineral flavor—Sancerre or Savenniéres from France's Loire Valley.

I prefer to eat artichokes slightly warm or at room temperature. While these can be served immediately after braising, the flavors seem to improve if they cool for an hour or two in the olive oil–wine braising liquid. You can also refrigerate them for a day or two after braising, just be sure to let them come to room temperature or warm them in a low oven before serving.

Serves 4 to 6 | *Braising Time: about 1 hour*

1 lemon

4 large globe artichokes (see "Shopping for Globe Artichokes," page 72)

1/4 cup extra-virgin olive oil

Coarse salt and freshly ground black pepper

2 garlic cloves, minced

2 tablespoons chopped flat-leaf parsley

1 tablespoon chopped fresh mint, preferably peppermint

1 tablespoon chopped fresh thyme

1/3 cup dry white wine or dry white vermouth

1/3 cup water

2 tablespoons freshly squeezed lemon juice or 1 tablespoon white wine vinegar

1. **Trimming the artichokes:** Fill a large bowl with water. Cut the lemon in half and squeeze the juice into the water. Drop the lemon halves into the water as well. Set aside. Pull the outer leaves from one artichoke, tearing them off where they break at the base, until you reach the tender pale yellow-green inner leaves that resemble a pointy flower bud. With a sharp knife, cut across these leaves just above where they meet the base. Then cut off all but 1 inch of the stem. Next, with a paring knife, peel the fibrous dark green outer layer from the stem—this is not unlike peeling broccoli stems, and you will be able to see clearly where the fibrous outer layer ends and the tender inner stem begins. Then work the knife around the bottom and sides of the base, trimming away all the dark green scales to reveal the pale artichoke bottom. Rub the cut surfaces of the artichoke with one of the lemon halves from the bowl of water (this slows down their tendency to turn a drab brown color). Stand the artichoke upside down on a cutting board so the stem is pointing upward, and slice down through the stem to cut the artichoke in half. With a melon baller or sharp-edged spoon, scoop away and discard the hairy choke that sits in the center of each half. Continue scraping until you reach the smooth surface of the artichoke heart. Finally, cut each half in halves or thirds to make wedges that are about 3/4 inch wide. Drop these into the lemon water. Repeat with the remaining artichokes.

2. **The braise:** When all the artichokes are ready, lift them from the water and spread out

on a clean dish towel or paper towel to drain. Pat dry. Heat the oil in a large deep skillet (10-inch) over medium heat. Add the artichokes, stir with a wooden spoon to coat with oil, and season with salt and pepper. Add the garlic, parsley, mint, and thyme and stir again to coat. Pour in the wine and water and let the liquid come to a gentle simmer. Cover, reduce the heat to low, and braise, stirring a few times, until the artichokes are tender enough to be easily pierced with a thin knife blade, about 1 hour. If at any time the liquid appears to be boiling too hard, lower the heat or set a heat diffuser beneath the pan.

3. The finish: With a slotted spoon, lift the artichokes from the pan and transfer them to a serving plate. Raise the heat under the pan and bring the braising liquid to a quick boil. Boil the liquid for a few minutes, until it is reduced to a syrupy glaze. Whisk in the lemon juice or vinegar, taste for salt and pepper, and drizzle this pan sauce over the artichokes. Serve warm or at room temperature.

Shopping for Globe Artichokes

Globe artichokes are the round, full artichokes, as opposed to the smaller, purple-tipped baby varieties. Choose ones that feel heavy and have tightly packed leaves. Squeeze an artichoke—it should squeak. If the leaves are too soft and tired to make any noise, it's a sure sign that the artichoke is past its prime. Avoid artichokes with black spots or withered-looking leaf tips. The peak of artichoke season is March through May, with a secondary season in the early fall.

Butter-Glazed Radishes →→

I am devoted to our local farmers' market and go every week no matter what else is on my schedule. The market doesn't start up until mid-May, because of the long Vermont winter, and even then the first few weeks offer mostly bedding plants and seedlings. One of the first local crops to appear are the multicolored bunches of radishes, which I gleefully scoop up. If you've never tasted a cooked radish, you've been missing out. They are sweet, mildly peppery, and pleasantly earthy. And best of all, their color runs into the braising liquid, leaving them and the buttery glaze a lovely rosy pastel. Just the thing to kick off spring. Many farmers also grow a second crop of radishes in the fall, so I make this again when the cold weather returns, as a farewell to summer.

Serves 4 | Braising Time: about 25 minutes

2 bunches small radishes (2 to 2 1/2 dozen, or about 1 pound; see "Shopping for Radishes," page 74)
2 tablespoons unsalted butter
1/3 cup chicken stock, homemade (page 448) or store-bought, or water

Large pinch of sugar
Coarse salt and freshly ground black pepper

1. **Trimming and washing the radishes:** Trim the radishes of their roots and pare off the greens, leaving 1/4 to 1/2 inch of the stems. (Taste a piece of the pared-off greens. If you like their peppery taste, wash them and save to add to salads; otherwise, discard them.) Soak the radishes in cold water for about 15 minutes to loosen any dirt that may be caught in the stems. (You certainly don't need to leave any of the green stems; I just think it looks nice and I enjoy the earthy taste they provide.) Drain and scrub the radishes. Cut any radishes that are more than 1 inch in diameter in half.
2. **The braise:** Place the radishes in a medium skillet (10-inch) that will hold them in a

single layer. Add the butter, stock or water, sugar, and salt and pepper to taste. Bring to a simmer over medium heat, cover, reduce the heat, and braise at a low simmer until the radishes are easily pierced with a metal skewer, 20 to 25 minutes.

3. The finish: Remove the lid, shake the pan to roll the radishes around, and continue simmering until the liquid reduces to a glaze and coats the radishes, another 5 minutes or so. Taste a radish for salt and pepper. Serve warm.

VARIATION: BUTTER-BRAISED RADISHES WITH CRESS

My friend and neighbor Robin Schempp is an amazing gardener, as well as a great cook, and when her radishes come up in the spring, so does a lacy green cress known as pepper-cress. Good in salads and tea sandwiches, cress also adds a sharp bite to Butter-Braised Radishes. Watercress works just as well, and I've made this many times with arugula, also an early spring crop. In Step 3, when the liquid has mostly evaporated, add 1 ½ to 2 cups loosely packed peppercress, watercress, or arugula leaves to the radishes. Season with 1 or 2 teaspoons rice wine vinegar, and stir and shake to wilt the greens. Taste for salt and pepper, and serve warm.

Shopping for Radishes

Radishes are a cool-weather crop, which means they are best in early spring and fall. The summer heat can make them excessively spicy hot and wooly in texture. At the market, seek out radishes with healthy, fresh-looking greens. Younger, crisper radishes will have smaller green tops. Avoid any bunches with very large or overly mature looking greens. For these braised radishes, choose bunches that are all more or less the same size so they cook at the same rate. Regular red radishes will do quite well, and those are the ones I normally use here. But it's also fun to try some of the more unusual varieties available at farmers' markets. If you're lucky enough to find the Easter Egg variety that comes in shades of pink, red, and purple, the dish will be prettier still. Another nice choice would be French Breakfast radishes, cylindrical bright red radishes with a white tip and a clean, sharp taste. As you taste different varieties, you'll discover that they possess different nuances of flavor but they all share that mildly peppery, earthy flavor that works so well in a quick braise.

Spring Vegetable Braise →→

This is what to make in the spring when you come home from the farmers' market charged with bags of the first baby vegetables of the season— artichokes, spring onions, fava beans, and carrots. Don't try to make this with the so-called baby vegetables sold in big supermarkets, which have been grown to stay small and then shipped halfway across the country. Since locally grown spring vegetables appear at different times and in varying combinations depending on where you live, think of this recipe as an outline rather than a specific formula. The basic technique is to start braising the tougher, more fibrous vegetables first (carrots and artichokes) and then, when they are just barely tender, add the more delicate types, such as peas and scallions, to braise for a few minutes more.

Follow your local market and make substitutions and additions according to what vegetables are the freshest. For instance, if there are no artichokes, add $1/2$ pound of marble-sized new potatoes. Spring turnips are also perfect here, especially the little round Japanese varieties. I sometimes add a few slivered cloves of green garlic along with the peas. And if you're fortunate to find all of these spring vegetables, go ahead and expand the medley, keeping in mind that as you add more, you'll have more servings.

The little bit of bacon to start and the crème fraîche to finish are decidedly French touches, and not surprisingly this recipe comes from a good friend, Randall Price, who lives and cooks in France. To my mind, it's one prime example of what makes French food so good—simple yet sublime.

wine notes

Youthful Sauvignon Blanc from New Zealand or South Africa with vibrant fruit and no oak.

¹/₂ lemon

1 pound baby artichokes (6 to 8), 2 to 3
    inches in diameter

1 cup shelled fava beans or shelled fresh
    peas (about 2 pounds fava beans in
    the pod or 1 pound peas in the pod)

1 tablespoon unsalted butter

¹/₄ cup ¹/₄-inch dice slab bacon (1 ounce;
    see "Slab Bacon," page 395)

¹/₂ pound baby carrots (8 to 10), scrubbed
    and greens removed

¹/₂ pound spring onions (6 to 8), about
    1 inch in diameter, or 6 thick scallions

Coarse salt and freshly ground black
    pepper

¹/₄ cup chicken stock, homemade (page
    448) or store-bought, or water, plus
    more if needed

¹/₄ cup crème fraîche

2 teaspoons chopped fresh tarragon

1. **Trimming the artichokes:** Fill a medium bowl with water. Squeeze the lemon into the water, and drop the spent lemon half into the water. Set aside. Pull the outermost leaves from one artichoke, tearing them off where they break at the base. (Since you can eat nearly all of a baby artichoke, don't tear away as many leaves as you would an ordinary globe artichoke.) With a sharp knife, cut the top 1 to 1 ¹/₂ inches off the artichoke. Many baby artichokes reveal a sort of "waist" or indentation when you peel away the outer leaves; if so, slice off the top at this indentation. Then trim the stem, leaving up to 1 inch. With a paring knife, trim the ragged edges from the artichoke, and pare away the fibrous outermost layer of the stem. Stand the artichoke upside down on a cutting board so the stem is pointing upward, and slice down through the stem to cut the artichoke in half. Look closely at the center, or choke. If it is hairy and fibrous looking, scoop it away with a sharp-edged teaspoon. If there is no visible choke, as is the case with some baby artichokes, then you are finished. Drop the halves into the lemon water. Repeat with the remaining artichokes.

2. **Peeling the fava beans, if using:** Taste a single fava bean. If the beans are small—thumbnail size—and particularly fresh, you probably won't even notice the thin skin encasing the bean. In this case, there's no need to peel them. If the beans are larger or older, you will notice a thicker, rubbery skin, which should be removed. Many recipes tell you to blanch the beans in boiling water and then shock them with cold water before peeling. This loosens the peel and makes it easier to remove, but it also softens the texture of the beans, something I prefer to avoid in this recipe. With such a small amount of fresh beans, I find the extra trouble of blanching the beans unnecessary, and the skins usually slip off

without too much frustration. If you have a sharp thumbnail, use this to slit open the casing where the little "eye" is and then simply peel off the casing. You can also use a paring knife, but be careful not to slice into the bean.

3.   Frying the bacon: Melt the butter in a wide shallow braising pan or deep skillet (12- to 13-inch) over medium heat. Add the bacon and fry, stirring often with a wooden spoon, until well browned and crisp on the outside but with some softness remaining inside, 4 to 6 minutes.

4.   Braising the tougher vegetables: Drain the artichokes and add them to the skillet, along with the carrots and spring onions, if using. Seasons with salt and pepper. Pour in the stock and bring to a simmer, then reduce the heat to medium-low so that the stock simmers gently and cover the pan. Braise, stirring once or twice, until the carrots and artichokes are just barely tender, 12 to 18 minutes. The timing will vary depending on the size and maturity of the vegetables.

5.   Braising the tender vegetables: Add the fava beans (or peas) and the scallions, if using. If the pan appears dry, add a few tablespoons of stock or water. Cover and continue to braise until all the vegetables are tender, another 4 to 5 minutes.

6.   The finish: Remove the cover, add the crème fraîche, and increase the heat to medium-high. Simmer rapidly until the crème fraîche thickens up and the vegetables take on an appealing fawn-colored glaze. Stir in the tarragon. Taste for salt and pepper. Serve hot or warm.

Braised Celery with Crunchy Bread Crumb Topping

Too often relegated to the soup pot or viewed as a tool for scooping up dip, celery has its own distinct character that turns fragrant, tender, and sweet when braised. After braising, it makes a tasty gratin, dusted with Gruyère, and Parmigiano-Reggiano too if you like, and bread crumbs and quickly baked until browned and crunchy. The best presentation for this celery is directly in the braising dish, so choose a handsome one.

Serves 4 | Braising Time: about 1 1/2 hours

- **2 tablespoons unsalted butter, at room temperature**
- **1 head celery (about 1 3/4 pounds)**
- **1 large shallot or 1 small yellow onion, finely minced (about 1/4 cup)**
- **1 1/2 teaspoons finely chopped fresh thyme or 1/2 teaspoon dried**
- **Coarse salt and freshly ground black pepper**
- **1/4 cup dry white wine or dry white vermouth**
- **1 cup chicken stock, homemade (page 448) or store-bought**
- **1/3 cup freshly grated Gruyère, or half Gruyère and half Parmigiano-Reggiano**
- **3 to 4 tablespoons fresh bread crumbs made from day-old rustic white bread**

1. **Heat the oven to 325 degrees.** Using about half the butter, generously butter a large gratin dish or baking dish (9- to 10-by-13- to 14-inch).
2. **Washing and trimming the celery:** Tear the celery stalks from the head. You should have about 10 or 12 sturdy outer stalks. Stop tearing off the stalks when you reach the shorter, pale, tender stalks, or the heart. Set it aside. Rinse the celery stalks, giving special attention to the inside of the base of each stalk, where dirt tends to lodge. You may need a vegetable scrubber to remove stubborn dirt. Trim off the top part of the stalk where it branches into leaves, and set the tops aside with the heart. Using a small paring knife or vegetable peeler, scrape the outside of each celery stalk to remove the fibrous strings that

run its length. Cut the stalks into 3- to 4-inch lengths. Arrange them in a layer in the baking dish. It's fine if the sticks overlap some; they will shrink and flatten into a single layer as they braise.

3.   **The aromatics:** Finely chop the reserved celery heart, with the celery tops and leaves. Melt the remaining butter in a medium skillet (10-inch) over medium-high heat. Add the shallot, thyme, and chopped celery heart and leaves. Season with salt and pepper. Sauté, stirring occasionally, until the vegetables are soft and beginning to brown, about 10 minutes. Pour in the wine and simmer until the pan is almost dry, about 3 minutes. Add the stock and simmer until reduced by half, another 6 minutes or so.

4.   **The braise:** Pour the celery-shallot-stock mixture over the celery sticks. Cover with foil and slide into the middle of the oven to braise until the celery has collapsed and feels very tender when prodded with a knife tip, about 1 hour and 15 minutes.

5.   **The finish:** Remove the celery from the oven, and increase the oven heat to 400 degrees. Sprinkle the cheese and bread crumbs over the celery, and return to the oven until the cheese is melted and the top is crusty and browned, about 10 more minutes. Serve hot or warm.

Cauliflower, Potatoes & Peas Indian-Style →→

About the best thing you can do to a head of cauliflower is cut it up into little florets and braise it with a mixture of the sweet and warming spices of Indian cuisine—cumin, ginger, chile, coriander, and turmeric. Ground turmeric may be the least recognizable in this gang, but it's worth seeking out (and buying a fresh jar if yours is years old). Besides lending an intense saffron color to the dish (it's the same spice that gives classic curry powder its color), turmeric imparts a deep, earthy flavor that works as an essential backdrop to the other bolder, sharper spices. Control the heat of the dish by seeding the green chile or not.

This dish makes a satisfying accompaniment for roasted chicken and lamb, or present it all by itself with bowls of basmati rice for a sensational vegetarian supper.

wine notes

Fruity, off-dry white such as Riesling from Germany or Chenin Blanc from California.

Serves 4 to 6 | Braising Time: 25 to 30 minutes

1 head cauliflower (1 1/2 to 2 pounds)

3 tablespoons ghee, clarified butter (see "Clarified Butter," page 82), or vegetable oil

2 teaspoons cumin seeds

2 teaspoons coriander seeds

1 tablespoon finely minced fresh ginger

1 small fresh green chile, such as serrano or jalapeño, seeded or not, depending on the level of heat you want

1/2 teaspoon ground turmeric

Coarse salt

1/2 pound red-skinned potatoes, scrubbed and cut into 3/4-inch chunks

2/3 cup water, plus more as needed

1/2 cup peas (6 ounces)—frozen are fine here

1 tablespoon extra-virgin olive oil or unsalted butter, melted

2 tablespoons chopped cilantro

1. **Cutting up the cauliflower:** Cut the cauliflower into florets, discarding the thick core. Cut into individual florets that are about 2 inches long and just about as wide. They should have enough bulk so they will cook in the same time as the potatoes.

2. **Frying the spices:** Heat the ghee, butter, or oil in a large skillet or shallow braising dish (12- to 13-inch) over medium-high heat. Add the cumin seeds, coriander seeds, ginger, and green chile, stir, and heat until the spices release their fragrance and begin to sizzle, about 10 seconds. *Don't turn away and let the spices burn.* Add the turmeric and about 1/2 teaspoon salt, stir, and immediately add the cauliflower and potatoes. Stir to coat the vegetables with the spices.

3. **The braise:** Pour in the water, cover, and reduce the heat to a low simmer. Cook, checking once or twice to make sure that the liquid in the pan hasn't dried up, until the cauliflower and potatoes are almost tender, 18 to 20 minutes. If the pan appears dry at any point, add about 1/4 cup more water. Stir in the peas, cover, and continue to simmer until all the vegetables are tender, another 5 minutes or so.

4. **The finish:** Uncover, increase the heat to medium-high, and bring any remaining liquid in the skillet to a boil. Pour in the 1 tablespoon oil or melted butter and stir gently so as not to break up the vegetables. Give the pan a shake to ensure that nothing is sticking, and cook until all the liquid has cooked away and the vegetables are beginning to brown, about 5 minutes. The vegetables will be infused with the spices so that the dish needs no sauce. Taste, and season with salt as needed. Stir in the cilantro and serve warm.

VARIATION: CAULIFLOWER, POTATOES & CABBAGE INDIAN-STYLE

Add 2 cups thickly shredded green cabbage (about 1/4 pound) in Step 2 with the potatoes, and braise with the cauliflower until tender, about 22 minutes. Omit the peas. Finish the same as in the recipe above.

Clarified Butter

If you sauté with butter over high heat, the butter smokes and burns, leaving an acrid burnt taste on the food and smell in the air. But in truth, it's not the butterfat that burns, it's the milk solids (the proteins that combine with butterfat to make butter smooth and creamy). The pure butterfat has a much higher smoke point and won't burn as readily. So, if you want to sauté in butter, you need to clarify it first, which means melting the butter and separating out the milk solids. The clear butterfat that you are left with is known as clarified butter (see below for instructions).

GHEE

Ghee is a style of clarified butter used in Indian cooking. Unlike ordinary clarified butter, for which the butter is only melted and the milk solids poured off, ghee is made by simmering the butter for a long time so that all the moisture evaporates and the clear butterfat takes on a toasted, nutty flavor. Beyond flavor, ghee possesses two advantages over fresh butter. When sautéing and panfrying at high temperatures, ghee, like clarified butter, won't burn the way whole butter does. Secondly, ghee can be stored at room temperature without turning rancid. Purchase jars of ghee in specialty food stores, or prepare your own (see below). It can also be mail-ordered; see Sources, page 456.

MAKING CLARIFIED BUTTER

Slowly melt 2 sticks (1/2 pound) unsalted butter in a small saucepan over low heat (it's awkward to clarify less than 2 sticks at a time, although it can be done). When the butter is completely melted and threatening to simmer, turn off the heat. There will be a creamy foam on the surface of the butter and a layer of white sediment in the bottom of the pan. Using a wide soupspoon, skim the foam from the surface, being careful not to jostle the pan, or you risk mixing the butterfat and solids. Once the surface is clear, slowly pour the clear butter from the pan, leaving the remaining milk solids behind. Clarified butter keeps for months in the refrigerator. Two sticks of butter will yield about 3/4 cup clarified butter.

MAKING GHEE

Gently melt 2 to 4 sticks (1/2 to 1 pound) unsalted butter in a small heavy-bottomed saucepan over low heat. (Since ghee simmers for a long time, you definitely need a minimum of 2 sticks; otherwise, it's too easy to burn the ghee.) When the butter is completely melted, increase the heat to medium and listen and watch as the butter begins to simmer and make a popping sound—like the sound of a drop of water dropped into hot fat. The popping comes from the water being released from the milk solids in the butter. Continue to watch as the milk solids fall to the bottom of the pot and a white foam rises to the surface of the butter. Push this foam aside with a wooden spoon so you can monitor the fallout of the milk solids. As they fall to the bottom of the pot, they will begin to brown— that is what gives ghee its distinctive nutty flavor. Let the ghee simmer until the popping noise has stopped and there is a layer of toasty brown particles on the bottom of the pot, about 10 minutes. Let the ghee cool and settle for 5 to 10 minutes, then decant it by pouring the clear liquid through a triple layer of cheesecloth into a jar. Ghee may be stored, covered, at room temperature, but I store it in the refrigerator out of habit, where it lasts for months. Expect to get about 3/4 cup of ghee from 2 sticks of butter.

Braised Cauliflower with Capers & Toasted Bread Crumbs →→

Cauliflower rarely wins a "what's your favorite vegetable?" contest, but it definitely deserves its due. Boiling or steaming it too often results in waterlogged florets that have lost their delicate, slightly peppery taste. Braising, on the other hand, deepens its intrinsic sweet flavor and renders cauliflower tender but not limp.

Browned butter, capers, and lemon are a classic combination, and the toasted bread crumbs provide the bonus of a good crunch. I braise the cauliflower with water or chicken stock, depending on how I plan to serve it or whether I've got stock on hand. Braised in chicken stock, the cauliflower will have a deeper, more savory character, more appropriate alongside roast chicken, beef, or lamb. Water produces a more subtle-tasting dish, better with seafood and veal.

wine notes

Crisp Italian white, such as Pinot Grigio, Soave Classico, or Vernaccia di Sangimignano.

Serves 4 to 6 | Braising Time: 15 to 20 minutes

1/2 cup fresh bread crumbs made from day-old rustic white bread

1 head cauliflower (1 1/2 to 2 pounds)

2 tablespoons unsalted butter

1 tablespoon extra-virgin olive oil

2 tablespoons capers, rinsed and drained

1/2 cup chicken stock, homemade (page 448) or store-bought, or water, plus more as needed

Coarse salt and freshly ground black pepper

1/2 lemon

1. **Toasting the bread crumbs:** Heat the oven to 325 degrees. Spread the bread crumbs in a single layer on a baking sheet. Bake, stirring once or twice with a pancake turner, until the crumbs are the color of pale toast and lightly crunchy, about 15 minutes. Set aside to cool.

2. **Trimming the cauliflower:** Cut the cauliflower into florets, discarding the thick core. Cut into individual florets that are about 1 ½ inches long and just about as wide. You want them small, but not trimmed so much that they are falling apart.

3. **Browning the cauliflower:** Heat the butter and oil in a large skillet (12-inch) over medium-high heat. When hot, add the florets and sauté, turning frequently, until they are speckled all over with nice bits of brown, about 8 minutes total. Add the capers, stir to distribute, and cook for another minute.

4. **The braise:** Pour in the stock or water, season with salt and pepper (go easy on the salt because of the capers), cover tightly, and reduce the heat to low. Simmer gently until the cauliflower is tender enough to be easily pierced with the tip of a knife, 15 to 20 minutes. If the liquid threatens to dry up at any point, add a splash of water.

5. **The finish:** When the cauliflower is tender, remove the lid and boil away any remaining liquid, shaking the pan so the cauliflower doesn't stick. Add a squeeze of lemon, and taste for salt and pepper. Stir in the bread crumbs and serve immediately.

VARIATION: PENNE WITH BRAISED CAULIFLOWER & CAPERS

Turn this cauliflower into a meal by boiling up ¾ pound of short tube-shaped pasta, such as penne, fusilli, or gemelli. When the pasta is al dente, drain it, reserving about 1 cup of the cooking water. In Step 5, don't boil away any remaining liquid. Add the pasta to the cauliflower before adding the bread crumbs, and add enough reserved pasta cooking water to moisten the dish. Drizzle with a bit of extra-virgin olive oil, stir in the bread crumbs, and taste for salt and pepper. A small handful of chopped flat-leaf parsley and some freshly grated Parmigiano-Reggiano cheese are good finishing touches. Serves 3 to 4.

Braised Leeks with Bacon & Thyme �

The tallest and most appealing member of the onion family, leeks offer the sweet taste of onion but with an earthier, more grassy, herbal character. The French refer to them as "poor man's asparagus," which doesn't really hold true anymore, since leeks now cost almost as much as asparagus pound for pound, but it is an indication of their delicate flavor. The best way I've found to prepare leeks is to braise them slowly in chicken stock until they collapse into utter tenderness. Braising reveals all their goodness and brings out a complexity of flavor that would be lost by boiling or steaming. I like the smoky, salty taste of bacon with the sweet leeks, but you can also braise these without it and they will still be delicious.

Braised leeks are good alongside grilled steaks, roast chicken, and sautéed salmon, as a singular first course on their own, or chopped up and added to pasta. Never worry about making too many braised leeks. Any leftovers belong in the leek and bacon tart (page 89).

wine notes

Youthful white with herbal flavors—Sauvignon Blanc from New Zealand or California.

Working Ahead

Braised leeks are infinitely versatile. Serve them hot, warm, at room temperature, or a little chilled. They keep for several days in the refrigerator.

Serves 6 | Braising Time: about 1 hour

4 slices thick-cut bacon (¹/₃ pound),
  cut into ¹/₂-inch-wide strips

1 teaspoon unsalted butter

4 to 5 pounds medium to large leeks (6 to
  8; see "Shopping for Leeks," page 88)

2 garlic cloves, peeled and cut lengthwise
  in half

Coarse salt and freshly ground black
  pepper

Freshly grated nutmeg

1 ¹/₂ tablespoons chopped fresh thyme
  (do not substitute dried)

1 cup chicken stock, homemade (page 448)
  or store-bought

¹/₂ lemon

1. **Frying the bacon:** Place the bacon in a medium skillet (8-inch), set over medium heat, and fry, stirring often with a slotted spoon, until mostly crisp but with some softness remaining, 8 to 10 minutes. Transfer the bacon to a plate lined with paper towels to drain, and set the skillet aside.

2. **Heat the oven to 325 degrees.** Butter a 13-by-9-inch baking dish with the butter.

3. **Trimming the leeks:** With a large knife, trim off the root ends of each leek—don't cut into the base of the leek, but do trim the root end flush. Unless the market has already done this, peel off one or two of the outer layers, getting rid of the heaviest green part and any tough white parts. Cut off the top of the leek at the point where the green turns from pale and smooth to dark and leathery—you should have at least 7 inches of leek remaining.

4. **Washing the leeks:** Cut the leeks lengthwise in half, without cutting completely through the root end. Wash the leeks thoroughly, holding them upside down under cold running water and flaring the layers to let the water run through to remove all the sand. Shake off the excess water and place the leeks in one layer in the baking dish. Tuck the garlic halves in the dish and season the leeks with salt, pepper, and nutmeg. Sprinkle on the thyme.

5. **The braising liquid:** Pour off as much fat as you can from the reserved skillet, without discarding any bacon drippings. Place over high heat, add the stock, and bring to a boil to deglaze the pan, scraping with a wooden spoon. Pour the hot stock over the leeks.

6. **The braise:** Cover the baking dish tightly with foil and place on a rack in the lower third of the oven. Braise the leeks for 30 minutes.

    Turn the leeks over with tongs and continue braising until the leeks are close to fork-tender, another 15 to 25 minutes. Scatter the reserved bacon over the leeks and continue braising for another 15 minutes, or until the leeks are soft enough to be easily pierced with the tip of a knife.

7. **The finish:** With tongs and a slotted spoon, transfer the leeks and bacon to a platter, and cover with foil to keep warm. If there is more than about 1/2 cup of juices remaining in the baking pan, pour them into a medium skillet or wide saucepan. Bring to a boil over medium-high heat and reduce the juices, adding any juices that have accumulated on the platter with the leeks, to about 1/4 cup. Add a generous squeeze of lemon juice, taste for salt and pepper, and spoon the juices over the leeks. Or, if there are only a few tablespoons of juices in the dish after braising, taste for salt and pepper and then simply pour them over the leeks along with a squeeze of lemon. Serve warm or room temperature.

VARIATION: GRATIN OF BRAISED LEEKS

In Step 6, when you add the bacon, pour over 1/2 cup heavy cream. Continue as directed until the leeks are done. Omit the lemon juice and skip Step 7. Instead, turn on the broiler to high, sprinkle 1/4 cup freshly grated Parmigiano-Reggiano cheese over, and broil until brown and the liquid is bubbly. Serve hot or warm.

Shopping for Leeks

Leeks are at their best in the fall and winter. You will see slim baby ones coming into the market in mid- to late summer, and these little leeks are good roasted or on the grill (give them a brief plunge in boiling water first, then brush with olive oil). But wait for the larger leeks of winter for braising. Shop for leeks that feel solid at the base, not at all squishy. The green top portion should be dark, not dried out. Inspect the white to see that it's smooth and bright, not split or slimy. Since the white and pale green parts are what you'll be cooking, look for leeks with a good amount of white. And, finally, watch out for large late-season (late winter/early spring) leeks that will have developed solid woody cores. These shoot-like centers are not anything you would want to eat, and they're an indication that the leek is way past its prime.

Some markets trim the long, floppy green tops off the leeks and sell straight, stubby leeks that are 9 to 10 inches long. If this is the case, you'll need slightly less than the 4 to 5 pounds called for in the recipe.

Braised Leeks & Bacon in a Tart →→

Yes, you could make a leek tart with steamed or boiled leeks, but it wouldn't have the same concentrated sweet flavor as one made with braised leeks (use leftovers from Braised Leeks with Bacon & Thyme, page 86). Although this tart falls into the category of quiches, there's much less eggy custard filling than in a traditional quiche. One devout quiche hater I served it to had seconds and then asked for the recipe.

wine notes

Rich, fruity white with a touch of mineral flavor—Pinot Gris or Pinot Blanc from Alsace.

Working Ahead

The pastry for the tart needs to rest and chill for at least an hour before rolling out (Step 2), so be sure to make time for this. It can also rest for as long as a full 2 days, if that suits your schedule. The baked tart can be served hot from the oven, warm, or even at room temperature.

Makes one 10- to 11-inch tart; serves 6 to 8

THE PASTRY

1 cup all-purpose flour, plus more
    for rolling out
1/2 teaspoon fine sea salt

6 1/2 tablespoons cold unsalted butter,
    cut into 1/2-inch bits
About 3 to 4 tablespoons ice-cold water

3 or 4 leftover braised leeks and bacon
   (page 86)

3 ounces Gruyère, grated (about 3/4 cup)

2 large eggs

1/4 cup crème fraîche

2/3 cup heavy cream or half-and-half

1 teaspoon chopped fresh thyme
   (do not substitute dried)

Freshly grated nutmeg

Coarse salt and freshly ground black
   pepper

1. **Making the pastry:** In a large bowl, combine the flour and salt. Drop in the cold butter and, with the tines of a fork or your fingertips, toss the butter in the flour so that all the pieces are coated. (If you have warm hands or aren't accustomed to making pastry, use a fork. Otherwise, you risk warming the butter, and the pastry won't be as flaky.) Still with the fork or your fingertips, mash the butter into the flour until it is all in small, flour-coated bits and the whole thing looks like dry oatmeal.

Sprinkle over 3 tablespoons cold water, and toss the mixture with the fork or your fingers to distribute the water evenly. Continue adding just a dribble of water (about 1/2 teaspoon) at a time until the pastry looks as though it will hold together loosely. Use your hands to squeeze the pastry into a disk. If it won't hold together, sprinkle over a little more water. Be careful, since too much water will result in a tough crust that shrinks as it bakes.

2. **Chilling and resting the pastry:** Shape the pastry into a disk (about 2 inches thick), and wrap it tightly in plastic. Chill in the refrigerator for at least an hour, and up to 2 days. (Leaving the pastry to chill is essential to relax the dough and distribute the moisture evenly. Pastry that doesn't chill long enough will tend to shrink more during baking.)

3. **Rolling out the pastry:** On a lightly floured surface, with a lightly floured rolling pin, roll the pastry out to a circle about 13 inches in diameter. Roll from the center out, and continually shift the pastry around on the work surface to be sure that it isn't sticking at all. Dust on more flour sparingly as needed, and keep your rolling pin lightly dusted as well. Lift the circle of dough by draping it over the rolling pin and transfer it to a 10- or 11-inch tart pan with 1-inch sides. Lower the crust into the tart pan, being sure to press it into the corners. Then nudge the crust down into the sides so that the sides are a tiny bit thicker than the bottom. Cut off any crust that extends above the rim by rolling the rolling pin across the top of the tart pan. Refrigerate the crust to firm up and rest again, about 40 minutes.

4. **Heat the oven to 375 degrees.** If you have a pizza stone, set it on a rack in the lower third of the oven.

5. **Blind-baking the tart crust:** Line the tart crust with parchment paper or foil so that

the paper reaches well above the sides. Fill the crust with the pie weights or dried beans. Spread the weights out evenly, being sure to get them into corners—this will help prevent the sides from collapsing. Bake the crust, on the pizza stone if using, until the pastry is set, 20 minutes. Remove the paper and weights, and return the crust to the oven to bake until toast colored and dried out, another 10 to 12 minutes. Set the crust on a cooling rack while you prepare the leeks and filling. Lower the oven heat to 350 degrees.

6. **Preparing the leeks:** Chop the leeks into 1 1/2 inch-pieces, and spread them out over the bottom of the prebaked tart shell. If there are any leftover braising juices, reserve them. Scatter the bacon over the leeks and then spread the cheese on top of this.

7. **The custard filling:** In a large measuring cup with a pouring spout, whisk together the eggs and crème fraîche until smooth. Add any reserved braising juices. Add the cream, season with the thyme, nutmeg, and salt and pepper, and whisk to combine. Pour this slowly over the leeks, bacon, and cheese.

8. **Baking the tart:** Bake the tart, again on the pizza stone, if using, until the filling is set and the top is slightly puffed and nicely bronzed in spots, about 40 minutes.

9. **Serving:** Let the tart sit for at least 15 minutes before serving. Serve hot, warm, or at room temperature.

Sweet Braised Whole Scallions →→

If you've never tasted slow-cooked whole scallions, you're in for a treat. This recipe comes in handy when stalwart scallions seem to be the only vegetable with any vitality left in the produce bins by late winter. It's also a favorite standby when I want a tasty side dish without making any real effort. Aside from trimming the scallions (removing the root end and only taking an inch or so off the top) and chopping a bit of tarragon, there's very little to do.

As the scallions braise, the sweet anise flavor of the tarragon mingles with their oniony juices, giving the whole dish a candy-like sweetness that is ideal alongside a grilled steak or roasted chicken. I like to place a dish of these on the Thanksgiving table too. If you can't find fresh tarragon, or simply don't care for its taste, substitute fresh parsley or omit the herb altogether. The scallions will still taste delicious.

Serves 6 | Braising Time: about 1 hour

2 1/2 tablespoons unsalted butter, at room temperature

1 pound scallions (about 5 bunches, or 3 dozen)

1/2 cup water

1 1/2 teaspoons coarsely chopped fresh tarragon (do not substitute dried) or 1 tablespoon chopped flat-leaf parsley

Coarse salt and freshly ground black pepper

1/2 lemon

1.   **Heat the oven to 350 degrees.** Using about 1 1/2 teaspoons of butter, generously butter a 9-by-13-inch baking dish.

2.   **Trimming the scallions:** Trim the root ends and 1 1/2 inches off the green tops of the scallions. Arrange half of the scallions in the baking dish so the bulb ends are lined up at one end and the greens are toward the middle. Place the other half of the scallions in the

opposite direction, so you end up with a double layer of scallion greens across the center of the dish and a single layer of bulbs at each end of the dish.

3.   **The Braise:** Pour the water into the dish. Cut the remaining butter into slivers and dot it over the top of the scallions. Season with the tarragon or parsley, salt, and pepper. Cover the dish tightly with foil, and slide onto the middle rack in the oven. Braise undisturbed until fragrant and tender, 35 to 40 minutes.

4.   **The finish:** Remove the foil from the dish, and increase the oven heat to 450 degrees. Roast the scallions for 10 minutes, then shake the pan back and forth to coat the scallions with the glaze that will have formed. Continue roasting until the liquid evaporates and the edges of the scallions are beginning to brown, another 5 minutes or so. Squeeze over a few drops of lemon juice to taste, and serve hot or warm.

Braised Shallot Confit →→

Braised shallots are one of those things that every resourceful cook should know about. When braised in a bit of red wine, Cognac, and fresh thyme, shallots turn unbelievably sweet and jammy—wonderful served alongside roast chicken or a juicy grilled steak. I also like to make extra to spread onto bruschetta and top with a little goat cheese. Or try these tucked into a sliced turkey sandwich on chewy country bread. So good.

Look for shallots that are all about the same size—preferably medium-sized, 1 to 1 ½ inches across—so they will braise evenly.

Working Ahead

The shallots can be made ahead and kept, covered, at room temperature for several hours or refrigerated for a few days. To serve, warm the shallots gently in a saucepan (adding a few drops of water if necessary) or simply bring them to room temperature.

Serves 4 | Braising Time: 40 to 45 minutes

3/4 pound shallots (see "Shopping for Shallots," page 195)

1 ½ tablespoons unsalted butter

Coarse salt and freshly ground black pepper

2 tablespoons Cognac, or other good brandy

½ cup dry red wine

1 ½ teaspoons chopped fresh thyme

1. **Trimming the shallots:** Peel the shallots, and trim off any bits of the root end that remain. Divide any large shallots in two—the halves should pull apart naturally, but you may need to peel off the first layer of shallot to separate them.

2. **Browning and flaming the shallots:** Melt the butter in a medium skillet over medium-high heat. Add the shallots, season with salt and pepper, and toss to coat. Sauté, tossing frequently, until the shallots are brown in spots and you can smell the aroma of

cooking onions, about 5 minutes. Add the Cognac. If you're cooking over gas, carefully tilt the pan and let the flame ignite the Cognac. On electric, hold a match to the pan to light the Cognac. Stand back as the flame flares up, then swirl the pan around and let the flame burn down. Simmer until there is only a glaze left on the bottom of the pan.

3. **The braise:** Add the wine and 1 teaspoon of the thyme and bring to a simmer, then reduce the heat to medium-low and cover the pan. Simmer until the shallots are completely soft and falling apart, 40 to 45 minutes. After the first 15 minutes, check to make sure that the pan is not dry, and add a few tablespoons of water if necessary. Check again 2 or 3 times as the shallots braise.

4. **The finish:** When the shallots are done, remove the lid and, over medium heat, boil down any liquid, shaking and stirring a few times, until a glaze forms on the shallots. Add the remaining $1/2$ teaspoon thyme, gently stir (expect the shallots to fall apart some), and taste for salt and pepper. Serve warm or at room temperature.

Shopping for Shallots

When shopping for shallots, I like to buy them from a bulk bin, not in those little mesh bags or cellophane boxes. This way I can give each one a little squeeze to determine that they aren't at all soft or spoiled and haven't sent up any green sprouts. Look for shallots with shiny, dry, tight skins. The most common supermarket shallots, known as red or orange shallots, have the same bronze-colored skin that we see on yellow onions. Gray shallots are a hard-to-find variety with superior flavor that you may see at specialty or farmers' markets. They are recognizable by their purple-gray skin and elongated shape. Buy them if you find them. Store shallots in a cool, dark, dry spot along with your onions and garlic for a week or so.

SEAFOOD

Braised Halibut Steaks with Creamy Leeks ✈

This is a two-part braise. First the leeks are braised in butter and white wine, and then the halibut steaks are set on top of the leeks and braised with a splash of heavy cream until just cooked through. The delicacy of the pearly white halibut against the sweetness of the pale green leeks makes this dish taste and look quite chefy—in the best sense of the word.

Don't substitute halibut fillets for the steaks in this recipe: the bone in the center of the steak protects the fish from drying out and contributes to the flavor. Halibut is most readily available from April through December. Salmon or swordfish steaks could easily stand in here.

wine notes

Crisp herbal white such as Sauvignon Blanc from New Zealand, or a dry Rosé from southern France.

Serves 4 | Braising Time: 45 to 50 minutes for the leeks, plus 18 to 20 minutes for the halibut

2 1/4 to 2 1/2 pounds halibut steaks, 1 1/4 inches thick—depending on the size of the halibut, this will be 2 or 4 steaks

Coarse salt and freshly ground black pepper

3 medium or 2 large leeks (about 1 1/2 pounds; see "Shopping for Leeks," page 88)

3 tablespoons unsalted butter

2 to 3 garlic cloves, minced

1 tablespoon chopped fresh thyme

1/2 cup dry white wine or dry white vermouth

1/4 cup heavy cream

1/2 lemon

1. **Seasoning the halibut:** Set the halibut steaks on a plate and season both sides with salt and pepper. If the kitchen is warm, refrigerate the fish while you prepare the leeks. The fish can be seasoned up to an hour before braising.

2. **Heat the oven to 350 degrees.**

3. **Trimming and washing the leeks:** Trim the root ends and dark green tops from the leeks, and discard (or save for stock). Cut the leeks lengthwise in half and then slice into 1/2-inch pieces. You should have 3 to 4 cups. Put the chopped leeks in a large bowl and fill it with water. Swish them around with one hand to loosen the dirt, then lift them out of the water and drain in a colander. Pour out the water, rinse the bowl to remove any grit from the bottom, and repeat; drain. Don't be tempted to skip this second rinse: most leeks come from the market with an impressive amount of sandy soil trapped between their leaves, and this double rinse is assurance that you won't ruin the dish with gritty leeks.

4. **Braising the leeks:** Melt the butter in a wide ovenproof skillet or shallow braising dish (12- to 13-inch) over medium heat. Add the leeks, garlic, and thyme, season with salt and pepper, and stir to coat the leeks with butter as thoroughly as you can. Add the wine and bring to a boil. Cover with a buttered round of parchment paper and a secure lid, and slide the skillet onto a rack in the middle of the oven to braise gently, stirring once after 20 minutes, until the leeks feel silky-tender when pierced with a fork, 45 to 50 minutes.

5. **Braising the halibut:** Arrange the halibut steaks over the braised leeks, and pour over the cream. Cover again with the parchment but not the lid. Return to the oven and braise until the halibut has just lost its translucence and pulls away from the bone cleanly when prodded with a fork, 18 to 20 minutes. (Overcooking will result in a somewhat cottony texture; not nice!)

6. **The finish:** Using a fish spatula (a slotted triangular spatula designed for lifting delicate pieces of fish) or other slotted spatula, gingerly transfer the halibut steaks to a shallow platter or a cutting board. Try to lift the fish without taking away too many leeks, but a few are bound to come along. Set the pan of leeks over a medium burner, and bring to a simmer. (If there's a handle on the pan, drape a dish towel or pot holder over it, so you won't automatically grab it and burn the inside of your hand.) Stir once or twice with a wooden spoon, and keep an eye out that the leeks don't begin to brown while you tend to the halibut. With a fork and small paring knife, peel back the skin from the perimeter of the steaks and then lift out the bones, trying your best to keep the steaks in one or two pieces. Cover loosely with foil to keep warm.

7. **Serving:** When the sauce around the leeks is creamy and nicely thickened but not completely dried out, add a squeeze of lemon. Taste the leeks for salt and pepper. Serve the halibut either on a bed of leeks or with the leeks spooned over, both good choices.

VARIATION: BRAISED HALIBUT STEAKS WITH SPINACH

Wash, stem, and rewash 1 pound of spinach, plunging the leaves into a large bowl of cold water, swishing them around with one hand, and then lifting them out and draining in a colander. Pour out the wash water, rinse the bowl, and repeat. After the second wash, taste a piece of spinach to be sure that you've removed all the sand. With its crinkly texture, fresh spinach often harbors a surprising amount of sand, which can ruin an otherwise good dish. (I prefer the more robust texture of larger spinach for braising, not the tender baby leaves that have become so popular for salads.)

Bring a large pot of salted water to a boil, and blanch the spinach for 2 to 3 minutes. Drain, plunge into a bowl of ice-cold water to stop the cooking, and drain again. Then, a handful at a time, squeeze the spinach dry. Coarsely chop the spinach and set aside.

Heat the oven to 350 degrees. Melt 2 to 3 tablespoons unsalted butter in a wide ovenproof skillet or shallow braising dish (12- to 13-inch) over medium heat. Sauté 1 finely chopped medium shallot until softened, about 3 minutes. Add the spinach a handful at a time, stirring as it wilts down. Season with salt, pepper, and a pinch of grated nutmeg. Sauté, stirring frequently, to evaporate any remaining water, about 4 minutes. Add $1/3$ cup dry white wine or dry white vermouth and bring to a simmer. Add the halibut and cream as in Step 5 and finish the braise in the oven as above.

Shopping for Fresh Fish

Since fish is more perishable than most meat or poultry, shopping for it requires a bit more vigilance. To begin with, seek out a good fish market. This may be a specialty store dedicated to selling seafood, or it may be the fish counter in your local supermarket. Either way, look for a market that smells clean. A fish market should not smell strongly of fish. That is a sign that things aren't being thoroughly cleaned at night. Also look for a market where you feel comfortable enough to browse at your own pace and to ask questions. Once you've found the market, get to know the people behind the counter and take advantage of their knowledge.

The first test for freshness is simply to judge what looks good. Fillets and steaks should be bright and shiny, moist but not watery, and certainly not dried out. Yellowing or graying edges are an indication that the fish was improperly stored or frozen, and its texture will have deteriorated. Whole fish should have clear eyes and shiny, taut skin. If the fish is displayed on ice, make sure there is some type of barrier (plastic or a tray) between the ice and skinless fillets or steaks. Direct contact between ice and delicate fish will draw off all moisture from the fish and ruin its texture.

Once you spot a piece of fish that looks fresh, the only true test is to smell it. The first few times you ask to do this, you may feel awkward leaning across the counter to discreetly sniff the piece of fish being proffered by a plastic-gloved hand, but if you've ever purchased fish that you thought looked fresh and then discovered at home that it wasn't that at all, you'll know how important it is to smell before buying. Fresh fish will have a faint, almost sweet, some say cucumber-like aroma. If the smell is at all assertive or chemical (the result of soaking in preservative solutions), move on.

Shopping for Previously Frozen Fish

There is a huge misconception about the quality of frozen fish in our marketplace. The problem is that many people think of frozen as the opposite of fresh, and this is simply not true when it comes to fish. The opposite of fresh is rotten, and thanks to advances in fish technology, much of the frozen fish sold today is worlds fresher than the so-called fresh. The issue with seafood is that it is highly perishable. When just caught or harvested, fish is, of course, at its peak of freshness. If properly handled and stored, most fish will maintain its quality for close to 10 days. After 10 days, fish is quite often still in the marketplace, but its quality has greatly deteriorated. Indeed, much of the "fresh" fish sold in markets has been around for twice that amount of time. If you consider the time involved in getting a piece of fish from the ship that brought it ashore to the docks, to the distributor, and finally to your market, you begin to understand the challenge of finding truly fresh fish.

Commercially frozen fish, however, is flash-frozen at sea at its absolute apex of freshness, immediately after being caught and cleaned. Flash-freezing involves high-tech industrial freezing systems that freeze individual pieces of fish in a matter of seconds. (Most large-scale commercial fisheries house these systems on large processing ships that stay at sea.) As soon as a piece of fish is cleaned, it is frozen and its freshness locked in. When fish is flash-frozen, the water in its tissue freezes in the tiniest of ice crystals that cause no real damage or change to the texture of the fish. As long as the fish is then kept frozen and thawed properly (overnight in a refrigerator), the texture and flavor will be excellent and very fresh.

If you have an aversion to frozen fish, it's most likely because you've had experience cooking poor-quality frozen fish—that was either poorly frozen or allowed to thaw and sit around for too long afterward, or both. Some lesser fish markets will sometimes freeze fish themselves because the fish has sat around for a few days not selling. When fish is frozen in an ordinary freezer (and not the flash freezer previously described), it freezes slowly and large ice crystals form that cut into the tissue and destroy its texture. (The water in all fish, meat, and poultry is contained within cell walls. If you rupture these cell walls, which is what large ice crystals do, the moisture will escape and the tissue will begin to dry out.) When poorly frozen fish is thawed, you'll see a great puddle of water around it—this is the moisture that the tissue can no longer retain since the cell walls have been cut open by large ice crystals. When cooked, the fish will be dry, cottony, and flavorless.

Many markets use labels such as "previously frozen" or "FAS" (frozen at sea) to indicate commercially frozen fish they have thawed themselves. If there are no such indicators, ask whoever is behind the counter. They should be able to tell you. You can also ask them when they thawed the fish. Ideally, you want fish that's only been thawed for a day or two. When buying previously frozen fish, use the same quality assessment as you would for fresh.

If you buy frozen fish, thaw it slowly, still wrapped, in the refrigerator. Kept frozen, it will keep for 4 weeks in your freezer.

Monkfish Braised with Cherry Tomatoes & Basil ➻

A quick and cheerful braise when you're craving something summery but the calendar's not cooperating. Thankfully, cherry tomatoes and fresh basil are easy to find year-round. To boost the sunny Mediterranean character of this dish, I add some chopped fresh fennel (at its best in the fall and spring), and a couple of ounces of pancetta. I use water here as the braising liquid rather than wine or stock to keep the flavors of the sauce bright. The tomatoes are added whole and then simmered until they begin to burst, creating a light, juicy sauce that may remind you of a pasta sauce. In fact, I do sometimes ladle this whole dish over pasta (see the variation that follows).

The lean and meaty character of monkfish makes it ideal for braising. Unfortunately, as the popularity of this delicious fish grows, so does the risk of its becoming overfished (see "A Note on Monkfish," page 106). If you cannot find monkfish or choose to avoid it, this recipe works beautifully with halibut, cod, and striped bass.

wine notes

Herbal, un-oaked white wine, such as Sauvignon Blanc from California, New Zealand, or South Africa; or a dry rosé or blush wine from France, California, or Australia (no White Zinfandels, as they tend to be off-dry to slightly sweet).

Serves 4 | Braising Time: about 8 minutes

3 tablespoons extra-virgin olive oil

2 thick slices pancetta (2 ounces), cut into 1-inch pieces

1 cup finely chopped fennel (about ¹/₂ bulb)

Coarse salt

Pinch of crushed red pepper flakes

¹/₄ cup water, plus more as needed

1 pint cherry or grape tomatoes

2 garlic cloves, minced

1 ¹/₂ pounds monkfish fillets (see "A Note on Monkfish," page 106)

Freshly ground black pepper

2 tablespoons shredded fresh basil

1. **Frying the pancetta:** Combine 1 tablespoon of the oil and the pancetta in a medium deep skillet (10-inch) and sauté the pancetta over medium heat, stirring so that it browns evenly, until it has rendered much of its fat and is cooked but not too crisp, about 5 minutes. With tongs or a slotted spoon, transfer to paper towels to drain.

2. **The aromatics and braising liquid:** Return the skillet to medium heat, add the fennel, and season with salt and the red pepper flakes. Stir with a wooden spoon to coat the fennel with the oil and pancetta drippings, and sauté for just a minute or two, until the fennel begins to sizzle. Add ¹/₄ cup water and stir and scrape the bottom to dislodge and dissolve any tasty cooked-on pancetta bits. Cover, reduce the heat to medium-low, and braise, stirring a few times, until the fennel is tender with just a little resistance, about 7 minutes.

    Add another tablespoon of oil to the pan, along with the tomatoes and garlic. Increase the heat to medium and sauté, uncovered, shaking and stirring frequently, until the tomatoes begin to burst, about 10 minutes. Stir often and scrape up the lovely caramelized crust that will develop on the bottom of the skillet. When about half of the tomatoes have burst, about 12 minutes, add another 2 to 3 tablespoons of water and the pancetta, cover, reduce the heat to medium-low, and let simmer, stirring occasionally, while you prepare the fish.

3. **Trimming the monkfish:** Inspect the monkfish. Most monkfish comes from the market with a thin grayish, rather slimy membrane covering the fish. This is a natural layer that exists between the skin and the pure white fillet, and it should be removed for aesthetic and textural reasons. Some markets trim this for you, but most do not. Using a sharp paring knife or fillet knife, trim away the membrane without cutting into the fish. Trim off any dark patches on the monkfish as well. Cut the monkfish fillet into 4 equal portions.

4. **Browning the monkfish:** Pat the monkfish fillets dry with paper towels, and season all over with salt and pepper. Heat the remaining tablespoon of oil in a medium nonstick skillet (9- to 10-inch) over medium-high heat. (A nonstick surface is especially useful for searing delicate fish so there's no worry of it sticking.) When the oil shimmers, add the fish and sauté until it has lost its raw appearance and the outside is pale golden, 4 minutes per side.

5. **The braise:** Transfer the fillets to the simmering tomato-fennel sauce. With a rubber spatula, scrape any oil or juices from the nonstick skillet onto the fillets. Cover and simmer

gently over low heat, turning the fillets after 4 minutes, until the fish is just cooked through, about 8 minutes total.

6. **Serving:** Transfer the monkfish to warm plates. Stir the basil into the sauce, taste for salt and pepper, and spoon it around the fish on each plate.

VARIATION: PASTA WITH BRAISED MONKFISH & CHERRY TOMATOES

While the monkfish cooks, boil 1 to 1 ½ pounds dried fettuccine or linguine in plenty of well-salted water until al dente. Collect about 1 cup of the pasta cooking water when you drain the pasta. Cut the braised monkfish into large chunks and gently toss it with the pasta, along with the sauce and as much of the reserved pasta cooking water as you need to make the dish moist but not soupy. Drizzle your best fruity extra-virgin olive oil over each serving. Purists may object to grated Parmigiano-Reggiano on pasta with fish, but if it tastes good to you, sprinkle some on. *Serves 4 to 6.*

A Note on Monkfish

Twenty-five years ago, few Americans had heard of monkfish and even fewer had tasted it. This lean, delicately flavored fish was considered a trash fish and discarded by fishermen because it had no commercial value. This began to change in the 1980s for two reasons. First, as more American cooks traveled to France to hone their skills, they discovered a world of unfamiliar ingredients, including monkfish, called *lotte*. The French prized this elegant, meaty fish as much as pricier catches like lobster and Dover sole, and with good reason—it is lean, easy to cook, and delicious. Around the same time, American fishermen were experiencing dwindling catches of popular seafood varieties, such as cod and scallops, and looking for other untapped species to fill their nets—and purses. And thus a market for monkfish was born.

Now, a quarter of a century later, monkfish shows up in seafood counters and on restaurant menus all across the country. Unfortunately, during the course of writing this book, the once plentiful supply of monkfish is now at risk of being overfished. The Seafood Watch at the Monterey Bay Aquarium has put a red alert on monkfish and recommends that consumers refrain from buying it. (For information on the Seafood Watch, see Sources, page 457). The good news is that the most recent research shows that portions of the monkfish stock are recovering. In the meantime, the best practice would be to substitute another lean, mild-tasting, firm-textured fish, such as halibut, cod, or striped bass.

Salmon Fillets Braised in Pinot Noir with Bacon & Mushrooms →→

One of the things I appreciate most about salmon, beyond its lush taste, is its versatility in the kitchen: you can grill it, roast it, sauté it, and, best of all, braise it. Braising eliminates any worries about having the delicate fish stick to a grill or sauté pan, and there's little risk of overcooking, since the braising temperature is so gentle. When braised, salmon fillets come out silky and succulent, cooked through with just a touch of pink at the center and not the slightest bit dry. I especially like to braise salmon in a hearty mix of bacon, mushrooms, and red wine. Whereas other milder types of fish would be overpowered by this treatment, salmon stands up beautifully and comes out tasting sweeter than ever—and the wine-based braising liquid becomes an instant, elegant sauce that marries perfectly with the fish.

This is one of those recipes that you can easily dress up or down depending on your appetite, the occasion, and your wallet. For the basic version, use everyday button mushrooms and a simple bottle of domestic wine. For something truly special, shop for chanterelle or other wild mushrooms and a fancier wine. Either way, you'll be pleased. Serve with a small mound of mashed potatoes and buttered snap peas.

wine notes

Although not written in stone, it's a good idea to enjoy the same kind of wine—even the same wine—used in the braise. Look for Pinot Noir with a touch of earthiness from California, Oregon, or New Zealand; or a red Burgundy with soft tannins, such as Volnay.

Serves 4 | Braising Time: 15 to 18 minutes

4 thick skin-on salmon fillets, preferably
    wild-caught, about 6 ounces each and
    1 1/2 inches thick (see "Shopping for
    Salmon," page 110)
1/4 pound (4 ounces) mushrooms—button
    mushrooms or a mix of specialty
    mushrooms, such as chanterelles or
    oyster mushrooms
5 slices thick-cut bacon (about 4 ounces),
    cut into 1/2-inch-wide strips
1 leek, finely chopped and thoroughly
    washed

1 carrot, finely chopped
1 small shallot, finely chopped
Coarse salt and freshly ground black
    pepper
2 cups light red wine, such as Pinot Noir
    or Beaujolais
Three 2- to 3-inch leafy fresh thyme sprigs
2 tablespoons unsalted butter
2 tablespoons chopped flat-leaf parsley

1. **Heat the oven to 375 degrees.**
2. **Removing any fish bones:** Run your finger down the flesh of the salmon fillets, near the center of the fillet. You will sometimes find a thin row of bones, called pinbones, that need to be removed. But many markets remove the pin bones themselves, so if you don't find any, don't be concerned that you're missing them: you'll notice them if they are there. The best tool for removing pinbones is a pair of pliers or strong tweezers: failing that, a small paring knife will do. If using pliers or tweezers, grab the end of each bone and yank it free. With a small knife, choke up on the blade of the knife with your thumb and fore-finger, snag the end of the bone between your thumb and the blade, and yank the bone free. Continue until you've removed all the pinbones. There may be anywhere from a few to a dozen wispy, soft bones in each fillet.
3. **The mushrooms:** Wipe the mushrooms clean with a damp paper towel. If they are very sandy, give them a quick rinse. (For more on cleaning mushrooms, see "Shopping for and Handling Cremini and Portobello Mushrooms," page 221.) Trim off the very base of the mushroom stems, then remove the stems and coarsely chop them. Set aside. Thinly slice the caps and set these aside separately.
4. **The aromatics and braising liquid:** Choose a deep ovenproof skillet or shallow brais-ing pan just large enough to hold the salmon fillets without crowding (I use a 12- to 13-inch pan). Add half the bacon to the cold skillet, set over medium heat, and cook, stirring occasionally, until the bacon has rendered much of its fat and is just beginning to brown, about 8 minutes. Don't let it become crisp. Add the leek, carrot, shallot, reserved mush-room stems, and salt and pepper to taste, and sauté, stirring often, until the vegetables are tender and beginning to brown, about 8 minutes. Pour in half the wine and add the

thyme. Bring to a rapid simmer and cook until the wine has reduced by about half, about 10 minutes. Add the remaining wine and return to a simmer for 5 minutes.

5.   **Meanwhile, prepare the bacon and mushroom garnish:** As the wine is reducing, place the remaining bacon in a medium skillet over medium heat and fry until crisp. Transfer to a small bowl with tongs or a slotted spoon and set aside. Pour off most of the grease from the skillet, add 1 tablespoon of the butter, and swirl the skillet, off the heat so that the butter doesn't burn or brown too quickly. Add the sliced mushroom caps and set the skillet over medium-high heat. Season with salt and pepper and sauté, shaking or stirring often. The mushrooms will throw off a fair amount of liquid: continue sautéing, stirring frequently, until all the liquid evaporates and the mushrooms are tender and nicely browned. Transfer the mushrooms to another bowl. Return the skillet to the stove, with the burner turned off—you will use the skillet later for finishing the sauce.

6.   **The braise:** Season the salmon on the top and sides with salt and pepper. When the braising liquid is ready, reduce to a gentle simmer and arrange the fillets skin side down in the simmering liquid. Cover tightly and slide the pan onto a rack in the middle of the oven. Braise the salmon for 15 to 18 minutes, checking once about halfway through to make sure that the liquid is simmering gently and to baste the fillets with the wine. If the liquid is simmering vigorously, lower the oven 10 or 15 degrees. (Since the salmon is delicate and cooks quickly, there is no need to turn it halfway the way you would a pot roast or other large cut.) Check for doneness by discreetly cutting into the thickest part of a fillet and peeking to see that it is opaque on the outside but still translucent toward the center. Remove the pan from the oven and, with a fish spatula or other slotted spatula, transfer the fillets to a platter to catch any juices. Cover loosely with foil and set in a warm spot.

7.   **The finish:** Strain the braising liquid into the reserved skillet, pushing on the vegetables to extract as much liquid as you can. Bring to a rapid simmer over medium-high heat. After a minute or two, lower the heat to medium, and when the simmer has slowed to a gentle one, whisk in the remaining tablespoon of butter. Stir in the parsley and taste for salt and pepper. Add the reserved crisped bacon and sautéed mushrooms to the sauce and heat through.

8.   **Serving:** Place the salmon fillets on dinner plates and spoon the sauce over the top.

Shopping for Salmon

Most of the fresh salmon sold in our markets is Atlantic salmon. This pretty pale pink fish has become more and more popular as a growing number of people recognize the health benefits of fish in their diets. Atlantic salmon is available year-round and at an affordable price. What many people do not know, however, is that all commercial Atlantic salmon is farm-raised. Salmon farming began many years ago in Norway, where salmon fishing has long been a way of life. Now there are salmon farms all over the world and, sadly, the quality of farm-raised salmon has deteriorated. As salmon farms grow in numbers, the pressure to produce fish as quickly and economically as possible prevails. Much of the farm-raised salmon that comes to market today tastes bland and flabby. In addition to the mediocre flavor of farm-raised salmon, I have trouble getting past the environmental damage that these industrial-sized fish farms can create. My solution is to shop for Pacific salmon, which is not farm-raised and is available only from late spring through the summer, sometimes into the early fall. Look for king, Alaskan, or Chinook—different names for the same fish. You may also come across sockeye, which is very similar to king and an excellent choice if you find it. Some markets simply use the names Pacific or wild salmon, both of which indicate good-tasting wild-caught fish.

When buying salmon fillets, avoid the tail portion, which is thin and narrow and will cook too quickly. Instead, ask for evenly sized pieces from the thicker upper part of the fillet, sometimes referred to as center-cut.

Tuna Steaks Braised with Radicchio, Chickpeas & Rosemary ✈

A much-beloved pantry staple in my house is *tonno ai ceci*, little jars of olive oil–packed tuna and chickpeas made by a company in Sicily called Flott. The combination of meaty tuna and nutty chickpeas is one I can't get enough of, and I confess that I occasionally eat it directly from the jar for a quick lunch. As much as I enjoy *tonno ai ceci*, I recently began to wonder if I couldn't improve on the combination by using fresh tuna. I start with thick tuna steaks that I braise along with chickpeas in a combination of rosemary-infused olive oil and chicken stock. The tuna comes out satiny, moist, and barely pink in the center, and the chickpea and radicchio garnish provides a tasty balance of sweet and bitter. I leave this braise soupy in the end, because I like the way the delicately flavored braising liquid moistens the rich-tasting tuna. Serve this warm in shallow pasta bowls with some crusty Italian bread, or at room temperature over a lightly dressed green salad, or as part of an antipasto. Either way, add a squeeze of lemon, a sprinkle of *fleur de sel*, and a thread of olive oil just before serving. Heads and shoulders above anything from a jar.

If your best extra-virgin olive oil is too dear to afford a full ⅓ cup, use a more generic one for the infusion in Step 1. But pull out the good stuff to drizzle on just before serving: it matters.

wine notes

Medium-rich white with herbal flavors and little or no oak—white Rhone blend of the Marsanne and Roussanne grapes; lightly-oaked Fumé Blanc; or a dry rosé from southern France or California.

If you're planning on serving this at room temperature, make it 1 to 2 hours ahead and let it sit at room temperature until ready to serve. Or make it 1 to 2 days in advance, cover, and refrigerate; allow an hour for the tuna to warm to room temperature before serving. The tuna doesn't reheat well, so if you do make this ahead of time, plan on enjoying it at room temperature.

Serves 4 | Braising Time: about 30 minutes

$1/3$ cup extra-virgin olive oil, plus more for drizzling

4 garlic cloves, cut into slivers

2 teaspoons coarsely chopped fresh rosemary

$1/4$ teaspoon crushed red pepper flakes

1 medium head radicchio (about 6 ounces)

1 cup chicken stock, homemade (page 448) or store-bought

1 tablespoon freshly squeezed lemon juice, plus more to taste

One 15 $1/2$-ounce can chickpeas, drained and rinsed (1 $1/2$ cups)

Coarse salt

1 $3/4$ pounds tuna steaks (usually 2 good-sized steaks), about 1 $1/4$ inches thick

Freshly ground black pepper

2 tablespoons coarsely chopped flat-leaf parsley

Fleur de sel or coarse sea salt

1. **Infusing the olive oil:** Combine the oil, garlic, rosemary, and pepper flakes in a medium high-sided skillet (10- or 12-inches). Heat over low heat, covered, until the garlic is fragrant, soft, and lightly golden, 4 to 5 minutes. Lift the lid frequently to check that the garlic isn't frying or browning; you want a gentle infusion of flavor into the oil. Set aside.

2. **The radicchio:** Cut the radicchio in half from core to top. With a small knife, carve out the small core. Place the halves cut side down on a cutting board and, using a larger knife, slice into $1/2$-inch-wide shreds. Add these to the infused olive oil. Return the skillet to medium heat and sauté, stirring occasionally, until the radicchio is wilted, about 5 minutes.

3. **Braising the chickpeas:** Add the stock, lemon juice, chickpeas, and a pinch of salt to the pan. Bring to a simmer, cover, and simmer gently for 8 to 10 minutes to meld the flavors.

4. **Braising the tuna:** Season the tuna steaks on both sides with salt and pepper. Set them on top of the chickpeas and radicchio, and reduce the heat to low. Cover and braise gently,

lifting the lid once or twice to check that the liquid is simmering quietly, not violently. If necessary, lower the heat, or set a heat diffuser beneath the pan. After 8 to 10 minutes, the tuna steaks should be cooked halfway through; judge this by seeing that the graying color of cooked tuna has advanced about halfway up the sides of the steaks. Slide a fish spatula or other slotted spatula under the steaks and turn them, lifting some chickpeas and radicchio too as you go so that the steaks are now smothered in a layer of chickpeas and radicchio. Replace the cover and braise gently until the steaks are just cooked through, another 6 to 8 minutes. Prod the center of a steak with a paring knife and peek to see that it's cooked to your liking. (I like this tuna best with only a faint trace of pink in the center.)

5.   **Serving:** Transfer the tuna steaks to a cutting board and divide into serving pieces. Set the tuna in warm shallow pasta bowls. Stir the parsley into the pan, taste for salt and pepper, and spoon the chickpea-radicchio garnish, along with plenty of liquid, over the tuna. Finish each serving with a squeeze of lemon juice, a thread of good olive oil, and a pinch of *fleur de sel* or coarse sea salt.

Tuna Pot Roast with Tomato, Basil & Capers →→

A pristine tuna steak heavily seared on the outside while left cool inside can be divine, and many of us have come to prefer our tuna cooked this way. But I confess that I actually prefer the slower, more thoroughly cooked tuna dishes of Italy and southern France. Cooks from these regions gently braise fresh tuna with vegetables and herbs until the fish is cooked all the way through and infused with the flavor of the sauce. The combination of the moist heat and the richness of the tuna means the fish does not dry out, but remains moist and almost creamy. If you've never slow-cooked a thick cut of top-quality tuna, you're in for a happy surprise.

I call this recipe pot roast because the tuna is left whole, then sliced after braising. Many markets pre-slice all their fresh tuna in the morning after deliveries. In that case, you'll want to call ahead and ask for a single large piece of tuna loin.

Serve the "pot roast" hot directly after braising accompanied by sautéed summer squash and pieces of warm focaccia. Or serve it at room temperature with roasted bell pepper strips, olives, an aged cheese, and a tomato salad for an outdoor summer lunch.

wine notes

Herbal white wine with little or no oak, such as Sauvignon Blanc or Fumé Blanc; or vibrant Italian white such as Pinot Grigio, Gavi, or Vernaccia; or dry rosé from France or California.

Working Ahead

Before braising, the tuna is seasoned with a mixture of anchovy, basil, and garlic and left to sit for 1 to 4 hours to allow the flavors to permeate the fish. Be sure to allow time for this essential step.

If you choose to make the pot roast ahead and serve it at room temperature, you can let it sit at room temperature for 1 to 2 hours until ready to serve. You can also make it 1 to 2 days in advance, cover, and refrigerate. Allow an hour for the tuna to warm to room temperature before serving. The tuna will dry out if you attempt to reheat it, so if you do make this in advance, serve it at room temperature.

Serves 4 to 6 | Braising Time: 20 to 25 minutes

THE BASIL-ANCHOVY PASTE

2 large garlic cloves, peeled

3 anchovies, minced

1 tablespoon finely chopped fresh basil,
   stems reserved

Coarse salt and freshly ground black
   pepper

THE BRAISE

1 3/4 to 2 pounds tuna loin in one piece,
   at least 3 to 4 inches thick

All-purpose flour for dredging (about
   1/4 cup)

1/4 cup extra-virgin olive oil

1/2 small yellow onion, sliced

1 small celery stalk with leaves, finely
   chopped

1 cup dry white wine or dry white
   vermouth

1 cup chopped ripe or canned tomatoes

Coarse salt and freshly ground black
   pepper

1/4 cup loosely packed shredded fresh basil
   leaves, stems reserved

1 tablespoon capers, rinsed and drained

1. **Season the tuna—1 to 4 hours in advance:** Coarsely chop 1 garlic clove and combine it with the anchovies and basil in a mortar. Season with salt and pepper, and crush and grind the garlic, anchovies, and basil into a paste using the pestle. (If you don't have a mortar and pestle, combine the ingredients on a cutting board and using a combination of chopping motion and smearing with the side of the blade, reduce them to a paste.) Slice the remaining garlic clove into slivers. With the tip of a sharp knife, make small incisions all over the tuna loin and stuff a sliver of garlic into each one. Smear the anchovy-garlic-basil paste over the entire surface of the tuna. Cover loosely with plastic and refrigerate for 1 to 4 hours.

2. **Dredging the tuna:** Spread the flour out on a plate. Roll the tuna loin, paste and all, in the flour. Some paste may come off, but don't worry. Lift the tuna loin out of the flour, and pat it to shake off the excess. Discard the leftover flour.

3. **Browning the tuna:** Add 2 tablespoons of the oil to a heavy high-sided lidded skillet or braising pan that will neatly hold the tuna without much room to spare, and heat over medium-high heat until the oil shimmers. Lower the tuna into the oil, using your hands or sturdy tongs, and sear it on all sides, turning with tongs, just until a pale brown crust forms, 2 minutes per side. Transfer the tuna to a plate, using a large spatula to lift it and a

pair of sturdy tongs to steady it so as to avoid piercing the fish with a fork. Discard the oil. Wipe out the pan with a paper towel.

4. **The aromatics and braising liquid:** Add the remaining 2 tablespoons oil to the pan and heat over medium heat. Add the onion and celery and sauté, stirring occasionally, until translucent and limp, about 8 minutes. Pour in the wine and simmer until reduced by about half, about 10 minutes. Add the tomatoes and season with salt and pepper. Tie the reserved basil stems together with kitchen string, then stir in the basil stems and capers and simmer for 2 minutes to meld the flavors.

5. **The braise:** Return the tuna to the pan, again using the spatula and tongs, cover, and reduce the heat to low. Lift the lid after a minute or two to make sure that the sauce is just barely bubbling. If it is simmering too vigorously, lower the heat or set a heat diffuser beneath the pan. Baste the tuna every 5 minutes or so, spooning the tomato braising liquid over the top. After 10 minutes, carefully turn the tuna using the spatula and a sturdy pair of tongs; do not grip too tightly with the tongs, or you may tear the tuna. Continue braising until the tuna is just cooked through, another 10 to 15 minutes. An easy doneness test is to insert a narrow blade or skewer into the center of the tuna. Wait a moment, then pull out the blade or skewer and touch it gingerly to your lip or the inside of your wrist. The blade or skewer should feel just warm to the touch, not cold and not scorching hot. You can also insert a small knife into the tuna and pull back the flesh to peek. The fish should be just cooked through but not at all dried out. Transfer the tuna to a serving dish, and cover loosely with foil to keep warm.

6. **The finish:** Remove the basil stems. Bring the sauce to a simmer, and taste it to evaluate its flavor and texture. If the sauce appears thin, boil to thicken it some, about 6 minutes. It should be thick enough to spoon over the tuna. Stir in the shredded basil and taste for salt and pepper.

7. **Serving:** If serving immediately, carve the tuna into thick slices or chunks and spoon the sauce over each. Or leave the tuna to cool in the braising liquid, then carve the tuna into slices or pull it into chunks and serve with the braising liquid.

VARIATION: TUNA POT ROAST WITH TOMATOES & BLACK OLIVES

As much as I enjoy tuna pot roast as is, I sometimes can't resist gilding the lily. I add a scant ¼ cup small unpitted black olives (such as Moroccan oil-cured or Niçoise) and 2 strips of orange zest, removed with a vegetable peeler (each about 3 inches by ¾ inch) to the braising liquid along with the capers and basil stems in Step 4. The olives add a lovely, briny, earthy note, and the orange sweetens the dish nicely.

Vietnamese Braised Scallops →→

Braising seafood, meats, and even tofu in a thick caramel sauce is a classic Vietnamese technique, referred to as *kho*. The dark caramel sauce, made with sugar, fish sauce, and shallots, is not at all sugary, but instead full of spicy-salty nuances—the perfect foil for sweet, meaty sea scallops. Since scallops are naturally tender, they braise less time than it takes to make the sauce. In place of scallops, thick chunks of any meaty white fish fillet, such as halibut, monkfish, or cod, would do well.

While the traditional vessel for *kho* is an earthenware crock that goes from the top of the stove to the table, a heavy-based skillet works just as well. To serve, set the scallops on a bed of jasmine rice and spoon the dark sauce over the top. Pass a bowl of thinly sliced cucumber dressed with rice wine vinegar at the table.

wine notes

Light-bodied white with a touch of sweetness and crisp acidity—off-dry Chenin Blanc from California or Washington state, or Riesling from Germany.

Working Ahead

The caramel braising sauce can be made weeks in advance and kept in a jar in the refrigerator until you're ready to braise (Steps 1 and 2).

Serves 4 | Braising Time: about 10 minutes

1/2 cup water (6 tablespoons if using
    Chinese brown sugar)

1/4 cup Asian fish sauce

1/3 cup granulated sugar or 2 1/2 ounces
    Chinese brown sugar (see "Chinese
    Brown Sugar," page 119)

2 shallots, minced

1 1/2 pounds sea scallops (see "Shopping
    for Sea Scallops," page 119)

1/2 teaspoon crushed red pepper flakes

2 scallions, thinly sliced, white and green
    parts kept separate

1. **Make the caramel:** Combine 1/4 cup water with the fish sauce in a glass measuring cup and set aside. If using granulated sugar, put it in a heavy-based skillet just large enough to hold the scallops in a single layer. Pour over the remaining 1/4 cup water and let it sit for a minute to soak in. Heat the skillet over medium heat until the sugar liquefies. You can shake or swirl the pan or stir with a wooden spoon once or twice so the sugar melts evenly, but don't stir constantly. Once the contents of the saucepan have liquefied entirely (the sugar will be clear with faint traces of amber around the edges), don't stir at all, or you risk crystallizing the sugar. If the sugar appears to be boiling unevenly, swirl the pan a little to even it out, but avoid disturbing it or swirling it too frequently. The sugar will begin to caramelize and darken quickly, so stay close by to monitor its progress. Continue to boil until the caramel is a deep reddish brown, but not black, 8 to 10 minutes. When the caramel begins to smoke a bit around the edges and smells very toasty, it is ready. You're after a very dark caramel—one that is very nearly burnt. If you've only ever made caramel for desserts, don't be afraid to take this one further. (Since this is such a shallow amount of caramel, I've never had any success using a candy thermometer for this dish. If you want to try, aim for a temperature in the range of 370 to 375 degrees.)

    If using Chinese slab sugar, combine it with 2 tablespoons water in the skillet over medium heat. Heat, stirring frequently with a wooden spoon to break up the sugar, until the sugar dissolves, about 4 minutes. Slab sugar eliminates the fear of having the sugar seize and crystallize, so there's no concern of overstirring. Reduce the heat to medium-low, and let the caramel bubble, stirring frequently, until it becomes a deep reddish brown, but not mahogany or black, 3 to 4 minutes.

2. **Adding the water and fish sauce:** Standing back and pouring slowly so the caramel does not boil over, add the water and fish sauce mixture. Don't worry if the caramel hardens; it will melt again as it boils. Stir and let the caramel boil until you have a smooth, thick sauce, about 4 minutes. Add the shallots, reduce the heat to low, and simmer for 2 minutes. Set the pan aside. (*You can make the caramel sauce ahead and keep it refrigerated in a jar for weeks.*)

3. **Trimming the scallops:** Examine the scallops. Most come with an opaque squareish hard bit attached to one side. This is a muscle that attaches the scallop to the shell and

while not inedible, it is neither sweet nor tender and is best removed. Do so by taking hold of this little muscle with one hand and pulling: it will strip off easily.

4. **Braising the scallops:** Bring the caramel sauce back to a very low simmer over medium-low heat in the same skillet you made it. Stir in the red pepper flakes and the white part of the scallions. Add the scallops in a single layer, partially cover, and simmer very gently for 4 or 5 minutes. Gently turn the scallops, using a small spatula or a pair of tongs, and continue to simmer until just cooked through, another 3 to 5 minutes. If unsure, nick a single scallop with a sharp thin-bladed knife and peek to check that there is just the slightest bit of translucence in the center.

5. **Serving:** Transfer the scallops to warm plates and spoon over some of the sauce. Garnish with the scallion greens and serve immediately.

Shopping for Sea Scallops

Be sure to buy "dry" sea scallops at the market. If they aren't labeled, ask. The less expensive, and much inferior, alternative is "wet" scallops, which have been soaked in a sodium phosphate solution to plump them and extend their shelf life. Besides bearing a label that should say something like "25 percent water added," wet scallops will look watery and milky. Not only do you end up paying for water that then leaks out the minute the scallops hit a hot pan, making sautéing them difficult, but the flavor of these scallops is chemical-tainted and rather nasty. If wet scallops are all you can find, change your menu.

Chinese Brown Sugar

The traditional basis for *kho* is an unrefined cane sugar, found in Asian markets as Chinese brown sugar or slab sugar, or as *panela* in Latin markets. This hard sugar comes in caramel-colored wafers or slabs that you dissolve in water to make a quick caramel. The same results can be obtained using ordinary granulated sugar cooked to caramel, the main difference being that there isn't the fear of having the sugar seize and crystallize with slab sugar, so there's not the concern of overstirring.

Mediterranean Squid & Shrimp Braise →→

There's only one rule that you need to know about cooking squid—you must
cook it either very quickly (no more than a few minutes) or very slowly.
Anything in between turns the squid tough and bouncy and no good at all. I
leave the quick cooking to restaurants and bars where I'm happy to nibble away
at a heaping plate of deep-fried calamari with drinks. For home cooking,
braising squid slowly is easier and gives you the opportunity to create a seafood
dinner with layer upon layer of flavor.

The braising liquid for this squid consists of a colorful mix of tomatoes,
garlic, onion, carrots, and celery that I brighten with the zests and juice of
orange and lime. I also include small potatoes to turn this into a satisfying one-
dish meal. And just a few minutes before serving, I toss in some shelled
shrimp, making the finished dish a real cornucopia of seafood and vegetables.
Since this braise comes out rather soupy, serve it in shallow pasta bowls. If
you've got guests with raging appetites, ladle the braise over linguine.

wine notes

Dry blush wines and rosés from southern France, California, or Australia.

Serves 4 | Braising Time: about 1 3/4 hours

1 1/2 pounds cleaned squid (or 2 1/4 pounds whole squid, cleaned; see "Buying and Cleaning Squid," page 123)	1/2 cup finely chopped yellow onion (about 1/2 small onion)
3 tablespoons extra-virgin olive oil	1/2 cup finely chopped carrot (1 small carrot)
3 to 4 garlic cloves, thinly sliced	1/2 cup finely chopped celery (1/2 stalk)

Coarse salt and freshly ground black
  pepper
1/2 cup dry white wine or dry white
  vermouth
2 strips orange zest, removed with a
  vegetable peeler (each about 3 inches
  by 3/4 inch)
1 strip lime zest, removed with a
  vegetable peeler (about 2 inches
  by 1/2 inch)
1/4 cup freshly squeezed orange juice
  (see "Bitter Oranges," page 122)
1/4 cup freshly squeezed lime juice

One 14 1/2-ounce can whole peeled
  tomatoes, drained and chopped
  (or 1 1/3 cups chopped, peeled, and
  seeded ripe plum tomatoes)
Pinch of crushed red pepper flakes
1/4 cup chopped flat-leaf parsley
3/4 pound small potatoes, preferably
  fingerlings or white creamers
1/4 cup small green olives, such as
  Picholine, not pitted
2 tablespoons capers, rinsed and drained
3/4 pound large shrimp (30 to 35 count per
  pound), peeled and deveined
2 tablespoons unsalted butter, cut into
  4 pieces (optional)

1. **Rinsing and cutting up the squid:** Fill a bowl with cold water and soak the squid for 5 minutes to freshen it and rid it of any of the slime that it tends to develop as it sits. Drain and rinse. If you didn't clean the squid yourself, sort through it, feeling to see if there are any hard round bits, or beaks that haven't been removed. Also reach into each body, or hood to check that the quill is gone, and remove and discard any that you find. Slice the bodies into 1-inch-wide rings, and chop the tentacles into 1/2-inch pieces. Lay the cut-up squid on a towel to dry.

2. **Sautéing the squid:** Heat the oil in a large deep lidded skillet (13-inch works well) over high heat until shimmering. Add the squid, a handful at a time (adding it all at once would lower the heat of the pan). Stand back a bit, since squid releases an impressive amount of liquid when it comes in contact with a hot pan and therefore splatters wildly. Immediately add the garlic. Sauté the squid, stirring and shaking the pan frequently, until it turns opaque and shrinks up, about 2 minutes. With a slotted spoon, scoop the squid out of the pan (don't worry if some garlic slices stick to the squid and some remain in the pan), and transfer it to a bowl. There should be a fair amount of liquid remaining in the pan.

3. **The aromatics and braising liquid:** Lower the heat to medium-high and add the onion, carrot, and celery to the liquid in the pan. Season with salt and pepper, stir, and return to a vigorous simmer. Add the white wine, orange and lime zests, and orange and lime juices, and let the liquid simmer vigorously until reduced by half, 7 to 10 minutes. Stir in the tomatoes, crushed red pepper, and 2 tablespoons of the parsley. Return to a simmer.

4. **The braise:** Add the squid to the braising liquid, turn the heat to very low, cover, and simmer gently for 30 minutes. Check on the squid after the first few minutes to make sure that the liquid maintains a lazy, not a rollicking, simmer. If you need to, lower the heat or place a heat diffuser under the pan.

5. **The potatoes, olives, and capers:** After 30 minutes, add the potatoes, olives, and capers. Stir so the potatoes are evenly distributed, replace the cover, and continue to simmer until the squid is tender and the potatoes are easily pierced with the tip of a knife, another 35 to 45 minutes.

6. **The finish:** Add the shrimp, leave the pan uncovered, and adjust the heat so the liquid simmers gently. Simmer just until the shrimp are cooked through, 4 to 5 minutes. Stir in the remaining 2 tablespoons parsley, and taste. If the sauce tastes too acidic or too sharp, stir in the butter. The small bit of butter will soften the acidity nicely. Taste again for salt and pepper. Remove the zests if you like, and serve in shallow bowls.

Bitter Oranges

The first time I made this dish, I was lucky enough to have received a few Seville oranges as a gift. Also known as bitter or sour oranges, these fragrant fruits are grown in the Mediterranean and Latin America. Once almost impossible to find in the United States, bitter oranges are now beginning to show up in specialty food shops and Latin markets. Look for them especially in the winter, when the citrus season is at its peak. Bitter oranges have the acidity of a lemon but the floral fragrance of an orange blossom. Their skins are knobbier and bumpier than the oranges we are used to, and they are not pleasant to eat out of hand. If you are a marmalade fan, you may already know that bitter oranges are used for the best marmalade.

If you do find bitter oranges in the market, use them in the Mediterranean Squid & Shrimp Braise (page 120). They will add a striking floral aroma to the dish. Simply replace the lime juice and zest (which I added to balance the sweetness of regular sweet oranges) with all bitter orange juice and zest.

Buying and Cleaning Squid

Most of the squid in fish markets today has been previously frozen in 5-pound blocks, then thawed before being sold. Fortunately, freezing and thawing squid does not alter or deteriorate its quality, so there is no need to go on a great hunt for fresh squid. What you do need to do before you buy is inspect the squid to determine that it hasn't been sitting thawed for too long. The squid should look shiny and bright, not dull or milky. The best test, as always, is to ask to smell the squid. It should have almost no smell, just a fresh clean whiff of ocean air.

Whether or not you buy cleaned squid may depend on what's available. It's the rare market that sells both. If given a choice, the cleaned squid should mean less work for you. Unfortunately, though, few markets do a very thorough job of cleaning squid, so it is always up to the cook to go back and pick out whatever the fishmonger left. In the end, I find it's easiest to clean it myself. Here's how:

Hold a whole squid in one hand (your left, if you're right-handed), grab the tentacles just where they connect to the body (or hood), and tug gently. The soft innards should come away with the tentacles. Cut off the innards where they are attached to the tentacles and discard. As you do so, you may notice a silvery-gray speck in the innards near the tentacles. This is the ink sac. Avoid nicking or tearing open the tiny sac, as it will spill an astonishing amount of black ink. Squeeze the top of the tentacles to pop out the small pea-shaped hard bit, called the beak, and discard. If the beak doesn't pop out, cut it out with a knife. Rinse the body under cold water, and reach inside with a finger to remove any remaining mushy innards and to search for the thin, glass-like blade known as the quill. Remove and discard. If you like, peel off any dark, grayish-purple membrane from the outside and discard. (Some cooks claim that the dark skin, or membrane, adds flavor to the squid and prefer what is called "dirty squid," or unpeeled squid. Other cooks—myself included—prefer to remove the membrane for aesthetic reasons. In my experience, there's not a great deal of difference in flavor, and indeed, most of the squid sold in markets today—both cleaned and whole—comes with the membrane already peeled off.) If the wings become unattached (these are flaps that extend from the hood), save them with the cleaned squid. Clean up and be sure to take the trash out soon after cleaning the squid, since discarded squid parts spoil extremely quickly and noticeably.

Squid Roulades Braised with White Wine & Tomatoes →→

Sweet-tasting and tender, squid make perfect little "pouches" for stuffing with a delicate mousse-like filling of white fish (such as pollock, cod, or flounder), bits of cooked shrimp, chopped-up squid tentacles, and plenty of parsley. Once they are filled, the real magic of this recipe begins. When you sear the stuffed squid in a few tablespoons of olive oil, they retract and shrink up into plump little pillows less than half their original size. No matter how often I make these, I still smile with amazement at witnessing this exaggerated transformation. Once they are seared and shrunken, you tuck the little pillows into a mix of white wine and grape tomatoes to simmer away until utterly tender. To serve, carve each little pillow into rounds, or roulades, revealing the light parsley-speckled filling encased in the rings of tender white squid. Lovely.

If you have a pastry bag, it makes the job of filling the squid a cinch. If not, I've had great success using a narrow teaspoon or demitasse spoon. The roulades make an elegant first course or light main course with a mound of steamed white rice or a swirl of buttered linguine.

wine notes

Crisp white with tangy fruit and herbal flavors like Pinot Grigio, Verdiccio, or Vernaccia; or a crisp, dry rosé or other blush wine.

Working Ahead

You can fill the squid (Steps 1 through 6) up to 4 hours ahead and keep them covered in the refrigerator.

After braising, the squid can sit for an hour or so in their braising liquid until ready to serve. This makes them ideal for entertaining. You can do all the work before your guests arrive, leaving you time to clean up the kitchen and put fresh flowers on the table. To serve, either reheat them before slicing over medium heat for a few minutes until the sauce comes to a simmer, or serve them lukewarm. Either way, the dish is a standout.

Serves 6 as a starter, 4 as a main course | Braising Time: about 1 hour

1 ½ pounds cleaned squid—12 to 16 3-inch-long bodies and a mix of tentacles (or 2 ¼ pounds whole squid, cleaned; see "Buying and Cleaning Squid," page 123, and "Shopping for Squid Suitable for Stuffing," page 127)

THE FILLING

¼ pound medium shrimp (35 to 40 count per pound), peeled and deveined

2 tablespoons extra-virgin olive oil

1 medium shallot, finely minced (2 heaping tablespoons)

Coarse salt and freshly ground white pepper

2 tablespoons chopped flat-leaf parsley

½ pound pollock, cod, or flounder fillets, cut into large chunks

⅓ cup well-chilled heavy cream

THE BRAISE

3 tablespoons extra-virgin olive oil

1 medium shallot, chopped (about 2 tablespoons)

1 cup dry white wine or dry white vermouth

Coarse salt and freshly ground white pepper

1 heaping cup grape tomatoes (about 6 ounces), halved lengthwise

½ lemon

2 tablespoons chopped flat-leaf parsley

1. **Rinsing and preparing the squid:** Fill a bowl with cold water and soak the squid for 5 minutes. Drain and rinse. Separate the bodies from the tentacles, and reach into each body to check that the brittle quill has been removed. If not, remove and discard it. Put the bodies in a bowl and refrigerate them for now. If you didn't clean the squid yourself, sort through the tentacles, feeling to see if there are any hard bits of what's referred to as the beak. Remove and discard any that you find. Chop the tentacles into ½-inch pieces and put in a bowl.

2. **The shrimp for the filling:** Slice the shrimp lengthwise in half and then chop the halves into ½-inch pieces. Add to the chopped squid in the bowl.

3. **The aromatics for the filling:** Heat the oil in a medium skillet (8-inch) over medium heat. Add the shallot and sauté, stirring occasionally with a wooden spoon, until tender, about 5 minutes. Add the chopped squid tentacles and shrimp and season with salt and white pepper. Increase the heat to high and sauté, stirring often, until the shrimp have turned pink and the squid tentacles are light purple, another 5 minutes so. Stir in the parsley and scrape the mixture into a bowl to cool.

4. **Making the fish mousse:** Place the pollock, cod, or flounder in a food processor. (If your kitchen is excessively warm, first chill the workbowl and chopping blade in the refrigerator for 20 minutes. Getting the mousse too warm can cause it to be grainy.) Pulse to coarsely chop the fish. Add the cream, 1/4 teaspoon salt, and a few grinds of white pepper and process, using the pulse button, until the fish is smooth and creamy. Do not overwork the fish, or the filling will be dry and spongy.

5. **Assembling the filling:** If the shrimp and tentacle mix is not yet cool to the touch, refrigerate the pureed fish while you wait. When it is cool, fold the mix gently but thoroughly into the pureed fish with a large rubber spatula.

6. **Stuffing the squid:** Choose a pastry bag that has an opening that is 3/4 to 1 inch across (if the opening is larger, fit the bag with a plain tip of that size), and scoop the filling into the bag. If you don't have a pastry bag, choose a narrow teaspoon or demitasse spoon that will easily fit inside the squid without tearing. Pipe or spoon the filling into the squid bodies until only about two-thirds full. It's critical that you don't overfill the squid, or they will burst or tear as they cook. Once filled, secure the openings with sturdy toothpicks or wooden skewers. Toothpicks are good for smallish squid, but if this doesn't seem secure, break a bamboo skewer into 2 1/2- to 3-inch lengths.

7. **Searing the squid:** Heat the 3 tablespoons oil in a medium skillet (9-inch works well) over high heat. Add as many squid as will fit and sear them, turning with tongs to cook all sides, until they shrink up to almost half their original size and are very lightly tinged with gold, about 4 minutes total. Don't expect the squid to brown—they won't. But the juices released from the squid will caramelize on the bottom of the skillet, forming a nice brown crust that will later add a sweet squid flavor to the braise. Transfer the squid with the tongs to a plate or dish as they're ready and sear the remainder.

8. **The aromatics and braising liquid:** When all the squid have been seared, pour off all but about 1 tablespoon of fat from the skillet and return it to medium heat. Add the shallot, stir, and cook for about 1 minute. Pour in the wine, scrape the bottom of the pan with a wooden spoon, and simmer, stirring and scraping, just long enough to dislodge and dissolve the browned crust from the pan.

9. **The braise:** Return the squid to the skillet. They should all now fit in a single layer. Season lightly with salt and white pepper, scatter over the grape tomatoes, and return to a

simmer. Cover, reduce the heat to low, and simmer gently, lifting the lid to turn each stuffed squid with tongs once or twice during braising, until very tender, 1 hour to 1 hour and 10 minutes. Check the skillet every so often to see that the liquid is gently simmering, not boiling furiously. Lower the heat as needed or set a heat diffuser under the skillet. (*At this point the squid may be left in the sauce in a warm spot for an hour or so until ready to serve.*)

10. **Serving:** When the squid are tender, lift them from the liquid with a slotted spoon or tongs and set them on a cutting board. Turn the heat under the braising liquid to high and let it boil to concentrate the flavor and reduce the volume just a bit, 5 to 10 minutes. Remove the toothpicks or skewers from the squid. Slice each squid on a sharp angle into thirds or quarters—the pieces should be about 1/2 inch thick. Arrange on dinner plates or a serving platter. Add a generous squeeze of lemon juice and the parsley to the sauce, and taste for salt and pepper. Spoon the sauce over the squid and serve.

Shopping for Squid Suitable for Stuffing

When buying squid for stuffing, you want squid that are neither too small nor too large. I occasionally see tiny squid with bodies (hoods) that are less than 2 inches long. These are really too small to stuff. Look instead for squid that are about 3 inches in length. You want 12 to 16 bodies for this recipe, but be sure to ask for a mix of tentacles and bodies so you can chop up the tentacles for the filling. They add flavor and juiciness.

POULTRY AND GAME

Quick Lemony Chicken with Prunes & Green Olives →→

This easy chicken braise simmers on top of the stove for about 35 minutes, making it ideal for a quick weeknight dinner. But don't let that stop you from making it for company. The winning combination of sweet prunes and green olives in a lemony braising liquid makes it distinctive enough for a fancy dinner party. Serve with mashed potatoes, a potato gratin, or buttered egg noodles.

wine notes

Medium-bodied white with youthful fruit and a touch of mineral flavor—Alsace Pinot Gris or Pinot Blanc, or Oregon Pinot Gris.

Serves 4 | Braising Time: 30 to 40 minutes

1/3 cup brined green olives, such as Picholine or Lucques

4 whole skin-on chicken legs (including thighs) or 4 thighs and 4 drumsticks (about 3 1/2 pounds total)

Coarse salt and freshly ground black pepper

All-purpose flour for dredging (about 1/2 cup)

2 tablespoons extra-virgin olive oil

1 cup dry white wine or dry white vermouth

1/4 cup white wine vinegar

1 garlic clove, peeled and smashed

4 strips lemon zest, removed with a vegetable peeler (each about 2 1/2 inches by 3/4 inch)

2 whole cloves

3/4 cup plump pitted prunes (see "Plumping Prunes," page 134)

1. **Pitting the olives:** If the olives are not pitted, remove the pits by smashing the olives one at a time with the side of a large knife, then slipping the pits out. If any flesh remains on the pits, slice it off with the knife. (You can use an olive pitter if you choose, but I've always found a knife faster and more efficient.)

2. **Separating chicken legs into thighs and drumsticks:** If using whole legs, separate the thighs from the drumsticks: Turn each leg skin side down and, with a sharp chef's or boning knife, cut along the line of yellow fat that runs between the thigh and drumstick. This line will direct you to the exact spot where the two parts are joined. Then cut down through the joint; it should be an easy cut. If your knife meets resistance, reposition the blade until you find the spot where it slides through easily.

3. **Dredging the chicken:** Rinse the chicken in cool water, and dry thoroughly with paper towels. Generously season all over with salt and pepper. Spread the flour in a wide shallow dish (a pie plate works well), and dredge half the chicken pieces one at a time, placing each one in the flour, turning to coat both sides, and then lifting it out and patting lightly to shake off any excess.

4. **Browning the chicken:** Heat the oil in a large deep skillet or shallow braising pan (12- to 14-inch works well) over medium-high heat until it shimmers. Place the dredged chicken pieces skin side down in the pan and sear, without disturbing, until a nut-brown crust forms on the first side, about 3 to 4 minutes. Turn the chicken with tongs and brown on the other side, another 3 to 4 minutes. While the chicken is browning, pat the remaining pieces dry again and dredge them in the flour. Transfer the seared chicken to a platter or large plate to catch the juices, and brown the remaining pieces. Set these aside with the others, and discard the flour.

5. **The aromatics and braising liquid:** Pour off the fat from the pan and quickly wipe out any black specks with a damp paper towel, being careful to leave behind any browned bits. Add the wine, vinegar, garlic, zest, and cloves to the skillet and stir with a wooden spoon to scrape up those prized browned bits stuck to the bottom of the skillet.

6. **The braise:** Return the chicken pieces to the skillet, arranging them so they fit in a snug single layer. Pour over any juices that have accumulated on the plate. Scatter over the prunes and olives. Cover tightly, and reduce the heat to low. Braise at a gentle simmer, basting occasionally and turning the pieces with tongs halfway through, until the chicken is tender and pulls easily away from the bone, 30 to 40 minutes. When you lift the lid to baste, check to see that the liquid is simmering quietly; if it is simmering too vigorously, reduce the heat or place a heat diffuser under the skillet.

7. **The finish:** Using a slotted spoon or tongs, transfer the chicken to a serving platter to catch the juices, and cover loosely with foil to keep warm. Skim any visible surface fat from the sauce with a wide spoon. Raise the heat under the skillet to high, and reduce the pan juices for 2 to 3 minutes to concentrate their flavor. The sauce should be the consistency of a thin vinaigrette. Taste for salt and pepper. Retrieve and discard the cloves and zest, if you like. Pour the juices over the chicken, and serve.

VARIATION: QUICK BRAISED CHICKEN
WITH MEYER LEMONS, PRUNES & GREEN OLIVES

When I find Meyer lemons in the market (see "Meyer Lemons," below), I love to use them in this braise. Their sweet floral perfume lends an appealing honeyed note to the dish. In place of the lemon peel, add ¼ cup chopped Meyer lemon, peel and all.

VARIATION: QUICK RED-WINE-AND-ORANGE-BRAISED
CHICKEN WITH PRUNES & BLACK OLIVES

For a darker, more rustic-looking dish, substitute red wine for the white wine and red wine vinegar for the white wine vinegar. Use orange or tangerine zest in place of the lemon zest, and black olives, such as Nyors or Niçoise, instead of green.

Meyer Lemons

A relatively new arrival on the produce scene, the Meyer lemon is a cross between a lemon and a mandarin orange that was developed more than one hundred years ago as an ornamental tree in China, then later grown in California. But it wasn't until the 1980s that California chefs discovered their goodness and began cooking with them. I adore the fragrance and flavor of Meyer lemons, and I eagerly anticipate their brief season each winter.

Meyer lemons have thin, smooth yellow-orange skins and are a bit larger, rounder, and less oblong than ordinary supermarket lemons (Eureka and Lisbon varieties). If you're at all unsure, scratch the skin—if it emits the fragrance of sweet citrus blossoms, it's a Meyer lemon. Although the fruit is not quite sweet enough to eat out of hand, chopped-up Meyer lemon can be added, peel and all, to salads, braises, stews, and other dishes. Since much of the floral character resides in its thin peel, don't be timid about including it.

Like most citrus, Meyer lemons appear in markets in the winter months, specifically November to March. Select ones that feel plump and heavy for their size, with smooth skin. Because of their thin skins, Meyer lemons are more perishable than standard varieties. Store them in a perforated plastic bag in the refrigerator and use them within a few days. Meyer lemons are grown on small farms and not usually sprayed or dyed, but it's always a good idea to wash the outside of fruit before using it. Rolling the lemon back and forth on a countertop before juicing will yield more juice.

Plumping Prunes

If the only prunes you can find are dry and leathery, you'll want to soak them overnight in room-temperature or slightly warm water to plump them up. Place them in a small bowl and pour over enough water to cover. Let the prunes sit until they are moist and plump, 8 to 12 hours. You can speed things up by using scalding water, but in my experience the hot water begins to break down the texture of the prunes and leave them a bit ragged.

You can also soak prunes in Cognac, port, wine, fruit juice, or any other liquid that you'll be adding to the dish you're making. As the prunes plump, they'll absorb the flavor of the liquid. Stock is not a good choice, however, because it is prone to spoilage and should not be left out on the counter overnight.

French Prunes

If you want to find the best prunes out there, look for ones imported from the Southwest of France (Agen to be exact). Labeled *"pruneaux d'Agen,"* these moist, fat prunes have a deliciously deep, almost caramelized taste. They're worth seeking out if you prize top-quality dried fruit. I love using them in braises because they hold their shape and remain decadently soft and sweet. I've not found a mail-order source for the prunes, but I sometimes find them in gourmet specialty shops. California prunes (now often labeled "dried plums") are actually the same variety of plum as those grown in France, but they tend to be a bit smaller in size and possess a less concentrated flavor.

Why Bone-In, Skin-on Chicken Parts Are Best for Braising

As much as it may speed things up in the kitchen to cook chicken off the bone, what you gain in time, you lose in flavor. Bone-in chicken, like all meat cooked on the bone, will retain more of its flavorful juices. Fortunately, chicken thighs, drumsticks, and breasts are all small enough that braising them on the bone takes only 40 to 60 minutes. This makes them ideal for quick weeknight braises.

As for the skin, it protects the meat from drying out during braising, especially during the browning step. The layer of fat beneath the skin also adds richness and flavor to the dish. One exception is Indian-style dishes. Indian cooks always remove the skin before cooking, originally because it was considered unclean, but now so that the spices come in direct contact with the meat. I use only thighs and legs in Indian-style dishes, because they are less prone to drying out than the white breast meat.

A Note on Chicken Skin

One of the biggest challenges when braising chicken and other poultry is preventing the skin from becoming flabby and unappetizing in the moist heat of a closed pot. This is especially true with the fattier thigh and leg pieces. The best solution I've found is to be especially patient and thorough when browning chicken before braising. In addition to making the skin attractive and tasty, a good sear renders off much of the fat, which is what makes the skin flabby in the first place. Another detail to watch is the amount of braising liquid. Avoid submerging chicken pieces completely in the braising liquid as this can leave the skin soggy. Ideally, there will be just enough liquid to come to where the skin meets the flesh. If the liquid is too deep, try reducing it before braising. In the end, however, no matter how well you sear chicken or how shallow the braising liquid, chicken will always emerge from a braising pot with somewhat soft skin—nothing like the crisp, dry skin that you get when you roast or panfry. In my mind, this is a small price to pay for tender, flavorful poultry. If it's really crispy skin you're after, you can brown the poultry after braising by briefly roasting in a hot oven, as in Braised Whole Chicken with Bread Stuffing & Bacon (page 183) or the Duck Legs Braised in Port & Dried Cherries (page 199).

As a final note on the issue of chicken skin, some chefs resort to braising it in the oven without a lid. This way the skin sits above the braising liquid and pan-roasts rather than braises. In creating the recipes for this book, I experimented with this nontraditional

(continued on next page)

method, and while it does produce a crispier skin, the meat does not absorb the surrounding flavors of the braising liquid the way it does when the pot is tightly sealed. For me, I'd rather have the skin a bit soft than lose the deeply infused flavor of a true braise.

Selecting Cuts of Chicken for Braising

The best cuts of chicken for braising are the dark-meat cuts, thighs and drumsticks. Because successful braising is all about the exchange of flavor between the braising liquid with the meat juices, the juicier the meat, the better-tasting the braise. Since thighs and drumsticks contain more fat and collagen than the white-meat breasts, they are tastier when braised. Chicken breasts are leaner and less moist by nature, so there won't be as much melding of flavors during the braise. Although a chicken breast will take nicely to a braise, it won't lend as much flavor to the sauce, nor will the meat take on much of the character of the sauce.

The other consideration is that chicken breasts are more prone to drying out than chicken legs. A chicken thigh or drumstick can cook 5 or even 10 minutes too long and still remain succulent, whereas a chicken breast can become dry in a matter of a few minutes. And breasts cook more quickly than legs. For these reasons, I've developed a couple of techniques to ensure that the dark meat and light meat cook evenly when braised together. When braising on top of the stove, I wait to add the breasts until 10 minutes into the braise. That way, they are done at the same time as the dark meat. This is not necessary in the gentler heat of the oven, where I manage by setting the chicken breasts on top of the darker meat. This evens out the cooking just enough so that all the parts are braised to doneness at the same time.

When dealing with whole chicken legs (drumstick and thigh), I separate them before braising because I find that they braise more evenly this way. Separating a whole leg into a thigh and drumstick is a simple operation described in Step 5 of "Cutting Up a Chicken," page 161.

Chicken *Do-Piaza* ✦✦

Indian-Spiced Chicken Smothered in Onions

Do-piaza is a classic Indian preparation in which chicken, meat, or shellfish braises in heaps of onions. And I mean heaps: traditionally, for 1 pound of chicken, a full 2 pounds of onions are used (*Do* means double, and *piaz* is onion). What drew me to the dish was the technique of pureeing half the raw onions in a blender with the spices and orange juice to make the braising liquid. The rest of the onions are then added at the very end to give the dish a refreshing taste and crunchy texture. The inspiration for this recipe comes from Julie Sanhi's exceptional cookbook, *Classic Indian Cooking.*

Including orange juice in the braise is not traditional, but I like the way the vibrancy of the citrus combines with the earthy, spicy flavors of ginger, garlic, turmeric, coriander, and cayenne. Drained yogurt is stirred in at the end to enrich and add body to the sauce.

Serve this saucy tangerine-colored chicken with steamed basmati rice or an Indian flatbread, such as *poori* or *paratha*.

wine notes

Fruity white that's off-dry to slightly sweet without any oak flavors—Chenin Blanc from California or Washington, or a slightly sweet Riesling from Germany.

Working Ahead

The yogurt needs to be drained for 4 to 6 hours ahead of time (Step 1). If you haven't the time or want to leave out the yogurt altogether, see the variation at the end of the recipe.

Serves 4 | Braising Time: 40 to 45 minutes

1 cup plain whole-milk yogurt

2 large white or yellow onions (about
    1 pound)

1/2 cup freshly squeezed orange juice

1/4 cup water

1 tablespoon grated fresh ginger

3 garlic cloves, coarsely chopped

2 teaspoons coriander seeds, lightly
    toasted and ground

1 teaspoon ground turmeric

1/4 teaspoon cayenne, or to taste, or
    1 small dried red chile

Coarse salt

8 bone-in, skinless chicken thighs (about
    3 pounds total)

2 tablespoons ghee, clarified butter
    (see "Clarified Butter," page 82), or
    vegetable oil

1. **Draining the yogurt—4 to 6 hours in advance:** Set a small mesh sieve over a tall medium bowl so that the bottom of the sieve sits at least 1 1/2 inches above the bottom of the bowl. Line the strainer with cheesecloth or sturdy paper towels, and pour the yogurt into the sieve. Set the assembly in the refrigerator to drain. After 4 to 6 hours, the yogurt will be the consistency of soft cheese and will have released about 1/4 cup of liquid. Discard the liquid.

2. **The onions and braising liquid:** Thinly slice 1 onion, place the slices in a strainer or colander, and rinse thoroughly with cold water. Set aside to drain over a bowl or in the sink. Coarsely chop the other onion and place it in a blender. Add the orange juice, water, ginger, garlic, coriander, turmeric, cayenne or chile, and 1 teaspoon salt. Blend on high speed until it becomes a smooth puree. (You can also do this in a food processor. The texture of the sauce will be a bit coarser but the flavor will be the same.)

3. **Browning the chicken:** Rinse the chicken pieces with cool water, and thoroughly dry them with paper towels. (Unless they are thoroughly dry, they won't brown and may stick to the pan when you sear them.) Season the chicken with salt. Heat the ghee, butter, or oil in a heavy-based lidded skillet (12- to 14-inch) or shallow braising pan (4-quart capacity) over medium-high heat. When the fat is almost shimmering, add the thighs, in batches so as not to crowd the pan, and brown lightly on both sides, turning with tongs, 6 to 8 minutes total per batch. Transfer to a large plate to catch the drips. When all the chicken is browned, pour off all but about a tablespoon of fat from the pan. Because the chicken is skinless, there won't be many browned bits on the bottom of the pan, but there will be some—be sure not to pour these off with the excess fat.

4. **Heating the braising liquid:** Return the pot to medium-high heat, and gradually pour in the orange-onion puree. Stand back as you do this, since it will sputter and splatter. Simmer for about 5 minutes, scraping the bottom and stirring occasionally with a wooden spoon.

5. **The braise:** Add the chicken to the sauce, along with any juices that pooled under it as it sat. Turn the pieces with tongs to coat with the sauce, and return to a soft simmer. Cover tightly, reduce the heat to low, and simmer gently. Check the pan after 10 minutes to make sure that the simmer is quiet and not turbulent; if the heat is too high, lower it or set the pan on a heat diffuser. After 20 minutes, turn the chicken pieces with tongs, and continue braising until the chicken is fork-tender, 40 to 45 minutes total time.

6. **The finish:** With tongs or a slotted spoon, transfer the chicken pieces to a platter to catch any drips, and cover loosely with foil to keep warm. Add the reserved onion slices to the pan and stir gently, working the onions evenly into the sauce. Replace the cover, and set aside, off the heat undisturbed for 5 minutes. This gives the raw onion slices just enough time to lose their bite while remaining crisp and mildly pungent.

Stir in the drained yogurt with a wooden spoon, working the thickened yogurt through the onions and sauce. Heat the sauce very gently over medium heat until the yogurt is warmed through. Do not let the sauce boil, or it will take on a curdled look. Taste for salt and cayenne. Return the chicken pieces to the pan, turning them to coat with the sauce and onions. Serve the chicken, spooning the onions and sauce over the top.

VARIATION: CHICKEN BREASTS *DO-PIAZA*

You can use bone-in skinless chicken breasts in place of the thighs. Braise them for only 30 to 35 minutes in Step 5.

VARIATION: CHICKEN *DO-PIAZA* WITH UNDRAINED YOGURT OR NO YOGURT

Step 1 may be skipped and undrained yogurt used. The sauce will be a bit thinner in taste and texture. Chicken *do-piaza* is also good without any yogurt at all, although it will be less creamy and rich.

Goan Chicken ✈

Chicken Thighs Braised with Cilantro, Mint & Ginger

A delectable example of successful fusion cuisine. Chicken thighs marinated in a spicy blend of herbs and chile pepper, braised in golden rum and chicken stock, and finished with a splash of heavy cream. Fabulous. The inspiration comes from an article I read on Goa, a state on the southwestern coast of India that used to be under Portuguese rule. I was so tempted by the descriptions of the food that I re-created a few of the dishes myself, and this reliable and satisfying braise quickly became part of my permanent repertoire.

Serve with a bowl of steamed basmati or jasmine rice to soak up some of the zesty, creamy sauce.

wine notes

Don't be misled by the oft-used adage "spicy wines with spicy foods." Often the so-called "spicy" wines have relatively high alcohol (14% or more) that will taste bitter and hot when paired with spicy food. Instead, look for a light-bodied white wine with a touch of sweetness and low-to-medium alcohol, such as Moscato d'Asti from the Piedmont region of Italy, or Spätlese-level Riesling from Germany.

Working Ahead

The chicken needs to marinate for 8 to 24 hours before braising (Step 1).

Serves 4 | Braising Time: about 30 minutes

8 bone-in chicken thighs (about 3 pounds
    total), skin-on or skinless

THE MARINADE

1/3 cup loosely packed cilantro leaves and
    tender stems, coarsely chopped
1/4 cup fresh mint leaves, coarsely
    chopped
2 tablespoons minced fresh ginger

1 jalapeño or serrano chile, seeded and
    minced
2 garlic cloves, minced
1/2 teaspoon coarse salt
3 tablespoons extra-virgin olive oil

THE BRAISING LIQUID

1/4 cup golden or amber rum (not dark),
    such as Mount Gay

3/4 cup chicken stock, homemade
    (page 448) or store-bought

3 tablespoons heavy cream
Freshly ground black pepper

1. **The marinade—8 to 24 hours in advance:** If the chicken thighs are skin-on, remove the skin: grab an edge of the skin with one hand and gently peel it back in one piece. With a sharp knife, trim away any large deposits of fat. Rinse the chicken with cool water, and dry it thoroughly with paper towels. Combine the cilantro, mint, ginger, chile, garlic, salt, and 1 tablespoon of the oil in a mixing bowl or gallon-size zip-lock bag. Add the chicken pieces, seal the bag, if using, and toss to coat. Refrigerate for 8 to 24 hours.

2. **Removing the marinade:** Remove the chicken from the marinade, scraping each piece clean with a small knife or rubber spatula as best you can, without being too fastidious. Return the herbs you scrape off to the marinade, and reserve the marinade.

3. **Browning the chicken:** Heat the remaining 2 tablespoons oil in a large heavy skillet or shallow braising pan (12- to 13-inch) over medium-high heat. Without wiping or drying the chicken pieces, add them to the skillet. (The oil from the marinade clinging to the pieces of chicken will enhance browning.) Sear undisturbed until the meat loses its raw appearance and develops a shiny brown crust on the first side, about 4 minutes. Turn with tongs and brown the other side for another 4 minutes or so. With tongs, transfer the chicken thighs to a large plate to catch the juices. Pour off and discard the excess fat from the pan, being careful not to discard any of the tasty brown bits on the bottom.

4. **The braising liquid:** Return the pan to medium-high heat and add the rum, stirring to deglaze. Stir in the reserved marinade, and boil, stirring to dislodge and dissolve any

cherished browned bits cooked onto the bottom of the pan, until the rum is reduced to a tablespoon or two, about 3 minutes. Add the stock and bring to a simmer.

5. **The braise:** Once the rum-stock mixture simmers, return the chicken thighs to the skillet, along with any juices they released while sitting. Cover, reduce the heat to low, and braise gently, checking during the first 5 minutes to make sure that the liquid is not simmering too turbulently. If it is, lower the heat or place a heat diffuser under the skillet. Continue braising at a quiet simmer, turning the pieces with tongs after 15 minutes, until the chicken is tender and there are no signs of pink remaining, a total of about 30 minutes.

6. **The finish:** Transfer the chicken to a serving dish to catch the juices, and cover loosely with foil to keep warm. Increase the heat under the pan to medium-high and boil to reduce the cooking liquid and to concentrate its flavor, about 5 minutes. Add the cream, return to a boil, and boil again until the sauce is thick enough to coat the back of a spoon, another 3 to 5 minutes. Taste for salt and pepper. Pour over the chicken and serve.

Chicken & Pork *Adobado* ✈

Philippine-Style Braised Chicken & Pork

Chicken and pork *adobado* is a traditional Philippine recipe that I prepare again and again simply because I can't resist the sweet-salty-sour taste of the delectably tender chicken and pork—and neither can anyone I serve it to.

The technique of making a Southeast Asian *adobado* has three distinct steps, but none are complicated. You start by marinating the meat—here, chicken thighs and country-style pork ribs—in a piquant vinegar-based sauce for 2 hours. Then you braise the meats together in this same sauce until fork-tender. Pretty standard stuff so far, but it's the third and final step that makes this dish truly exceptional. After braising, you quickly panfry the meats to give them a crisp, lacquered crust. The chicken and pork come out moist and tender on the inside and browned and glossy on the outside. Make a quick fresh tomato relish (recipe follows) and a pot of steamed rice, and you have an authentic and satisfying Filipino meal.

Traditional Filipino *adobado* is made with palm vinegar, a bright green vinegar with a sharp, citrusy taste made from palm sap. Because palm vinegar is hard to come by and it doesn't keep well, I substitute a good-quality white wine vinegar and a bit of lime zest to approximate the flavor. In the Philippines, chicken and pork are often braised together, and I love the way the juices of the two meld. But you can also make this with all chicken or all pork without any adjustments.

wine notes

Light and fruity red without too much tannin—lighter-style Shiraz (Syrah) or Shiraz-Grenache blends from Australia; or lighter, easy-drinking Zinfandels from California.

In order for the flavors of the garlic, vinegar, soy, lime, and spices to work their way into the chicken and pork, the meats need to marinate for 1 to 2 hours before braising. Don't exceed the 2 hours, however, or the acid in the marinade will turn the meat to mush.

Serves 6 | Braising Time: 45 to 50 minutes (plus 2 hours marinating)

6 garlic cloves, thinly sliced (scant 1/4 cup)

1/2 cup white wine vinegar

1/2 cup water

2 tablespoons soy sauce (not "lite")

2 teaspoons grated lime zest

2 bay leaves, each torn in half

2 teaspoons brown sugar (light or dark)

1/2 teaspoon coarse salt

1/2 teaspoon cracked black pepper

6 bone-in, skin-on chicken thighs (about
2 1/4 pounds total)

1 1/2 pounds boneless country-style pork ribs (see "Shopping for Country-Style Pork Ribs," page 365)

2 tablespoons peanut oil

Tomato Relish (recipe follows; optional)

1. **Prepare the marinade—1 to 2 hours in advance:** In a gallon-size zip-lock bag, combine the garlic, vinegar, water, soy sauce, lime zest, bay leaves, sugar, salt, and peppercorns. Zip the bag closed and shake and turn to dissolve the sugar and combine all the ingredients. Rinse the chicken thighs and pork ribs, and dry thoroughly with paper towels. Add the meats to the marinade in the bag, turning to coat, and set aside to marinate for 1 hour, turning every 20 minutes. If your kitchen is more than 75 degrees, marinate in the refrigerator for 2 hours.

2. **The braise:** Transfer the chicken and pork, along with all the seasonings and liquid, to a large lidded skillet or other shallow braising pan (12- to 13-inch or 4 1/2-quart capacity works well). Put the pan over medium-high heat and, as soon as bubbles appear, lower the heat to a quiet simmer and cover tightly. Every 10 to 15 minutes, lift the lid and turn the pieces of meat with tongs so that they braise evenly. Continue to braise at a gentle simmer until the chicken and pork are tender and the meat pulls easily away from the bone, 45 to 50 minutes total. If at any time the liquid is simmering too aggressively, lower the heat or set a heat diffuser beneath the pan.

3. **The sauce:** Using tongs, transfer the chicken and pork to a shallow platter to catch the juices. Skim the surface fat from the braising liquid, and bring to a boil over medium-high heat. Boil the sauce until reduced by about two-thirds to the consistency of a thin syrup,

12 to 15 minutes. Taste. It should be quite sharp and lively. I don't remove the bay leaves, because I like to encounter them as I eat, but do as you like. Keep the sauce warm over low heat.

4. **Meanwhile, brown the meat:** Heat the oil in a large sauté pan, preferably nonstick, over medium-high heat. (Because the pieces of chicken and pork will be a bit sticky with sauce even after you dry them off, a nonstick pan makes the job of frying them easier and less messy. If you don't have nonstick, any heavy-based sauté pan will do.) Pat the chicken and pork thoroughly dry with paper towels. When the oil is shimmering, add as many pieces of meat (skin side down for the chicken) as will fit without crowding and fry until they acquire a crisp, lacquered crust, about 3 minutes a side. The meat will splatter quite a bit as it fries; if you own a splatter screen, this is a good time to bring it out. Transfer to the same large plate, and repeat with the remaining pieces of chicken and pork.

5. **The finish:** Slip the browned meat into the sauce, and add any juices that have seeped onto the platter. With tongs, turn each piece of meat to coat with sauce, and heat through over medium-high heat. Serve over rice, and spoon the sauce on top. Pass the relish, if using, at the table.

TOMATO RELISH

Not unlike a salsa, this fresh garnish brings a vibrant contrast to the meaty *adobado*.

Serves 6

3/4 cup finely chopped white onion (about 3 ounces)

2 ripe tomatoes (about 1 pound), cored and chopped into 1/4-inch dice

1/3 cup loosely packed chopped cilantro leaves and tender stems

1 tablespoon freshly squeezed lime juice, plus more if needed

Coarse salt

1. Put the onion in a strainer, and rinse well with cold water (this removes much of the harsh bite of raw onion). Transfer to the center of a clean dish towel. Bring up the edges and squeeze the onion to eliminate as much moisture as you can.

2. Place the onion in a medium bowl. Add the tomatoes, cilantro, and lime juice and stir to combine. Season with salt. Taste, and add additional lime juice or salt as needed.

Soy-Braised Chicken Thighs with Star Anise & Orange Peel →→

This quick braise was inspired by the aromatic syrupy soy sauce used in Indonesia, *ketjap manis* (see pages 149 and 446). Since I don't always stock it in my pantry, I've come up with a way to get its spicy-sweet-fragrant taste with regular soy sauce and a handful of other easily found ingredients. The flavors penetrate the chicken as it braises, and the falling-off-the-bone-tender thighs emerge coated with a dark, glossy sauce. Serve this with steamed basmati rice and sautéed bok choy, spinach, or watercress.

wine notes

White wine with luscious fruit and crisp acidity—Pinot Gris from Alsace or Oregon; or an off-dry Riesling from Alsace, Austria, or the Rheingau and Pfalz regions of Germany.

Serves 4 | *Braising Time: 30 to 35 minutes*

2 tablespoons soy sauce
   (see page 445)
2 tablespoons rice wine vinegar, plus more
   if needed
2 tablespoons Asian fish sauce
1 tablespoon brown sugar (dark or light)
1/4 cup plus 1 tablespoon chicken stock,
   homemade (page 448) or store-
   bought, or water, or as needed
8 bone-in, skin-on chicken thighs (about
   3 pounds total)

3 scallions
3 tablespoons peanut oil
3 garlic cloves, minced
1 tablespoon grated fresh ginger
1 dried small red chile pepper, such as chile
   de arból
3 strips orange zest, removed with a
   vegetable peeler (each about 3 inches
   by 3/4 inch)
1 whole star anise
2 teaspoons cornstarch

1. **Heat the oven to 325 degrees.**

2. **The braising liquid:** In a small bowl, stir together the soy sauce, vinegar, fish sauce, sugar, and 1/4 cup stock or water. The sugar won't completely dissolve at this point, but just stir to mix. Set aside.

3. **Browning the chicken:** Rinse the chicken pieces with cool water and thoroughly dry them with paper towels. (Moist chicken will stick to the pan and won't sear properly.) Heat 2 tablespoons of the oil in a large ovenproof skillet or other heavy lidded braising pot (12-inch or 4- to 5-quart) over medium-high heat until the oil shimmers. Add half the chicken pieces, skin side down, and sear, without disturbing, until the skin is crisp and bronzed, about 6 minutes. Lift a corner of a chicken thigh to see that it's nicely browned before turning the pieces carefully, so as not to tear the skin. Brown the other side, another 6 minutes or so. Transfer the chicken to a large plate to capture any juices. Pat the other 4 thighs dry, and sear them until crisp and bronzed as you did with the first batch. Add these to the plate with the others.

4. **The aromatics:** Coarsely chop the scallions, separating the white and green parts. Set the greens aside for the finish. Pour off and discard all the fat from the pan. Return the pan to medium heat, add the remaining tablespoon of oil, and then add the white part of the scallions, the garlic, ginger, and chile pepper. Stir and cook just until you can smell the garlic and ginger, about 30 seconds. Pour in the reserved soy mixture and stir to combine. Add the orange zest and star anise.

5. **The braise:** Set the chicken thighs in the pan, and add any juices that have accumulated on the plate. Cover the pan with parchment paper, pressing down so that the paper nearly touches the chicken and the edges extend about an inch over the sides of the pan. Cover with a secure lid and set the pan in the lower third of the oven. After 15 minutes, turn the chicken pieces with tongs and check to make sure that there's at least 1/4 inch of liquid in the pan. If not, add a few tablespoons of stock or water. Continue braising at a quiet simmer until the chicken is fork-tender and pulling away from the bone, a total of 30 to 35 minutes.

6. **The finish:** With a slotted spoon, transfer the chicken to a serving platter, without crowding the pieces too closely, and cover loosely with foil to keep warm. I like to retrieve the star anise and chile pepper from the braising liquid so no one will bite into one of these. Set the pan over medium-high heat and bring to a simmer. Skim off any surface fat that pools on the braising liquid. Add the scallion greens. Put the cornstarch in a small bowl, add the remaining tablespoon of stock or water, and whisk briskly with a fork or small whisk to combine and smooth out any lumps; this mixture is known as a slurry. Pour the slurry into the simmering liquid, stirring so that it is incorporated evenly. The liquid will immediately thicken to a glossy sauce with the consistency of maple syrup. Pour any juices

the chicken thighs have released into the sauce, and simmer for just another minute. Don't leave the sauce to simmer for too long, or it may become overly salty. Taste for soy and rice wine vinegar. Keep in mind that the sauce should reflect the Asian appreciation for salt, but if it tastes too salty for you, a splash of vinegar will balance it. Spoon the sauce over the chicken thighs and serve.

Ketjap Manis

This thick, syrupy, soy-based condiment, also spelled *kecap manis*, is a staple in parts of southeast Asia, particularly Indonesia. Traditionally sweetened with palm sugar and seasoned with a number of aromatic spices, including garlic, star anise, and the aromatic leaves of a laurel-like tree, culinary scholars tell us that this exotic sauce was a precursor to today's sweet tomato ketchup. Shop for tall glass bottles of *ketjap manis* at Asian markets on the shelf with the other soy sauces. (For more on soy sauces, see page 445.) If you do have ketjap manis in your pantry, use it in equal measure in place of the dark soy sauce in the above recipe, and omit the brown sugar.

Chicken Breasts Braised with Hard Cider & Parsnips ✈

I'm always surprised that more food lovers don't get excited about hard cider. Made from fermented sweet cider, hard cider is a wine-like drink that can be delicate, crisp, and delicious. In the kitchen, I often use it in place of wine to deglaze and build a braising liquid. It adds a subtle note of fruit that is particularly good with parsnips and rosemary. When shopping for cider, look beyond the imports from France and England for a bottle from any one of the number of American or Canadian fruit growers now producing interesting cider in places like New England, New York, California, Ontario, and British Columbia. I've become quite fond of a crisp, dry cider from Flag Hill Farm in Vermont made on a 250-acre family farm and orchard near the Connecticut River. Hard cider can be either bubbly (like champagne) or still (like wine). Both work well in this recipe, but since the effervescent kind tends to cost more and the bubbles disappear during braising, I generally cook with still cider. If you've never tasted hard cider, be sure to pour yourself a chilled glass. Sip it as an alternative to white wine for an aperitif or with a meal.

Even though chicken breasts don't need to be braised to become tender, I use them here because I like the way their delicate white meat pairs with the sweet flavor of parsnips, cider, and fresh rosemary. Once the chicken breasts are cooked through, the cider-based braising liquid gets spooned over as a flavorful sauce. The parsnips become the perfect side vegetable. This elegant dish needs no accompaniment other than a pretty table setting and a few candles.

cider and wine notes

Look no further than a glass of the same hard cider used in the recipe. If you must have wine, choose a light, slightly sweet, high-acid white, such as German Kabinett Riesling.

2 teaspoons extra-virgin olive oil

4 slices thick-cut bacon (about 4 ounces), cut into 1/2-inch wide strips

4 bone-in, skin-on chicken breasts (about 3 pounds total)

Coarse salt and freshly ground black pepper

1 large shallot, minced (about 3 tablespoons)

2 1/2 cups hard cider (still or bubbly)

1 tablespoon finely chopped fresh rosemary

1 pound parsnips, peeled, any woody core removed (see "Shopping for Parsnips," page 153), and cut into sticks about 3 inches by 1/2 inch

1. **Heat the oven to 325 degrees.**

2. **Crisping the bacon:** Combine the oil and bacon in a large deep lidded skillet or shallow braising pan (4-quart capacity is ideal). Heat over medium heat, stirring a few times, until the bacon renders most of its fat and is just crisp, about 6 minutes. With tongs or a slotted spoon, transfer the bacon to a paper towel–lined plate to drain. Set the pan aside.

3. **Browning the chicken:** Rinse the chicken breasts under cool running water and dry them thoroughly with paper towels. (Be sure to dry the chicken thoroughly, or it won't brown properly and will threaten to stick to the pan during searing.) Pour off and discard all but about 2 tablespoons of the olive oil and rendered bacon fat from the pan. Heat the remaining fat over medium-high heat. Season the chicken pieces all over with salt and pepper. Place them skin side down in the pan and brown, without disturbing, for a few minutes. Then peek underneath by lifting the edge of the chicken with a pair of tongs to see if the skin is crisp and bronzed. Once the skin is nicely browned, about 4 to 5 minutes, turn with tongs and brown the other side as well, another 4 to 5 minutes. If the breasts are extremely plump, stand them on the wide rounded edge, leaning them against the sides of the pan or holding them upright with the tongs, and brown this edge, about 2 minutes. Transfer to a large plate or tray to catch the juices, and set aside.

4. **The aromatics and braising liquid:** Add the shallot to the pan, still over medium-high heat, and let it sizzle, stirring, for a minute. It will brown quickly—be careful not to let it burn. Quickly pour in 2 cups of the hard cider to deglaze, and scrape the bottom of the pan with a wooden spoon to dislodge and dissolve the browned bits that will flavor the sauce. Let the cider boil to reduce down to about 1/2 cup, 10 to 15 minutes. Add the rosemary and the remaining 1/2 cup cider and boil down again until there's about 3/4 cup total,

another 6 to 8 minutes. The cider won't become thick, but you will be concentrating the combined flavors of fruit, bacon drippings, chicken drippings, and rosemary in the process.

5. **The braise:** Add the parsnips and season with generous grindings of black pepper and a pinch of salt. Sprinkle the bacon over the parsnips, and arrange the chicken pieces on top, skin side down. Cover with parchment paper, pressing down so that the paper nearly rests on the chicken pieces and hangs over the sides of the pan by about an inch, and set the lid in place. Slide the pan onto a rack in the lower third of the oven to braise at a gentle simmer. After 25 minutes, turn the chicken pieces, and check the liquid. If it is simmering too ferociously, lower the oven temperature 10 or 15 degrees. Continue braising until the meat at the thickest part of the breast is cooked through when you make a small incision with a knife, another 20 to 25 minutes.

6. **The finish:** Transfer the chicken to a good-looking platter or serving dish. Spear a few parsnips gently with the tip of a sharp knife, and if they are tender throughout, remove them with a slotted spoon and arrange them alongside the chicken. If they are not yet tender, leave them in the pan. Degrease the sauce as necessary by skimming the surface with a large spoon, and then taste. If the sauce tastes a bit weak and/or if the parsnips are not tender, set the pan over medium-high heat and simmer until the parsnips are easily pierced but not falling apart and the sauce has a concentrated, sweet flavor, 5 to 8 minutes. You want the sauce to be thicker than stock, but not thick enough to coat a spoon. Taste for salt and pepper. If you haven't already, scoop out the parsnips and arrange them around the chicken. Ladle the sauce over the chicken and parsnips.

Shopping for Parsnips

I think parsnips deserve a hallowed spot in the vegetable kingdom because of the unexpected sweetness and delicate soft texture they provide in the dead of winter. Many New Englanders will tell you that spring-dug parsnips taste sweetest of all because the sugar level rises when parsnips are left underground all winter. In my experience, any parsnip that has been harvested after a hard frost will be plenty sweet.

The only drawback to parsnips is that you must be wary of the woody, fibrous core that develops during storage. Fortunately the core is easy to spot and remove, leaving the rest of the parsnip perfectly good for cooking and eating. After peeling the parsnip, cut it lengthwise into quarters. Look at the core of each quarter, and if you notice a differentiation in color and texture (if it's slightly darker and definitely more dense and fibrous), you'll want to remove it. Left in, the core will remain stringy and unpleasant to eat no matter how long you cook the parsnip. To remove the core, simply pry it out of the quartered root with the tip of a paring knife. It may take some coaxing, but it will eventually pop out.

When buying parsnips, look for medium-sized ones about the size of plump carrots (6 to 7 inches long and 1 1/2 to 2 inches thick at the top). Too skinny or short, and they are too much work to peel for little reward; too large, and the woody core may make up almost the entire root. Parsnips begin to appear in markets in the late fall, after the first good frost, and remain through late spring. Look for ones that are firm and not split or drying out. They should feel heavy in your hand and not at all damp or slimy. Avoid parsnips with green tops beginning to sprout—this means that they are past their prime and may have a wooly texture.

Red Pine Chicken →→

Pork-Filled Chicken Breasts Braised in Soy

The name "Red Pine" describes the tawny reddish appearance of these bone-less, skinless chicken breasts after braising in a soy-based sauce. When my friend, and supremely talented Chinese chef, Steve Bogart first explained this recipe to me, I couldn't imagine how the ground pork filling would stay in place, since it's spread flat on one side of the chicken, not rolled up in or stuffed into it in any way. Yet not only does the pork filling stay in place, it acts as a conduit so the chicken cooks not by direct contact with the braising liquid, but by the gentle heat coming up through the rich filling. The result is an astonishingly tender and moist chicken breast infused with the flavors of soy, ginger, and star anise.

At his restaurant, The Single Pebble, in Burlington, Vermont, Steve slices each chicken breast on an angle and fans the slices out onto a bed of sautéed spinach. He sometimes garnishes the dish with slices of hard-cooked egg and calls it Bright Moon Red Pine Chicken. When I make this at home, I don't want to interfere with the exciting flavor of the pork-filled chicken breasts, so I leave out the egg.

wine notes

Young fruity red without too much oak flavor, such as a fruity Zinfandel, a lighter-style Australian Shiraz, or a recent vintage of Italian Barbera.

Serves 4 | Braising Time: about 35 minutes

THE FILLING

6 ounces ground pork, preferably not
    too lean

2 tablespoons water

Scant 1/2 teaspoon coarse salt

3/4 teaspoon sugar

THE BRAISE

4 small boneless, skinless chicken breasts
    (about 1 1/2 pounds total)

Cornstarch for dusting

2 tablespoons soy sauce (not "lite")

1 tablespoon dark mushroom soy sauce
    (see "Dark Mushroom Soy Sauce,"
    page 156)

2 tablespoons minced fresh ginger

1/2 cup chicken stock, homemade (page
    448) or store-bought

1 1/2 tablespoons Shaoxing rice wine or
    dry sherry

1 tablespoon sugar

4 whole star anise

1 tablespoon peanut oil

THE SPINACH

1 tablespoon peanut oil

1 1/2 pounds spinach, tough stems
    removed, leaves washed but not dried

Coarse salt and freshly ground white
    pepper

1. **The filling:** In a medium bowl, combine the ground pork, water, salt, and sugar. Mix gently with your hands to combine, without overworking the mixture, and set aside.

2. **Pounding the chicken:** Rinse the chicken breasts with cool water and dry them thoroughly with paper towels. Lay the chicken breasts out on a work surface. Remove any chicken tenders (the thin strip of meat sometimes dangling from the side where the bones were) and reserve for another use. Gently pound the chicken with the bottom of a small saucepan or the side of a large knife to even the thickness to about 1/2 inch. As you pound, dust the top of the chicken breasts with a little cornstarch. This keeps the chicken from sticking to the saucepan or knife and will later help the filling adhere to the chicken.

3. **Spreading the filling:** With your hand, scoop one quarter (about 2 tablespoons) of the filling onto the rough side (the side where the bones were) of each breast, and spread it to the edges to form an even 3/8-inch, thick layer. Using your fingers, sprinkle the filling with a bit more cornstarch, then, with your cornstarch-covered fingers, pat down the filling lightly so it stays in place. (The cornstarch keeps your fingers from sticking to the filling and in the process also adds a bit more cornstarch to help the filling hold together.)

4. **The braising liquid:** In a small bowl, combine the soy sauces, ginger, stock, wine, sugar, and star anise. Stir until well mixed, and set aside.

5. **Browning the chicken:** Heat the oil in a large skillet (I like to use a 12-inch nonstick pan as insurance that the delicate chicken or filling won't stick) over medium-high heat until it shimmers. Holding a filled chicken breast filling side up in your hand, lower it into the pan, still filling side up. Add the remaining breasts so they are close together but not touching. Sear without disturbing until the chicken firms up slightly and becomes lightly golden on the bottom, about 4 to 5 minutes. When the edges of the chicken and filling have turned opaque, peek underneath by lifting with a flat spatula to check that the chicken is golden brown. Carefully turn the chicken breasts with the spatula so they are filling side down, and cook for 1 to 2 minutes to set the pork filling. Don't worry that it's not browned.

6. **The braise:** Reduce the heat to very low and, leaving the chicken breasts filling side down, pour in the prepared braising sauce. Baste the chicken every few minutes as it braises by splashing the sauce over the top of each breast with a soupspoon. This braise is not a fix-and-forget-it enterprise, you really must stand close by and baste regularly. Braise without shifting the pieces of chicken and without letting the sauce boil or even simmer— all you want to see are small puffs of steam rising up off the surface but no bubbles breaking through. If you allow the sauce to simmer, the chicken and pork will cook too quickly and may easily dry out. Continue gently braising and basting until the chicken and pork are cooked through, about 35 minutes. Check for doneness by making a small cut in the chicken with a sharp paring knife to peer inside and see that it is cooked through but is still juicy.

7. **The spinach:** While the chicken braises, heat the oil in a large skillet (12-inch) over medium-high heat. When it is hot, add the spinach a handful at a time and sauté briskly, tossing with tongs, until wilted, 2 to 3 minutes. Season with salt and pepper, and set aside on the back of the stove to keep warm.

8. **The finish:** With a slotted spatula or large spoon, lift the chicken with the filling from the sauce and set on a carving board. Slice each piece on an angle into 4 or 5 pieces. Make a bed of wilted spinach on each plate, and fan out the chicken on the spinach. Spoon some of the braising liquid over the top, and serve.

Dark Mushroom Soy Sauce

If you can't find dark mushroom soy sauce (or just don't want to buy a whole bottle for one recipe), substitute regular soy sauce and add 1 teaspoon dark molasses. The finished sauce won't have quite the same meaty intensity of the one made with mushroom soy, but it will still be plenty earthy. (For more on soy sauce, see page 445.)

Coq au Vin ✈

I had the good fortune to spend several summers in a seventeenth-century château in the heart of Burgundy during the 1980s and 1990s while working for Anne Willan at her cooking school, La Varenne. Many chefs from the surrounding countryside came through the château's kitchens to teach, bringing their own versions of this Burgundian classic. Coq au vin is real French country cooking, and several of the local chefs insisted it be made only with an old rooster (the *coq* of the name). Others told us you must add the rooster's blood to thicken the sauce properly. Since then, I've created my own version that preserves the spirit and essence of the original but is something I can easily make at home. To start, I buy a naturally raised chicken, because it tastes better and juicier than an ordinary supermarket chicken. Then it's a matter of searing the chicken carefully to develop a dark caramelized crust on the meat and on the bottom of the pot, and then deglazing with a combination of Cognac and red wine. The garnish of bacon, sautéed mushrooms, and glazed baby onions adds the crowning touch that makes this unmistakably Burgundian. From the aromas reaching up out of the oven to the taste on the plate, this transports me right back to Burgundy every time I make it.

On its native turf, coq au vin is braised in a *vin ordinaire* (or table wine) from one of the many small vineyards that dot the countryside. To best match this flavor, I look for a light dry red wine, with some amount of fruit, such as a Beaujolais or domestic Pinot Noir.

The chefs I knew in Burgundy used to make fresh egg pasta cut into wide strips to soak up the delicious dark, winey sauce, but I am just as happy with a heap of buttered egg noodles or mashed potatoes and a crusty baguette. Fried Croûtes (page 168) also make a fine garnish.

Coq au Vin and red Burgundy is one of the all-time great food and wine pairings. Look for village-level Burgundies from Volnay, Pommard, or Beaune. Alternatively, try a Beaujolais Villages, or Pinot Noir from California, Oregon, or New Zealand.

Serves 6 | *Braising Time: 1 to 1 ¹/₄ hours*

¹/₄ pound slab bacon (see "Slab Bacon," page 395), rind removed, cut into ¹/₂-inch dice

One 4 ¹/₂- to 5-pound chicken, cut into 8 pieces, wing tips, back, neck, and giblets (except the liver) reserved (see "Cutting Up a Chicken," page 161)

Coarse salt and freshly ground black pepper

All-purpose flour for dredging (about ¹/₂ cup)

3 tablespoons unsalted butter

1 large yellow onion (about 8 ounces), chopped into ¹/₂-inch pieces

1 carrot, chopped into ¹/₂-inch pieces

1 tablespoon tomato paste

2 tablespoons Cognac or other good brandy

One 750-ml bottle dry, fruity red wine

2 garlic cloves, peeled and smashed

1 bay leaf

1 tablespoon chopped fresh thyme or 1 teaspoon dried

2 tablespoons chopped flat-leaf parsley

1 cup chicken stock, homemade (page 448) or store-bought

THE GARNISH

10 ounces pearl onions (about 24 ³/₄-inch onions; frozen pearl onions, not thawed, may be substituted)

2 ¹/₂ tablespoons unsalted butter

³/₄ pound cremini mushrooms, quartered

Coarse salt and freshly ground black pepper

2 tablespoons chopped flat-leaf parsley

1. **The bacon:** Place the diced bacon in a cold, large Dutch oven or other heavy lidded braising pot (7-quart works well), set oven medium heat, and cook the bacon, stirring often with a slotted spoon, until well browned and crisp on the outside but with some softness remaining inside, 12 to 15 minutes. Transfer the bacon to a plate lined with paper towels. Set the pot with the rendered bacon fat aside off the heat.

2. **Heat the oven to 325 degrees.**

3.   **Dredging the chicken:** Rinse the chicken pieces with cool water and pat dry with paper towels. Season on all sides with salt and pepper. Spread the flour in a wide shallow dish (a pie plate works well), and dredge half the chicken pieces one at a time, placing each one in the flour, turning to coat both sides, and then lifting and patting lightly to shake off any excess.

4.   **Browning the chicken:** Add 1 tablespoon of the butter to rendered bacon fat in the pot and place over medium-high heat. When the butter has melted, ease in the dredged pieces of chicken, skin side down, without crowding. Sear on both sides, turning once with tongs, until a deep golden brown crust forms, 7 to 10 minutes total. Transfer the chicken to a large platter to catch the juices. Dredge the remaining chicken pieces, and discard the flour. Add another 1 tablespoon butter to the pot. Sear the dredged chicken as you did the first batch, turning once with tongs, until golden, 6 to 9 minutes. The second batch of chicken pieces may brown faster; lower the heat a bit if the skin begins to burn at all. A thick ruddy crust will have formed on the bottom of the pot that will later contribute great depth of flavor to the sauce. Transfer the chicken to the platter, and pour off the fat from the pot without discarding the tasty browned bits. Return the pot to medium heat.

5.   **The aromatics and braising liquid:** Add the remaining tablespoon of butter to the pot and melt it over medium heat. Add the onion and carrot, and toss to coat the vegetables in the butter. Sauté, stirring once or twice with a wooden spoon, until the vegetables are beginning to soften and are flecked with brown, about 5 minutes. The brown crust on the bottom of the pot will continue to cook and may soften from the vegetable juices released into the pot. Add the tomato paste and stir to smear the paste through the vegetables. Add the Cognac and bring to a boil to deglaze, scraping the pot with a wooden spoon to dislodge the precious crust. Simmer, stirring a few times, until the liquid is almost all gone. Raise the heat to high, add the red wine, garlic, bay leaf, thyme, and parsley, and bring to a boil. Lower the heat to medium-high and simmer rapidly until the wine reduces by about half, about 15 minutes. Stir in the reserved bacon and the stock and bring to a boil. Using a ladle, scoop out about 1/2 cup of braising liquid and set aside for later cooking the pearl onions.

6.   **The braise:** Add the chicken pieces to the pot in this order: place the legs, thighs, and wings, and the wing tips, back, neck, heart, and gizzard (if using) in the pot first, then put the breast pieces on top of them, skin side down. (Keeping the breast pieces on top protects them from overcooking and drying out.) Pour in any juices that collected as the chicken sat, and bring to a simmer. Cover the chicken with parchment paper, pressing down so that the paper nearly touches the chicken and extends over the sides of the pot by about an inch. Cover with the lid, and place on a rack in the lower third of the oven to braise. After 15 minutes, turn the breast pieces over with tongs. At the same time, check that the liquid is

simmering quietly. If not, lower the oven temperature by 10 or 15 degrees. Continue braising gently for another 45 to 60 minutes, or until the breasts and dark meat are fork-tender.

7.   **While the chicken braises, cook the garnish:** If using fresh onions, bring a pot of
water to a boil. Add the onions and bring the water back to a boil. Boil the onions for 2
minutes, drain, and rinse with cold water. Using a small paring knife, slip off the onion
skins, and pat the onions dry. (If using frozen onions, skip this step: frozen onions have
already been blanched and peeled.)

Heat 1 tablespoon of the butter in a large skillet (preferably a 12-inch nonstick for the
best glaze on the garnish) over medium heat. Add the blanched onions (or still-frozen
onions) and sauté, stirring and shaking frequently, until tinged with brown, 3 to 4 minutes.
Season with salt and pepper, add the reserved 1/2 cup of braising liquid, cover, and simmer,
shaking the pan frequently, until the onions are tender when pierced with the tip of a
knife, about 12 minutes (or 3 to 4 minutes if using frozen). Remove the lid, increase the
heat to medium-high, and boil to reduce the liquid to a glaze. Transfer the onions and
liquid to a small bowl, scraping the pan with a rubber spatula as best you can. Return the pan
to medium-high heat and add the remaining 1 1/2 tablespoons of butter. When the butter
stops foaming, add the mushrooms, season with salt and pepper, and sauté briskly. The
mushrooms may release a lot of liquid at first. Continue to sauté, stirring occasionally, until
the liquid has evaporated and the mushrooms develop an attractive chestnut brown sear,
about 10 minutes. Remove from the heat and return the onions and liquid to the skillet.
Set aside.

8.   **The finish:** When the chicken is fork-tender and pulling away from the bone, transfer
the breast, thigh, leg, and wing pieces to a deep platter or serving dish (discard the wing
tips, back, neck, heart, and gizzard), and cover loosely with foil to keep warm. Let the
braising liquid settle for a moment and then, with a wide spoon, skim off as much surface
fat as you can without being overly fastidious. Place the pot over high heat and bring the
juices to a boil. Reduce the juices until thickened to the consistency of a vinaigrette, about
10 minutes. Remove and discard the bay leaf if you like.

Lower the heat, add the reserved onion-mushroom garnish, and heat through, about 4
minutes more. Spoon the sauce over the chicken pieces, sprinkle with the chopped parsley,
and serve.

Cutting Up a Chicken

Whenever a recipe calls for chicken parts, I encourage you to buy a whole chicken and cut it up yourself, for several reasons. For one thing, a whole chicken is a good deal less expensive than parts. Plus, packaged chicken parts tend to vary in size, which can make them difficult to cook evenly. When you cut up a whole chicken, you're guaranteed evenly sized pieces. It's also near to impossible to find packaged chicken parts that aren't either all legs or all breasts. But the most important reason to butcher a whole chicken at home is that you'll be rewarded with all those tasty, sauce-building pieces (namely the wing tips, the back, the neck, and the giblets) that are missing from packaged parts. If you're still not convinced about undertaking the task, all the recipes in this book that call for a cut-up chicken can be made with an assortment of packaged parts, preferably thighs and legs. Just shop for as evenly sized pieces as you can.

Cutting up a whole chicken is not a complicated enterprise, and, as with any acquired skill, the more you do it, the greater dexterity you'll develop. To start, you'll need a sharp sturdy chef's knife, and it's helpful to have a sharp pair of poultry shears on hand. Here's how I go about cutting up a 3 ½- to 5-pound chicken:

1. Set up a thoroughly cleaned large cutting board (at least 12 by 18 inches) in a work area that is clear of other foods. Raw chicken is something you need to isolate and to be able to thoroughly clean up after, knives, hands, surfaces, and all.

2. Retrieve the packet of giblets, usually tucked inside the cavity. Of these, I typically keep the neck, heart, and gizzard to add to braises or to freeze for stock. The liver can be saved and sautéed, but it will cloud stocks and sauces. Pull out any large deposits of fat found near the opening of both the neck and body cavity. These can be collected and rendered (see "Making Schmaltz," page 187) or discarded. Rinse the chicken inside and out with cool water and dry it inside and out with paper towels.

3. Set the chicken on its back on the cutting board so the wings face you. Pull on the wing tip to unfold the joints, and cut off the outermost segment of each wing. Reserve the wing tips with the back, neck, heart, and gizzard.

4. Turn the bird so the legs are near you. Tug at one drumstick to pull the leg away from the body, and, with the tip of the knife, cut through the skin that bridges the body to the leg. Cutting the skin closer to the leg will leave the breast skin most intact. Once you've cut through the skin, you will have exposed the joint where you can cleanly separate the leg from the body. To best judge where to cut, put down the

(continued on next page)

knife, and bend the leg back away from the body, popping the leg joint. This will expose the ball-and-socket joint and show you right where to cut. Pick the knife up and separate the leg from the body, cutting right through this joint, and cutting as close to the backbone as possible. This is an easy cut and should not require any real force on your part. If you find yourself wrestling with bone, position the knife and try again. The idea is to separate the joint by cutting through cartilage, not bone. Repeat with the second leg.

5. Set one leg skin side down on the cutting board. Locate the strip of white-to-yellow fat that runs crosswise, separating the leg from the thigh. With the knife, cut firmly along this line and down through the joint. Again, you should not have to cut through any bone, just the cartilage that secures the joint. Repeat with the second leg.

6. The next step requires your most aggressive cutting, as you separate the backbone from the breast. If you have poultry shears, they work well here. If not, the chef's knife will do the job. If using shears, turn the chicken over so you are looking at the back. Starting from the leg end, cut up one side of the back and continue cutting up through the rib bones until you reach the neck. You are aiming to isolate the bony back portion and leave the breast intact. Repeat on the other side. Or, if you are using a chef's knife, stand the carcass up so that the leg end is facing up. With the knife, whack though the ribs on both sides of the backbone to separate it from the breast. When you get to the neck, you'll have to cut away on either side to free the entire backbone. Set the backbone aside with the wing tips and other bits.

7. Lay the breast skin side up on the cutting board, and straighten the skin over the breast so it's not pulled to one side or stretched. Using your sturdy knife and steady pressure, cut down through the center of the breast, separating it into two halves, each with a wing bone attached.

8. Grab one wing in your noncutting hand and wiggle it against the breast so that you can feel where the shoulder socket joint is. Holding the knife in your other hand, and pressing the wing against the breast, cut at an angle to separate the wing from the breast by slicing through the joint and slicing a 1/2- to 1-inch piece of breast away with it. Tug on the wing to open the joint as you slice through the cartilage: the wing with the small piece of breast meat should release. If you strike solid bone, reposition the knife and try again for the socket. Repeat with the other breast half. You will now have 8 pieces of chicken: 2 thighs, 2 drumsticks, 2 breasts, and 2 wings: enough to serve 4 to 6 people, depending on the size of the bird.

9. After cutting up the chicken, there are a few choices of how to deal with the trimmings. For starters, the back should be split in two just above where the legs were attached—depending on how efficiently you cut up the chicken, you may see two pockets of meat here known as the "oysters." The top half is smaller and bonier and isn't much good for anything but the stockpot; I don't usually add it to a braise since it takes up room and doesn't contribute as much flavor as other parts. But I do like to include the meatier bottom portion in my braises. I remove it before serving, since it's not really a piece for the dinner table, although there are some sweet bits there to nibble on—I like to think of it as a cook's treat, and I pry the little oysters of dark meat out to snack on while I finish the sauce.

As for the wing tips, I toss these into the braising pot along with the neck and gizzard to add flavor and body. Just be sure to remove and discard them before serving.

Chicken Fricassee with Artichokes & Mushrooms ⇢

In the lexicon of classic French cooking, *fricassee* refers to chicken pieces that are cooked gently in butter to enhance their flavor but without browning the skin, then braised slowly in stock and/or wine, and finally enriched with cream. When prepared with care, the pale, ivory-colored dish is both elegant and soulful. Many fricassees call for stock, but it must be a very pale and light-flavored stock to maintain the color and delicate flavor of the dish. I simplify things by using just white wine. The wine gives the dish a lighter, sharper character than a stock-based braise, which better complements the flavors of the mushrooms and the artichokes.

A French fricassee calls for thickening the sauce with egg yolks mixed with cream, which can be tricky, since there's always the risk of curdling. Again, I make life easier by using crème fraîche as an enrichment and thickener. A half cup of thick, tangy crème fraîche elevates the flavor of the entire dish.

I make this dish with canned artichoke bottoms and love the results. Even though I tend to be a real stickler for fresh seasonal produce, canned artichoke bottoms (not hearts) are a pantry staple in my house. These saucer-shaped rounds have a lovely texture (without any of the fibrous leaves that hearts so often have) and a sweet flavor that makes a great addition to many dishes (try them in stews, omelets, or salads). If fresh globe or baby artichokes are in season, and you're up for the task of trimming and parcooking them, consult the variation that follows the recipe.

Serve with plain boiled potatoes and, for an added French accent, a few Fried Croûtes (page 168).

wine notes

Full-bodied dry white, such as Chardonnay (that isn't overly oaked), dry Riesling, or Pinot Gris.

One 3 1/2- to 4-pound chicken, cut into
  8 pieces, wing tips, back, neck, and
  giblets (except the liver) reserved (see
  "Cutting Up a Chicken," page 161), or
  2 3/4 pounds legs and thighs
Coarse salt and freshly ground black
  pepper
All-purpose flour for dredging (about
  1/2 cup)
4 tablespoons unsalted butter
One 14-ounce can artichoke bottoms
  (not artichoke hearts), drained, rinsed,
  and quartered; if using fresh
  artichokes, see the variation that
  follows, page 166

3/4 pound (12 ounces) button mushrooms,
  quartered, or halved if small
1 medium yellow onion (about 6 ounces),
  thinly sliced
1/4 cup Cognac, or other good brandy
1 1/4 cups dry white wine or dry white
  vermouth
Two 2- to 3-inch leafy fresh thyme sprigs
One 2- to 3-inch leafy fresh marjoram
  sprig
1 garlic clove, minced
1/2 cup crème fraîche
1/2 lemon (optional)

Fried Croûtes (recipe follows; optional)

1. **Heat the oven to 325 degrees.**
2. **Dredging the chicken:** Rinse the chicken pieces under cool water and dry well with paper towels. Generously season the chicken all over with salt and pepper. Spread the flour in a wide shallow dish (a pie plate works well). Dredge half the chicken pieces one at a time, placing each one in the flour, turning to coat both sides, and then lifting and patting lightly to shake off any excess.
3. **Searing the chicken:** Heat the butter in a Dutch oven or heavy lidded braising pot (4-quart works well) over medium heat. When the butter stops foaming, add the dredged chicken pieces skin side down and cook until the skin is an even blond color but not at all brown, about 4 minutes. Turn with tongs and cook the second side until blond but not browned, another 4 minutes or so. Transfer to a large plate or tray to catch any drips. While the first batch of chicken is cooking, dredge the remaining pieces in the flour. Discard the remaining flour. Cook the second batch of chicken, again without browning, for about 4 minutes per side. Set aside with the rest.
4. **The aromatics:** Return the pot to medium heat—there will still be enough butter in the bottom for the aromatics. Add the artichokes, mushrooms, and onion to the pot, stir them around with a wooden spoon, and season with salt and pepper. Cook until the vegetables have absorbed the remaining butter and begin to soften, about 5 minutes. Transfer the vegetables to the platter with the chicken.

5. **Flaming the Cognac and building the braising liquid:** Increase the heat to medium-high. Add the Cognac, and carefully ignite it with a match or by tilting the pan and letting the gas flame lick over the edge. Stand back, and be careful, as the flames can be high. Let the flames die down, about 2 minutes. Scrape the bottom of the pot with a wooden spoon as the Cognac boils to dislodge any lovely browned bits cooked onto the bottom of the pan from the chicken. Add the wine and bring to a boil. Simmer to reduce the liquid by about one quarter, 8 to 10 minutes.

6. **The braise:** Add the chicken pieces to the pot in this order: Place the legs, thighs, and wings, and the wing tips, back, neck, heart, and gizzard (if using) in the pot first, then put the breast pieces on top of them, skin side down. (Setting the breasts on top protects them from overcooking.) Or, if you're using all legs and thighs, fit them in the pot as evenly as possible. Add the vegetables to the pot, along with the thyme, marjoram, garlic, and any juices that have collected on the platter. Cover the pot with parchment paper, pressing down on the paper so that it nearly touches the chicken and extends over the sides of the pot by about an inch. Then cover tightly with the lid. Slide onto a rack in the lower third of the oven and braise gently for 15 minutes. Turn the breast pieces over and continue braising gently until the chicken is fork-tender, another 40 to 45 minutes (a total of 60 to 65 minutes). As you lift the lid to turn the chicken pieces, check that the liquid is simmering quietly; if not, lower the oven heat by 10 or 15 degrees.

7. **The finish:** With a slotted spoon or tongs, lift the chicken pieces and most of the mushrooms and artichokes from the pan and transfer them to a serving platter or other shallow dish, without stacking. Don't worry if you can't get every last mushroom or artichoke bottom. Discard the wing tips, back, neck, heart, and gizzard, if using. With a wide spoon, skim as much surface fat as you have the patience for from the braising liquid. Set the sauce over medium-high heat and bring to a strong simmer. Lift out and discard the herb sprigs. Let the sauce simmer vigorously to reduce in volume and concentrate in flavor for about 5 minutes. Add the crème fraîche and continue to simmer to reduce to the consistency of a thin cream soup, another 5 minutes or so. Taste for salt and pepper. If the sauce tastes flat, add a squeeze of lemon. Serve the chicken, artichokes, and mushrooms and spoon the sauce over the top. Garnish each plate with 2 fried croûtes, if using.

VARIATION: CHICKEN FRICASSE WITH FRESH ARTICHOKES

The peak season for artichokes is spring, March through May. If you are making this in season, substitute 6 globe artichokes or 8 baby artichokes for the canned. With larger globe artichokes, trim as directed in Step 1 of Roman-Style Artichoke Bottoms (page 70). For baby artichokes, follow the directions in Step 1 of Spring Vegetable Braise (page 75). Once they are trimmed, cut globe artichokes into quarters or cut baby artichokes into halves—be sure to scrape away all traces of the hairy center, or choke. Then whisk 2 tablespoons all-purpose flour and the juice of 1/2 lemon into 2 1/2 quarts water in a medium pot. Add a good pinch of salt, and bring to a boil over medium-high heat. Add the artichokes and blanch for 8 minutes. (The technique of adding the flour and water is French and referred to as cooking *à blanc*. It helps the artichokes maintain their pale green color.) Drain, and add the artichokes to the braise as directed in Step 4 above.

FRIED CROÛTES

Serve a pair of these crispy, golden toasts alongside most any saucy braised dish. I like to cut the bread into neat triangles, but feel free to make oval, round, or even heart-shaped ones with a cookie cutter. You can also dress up the croûtes by dipping one corner or edge in the sauce and then in chopped parsley just before serving. Very pretty, and very French.

Makes 12 croûtes

Six ¼-inch-thick slices fine-crumbed sandwich bread, such as Pepperidge Farm

Extra-virgin olive oil or peanut oil for pan frying

1. Trim the crusts from the bread, and cut each slice on the diagonal into 2 triangles.
2. Pour ¼ inch of oil into a large skillet (12-inch) and heat over medium heat. When the surface of the oil shimmers, add as many pieces of bread as will fit without crowding. Fry, turning once with tongs, until crisp and golden on both sides, 1 to 2 minutes per side. Drain on a paper towel–lined tray. Repeat with the remaining pieces. Serve within 4 hours.

Moroccan Chicken with Green Olives & Preserved Lemons →→

Chicken braised with olives and lemons is a classic Moroccan dish, and there are countless ways to prepare it. Some recipes are simpler than my version and some grander, but this is the one I rely on when I crave food that tastes familiar and exotic at the same time. The familiar is the comforting taste of chicken braised in a sweet onion-based sauce. The exotic is the combination of ginger, cumin, red pepper, saffron, and the salty piquancy of preserved lemons.

The technique of including the chicken liver in the braise and then mashing it up to add to the finished sauce comes from Paula Wolfert's venerable cookbook *Couscous and Other Good Food from Morocco*. If you are not a fan of chicken liver, I urge you to try it here anyway. It won't make the sauce taste at all livery. Instead, it contributes an earthiness and depth that you won't be able to identify but will savor.

If you haven't made preserved lemons (see page 173) in advance and don't have access to a good Middle Eastern market that sells them, the dish will still be wonderful, although not as aromatic. Don't substitute regular lemon peels for the preserved, they're not the same thing at all.

Couscous is traditional with this dish.

wine notes

Dry, medium-to-full bodied white with youthful fruit and a touch of earthiness, such as a dry Riesling from Austria, Alsace, or southern Germany.

Working Ahead

I can never decide if I prefer to eat Moroccan chicken right away or the day after I've made it. The preserved lemon tends to stand out from the other flavors when the dish is first made. If the chicken sits overnight in the refrigerator, the combined tastes of the spices, lemons, and olives meld together.

To reheat, arrange the chicken pieces in a shallow baking dish, and scrape the sauce over the top. Cover and heat at 325 degrees until warm throughout, about 20 minutes.

Serves 4 to 5 | *Braising Time: about 45 minutes*

THE SPICE MIX

1/2 **teaspoon ground ginger**

1/2 **teaspoon cumin seeds, toasted and ground**

1/2 **teaspoon freshly ground black pepper**

1/4 **teaspoon sweet pimentón (smoked Spanish paprika) or sweet Hungarian paprika (see "Hungarian Paprika and Pimentón," page 357)**

1/4 **teaspoon crushed red pepper flakes**

1/8 **teaspoon saffron threads, crumbled**

THE BRAISE

1/2 **cup green olives in brine, such as Lucques or Cerignola, not pitted**

One 3 1/2- to 4-pound chicken, cut into 8 pieces, wing tips, back, neck, and giblets reserved (see "Cutting Up a Chicken," page 161), or 2 3/4 pounds legs and thighs

2 **tablespoons extra-virgin olive oil**

1 **tablespoon unsalted butter**

Coarse salt

1 **medium yellow onion (about 6 ounces), thinly sliced**

3 **garlic cloves, thinly sliced**

3/4 **cup water**

1 **lemon, halved**

1/4 **cup mixed chopped flat-leaf parsley and cilantro**

1 **whole (4 quarters) Salt-Preserved Lemon (recipe follows)**

Freshly ground black pepper

1. The spices: In a small bowl, stir together the ginger, cumin, black pepper, pimentón or paprika, red pepper, and saffron. In another bowl, cover the olives with cool water, and set aside to soak.

2. Browning the chicken: Rinse the chicken pieces with cool water, and dry them thoroughly with paper towels (otherwise they won't brown well—moist meats steam and tend to stick to the pan). Heat the oil and butter in a large deep-sided skillet or shallow braising pan (4-quart capacity) over medium-high heat. While the oil and butter heat, season half the chicken pieces lightly with salt (keep in mind that the olives and preserved lemons will add saltiness). When the butter is sizzling, add the salted chicken pieces skin side down and sear, without disturbing, until the skin is crisp and evenly browned, about 4 minutes. Peek by lifting one edge with tongs to see that the skin side is browned, then turn with tongs and brown the second side, another 4 minutes or so. Transfer the browned chicken to a platter or tray to collect any drips. Pat the remaining chicken pieces again with paper towels just to be sure they are as dry as possible, and lightly salt both sides. Add these pieces to the pan skin side down and sear them as you did the first batch, transferring them to the platter with the other chicken when they are browned.

3.   **The aromatics:** Pour off all but about 1 tablespoon of fat from the pan and return the pan to medium heat. Add the onion and garlic, stir with a wooden spoon, and sauté until you can smell their fragrance and they begin to soften, about 3 minutes. (The bottom of the pan will develop a walnut-colored crust.) Add the spice mix, stir, and sauté for a minute longer.

4.   **The braising liquid:** Pour in the water to deglaze the pan, and stir and scrape the bottom with a wooden spoon to dislodge and dissolve the flavorful cooked-on crust.

5.   **The braise:** When the water boils, return the chicken legs and thighs, and the wing tips, back, neck, heart, and gizzard, if using, to the pan. Tuck the liver, if using, between the pieces. Cover, reduce the heat to low, and braise the chicken for 10 minutes. Uncover the pan, and if the liquid is simmering too forcefully, lower the heat to a quiet simmer, or set a heat diffuser under the pan. Turn the legs and wings over with tongs, and place the chicken breast pieces skin side up on top of the legs and wings. (Adding the chicken breasts after 10 minutes prevents them from overcooking and drying out. If you're using all legs and thighs, add them all at the start.) Squeeze the juice from one lemon half over the chicken, and sprinkle over half the chopped herbs. Continue to braise gently for 20 minutes more.

6.   **While the chicken braises, prepare the olives and preserved lemons:** Drain and rinse the olives. Remove the pits by crushing them one by one with the side of a large knife and pulling out the pit. Most olives will remain in one piece, like an open book, but it's fine if some olives break in two. (You can use an olive pitter if you choose, but I've always found the knife faster and more efficient.) Rinse the preserved lemon quarters under cool water, and remove and discard the pulp. Chop the peel into 1/2-inch pieces.

7.   **Adding the olives and preserved lemons:** After the chicken has braised for a total of 30 minutes (20 minutes after you added the breasts), lift the lid, add the olives and preserved lemons, and turn the chicken pieces again.

8.   **Optional step, if using the liver:** Remove the liver from the pan, place it in a small bowl, and mash it to a paste with a fork. Set aside.

9.   **Continuing the braise:** Replace the lid and continue to braise until the juices from the legs run clear when pierced with the tip of a sharp knife, another 10 to 15 minutes (for a total of 40 to 45 minutes). Transfer the chicken pieces to a serving dish or tray to catch the

juices, and discard the wing tips, back, neck, heart, and gizzard, if you used them. Cover the chicken loosely with foil to keep warm.

10. The finish: Increase the heat under the braising liquid to medium-high and bring to a boil. Return the liver, if using, to the skillet and stir it into the sauce. Squeeze in the juice from the other half of the lemon. Simmer the sauce until it reduces just a bit, about 5 minutes. Add the remaining herbs. Taste for salt and pepper. Spoon the sauce over the chicken and serve.

SALT-PRESERVED LEMONS

Salt-preserved lemons are staples of Moroccan cooking. Even though they require a three-week wait, they're worth it. I prefer using small lemons for this, about 2 to 3 inches long, because they fit more neatly in the jar. If your market only stocks jumbos, ask about special-ordering small lemons. And since you'll be eating the peel, it's safest to buy organic lemons that you know are free of any harmful sprays.

Makes 1 pint (3 preserved lemons)

3 small lemons (about 4 ounces each),
    preferably organic
2/3 cup freshly squeezed lemon juice (from
    about 3 small lemons)

1/4 cup coarse salt

1. Wash a wide-mouth 1-pint glass jar and lid in very hot soapy water. Rinse well. Leave them to dry upside down on a clean towel.

2. Rinse the lemons and scrub them with a vegetable brush. If the lemons aren't organic, you might want to use a little dish detergent to remove any pesticide residue. Rinse well. Cut the lemons lengthwise into quarters and place them in a bowl. Add the salt and toss the lemons with a rubber spatula to coat them with the salt.

3. With clean hands, arrange the lemon quarters in the jar, compacting them as best you can. After you've fitted half the lemon quarters in the jar, sprinkle over some of the salt from the bottom of the bowl, then fill the jar with the remaining lemon quarters. When all the lemons are in the jar, use a rubber spatula to scrape the remaining salt from the bowl into the jar.

4. Pour enough lemon juice into the jar to cover the lemons, leaving about 1/2 inch head-space. Wipe the rim with a damp paper towel. Screw on the lid tightly.

5. Set the jar in a dark cupboard to pickle for at least 3 weeks. Turn the jar on end every 10 days or so to redistribute the salt, and let it sit for a few hours, then turn the jar upright again.

6. To use the preserved lemons, pull a lemon quarter from the jar with clean fingers or tongs. Rinse under cool water and slide off the pulp. Use only the pickled peel. Once you've opened the jar, store the lemons in the refrigerator for up to 1 year.

Chicken & Dumplings ✈

Chicken and dumplings is one of those great American braised classics, like pot roast, that used to regularly grace the Sunday dinner table. The traditional recipe starts by cutting a whole chicken into serving pieces, then braising it in seasoned water until done. As the chicken simmers, you whip up a dumpling batter (a sort of wet biscuit dough), then drop the batter in spoonfuls onto the simmering chicken during the last 15 minutes of braising. In the end, you've got a full-course meal of chicken, dumplings, and sauce.

As much as I love the notion of a classic chicken and dumplings, I've too often been disappointed with pieces of tough chicken, dumplings as dense as doorstops, and a watery sauce. So I developed a recipe that delivers tender, moist chicken fragrant with hints of lemon, nutmeg, and Riesling; dumplings as light as gnocchi; and an elegant, creamy sauce. I use stock and wine in place of water for the braising liquid and add plenty of aromatics.

I sometimes add fresh herbs to the dumplings to brighten the dish even more, but they are very good without. Watermelon pickle and/or succotash would be very fitting side dishes.

wine notes

Enjoy the same bottle of dry Riesling, Fumé Blanc, or Sancerre used in the recipe, or a full-bodied, dry Chardonnay with moderate oak flavors from California or Australia.

Serves 4 to 5 | *Braising Time: about 40 minutes*

One 3 1/2- to 4-pound chicken, cut into
    8 pieces, wing tips, back, neck, and
    giblets (except the liver) reserved (see
    "Cutting Up a Chicken," page 161), or
    2 3/4 pounds legs and thighs
Coarse salt and freshly ground black
    pepper
4 tablespoons unsalted butter
1 medium yellow onion (about 6 ounces),
    chopped into 1/2-inch pieces
2 medium celery stalks, chopped into
    1/2-inch pieces

1 large shallot, chopped into 1/2-inch
    pieces
2 strips lemon zest, removed with a
    vegetable peeler (each about
    2 1/2 inches by 3/4 inch)
Scant 1/4 teaspoon freshly grated nutmeg
1 cup dry Riesling, Fumé Blanc, or Sancerre
1 cup chicken stock, homemade (page 448)
    or store-bought

THE DUMPLINGS

1 cup all-purpose flour
1 teaspoon baking powder
1/2 teaspoon coarse salt
1 tablespoon chopped flat-leaf parsley
1 tablespoon finely chopped fresh chives
    or minced scallion greens

Scant 1/8 teaspoon freshly grated nutmeg
1 large egg, at room temperature
6 to 8 tablespoons whole milk, at room
    temperature
2 tablespoons unsalted butter, melted
    and cooled

THE LIAISON

2 large egg yolks
1/2 cup heavy cream
Coarse salt and freshly ground black
    pepper

1/2 lemon
2 tablespoons chopped flat-leaf parsley

1. Searing the chicken: Rinse the chicken pieces with cool water and dry them thoroughly with paper towels. Season all over with salt and pepper. Heat 2 tablespoons of the butter in a large deep lidded skillet or shallow braising pan (12- to 13-inch) over medium-low heat. Add the chicken pieces skin side down, in batches so as not to crowd the pan, and gently sear until the chicken is evenly blond (do not let the chicken brown) and no longer raw-looking, about 4 minutes. Turn the pieces over with tongs and cook on the second side for another 4 minutes, again without browning. Transfer the chicken to a plate and set aside. Repeat with the remaining chicken.

2.   **The aromatics:** Pour off and discard all the fat from the pan. Add the remaining 2 tablespoons butter and heat until the foam subsides. Add the onion, celery, shallot, lemon zest, nutmeg, and a sprinkling of salt and pepper and sauté until the vegetables are softened, about 4 minutes. Add 1/2 cup of the wine and bring to a gentle boil. Reduce the wine by three quarters, about 7 minutes. Add the remaining 1/2 cup wine, bring back to a gentle boil, and boil for another 6 to 7 minutes. Add the stock and bring just to a simmer.

3.   **The braise:** Return the legs and wings, and the wing tips, back, neck, heart, and gizzard, if using, to the pan, arranging them in one layer. Lower the heat to medium-low, cover the pan, and cook the chicken for 10 minutes. Uncover the pan, and if the liquid is simmering too turbulently, lower the heat to a quiet simmer, or set a heat diffuser under the pan. Turn the legs and wings over and place the chicken breast pieces skin side up on top of the legs and wings. (Adding the breasts partway through the braise ensures that they won't overcook and dry out. If you're using all legs and thighs, add them all at the start.) Cover the pan and continue to braise at a lazy simmer for another 25 to 30 minutes, until the juices from the legs run clear when pierced with the tip of a sharp knife.

4.   **While the chicken braises, make the dumplings:** Place the flour, baking powder, salt, parsley, chives or scallion greens, and nutmeg in a medium bowl. Whisk together to blend, and make a well in the center. Add the egg and 6 tablespoons of the milk and whisk together, gathering in the flour as you whisk. Add some or all of the remaining 2 tablespoons of milk if the batter is very stiff at this point; it should be wet enough to mix but not slushy. Slowly pour in the melted butter in a steady stream, continuing to whisk gently just until all the ingredients are incorporated. Scrape the sides of the bowl once or twice while you whisk the dough. It is important not to overmix, or the dumplings will be dense and springy, not tender. Leave the dough in a loose, shaggy mass, and set it aside.

5.   **Cook the dumplings:** When the chicken has finished braising, transfer the pieces to a serving platter large enough to later hold the dumplings and the sauce without crowding. Remove and discard the wing tips, back, neck, heart, and gizzard as you come across them, if you used them. Cover the chicken loosely with foil to keep warm, and set aside. Strain the pan juices into a bowl, pressing down lightly on the aromatics to extract as much liquid as you can before discarding them, and then return the juices to the skillet. Let sit for a minute, and spoon off any surface fat. Return the pan to medium heat and bring the juices to a simmer. With two regular tablespoons or soupspoons, form 8 dumplings with the dough and lower them gently into the simmering juices. Let the dumplings poach, uncovered, until they become firm on the bottom and hold their shape, about 5 minutes. Gently roll the dumplings over using a slotted spoon and poach the second side for another 5 minutes. Transfer the dumplings to the platter with the chicken and cover to keep warm.

6.   **While the dumplings poach, prepare the egg-and-cream liaison:** Combine the egg

yolks, cream, and a generous pinch each of salt and pepper in a small bowl. Whisk until smooth. (This mixture, known as a liaison, is a classic French technique for thickening and enriching sauces just before serving.)

7. **The finish:** When the dumplings are done and on the platter, reduce the heat to low to finish the sauce. You will need a ladle, whisk, and wooden spoon. Ladle some pan juices slowly into the egg mixture, whisking continuously. Then reverse the process and slowly pour the warmed yolk-cream mixture into the pan juices, whisking continuously. This technique, known as tempering, prevents the yolks from curdling or scrambling, which they would if added directly to the hot liquid. When they are incorporated, switch from the whisk to the wooden spoon and continue stirring and gently cooking until the sauce thickens and coats the back of the spoon. Watch carefully, and do not let the sauce come close to a boil or it will curdle. As soon as it has thickened, remove the sauce from the heat. Taste for salt and pepper. If the sauce tastes too eggy or bland, add a long squeeze of lemon. Quickly spoon the sauce over the chicken and dumplings, sprinkle with the chopped parsley, and proudly carry the platter to the table.

Vietnamese Braised Scallops, page 117, over rice

Braised Whole Chicken with Bread Stuffing
& Bacon, page 183, with gravy on the side

Moroccan Chicken with Green Olives &

Preserved Lemons, page 169

Short Ribs Braised in Porter Ale
with Maple-Rosemary Glaze, page 247,
with golden beets

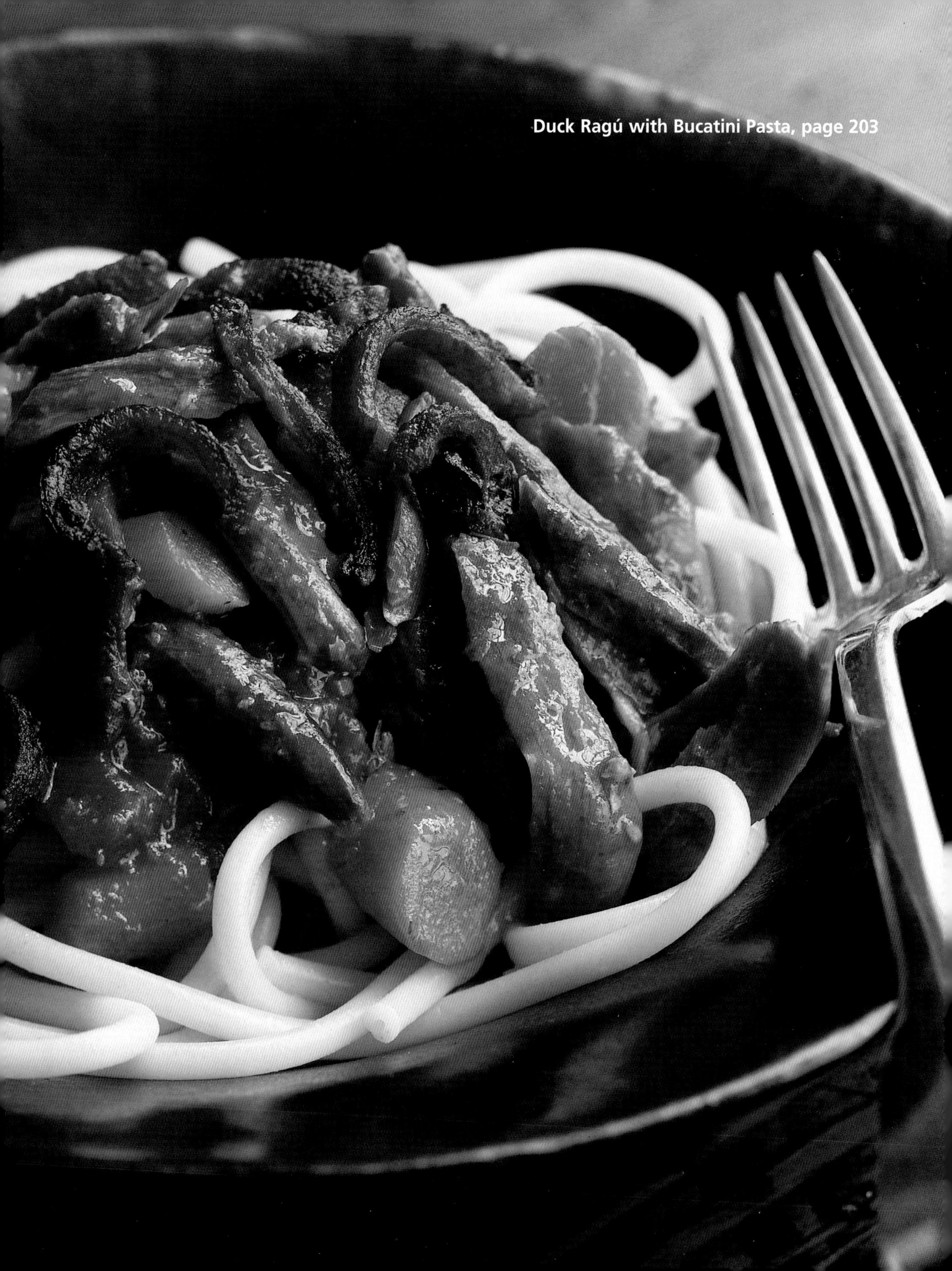
Duck Ragú with Bucatini Pasta, page 203

Boneless beef chuck blade pot roast,
tied before braising, page 258

Zinfandel Pot Roast with

Glazed Carrots, Parsnips & Fresh Sage, page 264

Bisteces Rancheros, page 222

Whole Chicken Braised with Pears & Rosemary ➼

A lovely alternative to roast chicken. Even better, in fact, because the chicken makes its own pear-and-rosemary-scented sauce as it braises. The secret is stuffing a quartered pear and a few branches of rosemary into the cavity before braising. As the chicken simmers to tenderness, the pear juices flow into the meat, giving it a subtle sweetness. The pear-enriched chicken drippings mingle with the braising liquid to create a complex sauce with a hint of fruit and a whiff of rosemary. To suit the elegant flavors in this dish, I take the time to strain the sauce before serving and make a garnish of balsamic-glazed pears to add to the smooth sauce. Not only do the pears look beautiful in the sauce, but their flavor perfectly complements the juicy braised chicken.

Make this dish in the fall when pears are in season. Look for Bosc or Forelle varieties, just ripe enough to be sweet but not so soft that they will collapse during braising.

Serve with rice pilaf, buttery polenta, or celery root and potato puree.

wine notes

Crisp white with herbal flavors, such as Sauvignon Blanc from New Zealand or Sancerre from France's Loire Valley; or a dry Riesling from Alsace or Austria.

Serves 3 to 4 | Braising Time: 1 1/4 hours

THE BRAISE

One 3 3/4- to 4 1/4-pound chicken, neck,
 heart, and gizzard reserved
Coarse salt and freshly ground black
 pepper
1 just-ripe pear, preferably Bosc or Forelle
Three 3-inch leafy fresh rosemary sprigs
2 tablespoons unsalted butter
1 tablespoon extra-virgin olive oil

1 1/3 cups finely chopped leek, white and
 pale green part only (1 large or
 2 medium)
1/4 cup finely chopped shallots (2 medium)
1/4 cup dry white wine or dry white
 vermouth
1/2 cup chicken stock, homemade (page
 448) or store-bought
1 tablespoon white wine vinegar

THE PEAR GARNISH

2 just-ripe pears, preferably Bosc or Forelle
2 tablespoons unsalted butter
2 teaspoons sugar
1 teaspoon finely chopped fresh rosemary

Coarse salt and freshly ground black
 pepper
1 tablespoon balsamic vinegar

1. **Heat the oven to 300 degrees.**

2. **Truss the chicken:** Rinse the chicken inside and out with cool water, and dry it inside and out using paper towels. Tear out any large lumps of fat from the chicken and discard. Cut the last two joints off each wing and reserve along with the neck, heart, and gizzard (discard the liver or save for another use). Season the chicken inside and out with salt and pepper. Cut the pear into quarters (peel left on and not cored), and stuff these into the cavity, putting 2 quarters in stem side first, the others blossom side first. Slide in 2 rosemary sprigs alongside the pear. Using a length of kitchen string about 24 inches long, truss the chicken: Loop the middle of the string around the ends of the two drumsticks to pull them together. Next, bring the ends of the string back along the sides of the chicken, running the string between the leg and the breast on both sides, then turn the chicken over and snag the string over the base of the neck so that it won't slide down the chicken's back. Knot the string securely. Trim off the string close to the knot.

3. **Brown the chicken:** Heat 1 tablespoon of the butter and the oil in a medium Dutch oven (a 3-quart oval oven works well) or deep flameproof roasting pan (3- to 4-inch sides) over medium-high heat. Pat the surface of the chicken dry again with paper towels (the drier it is, the better it will brown). When the butter stops foaming, pick up the chicken and gently lower it breast side down into the hot pan. Brown the chicken without disturbing it for about 4 minutes, then nudge one side with a wooden spoon and peek to see whether the skin has developed a deep brown color. If so, maneuver the chicken onto one

side; I use two flat wooden spoons for this operation—they turn the chicken without tearing into the skin. If not, sear for another minute or two. Continue browning and turning until all four sides (breast, back, and sides) are an appealing roasted brown, 12 to 18 minutes total. Lift the chicken, either with the wooden spoons or with a thick dish towel to protect your hands, and set it aside on a large plate. Add the reserved wing tips, neck, heart, and gizzard to the pan and sauté, stirring occasionally, until they brown in spots, about 7 minutes. Remove and set aside with the chicken.

4. **The aromatics and braising liquid:** Pour off all the fat from the pot and discard. With a damp paper towel, wipe out any burnt specks from the bottom of the pan, being careful to leave behind all the delicious caramelized bits. Return the pot to medium heat and add the remaining tablespoon of butter. Add the leek, shallots, and remaining rosemary sprig, season with salt and pepper, and sauté, stirring occasionally with a wooden spoon, until the vegetables have softened and are releasing their juices, about 7 minutes. Pour in the wine, raise the heat again to medium-high, and boil, stirring, until the wine is reduced by about half, about 2 minutes. Add the stock and white wine vinegar, and boil for 2 more minutes to meld the flavors.

5. **The braise:** Using your hands, place the chicken on top of the vegetables, breast side up, and pour in any juices that seeped onto the plate where it rested. Tuck the neck, wing tips, and giblets alongside the chicken. Cover with parchment paper and press down on the paper so that it nearly touches the chicken and extends about an inch over the sides of the pot. Then set a tight-fitting lid in place. Slide the pot into the lower third of the oven. Braise, basting every 20 minutes with a large spoon, until the juices run clear when you prick the side of the thigh with a thin blade and an instant-read thermometer registers 170 degrees when you insert it between the breast and the thigh, about 1 hour and 15 minutes. When you lift the lid to baste, check to see that the liquid is at a slow simmer; if it appears to be simmering too furiously, reduce the oven heat by 10 or 15 degrees. (There's no need to turn a whole chicken during braising. The quicker-cooking white meat sits above the liquid, where it braises more slowly, while the slower-cooking dark meat sits in the braising liquid, where it braises more quickly. In the end, the whole turns out perfectly.)

6. **Meanwhile, prepare the pear garnish:** Peel the pears, cut them into quarters, remove the cores, and then cut each quarter crosswise into 1/2-inch-thick slices. Heat the butter in a large skillet (10- to 12-inch), preferably nonstick, over high heat. When the butter stops foaming, add the pears and toss with a heat-resistant rubber spatula to coat with the butter. Add the sugar, rosemary, and salt and pepper to taste. Sauté briskly, shaking the skillet and turning the pears frequently with the spatula, until they begin to caramelize on all surfaces, about 5 minutes. Add the balsamic and continue to shake and stir until the vinegar has reduced to a glaze that coats the pears, barely 30 seconds. Transfer the pears to a large

plate, spreading them out so they will stop cooking and do not steam and become mushy while you finish the sauce.

7. **The finish:** Remove the chicken from the pot by spearing a meat fork into the cavity, tipping the chicken toward you so that the juices run back into the pot, and lifting gently, and set the chicken on a carving board. Cover loosely with foil to keep warm. Strain the braising liquid into a small saucepan, pressing down lightly on the vegetables and giblets to extract as much liquid as you can. Discard the vegetables and giblets. Using a wide metal spoon, skim the clear surface fat from the sauce. Set the sauce over medium-high heat and bring to a gentle boil. Simmer the sauce to concentrate the flavor and give it some body, about 6 minutes. The sauce should be the consistency of a thick vinaigrette. Taste for salt and pepper. Add the pear garnish to the sauce to warm through.

8. **Serving:** Carve the chicken, and spoon some sauce and pears over each serving.

Braised Whole Chicken with Bread Stuffing & Bacon ⇥

Braising a plump roasting chicken makes a comforting family dinner. It's also just the dish to serve to guests when you want them to feel like family. What I love about braising a chicken is that there's none of that fuss over turning the bird to roast evenly or worry about getting the timing just right. The moist, gentle heat cooks the bird through to tender doneness in about 2 hours, and it doesn't threaten to dry out if you happen to braise it a few minutes too long. Plus, you end up with a perfectly balanced sauce that you quickly whir in the blender to make smooth and creamy. The bread stuffing accented with sliced ham, pine nuts, and raisins tastes so good that I make extra to bake alongside the chicken, just to be sure there's plenty to go around.

The only challenge in braising such a large bird is getting the outside browned. Its size and the stuffing make it too unwieldy to brown on top of the stove. I solve this by briefly roasting the chicken *after* braising. This way, the strips of bacon draped over the top of the chicken, which basted the meat as it braised, become all crisp and brown. Splendid.

wine notes

Medium-bodied red with youthful fruit, a touch of earthiness, and bright acidity—Pinot Noir from California, Oregon, or New Zealand; lighter-style red Burgundy; Cru Beaujolais; or Italian Barbera.

Serves 6 | Braising Time: about 2 hours

THE STUFFING

4 tablespoons rendered chicken fat or
  unsalted butter (see "Making
  Schmaltz," page 187)
1 1/2 cups finely chopped yellow onion
  (1 large)
2/3 cup finely chopped inner celery stalks
  with leaves (4 small stalks)
2/3 cup finely chopped good-quality baked
  ham (4 thin slices), such as Black
  Forest or Westphalian

1/3 cup pine nuts, lightly toasted
1/3 cup currants, soaked in warm water for
  20 minutes and drained
1/2 cup coarsely chopped flat-leaf parsley
5 cups 3/4-inch bread pieces with crust—
  torn from a slightly stale rustic white
  loaf, preferably not sourdough (about
  8 ounces)
Coarse salt and freshly ground black
  pepper

THE BRAISE

One 6- to 7-pound roasting chicken, neck,
  heart, and gizzard reserved
Coarse salt and freshly ground black
  pepper
2 to 2 1/4 cups chicken stock, homemade
  (page 448) or store-bought
1 tablespoon unsalted butter or rendered
  chicken fat
1 tablespoon extra-virgin olive oil
1 large or 2 small carrots, coarsely
  chopped
2 celery stalks, coarsely chopped

1 large yellow onion (about 8 ounces),
  coarsely chopped
1 teaspoon chopped fresh rosemary
1 teaspoon chopped fresh thyme
2 bay leaves
3 strips lemon zest, removed with a
  vegetable peeler (each about
  2 1/2 inches by 3/4 inch)
1/2 cup dry white wine or dry white
  vermouth
5 strips lean bacon
1/4 cup heavy cream (optional)

1. **The stuffing:** Melt the fat or butter in a medium skillet (8-inch) over medium-low heat. Add the onion and celery and sauté, stirring once or twice, until translucent and soft, about 7 minutes. Transfer to a medium bowl. Add the ham, pine nuts, drained currants, parsley, and bread to the onion-celery mix and toss with a large spoon to distribute the ingredients evenly. Season with salt and pepper and toss again.

2. **Heat the oven to 325 degrees.**

3. **Stuffing the chicken:** Rinse the chicken inside and out under cool running water. Drain and then dry inside and out with paper towels. If you have not already removed the fat for rendering (See "Making Schmaltz," page 187), pull any lumps of chicken fat from the opening of the cavity and discard. Chop off the last 2 joints of the wings with a cleaver or large kitchen knife, and reserve them with the neck, heart, and gizzard. Season the chicken

inside and out with salt and pepper, and scoop enough stuffing into the cavity to fill it generously without jamming it full; the stuffing needs some room to expand as the chicken braises. Butter a small baking dish large enough to hold the remaining stuffing. Fill the dish with the leftover stuffing, and pour over $1/2$ to $3/4$ cup of the stock, enough to barely moisten the stuffing. Cover with foil and set aside.

4. **Trussing the chicken:** Using a length of kitchen string about 30 inches long, truss the chicken: Loop the middle of the string around the ends of the two drumsticks to pull them together. Now bring the ends of the string back along the sides of the chicken, running the string between the leg and the breast on both sides, then turn the chicken over and snag the string over the base of the neck so that it won't slide down the chicken's back. Knot the string securely and trim off close to the knot.

5. **The aromatics and braising liquid:** Heat the butter and oil in a large Dutch oven (a 9 $1/2$-quart oval works well) or deep flameproof roasting pan (3- to 4-inch sides) over medium-high heat. When the butter stops foaming, add the carrots, celery, onion, wing tips, neck, heart, and gizzard (discard the liver or save it for another use). Stir with a large wooden spoon to coat the vegetables in fat, and sauté until the vegetables begin to brown in spots, about 10 minutes. Add the rosemary, thyme, bay leaves, lemon zest, and salt and pepper to taste. Sauté for another minute. Pour in the wine and bring to a rapid simmer.

6. **The braise:** Set the chicken on top of the vegetables. Lay 4 strips of bacon lengthwise from head to tail over the chicken to cover the entire breast. Cut the remaining strip of bacon in half and drape one half over each leg. Gently pour the remaining 1 $1/2$ cups stock over the bacon. Once the stock begins to boil, lay a sheet of parchment paper over the chicken and tuck the edges around the chicken. Cover the pan tightly with the lid or with a sheet of heavy-duty foil. Slide the pan onto a rack in the lower part of the oven. Braise at a gentle simmer, basting every 30 to 40 minutes by spooning some of the braising liquid over the breast and legs. When you lift the lid or foil to baste, check to see that the liquid is at a slow simmer; if it appears to be simmering ferociously, reduce the oven heat by 10 or 15 degrees. Continue braising until the juices run clear when you prick the center of a thigh with a thin blade and an instant-read thermometer inserted between the thigh and the breast registers about 170 degrees, 1 $3/4$ to 2 $1/4$ hours. (You do not need to turn the chicken during braising. Since the dark meat, which takes longer than white meat to cook, sits in the liquid at the bottom of the pot, it will cook more quickly than the white meat above it. In the end, both white and dark meat are done at the same time. Another benefit of braising.)

7. **Meanwhile, heat the remaining stuffing:** When the chicken is almost done (1 $1/2$ to 2 hours into braising), put the dish of stuffing into the oven alongside it or on a rack above it to heat through, about 25 minutes.

Transfer the chicken to a sturdy baking sheet or half sheet pan and loosely cover it with foil so it doesn't cool too much. Increase the oven temperature to 475 degrees. If the dish of stuffing is heated through, remove it and set aside in a warm place. If it needs more time, leave it in the oven for a little while. Don't forget about the stuffing, however, as it will burn if left too long at 475 degrees.

8. **The sauce:** While the oven is heating, tilt the braising pan so that all the juices pool in one end, and skim off as much of the surface fat as you can with a wide metal spoon. Retrieve the bay leaves, lemon zest, wing tips, neck, heart, and gizzard with tongs and discard. Transfer the vegetables and cooking juices to a blender. With the blender lid ajar, puree until smooth (see "Pureeing Hot Liquids in a Blender," page 309). Pour the sauce into a medium saucepan and bring to a simmer over medium-high heat. Stir in the cream, if using. (The cream will round out the flavor of the sauce and impart a silky luxurious texture.)

9. **While the sauce is simmering, brown the chicken:** Slide the chicken onto a rack in the middle of the oven to roast until the bacon begins to brown, 10 to 12 minutes. At the same time, remove the foil from the dish of stuffing, and return to the oven to roast until the top becomes browned and crusty, about 10 minutes. If there's room on the oven rack for the stuffing next to the chicken, slide it onto the same rack; otherwise, put the stuffing beneath the chicken.

10. **Finish the sauce:** Taste the simmering sauce and assess its consistency. With or without the cream, it should be saucey but not too thick. If you want it a bit thicker, increase the heat and simmer vigorously to reduce. Otherwise, turn the heat to low to keep the sauce warm. Season to taste with salt and pepper.

11. **Serving:** Transfer the chicken to a carving platter. Remove the trussing string and carve into serving pieces, making sure to give everyone a few bits of crisp bacon. Scoop some stuffing onto each plate, and ladle the sauce over the top. Pass the remaining sauce at the table.

Making Schmaltz (Rendered Chicken Fat)

Large roasting chickens typically come with two or more large deposits of fat in their cavities. Rather than just tossing these out, I like to render them to make the golden, nutty-flavored chicken fat, or *schmaltz*, that I then use to sauté the vegetables for the stuffing and/or the braise—depending on how much I end up with.

Pull the large lumps of fat from the chicken and chop the fat into 1/4-inch pieces. Heat a teaspoon of extra-virgin olive oil or peanut oil in a small heavy-bottomed saucepan or skillet over low heat. Add the chicken fat and melt it slowly until it renders a clear, golden liquid fat and the small solid bits that remain turn golden brown, about 20 minutes. Strain the fat into a jar. (The crunchy little solid bits that you strain out make a nice cook's snack or can be tossed onto a salad as you would crisp bacon.) The fat will keep for weeks in the refrigerator. Since chickens vary widely in how much fat they come with, it's hard to predict the yield. A 6- to 7-pound roaster will typically provide close to 1/4 cup of rendered fat. If there's not enough for your recipe, use unsalted butter or extra-virgin olive oil to make up the remainder.

Braised Cornish Game Hens with Sage Stuffing →→

With their meaty sage-scented stuffing and rich cream sauce, these braised hens hardly need any other embellishment. But if I'm making them for a dinner party, I like to add a little something on the plate, such as a neat stack of blanched and buttered haricots verts or a tangle of lightly dressed watercress.

Cornish hens range in size from 1 pound to as much as 2 pounds. The smaller ones are perfect for a single serving, and they make a very elegant presentation. Larger hens are generally too much for one serving. When all I can find are 2-pound hens, I'll braise only two, and then split each in half with a large chef's knife or poultry shears after braising, to serve 4 people. The presentation isn't as tidy, but it's better than serving gargantuan portions to your guests.

wine notes

Earthy, medium-bodied red wine—red Burgundy, Cru Beaujolais, Chianti Classico Riserva, or Vino Nobile di Montepulciano.

Serves 4 | Braising Time: 1 hour and 10 minutes

THE STUFFING

1 thick slice slightly stale chewy white bread, such as a country loaf or rustic Italian bread, preferably not sourdough

1/4 cup whole milk

1 tablespoon unsalted butter

1/4 cup minced shallots (2 medium)

1 tablespoon chopped fresh sage

2 tablespoons chopped flat-leaf parsley

1 large egg yolk

1/2 pound ground pork, preferably not too lean

1/2 pound ground veal

Coarse salt and freshly ground black pepper

1/8 teaspoon ground allspice

Pinch of freshly grated nutmeg

1 tablespoon extra-virgin oil

2 1/2 tablespoons unsalted butter

4 small (about 1 pound each) or 2 large (about 2 pounds each) Cornish game hens

Coarse salt and freshly ground black pepper

1 cup sliced (about 1/4-inch-thick) shallots (6 to 8)

1/2 cup dry white wine or dry white vermouth

1 cup chicken stock, homemade (page 448) or store-bought

1/3 cup heavy cream

1/2 lemon

2 tablespoons chopped flat-leaf parsley

1. **Heat the oven to 325 degrees.**

2. **Soaking the bread for the stuffing:** Remove any extremely tough portions of crust from the bread (usually the bottom crust), and tear the rest of the slice into 1/2-inch pieces. You should have about 1/2 cup. Place the bread bits in a medium bowl and pour over the milk. Stir with your fingers or a small wooden spoon to moisten the bread, and let soak while you cook the shallots.

3. **The aromatics for the stuffing:** Heat the butter in a small skillet over medium heat. Add the minced shallots and cook, stirring occasionally, until softened, about 5 minutes. Stir in the sage and remove from the heat.

4. **Assembling the stuffing:** Squeeze the bread to extract the excess milk, then discard the milk, wipe out the bowl, and return the bread to it. Stir in the cooked shallots, chopped parsley, egg yolk, ground meats, 1/2 teaspoon salt, a few grinds of black pepper, the allspice, and nutmeg. Work the stuffing gently with a wooden spoon and then with your hands to mix everything together without pulverizing it. It will be quite moist and hold together loosely.

5. **Stuffing and trussing the hens:** Rinse the hens under cool water and drain. Pat dry with paper towels, inside and out. Season the hens inside and out with salt and pepper. Stuff one quarter of the stuffing into each hen. Fold the wing tips back and over the top of the hens so that they tuck neatly under the neck. You'll have to force the wing tips to bend this way, but once done, they will remain in place. With kitchen string, tie the legs together for a simple truss—this will help keep the stuffing inside the hen.

6. **Browning the hens:** Pat the hens dry again (damp poultry will stick to the pan and the skin will tear). Heat the oil and 1/2 tablespoon of the butter in a large skillet (12-inch) over medium-high heat until it shimmers. Add the hens, breast side down, and brown them, tilting the breasts first to one side and then to the other to brown both sides, then finish by turning them over to brown the back, about 10 minutes total. Large kitchen tongs or two

long wooden spoons are good tools for this browning-and-turning operation. Handle the hens carefully as you sear and turn them, trying not to tear the skin. But don't worry if the skin tears a little—they won't be quite as pretty on the plate, but this won't affect the taste at all. With tongs, transfer the birds to a 3-inch-deep roasting pan or baking dish big enough to hold them in a snug single layer. Pour off the fat from the skillet, and wipe it quickly with a damp paper towel to clear out any burnt bits. Do be sure to leave behind the caramelized drippings that are so essential to sauce building.

7.   **The aromatics and braising liquid:** Melt the remaining 2 tablespoons butter in the skillet over medium heat. Add the shallots and sauté, stirring often, just until tender, about 5 minutes. Pour in the wine, stir to scrape up the precious browned bits from the bottom, and let come to a boil. Add the stock and return to a boil. Pour the braising liquid over the birds, and cover tightly with foil.

8.   **The braise:** Slide the hens into the lower part of the oven. Braise for 30 minutes. Check that the braising liquid is simmering gently; if it is simmering aggressively, reduce the oven heat by 10 to 15 degrees. Continue braising until the juices run clear when you prick the thigh with a knife and a meat thermometer inserted deep into the stuffing reads 160 degrees, about 40 more minutes. (You don't need to turn whole poultry during braising. In fact, it helps it cook evenly, with the quicker-cooking white meat above the level of the braising liquid, where it braises more slowly. The slower-cooking dark meat submerged in the braising liquid braises a bit more quickly. In the end, both white and dark meat are done at the same time.)

9.   **Finishing the sauce:** Transfer the hens to a cutting board with a moat around the edges to catch the juices or to a large platter. Cover loosely with foil to keep warm. With a wide spoon, skim as much surface fat from the braising liquid as you have patience for. If the pan is flameproof, set it over a medium-high burner and bring the pan juices to a brisk simmer. Alternatively, scrape the juices and drippings into a wide saucepan. Boil the braising liquid to concentrate the flavor until it is the consistency of a vinaigrette and you're pleased with the intensity of flavor, 6 to 10 minutes. Add any juices that have seeped from the hens as they rested. Then add the heavy cream and simmer rapidly for another 2 to 3 minutes. Season with a healthy squeeze of lemon and the chopped parsley, and taste for salt and pepper.

10. **Serving:** If you are serving one hen per person, set one on each dinner plate and spoon some sauce over the top. For demi-portions, cut the hens in half from head to tail, cutting cleanly through the breastbone and backbone: you'll need a sturdy 10-inch chef's knife or poultry shears and a bit of determination to do this well. It's not at all difficult, but you can make a mess of the bird if you hesitate or saw away at it: If using a knife, set each hen breast side up on the cutting board, and aim to halve the bird with a swift deliberate cut

though the breastbone and backbone. If using shears, snip first though the breastbone, then turn the hen over, holding it together as best you can, and snip down the backbone. Set each half, stuffing side down on a warm dinner plate, and tuck in any stuffing that may have fallen out under the bird. Spoon over some of the sauce, and pass the remaining sauce at the table.

Braised Turkey Thighs with Onions & Buttercup Squash →→

All the goodness of Thanksgiving dinner together in one dish, but without the pressure of having to roast an entire bird and prepare countless side dishes. As the turkey thighs braise in a fragrant blend of herbs, vegetables, freshly squeezed orange juice, and stock, you prepare a colorful mix of sautéed buttercup squash and sweet onion. Once the turkey is tender, it rests while the squash and onion mixture finishes cooking in the braising liquid. In the end, you've got a handsome dish resplendent with the flavors of autumn.

Most markets now sell a selection of turkey parts, but of all the ways to buy turkey—cutlets, breast, thighs, and ground—there's no contest for the most flavorful. Even if you're not a "dark meat" person on Thanksgiving, you can't deny the moist tenderness of braised turkey thighs. And they don't get at all oily or ropy, the way they often do when roasted.

Serve with warm biscuits or soft rolls and cranberry chutney or sauce.

wine notes

As with Thanksgiving dinner, braised turkey pairs well with a wide range of wines—dry fruity whites without oak (Riesling from Germany and Alsace), dry rosés from France and California, and medium-bodied reds (Pinot Noir from California and Oregon).

Serves 4 to 6 | Braising Time: about 1 1/4 hours

THE BRAISE

1 tablespoon unsalted butter

¹/₄ pound pancetta (about 8 thin slices),
   sliced into 1-inch-wide strips

4 bone-in, skin-on turkey thighs (3 ¹/₃ to
   4 pounds total)

Coarse salt and freshly ground black
   pepper

1 medium yellow onion (about 6 ounces),
   coarsely chopped

1 medium carrot, coarsely chopped

1 celery stalk, coarsely chopped

2 large garlic cloves, peeled and smashed

Three 4-inch leafy fresh thyme sprigs

Two 6-inch leafy fresh sage sprigs

1 bay leaf

¹/₂ cup freshly squeezed orange juice

1 cup chicken stock, homemade (page 448)
   or store-bought

THE ONION-SQUASH GARNISH

Rendered pancetta fat (from Step 2)

Extra-virgin olive oil, if needed

2 large sweet onions (about 1 pound),
   such as Vidalia or Oso Sweet, coarsely
   chopped (see "Sweet Onions," page
   195)

2 large garlic cloves, minced

Coarse salt and freshly ground black
   pepper

1 tablespoon unsalted butter

1 small buttercup or butternut squash
   (about 2 pounds), peeled, seeded, and
   cut into 1-inch chunks

¹/₄ cup chopped flat-leaf parsley

2 tablespoons loosely packed chopped
   fresh sage

1. **Heat the oven to 300 degrees.**

2. **Crisping the pancetta:** Melt the butter in a large skillet or shallow braising pan (12-inch) over medium-high heat. Add the pancetta slices and sauté until crisp and brown, 8 to 10 minutes. Transfer the pancetta to a plate lined with paper towels to drain. Pour all but 1 tablespoon of the fat into a small jar or ramekin and reserve it for the onion-squash garnish. Set the pan aside.

3. **Browning the turkey:** Rinse the turkey thighs with cool water, and dry with paper towels. Season all over with salt and pepper. Return the skillet to medium-high heat and sear the thighs on both sides until they are a deep golden brown, about 6 minutes per side. Do this in two batches if necessary, so as not to crowd the skillet, and remember to dry the second batch of turkey again before adding it to the skillet, because it won't brown well if it's damp. Transfer the turkey thighs to a plate and set aside. Pour off all but 1 tablespoon of the fat, and discard it.

4. **The aromatics and braising liquid:** Return the skillet to medium-high heat. Add the onion, carrot, celery, and garlic, sprinkle lightly with salt and pepper, and toss well. Sauté

until the vegetables are browned in spots, 4 to 5 minutes. Add the thyme, sage, bay leaf, and orange juice. Deglaze the skillet by bringing the orange juice to a strong simmer and scraping the bottom of the pan with a wooden spoon to dislodge and dissolve any treasured cooked-on bits. Continue simmering until the orange juice is reduced by about half, about 2 minutes. Add the stock and bring to a simmer.

5. **The braise:** Return the turkey thighs, skin side down, to the skillet and pour in any juices from the plate. Cover with parchment paper, pressing down so that the paper nearly touches the turkey and the edges of the paper reach over the sides of the skillet. Then cover with a tight-fitting lid or a large piece of foil, and slide the skillet into the lower third of the oven. Braise at a gentle simmer for 30 minutes, checking after the first 10 or 15 minutes that the liquid is simmering peacefully. If it is not, lower the oven heat 10 to 15 degrees. After the first half hour, turn the thighs over with tongs and continue braising for another 30 to 40 minutes, or until tender and the juices run clear when you prick the thighs with a knife and a meat thermometer registers about 170 degrees.

6. **While the turkey thighs braise, prepare the garnish:** Measure the reserved pancetta fat and spoon 2 tablespoons of it into another large skillet. If there's less than 2 tablespoons, add enough olive oil to make up the difference. Heat over medium-high heat until the fat slides easily across the pan. Add the onions and garlic, sprinkle with salt and pepper, and toss the vegetables in the fat. Sauté, stirring often, until well browned, about 12 minutes. Transfer to a plate and set aside. Add the butter to the skillet and melt it. Add the squash, toss to coat with butter, and sauté, tossing often, until browned, about 10 minutes. Remove from the heat and set aside until the turkey is done.

7. **Straining the braising liquid:** When the turkey is tender, remove the thighs from the skillet and set them on a platter or a deep serving dish. Cover loosely with foil to keep warm. Strain the braising juices into a bowl or measuring cup, pressing on the vegetables to extract all the juices. Discard the vegetables. Let the juices settle for a minute or two, and skim the clear surface fat from the juices using a wide spoon. Alternatively, you can separate the fat from the juices using a gravy separator.

8. **Braising the garnish:** Return the squash to medium-high heat. Add the reserved onion-garlic mixture, toss to combine, and sauté for 2 minutes. Add the skimmed braising juices to the skillet, along with 2 tablespoons of the parsley and the sage. Stir well to combine, reduce the heat to low, cover, and cook until the squash is tender when pierced with the tip of a sharp knife, about 15 minutes. If you have trouble maintaining a gentle braise, place the skillet on a heat diffuser.

9. **The finish:** Crumble the reserved pancetta with your hands. Uncover the skillet, raise the heat to high, add the crumbled pancetta, and bring to a rapid simmer. Simmer the gar-

nish for 2 minutes to thicken it up some and meld all the flavors. Taste for salt and pepper. Spoon over the turkey thighs, sprinkle the dish with the remaining 2 tablespoons parsley, and serve.

VARIATION: BRAISED TURKEY THIGHS WITH ONIONS & APPLES

An alternative and equally delicious autumnal preparation for braised turkey thighs.

- Reduce 2 cups of apple cider to 1/2 cup and use in place of the orange juice.
- Replace the squash with 4 tart apples (about 1 1/2 pounds), quartered, peeled, cored, and cut crosswise into 1/2-inch slices. In Step 6, sauté the apple slices in 2 tablespoons butter until tender and well browned, about 7 minutes. Mix with the onions and set aside.
- Replace the sage in the braise and the garnish with fresh marjoram.
- In Step 8, add the skimmed braising juices to the onion-apple garnish, along with the 2 tablespoons of parsley, and just heat through (omit the cooking together for 15 minutes). Crumble over the pancetta and continue with the recipe.

> ## Sweet Onions
>
> Sweet onions, such as Vidalia, Oso, Walla Walla, and Texas, may look similar to ordinary onions, but they are only sold fresh, not dried and cured for long storage like everyday yellow and white onions. The season for sweet onions is generally spring and summer, but some varieties reach into the fall. If you're making this turkey recipe late in the fall or winter when sweet onions are no longer available, substitute large yellow onions. The dish will still be excellent.
>
> When shopping for sweet onions, look for firm onions without any soft spots or shriveling. Avoid those that display any signs of green sprouts or an assertive oniony smell. Fresh onions should be used within several days of buying. Unlike yellow and white onions, sweet onions are not good keepers.

Burgundian Quail Braised with Grapes ➝

During the years I worked and toured in Burgundy, I would hear stories about flocks of quail that used to inhabit the vineyards, taking shade under the leafy grapevines. Although I never actually spotted any quail, I did find much evidence of this alliance in the cooking of the region. Burgundian cooks often roast quail wrapped in grape leaves and serve them in a sauce of white wine and grapes. Some recipes for grilled quail suggest throwing dried grapevines onto the coals to add flavor to the smoke. My favorite approach to this combination is to braise quail with table grapes and a sweet dessert wine. I've had splendid results with Muscat Beaumes-de-Venise from the Côtes du Rhone region. Vin santo from Italy also works quite nicely, as do some of the late-harvest dessert wines from California. Feel free to substitute any light-bodied sweet wine you like, but avoid wines as strong as Marsala, which would eclipse the other flavors.

Restaurants usually serve two quail per person as a main course (and one as an appetizer), but I think two quail are too much for all but the most robust appetites, while one seems paltry. I split the quail after braising (not before, since they retain more juices when cooked whole) and serve one and a half per person as a main course. Besides being just the right amount, a split quail requires a bit less knife-and-fork maneuvering at the table. Very good with polenta or sautéed potatoes.

wine notes

Medium-bodied red with youthful fruit and medium tannins—red Burgundy, Cru Beaujolais, or Pinot Noir from Oregon or California.

Serves 4 | *Braising Time: about 15 minutes*

6 quail (about 5 ounces each; see "Shopping for Quail," page 198)

Coarse salt and freshly ground black pepper

3 tablespoons extra-virgin olive oil

1 tablespoon unsalted butter

1 medium shallot, finely chopped

1/4 cup finely chopped pancetta (about 1 ounce)

Generous 1 tablespoon chopped fresh thyme

3/4 cup sweet white wine, such as Muscat Beaumes-de-Venise or vin santo

1 pound green or red grapes, preferably seedless and a bit tart, such as Red Flame or Thompson (see "Shopping for Grapes," page 198)

1. **Seasoning the quail:** Rinse the quail inside and out with cool water, then dry thoroughly with paper towels. (If left damp, the quail won't brown well and the skin may stick to the pan and tear.) Season inside and out with salt and pepper.

2. **Browning the quail:** Heat the oil in a wide deep skillet or shallow braising pan (12-inch) over medium-high heat. When hot, add half the quail, setting them down on one side of the breast, and brown them, turning with tongs to brown all three sides (two sides of the breast and the back), 3 to 4 minutes per side. Be sure to let the quail cook undisturbed for the first 2 minutes on a side—the skin may stick and tear if you try to move it too soon. Set aside on a plate, without stacking, and continue with the remaining quail.

3. **The aromatics and braising liquid:** Pour off all the oil from the skillet, leaving behind any drippings or browned bits that you will use to build the flavor of the braise. Return the pan to medium heat, and add the butter. As soon as the butter melts, and before it browns, add the shallot and pancetta, stir with a wooden spoon, and sauté until the shallot is softened and the pancetta has rendered some of its fat, about 4 minutes. Add the thyme and sauté until just fragrant, about a minute. Pour in the wine, bring to a boil, and scrape the bottom of the pan to dislodge and dissolve the cooked-on bits. Add the grapes and let the liquid come to a boil once again.

4. **The braise:** Return the quail to the pan, nestling them breast side up in among the grapes. If the pan is crowded, arrange the quail so the legs overlap or intertwine. (Since the skinny legs cook more quickly than the breasts, pushing the leg ends together will actually help the quail cook evenly.) Cover, reduce the heat to a quiet simmer, and braise, checking after about 3 minutes to make sure that the liquid is simmering with an occasional quiet bubble, not a churning boil. If necessary, turn down the heat slightly, or set the pan on a heat diffuser. After 8 minutes, turn the quail with tongs, baste with the sauce, and continue to braise gently for another 7 minutes (15 minutes total). The quail should be rosy and juicy inside. Overcooking quail gives it an unpleasant livery taste. Transfer the quail to a cutting board with a moat to catch the juices or to a shallow platter.

5. **The finish:** Bring the grapes and braising liquid to a boil and cook, uncovered, to concentrate the flavors and reduce the liquid to a saucy consistency (similar to a vinaigrette), about 5 minutes. The grapes should begin to collapse but still maintain their shape. Taste

for salt and pepper. I tend to season this sauce assertively with salt and pepper to balance its sweetness: don't be timid.

Meanwhile, using clean poultry shears or a strong sharp knife, split the quail in half by cutting down through the backbone and again through the breastbone. Collect all the rosy juices that escape. Return the quail to the sauce, arranging them bone side down, and pour over the collected juices. Simmer to heat the quail through, about 3 minutes. Serve warm with the grapes and sauce spooned over the top.

Shopping for Quail

These little birds with lean dark meat and a delicate game flavor are commercially raised in many parts of the country, so they are plentiful and reasonably priced. If your local meat market doesn't carry quail, ask. They may be able to special-order them quite easily. Otherwise, consult the Sources (page 455) to mail-order.

Quail may be sold fresh or frozen, and in my experience, the quality is equal. If you do buy frozen quail, just be sure to let it defrost slowly (a day or two) in the refrigerator in its original packaging. Rushing things by thawing the quail under warm water will leach away much of its subtle taste. If you've hunted quail, or know a hunter who has shared his bounty with you, then you may have tasted *bobwhite quail*, the native American species. Most commercially raised quail is a somewhat smaller but equally delicious variety known as *coturnix*.

Shopping for Grapes

The fresh bunches of sweet green, red, and blue-black grapes sold in produce departments all over the country are called "table grapes," to distinguish them from wine grapes, which are similar varieties but grown as much for their acidity and tannin as for their sweetness. Most table grapes come from California and are available from May through January. During this long season, different varieties appear during various times, but few markets bother labeling grapes beyond the basic red or green. Flame Seedless are a sweet red grape variety available from May all the way through December, and Tudor Premium Red are a similar sweet, red seedless, variety that appears in September and lasts till December. If your market does label table grapes by variety, a few other good red ones to be on the lookout for are Ruby Seedless and crimson. As for green, try Thompson Seedless, Sugarone, or Perlette (these last two are only available in the summer).

Duck Legs Braised in Port & Dried Cherries ➻

Few things match the pleasure of slow-cooked duck legs. If you've eaten duck confit (the classic French preparation whereby duck legs are simmered in duck fat until they are entirely fall-apart-tender and unbelievably succulent), then you've a notion of what I'm talking about. But, as good as confit can be, I prefer braised duck legs both for their ease of preparation and for their taste. Whereas confit requires a vat of duck fat as a cooking medium, a braise can be made with a simple cup or two of flavorful liquid—in this case, port and a bit of stock.

Some recipes recommend two duck legs per serving. I find that one is enough, especially when using Moulard (see "Shopping for Duck," page 202). If you're concerned, you can always toss in two more legs to divide up for any-one looking for a second helping. Serve with creamy polenta or a puree of sweet winter squash, such as butternut or Delicata.

wine notes

Youthful red with concentrated fruit and medium tannins, such as recent vintages of deeply flavored Australian Shiraz or a rich California Zinfandel.

Working Ahead

Much of the flavor of this braise comes from rubbing the duck legs with a spice rub and letting them sit overnight (Step 2). The cherries should also soak overnight to plump (Step 3).

Serves 4 | Braising Time: about 2 hours

4 large Moulard duck legs, including thighs
    (about 12 ounces each; see
    "Shopping for Duck," page 202)

THE SPICE RUB

1 teaspoon coriander seeds, lightly
    toasted
	1 tablespoon chopped fresh thyme or
	    1 teaspoon dried

1/2 teaspoon black peppercorns	**1 1/2 teaspoons coarse salt**
1/2 teaspoon allspice berries	

THE BRAISE

1/2 cup (3 ounces) dried Bing cherries (with
    no sugar added)
	1 cup chicken stock, homemade (page 448)
	    or store-bought

1 cup tawny port	**Coarse salt and freshly ground black**
1 large shallot, thinly sliced	**pepper**
1 bay leaf	

1. **Trimming the duck—the day before:** Trim the duck legs of as much excess fat as you can without cutting into the skin or the meat. If you've never trimmed duck legs before, proceed slowly to avoid trimming off the skin with the fat. Unlike chicken, duck skin and fat can be hard to distinguish. After removing a maximum of fat, trim off any loose flaps of skin as well. Depending on the duck, there may be as much as 4 ounces of fat to trim off each leg. Collect the fat to render at another time and use it for sautéing potatoes or other vegetables, or discard.

2. **The spice rub:** In a small mortar or spice grinder, combine the coriander, black pepper-corns, and allspice and grind to a coarse powder. Add the thyme and salt and mix. Sprinkle this spice mixture all over the duck legs and rub so the seasonings adhere. Arrange the duck legs in a single layer in a baking dish, cover with plastic, and refrigerate overnight.

3. **Plumping the cherries—the day before:** In a small bowl, pour the port over the cher-ries. Set aside to plump overnight.

4. **Heat the oven to 325 degrees.**

5. **Browning the duck:** Pat the surface of the duck dry using paper towels, being careful not to wipe off the spices. Heat a large heavy skillet (10- to 12-inch) over medium-high heat: If you have a cast-iron skillet, this is a good place to use it. Because it holds heat so well, it sears the duck legs without having the skin stick or tear. If you don't have cast iron, choose the heaviest skillet you have. Don't worry that there's no fat in the pan; the duck legs will quickly throw off enough to get things sizzling. When the skillet is hot but not

scorching, add as many duck pieces skin-side down as will fit without crowding. Sear the duck, without disturbing, until the skin is crisp and taut, about 7 minutes. Lift one edge with tongs to peek to see that the skin is crisp before turning. Panfry the other side just until spots of brown appear, another 3 to 4 minutes. Transfer the duck to a shallow braising pan (4- to 5-quart). Pour off all the excess fat and repeat with the remaining duck legs. Pour off the fat, this time reserving 2 teaspoons in a small jar or ramekin, and remove any black specks from the skillet with a damp paper towel. Don't clean away any tasty cooked-on browned bits that will later add depth of flavor to the braising liquid.

6. **The aromatics and braising liquid:** Return the skillet to medium heat, add the reserved 2 teaspoons duck fat and the shallot, and sauté until the shallot begins to soften, 1 to 2 minutes. Add the cherries and their soaking liquid, increase the heat to medium-high, and simmer to reduce the liquid by half, about 5 minutes. Add the bay leaf and stock and reduce again by half, another 8 minutes.

7. **The braise:** Pour the reduced port-stock mixture over the duck legs. Cover with parchment paper, pressing down on the paper so it nearly touches the duck and extends over the sides of the pan by about an inch. Cover with a tight lid. Slide into the middle of the oven to braise at a gentle simmer. Lift the lid of the braising pan during the first 30 minutes to check that the liquid isn't simmering too forcefully. If it is, lower the oven temperature 10 or 15 degrees. After 1 hour, turn the duck legs with tongs. Continue braising gently until the duck is fork-tender and pulling away from the bone, another hour or so (about 2 hours total). Remove the duck from the oven, and, with tongs, arrange the legs skin side up in a single layer on a half sheet pan or broiler pan. Cover loosely with foil to keep warm. Increase the oven heat to 475 degrees.

8. **Degreasing the sauce:** Duck legs release a substantial amount of fat when braised, and if you own a gravy separator, this is a good opportunity to bring it out. Pour the braising liquid into the separator, and then pour the liquid into a medium saucepan (2-quart), leaving the clear fat behind. If you don't have a gravy separator, pour the braising liquid into the saucepan and skim the surface fat with a wide metal spoon.

9. **Reducing the sauce:** Set the saucepan over medium-high heat and simmer rapidly until reduced to a syrupy sauce, about 3 minutes. Taste for salt and pepper, and lower the heat below a simmer to keep warm.

10. **Meanwhile, crisp the duck:** Once the oven has preheated, remove the foil and slide the pan of duck legs onto a rack in the middle or upper part of the oven and roast until the skin on top is crispy and sizzling, 8 to 10 minutes. Transfer to warm plates or a handsome serving platter.

11. **Serving:** Spoon the dried cherry and port sauce over the top of the duck. Serve.

Shopping for Duck

The two types of duck most available are Pekin (or Long Island) and Moulard. The Pekin (not Peking) is a smaller, more delicate variety found in most supermarkets and sometimes labeled as duckling. Pekin ducks weigh about 5 pounds and make an excellent choice for roasting whole, but for braising, look for the larger, meatier Moulard. A French hybrid cross of female Pekin and a male Muscovy duck, Moulard ducks are the ones raised for *magrets* (their fat, deep-hued breasts), hefty legs used for confit, and, of course, the rich liver known as foie gras. Moulard ducks may not be as readily available as Pekin. If you have a specialty butcher or gourmet market, look there; otherwise you can mail-order them with little hassle. See Sources, page 455.

Duck Ragù with Pasta �>➤

This is one of my favorite ways to serve duck. By pulling the tender braised meat off the bone and adding it to the fragrant pasta sauce, I feel as if I'm coddling my guests, saving them the work of knife-and-fork eating. To me, this is comfort food.

Duck skin emerges from the braise velvety and soft, and there are a couple of options for what to do with it. The most traditional approach is to shred it with the meat and allow it to further enrich the sauce. You can also turn the soft skin into cracklings (described in Steps 10 and 11 of the recipe) to serve as a garnish to either the pasta or an accompanying salad.

My favorite dried pasta shapes for this meaty sauce are long, thin noodles, such as bigoli, bucatini, or spaghetti. If, like some people I know, you almost always prefer short tubes, penne or penne rigate are also excellent.

wine notes

Medium-bodied red with spice flavors, a touch of earthiness, and bright acidity—Chianti Riserva, Rioja Reserva, or Rioja Gran Reserva.

Working Ahead

After braising, let the duck legs cool for a bit in the braising liquid (Step 7). This leaves them cool enough to handle, but it also improves their taste as they absorb flavors from the surrounding braising liquid. You can also leave the duck legs to sit for up to 2 days in the braising liquid (covered and refrigerated) before making and serving the ragù.

Serves 4 to 5 | Braising Time: about 2 hours

4 large Moulard duck legs, including
thighs (about 12 ounces each; see
"Shopping for Duck," page 202)
Coarse salt and freshly ground black
pepper
1 tablespoon extra-virgin olive oil
1 medium yellow onion (about 6 ounces),
chopped into 1/2-inch pieces
2 carrots, sliced into 1/2-inch rounds
1 celery stalk, chopped into 1/2-inch pieces
4 garlic cloves, thinly sliced
1 1/2 tablespoons chopped fresh rosemary

1/4 teaspoon ground allspice
2/3 cup dry white wine or dry white
vermouth
3/4 cup chicken stock, homemade (page
448) or store-bought
One 14 1/2-ounce can whole peeled
tomatoes, chopped, juice reserved
2 bay leaves
Red wine vinegar to taste
1 pound dried pasta, such as bigoli,
bucatini, spaghetti, penne, or penne
rigate

1. **Trimming the duck:** Trim the duck legs of as much excess fat as you can without cutting into the skin or the meat. If you've never trimmed duck legs before, proceed slowly to avoid trimming off the skin with the fat. Unlike chicken, duck skin and fat can be hard to distinguish. After removing as much fat as you can, trim off any loose flaps of skin as well. Depending on the duck, there may be as much as 4 ounces of fat to trim off each leg. Collect the fat to render at another time to use for sautéing potatoes or other vegetables, or discard. If the surface of the duck legs is at all moist, dry with paper towels (moist meat won't brown well). Season generously all over with salt and pepper.

2. **Heat the oven to 325 degrees.**

3. **Browning the duck:** Heat a large wide braising pan (4- to 5-quart) over medium-high heat: If you have a wide cast-iron braising pot, it works especially well during the browning step, since the heavy bottom holds the heat to sear the duck effectively without having the skin stick. If you don't have cast iron, just choose a pot with a good heavy base. Don't worry about the pan scorching without any fat to start; the duck legs will quickly throw off enough to get things sizzling. When the pan is hot but not scorching, add as many duck pieces skin side down as will fit without crowding. Sear the duck until the skin is crisp and taut, about 7 minutes. Lift an edge with tongs to peek underneath to see that the skin is brown before turning with tongs. Panfry the other side just until spots of brown appear, another 3 to 4 minutes. Transfer the duck legs to a large plate or tray. Pour off the excess fat and repeat with the remaining duck legs.

4. **The aromatics:** Pour off the fat and, with a damp paper towel, wipe any charred bits from the pan, being careful to leave behind the precious caramelized drippings. Return the pan to medium heat and add the olive oil. Add the onion, carrots, and celery, and season with salt and pepper. Sauté, stirring a few times with a wooden spoon, until the vegetables

are softened and browned on the edges, 7 to 8 minutes. Add the garlic, rosemary, and all-spice, stir to combine, and sauté until fragrant, another minute.

5. **The braising liquid:** Add the white wine, bring to a simmer, and stir with a wooden spoon, scraping up any cooked-on tasty browned bits stuck to the bottom of the pan. Simmer to dissolve the browned bits and to reduce the wine by half, about 6 minutes. Pour in the stock and simmer again to reduce by half, another 6 minutes. Add the tomatoes and their juice to the pan, stir so they blend into the sauce, and let simmer for 2 to 3 minutes to meld the flavors.

6. **The braise:** Return the duck to the sauce. Tuck the bay leaves between the pieces. Cover with parchment paper, pressing down so the paper nearly touches the duck and the edges hang over the sides of the pan by about an inch. Then cover with a lid. Slide onto a rack in the middle of the oven to braise until fork-tender, about 2 hours. Lift the lid of the braising pan during the first 30 minutes to check that the liquid isn't simmering too vigorously. If it is, lower the oven temperature 10 or 15 degrees.

7. **Letting the braise rest:** Let the duck cool in the braising liquid for 20 minutes to 1 hour. (You can also refrigerate it overnight in a covered bowl or pot. If you braised the duck legs in a cast-iron pan, transfer them, along with their braising liquid to a nonreactive vessel, such as a stainless steel pot or bowl.)

8. **The sauce:** Shortly before you're ready to serve the ragù, bring a large pot of water to a boil for the pasta. Meanwhile, with tongs or your fingers, pull the duck legs from the sauce and set aside. Skim as much surface fat as you can from the sauce. (If you've chilled the braise overnight, scrape off the solidified fat with a large spoon.) I like to leave a thin layer of fat to enrich the sauce, but this is a matter of personal preference. (If you've chilled the braise in a bowl, transfer it to a large saucepan; otherwise, heat it in the braising pan.) Set the sauce over medium-low heat and bring it to a low simmer. Taste. If it seems at all thin or weak, raise the heat and simmer to concentrate its flavor. Add a generous splash of red wine vinegar, and adjust the salt and pepper to taste. I find that this sauce tastes best with a bracing amount of freshly ground black pepper. Keep warm, but not boiling away, as you ready the duck.

9. **Shredding the duck:** Tear the skin off the duck legs and reserve. Pull the duck meat from the bones and, using your fingers, shred it into bite-sized hunks. Return the meat to the sauce, stir, cover, and simmer until the sauce is quite thick and meaty, about 10 minutes. Quickly skim off any remaining surface fat. Keep warm.

10. **Meanwhile, prepare the duck skin:** Now, for the skin, you have a choice: You can either cut it into small bits and return it to the sauce with the meat or make duck cracklings. Since both options are tempting, I often do both, adding some skin to the ragù to enrich the whole sauce, then garnishing it with little crispy, crunchy cracklings.

To make duck skin cracklings: Cut the skin into ½-inch pieces. Heat a medium (large if you're using all the skin) heavy skillet (cast iron is best) over medium-high heat. Add the duck skin and fry, stirring frequently, until the skin turns crisp and renders most of its fat, 6 to 8 minutes. With a slotted spoon, transfer the cracklings to a paper towel to drain. Sprinkle with salt while still warm. You can then serve the cracklings sprinkled over the ragù as a garnish; but they are also very good on a tossed green salad; and there is no finer snack for the cook.

11. **Choose between two methods for finishing:** The method that best shows off the meat sauce, and the one you'll most often find in restaurants, is to divide the pasta among warm bowls or plates and ladle a helping of ragù on top (see photograph, between pages 306 and 307). This leaves your guests to admire the glory of the braised duck ragù and then to toss it with the pasta themselves as they eat. For the second method, you add the drained pasta to the meat sauce in the kitchen, toss them together, and then serve the pasta already sauced. This less glamorous presentation is the more traditional home-style way of serving ragù, and it has the benefit of making sure that the meat sauce is evenly distributed so that the pasta doesn't dry out. The choice is yours.

12. **The restaurant method for serving:** When the pasta water reaches a full boil, add a handful of salt (about 2 tablespoons), drop in the pasta, and boil, stirring once or twice, until al dente. Drain, reserving about 1 cup of the pasta cooking water. Divide the pasta among four or five warm pasta bowls or plates. Add a bit of the reserved pasta cooking water as needed to loosen the sauce. Ladle the sauce over the pasta, and sprinkle some cracklings over each serving, if you like. Serve immediately.

The home-style method for serving: When the pasta water reaches a full boil, add a handful of salt (about 2 tablespoons), drop in the pasta, and boil, stirring once or twice, until al dente. Drain, reserving about 1 cup of the pasta cooking water. Add the cooked pasta to the ragù in the pan, stirring so the meat sauce covers all the pasta. Add a bit of the reserved pasta cooking water as needed to loosen the sauce. Serve immediately in warm pasta bowls. Sprinkle some cracklings over each serving, if you like.

Braised Rabbit with Roasted Red Peppers & Merguez Sausage ✈

Every time I make this dish, I marvel at the play of flavors between the delicate rabbit, the sweet roasted peppers, the smoky pimentón, and the spicy sausage. In a word, this dish is spectacular, and it's one that will please even the most jaded palates.

If you're unfamiliar with merguez, it's a fresh lamb (or sometimes beef) sausage spiced with harissa, a fiery red pepper and spice paste, that originated in North Africa and then traveled to Spain and France. You can now find fresh merguez in ethnic and gourmet meat markets in most cities.

To get the most flavor, I buy whole rabbits and cut them up myself. This way I'm left with a small heap of rabbit bones that I roast and then simmer into a rich rabbit stock to use as the braising liquid. This little bit of butchery is not complicated, and I've outlined the procedure below. If, however, you're not up for the task, there are two options. Ask the butcher to cut each rabbit into 5 serving pieces (4 legs and the saddle) and to save the bones and scraps for you. Or buy 6 rabbit legs and follow the variation for shortcut braised rabbit (page 212).

wine notes

Fruity red wines from southern Spain or the southern Rhone Valley made from a Grenache blend.

Working Ahead

Although the actual braising time is little more than an hour, the rabbit stock takes about 2 hours before you begin the braise (Step 5). If you want to divide the work up over a couple of days, cut up the rabbits (Step 2) and make the stock (Step 5) a day or two in advance. You can also roast and peel the red peppers (Steps 6 & 7) ahead of time. Keep the strained stock and peeled peppers covered and refrigerated for 1 to 2 days until you're ready to make the braise. To finish, marinate the rabbits (Step 4) for 2 hours before searing and braising.

As with most braises, this dish improves when left to sit overnight after braising. Complete the recipe through Step 14, then cool, cover, and refrigerate. To serve, gently reheat the rabbit in its braising liquid in a 325-degree oven for about 20 minutes.

Serves 6 | *Braising time: about 1 hour and 10 minutes*

2 rabbits (2 ¹/₂ to 3 ¹/₂ pounds each;
    see "Shopping for Rabbit," page 213)

THE MARINADE

2 tablespoons extra-virgin olive oil

1 tablespoon sherry vinegar

1 ¹/₂ teaspoons coarse salt

¹/₂ teaspoon crushed red pepper flakes

THE STOCK

1 medium yellow onion (about 6 ounces),
    thickly sliced

1 medium carrot, thickly sliced

2 garlic cloves, unpeeled, smashed

Small handful of parsley stems

6 black peppercorns

1 bay leaf

Coarse salt

3 cups chilled chicken stock, homemade
    (page 448) or store-bought, or water,
    or as needed

THE BRAISE

2 large red bell peppers (6 to 7 ounces
    each)

3 tablespoons extra-virgin olive oil

1 medium yellow onion (about 6 ounces),
    finely chopped

1 celery stalk, finely chopped

4 garlic cloves, thinly sliced

1 teaspoon pimentón or paprika (sweet or
    hot); see "Hungarian Paprika and
    Pimentón," page 357)

1 tablespoon tomato paste

6 tablespoons dry sherry

¹/₄ cup chopped flat-leaf parsley

¹/₂ pound fresh merguez sausage, cut into
    1-inch pieces

Coarse salt and freshly ground black
    pepper

Reserved livers and kidneys

Coarse salt and freshly ground black
    pepper

2 tablespoons extra-virgin olive oil

1/4 cup dry sherry

1. **Heat the oven to 450 degrees.**

2. **Cutting up the rabbits:** Lay a rabbit on its back. Spread open the chest cavity and look
to see if the kidneys and liver are intact. (Some markets remove these innards, so you may
not always find them.) If they are attached, save them only if they are shiny and fresh looking: Gently tug out the kidneys and liver, using a sharp knife if needed to release them.
Place them in a small bowl, cover, and refrigerate. Now, pull out one of the large hind legs
to expose the spot where the leg connects to the backbone. Using a boning knife, separate
the leg from the body, cutting around the top of the leg meat so that you leave as little as
possible on the carcass. Cut down though the joint just below the hip bone, where the leg
bone meats the backbone. As you remove the leg, you will leave a long "tail" of the backbone connected to the body. Repeat with the second leg. Place the 2 hind legs in a large
stainless steel bowl.

    Pull on one front leg to extend it, and identify where the shoulder muscle rides on the
rib cage. You'll want to remove this muscle with the foreleg. With your boning knife, separate the front leg from the body by cutting between the muscle and the ribcage so that
the muscle comes away with the leg. Press back the leg to expose the joint where it connects, and cut through this joint. Repeat with the other leg. Add these to the bowl with
the hind legs.

    Turn the rabbit belly side up on the cutting board and identify the meaty portion in the
center of the carcass referred to as the saddle. Using a cleaver or heavy chef's knife, chop
above and below this saddle portion: these cuts will be just above the hips and below the
ribs. If you're having trouble getting your cleaver or knife through the backbone, use both
hands to snap the backbone; this will make cutting through it easier. Trim off the 2 thin
belly flaps that hang off the saddle, and set aside. You should now have a 3- to 4-inch-long
rectangular chunk that contains a portion of the backbone flanked by the loin on either
side. Add this to the bowl with the legs.

    With the cleaver or heavy knife, chop the remaining carcass into 2- to 3-inch chunks.
Set these aside with the belly flaps.

    Repeat with the second rabbit. You will now have 4 meaty hind legs, 4 skinny forelegs,
and 2 saddles, along with a pile of chopped-up bones and belly flaps for the stock.

3. **Roasting the bones for the stock:** Place the chopped-up carcass and belly flaps in a
lightly oiled medium roasting pan or baking dish. Slide it into the oven and roast, turning

the bones once or twice with tongs, until they are lightly browned and sizzling, 30 to 35 minutes.

4.   **While the bones roast, marinate the rabbit:** Season the rabbit pieces in the bowl with the olive oil, sherry vinegar, coarse salt, and red pepper flakes. Toss with your hands to coat. Cover and refrigerate until the stock is ready, about 2 hours.

5.   **Making the stock:** Once the bones are roasted, transfer them with tongs to a large saucepan or small stockpot. Add about 1/4 cup water to the roasting pan and scrape with a wooden spoon to deglaze any drippings. When the drippings are dissolved, pour the sea-soned water onto the bones. Add the onion, carrot, garlic, parsley stems, peppercorns, bay leaf, and a pinch of salt. Pour in enough cold stock or water to barely cover the bones. Bring to a simmer over medium heat. Regulate the heat to maintain a gentle simmer— bubbles should break on the surface of the stock regularly but it should not boil—and sim-mer until the stock has a sweet, rich flavor, about 1 1/2 hours.

Strain the stock into a medium saucepan or other heat-resistant container. Set aside.

6.   **While the stock simmers and the rabbit marinates roast the red peppers:** Set the red peppers directly on a gas burner and turn the flame to high. Roast, turning with tongs as each side chars, until all sides are blistered and charred, about 15 minutes total. (If you don't have a gas burner, roast the peppers on a hot grill or under the broiler, turning with tongs until completely blistered and charred.) Transfer the peppers to a medium bowl, cover tightly with plastic wrap, and set aside until cool enough to handle.

7.   **Peeling the peppers:** When the peppers are cool, slip off the charred skin with your fingers. Don't rinse the peppers under the faucet, because this would wash away too much flavor. If the charred skins are making a mess, hold the pepper in one hand over the sink near the running faucet, wet your other hand under the running water, and slip off the skin with your wet hand, then rinse your hand and continue. Once both peppers are peeled, slice them open, cut away the stems and remove all the seeds. Cut the peppers into 2- by 1/4-inch strips and set aside.

8.   **Heat the oven to 300 degrees.**

9.   **Searing the rabbit legs:** Once the stock and peppers are ready and the rabbit has mar-inated for 2 to 3 hours, heat 2 tablespoons of the oil in a shallow braising pan (4-quart works well) or large skillet (12-inch) over medium-high heat. Add the rabbit pieces in batches (without scraping off the marinade) so as not to crowd the pan, and sear, without disturbing, until a slick golden crust forms on the first side, 5 to 7 minutes. Using tongs, lift the edge of a piece of rabbit to check that it's well seared. Once it is, turn and sear the sec-ond side, another 6 minutes or so. Transfer the seared rabbit back to the bowl you used to marinate it.

10. **The aromatics and braising liquid:** Pour off all but a few teaspoons of fat from the pan and discard. Return the pan to medium-high heat and add the onion and celery. Sauté, stirring frequently, until the vegetables begin to soften and are tinged with brown, about 6 minutes. Add the garlic, pimentón or paprika, and tomato paste, stir, and sauté until you can smell the garlic, 1 to 2 minutes. Pour in ¼ cup of the sherry, bring to a boil, and boil until reduced to a wet paste, about 4 minutes. Add the strained rabbit stock and return to a boil. Adjust the heat to a strong simmer and reduce, stirring occasionally, until there is only about ¼ inch (or 1 cup) remaining in the pan, about 15 minutes.

11. **The braise:** Add the rabbit legs to the simmering liquid, along with half the parsley. Place the 2 saddles on top. Cover with a piece of parchment, pressing down so the paper nearly touches the rabbit and the edges of the paper hang over the edge by about an inch. Set a secure lid in place, and slide onto a rack in the middle of the oven. Braise gently, turning the legs with tongs about halfway through, until the meat is almost pulling away from the bone, about 1 hour.

12. **While the rabbit braises, prepare the sausages and peppers:** Heat the remaining 1 tablespoon of oil in a large skillet (12-inch) over medium-high heat. Add the sausage and fry, turning with tongs, until cooked and browned on all sides, about 6 minutes. Transfer to a plate. Pour off and discard the excess fat (most merguez sausage produces quite a bit). Return the skillet to medium heat. Add the pepper strips and the remaining 2 tablespoons sherry, stir, and heat for a minute or two, until the peppers begin to heat through. Return the sausage to the pan, season with salt and pepper, and stir to combine. Remove from the heat and set aside in a warm spot.

13. **Sautéing the liver and kidneys (optional):** If the rabbits come with their livers and kidneys intact, I like to sauté up these bits and serve them alongside the braise. If you've never tasted rabbit liver or kidneys, imagine them to be much like chicken liver, only a bit leaner. Before sautéing, rinse the livers and kidneys under cool water and pat dry. With a sharp paring knife, separate the livers into 3 lobes. Season the livers and kidneys with salt and pepper. Heat the olive oil in a medium skillet over high heat. Add the livers and kidneys and sear, undisturbed, until firm on the first side, about 2 minutes. Turn with a spatula and cook the second side until firm and the juices begin to run, another minute or so. You want the livers and kidneys to remain barely pink on the interior. Transfer them to a plate. Add the sherry to the pan, stir to dislodge any cooked-on bits, and reduce to a glaze, about 2 minutes. Pour over the livers and kidneys, and keep in a warm spot until ready to serve.

14. **The finish:** When the rabbit is almost tender, after about 1 hour, remove the pan from the oven and add the sausage-pepper mix. With a wooden spoon, stir gently to blend the ingredients, but be careful not to tear the tender rabbit meat. Return the parchment paper

and the lid, and slide the pan back into the oven to braise until the rabbit is fork-tender and the flavors are melded, another 10 minutes. Uncover the braise, stir in the liver and kidney, if using, and sprinkle the remaining 2 tablespoons parsley over the top.

15. **Serving:** You can either serve the rabbit family-style directly from the braising dish, or serve up individual portions. Each person should get either a hind leg or one of the saddles. Then give the forelegs to whoever has the biggest appetite.

VARIATION: SHORTCUT BRAISED RABBIT
WITH ROASTED RED PEPPERS & MERGUEZ SAUSAGE

If you don't have the 2 hours to make the rabbit stock, skip Steps 3 and 5. Use 2 cups chicken stock, homemade (page 448) or store-bought, in place of the rabbit stock, and proceed as directed.

VARIATION: BRAISED RABBIT RAGÙ
WITH ROASTED RED PEPPERS & MERGUEZ SAUSAGE

As much as I love braised rabbit on the bone, I also love to shred the meat and turn the braise into an incredibly good pasta sauce. (This is also a great way to make use of leftover braised rabbit. Adjust the amount of pasta accordingly.) Follow the recipe through Step 14, then let the rabbit cool in its braising juices. You can cover and refrigerate it for 1 to 3 days at this point.

To serve, tear the rabbit meat from the bones, and shred the meat into bite-sized pieces. Place the meat in a large skillet or saucepan and add the peppers, sausage, and braising liquid. Heat gently over low heat. Meanwhile, bring a large pot of salted water to a boil. Cook 1 ½ pounds fettuccine or pappardelle until al dente; drain, reserving about 1 cup of the pasta cooking water.

Add the cooked pasta to the rabbit sauce, tossing with tongs to coat the pasta with the meaty sauce and adding some of the reserved pasta cooking water as needed to thin the sauce. *Serves 6.*

Shopping for Rabbit

The rabbit sold in markets (or through mail-order) today is all farm raised. The fine-grained meat is pale in color—much like chicken breasts—and its taste is mild and sweet. It may be a cliché to say "it tastes like chicken," but there is an undeniable similarity between the two. To my taste, rabbit is the more delicate and elegant. Shop for a rabbit that is in the 3-pound range, what's called a fryer. Anything over 4 pounds is referred to as a roaster, and I find the individual pieces are unwieldy for serving.

Depending on where you live, you may or may not be able to find rabbit at your meat market. I've had the best luck at upscale gourmet markets. Rabbit is also available through mail-order (see Sources, page 455).

BEEF

Top Blade Steaks Smothered in Mushrooms & Onions →→

James Beard wrote that smothered steaks were a "minor classic in American food." It's my guess that he relegated them to second-class status because traditional recipes, Beard's included, called for top round steaks—a cut that becomes dry and leathery when braised and really needs to be smothered in a thick coating of gravy to make it palatable. Switching from top round to top blade transforms the dish into a major classic. Adding sweet paprika and dry sherry to the braising liquid and sweet cream to the finished sauce further elevates it. Think of these as smothered steaks with a makeover.

Equal amounts of cremini and portobello mushrooms provide a balance of savory mushroom flavor and meatiness. If you can't find portobello mushrooms (or if you just don't like their look or price), use all cremini. Or if you can't find cremini, regular button mushrooms will do. On occasion, when I find good-looking wild or specialty mushrooms at the market (such as chanterelles or oyster mushrooms), I use them in place of the portobellos to add another dimension of flavor.

These steaks are good with buttered egg noodles and something green, such as steamed green beans or sugar snap peas.

wine notes

Grenache blend from the southern Rhone Valley (Chateauneuf-du-Pape, Vaqueyras, and Lirac), or a rich Zinfandel or Shiraz.

Serves 6 | Braising Time: 1 1/4 to 1 1/2 hours

Six ³/₄- to 1-inch-thick boneless top blade steaks (about 2 ³/₄ pounds; see "Shopping for Top Blade Steaks," page 220)

Coarse salt and freshly ground black pepper

All-purpose flour for dredging (about ¹/₂ cup)

2 tablespoons unsalted butter

2 tablespoons extra-virgin olive oil

³/₄ pound cremini or button mushrooms, sliced about ¹/₄ inch thick (see "Shopping for and Handling Cremini and Portobello Mushrooms," page 221)

4 medium portobello mushrooms (about 12 ounces or ³/₄ pound), sliced about ¹/₄ inch thick (see "Shopping for and Handling Cremini and Portobello Mushrooms," page 221)

2 large yellow onions (about 1 pound total), sliced about ¹/₄ inch thick

1 tablespoon chopped fresh thyme or 1 teaspoon dried

1 ¹/₂ teaspoons sweet Hungarian paprika

¹/₂ cup plus 4 teaspoons dry sherry

¹/₄ cup heavy cream

¹/₂ lemon

2 tablespoons chopped flat-leaf parsley

1. **Dredging the steaks:** Using a meat mallet or straight rolling pin, pound the steaks to a ¹/₂-inch thickness. Season all over with salt and pepper. Put the flour in a shallow dish (a pie plate works well) and dredge half the steaks one at a time, by placing each one in the flour, turning to coat both sides, and lifting and patting lightly to shake off any excess. Set the steaks on a large plate or sheet of wax paper, without stacking.

2. **Browning the steaks:** Heat 1 tablespoon of the butter and 1 tablespoon of the oil in a large deep skillet (12-inch) over medium-high heat. Sear the dredged steaks until nicely browned on both sides but not cooked through, about 4 minutes per side. Transfer the steaks to a platter as they are browned. Dredge and brown the remaining steaks, and discard the remaining flour. If there are any burned bits of flour in the pan, wipe them out with a damp paper towel, but do your best to leave behind the precious caramelized bits that aren't scorched—these will contribute intense beefy flavor and a deep color to the braising liquid.

3. **Sautéing the mushrooms:** Add another ¹/₂ tablespoon each of butter and oil to the pan and heat over medium-high heat. When hot, add the mushrooms, season lightly with salt and pepper, and sauté, stirring occasionally, until tender and just starting to brown, 15 to 20 minutes. At first the mushrooms will throw off a good deal of liquid, then, as they sauté, the liquid will evaporate and the mushrooms will begin to brown. Transfer the mushrooms to a wide bowl.

4. **Sautéing the onions:** Return the skillet to medium-high heat and add the remaining ¹/₂ tablespoon each of butter and oil. When hot, add the onions, thyme, and paprika, season lightly with salt and pepper, and sauté, stirring, until the onions are soft and almost

translucent, about 8 minutes. Pour in the ½ cup sherry and bring to a boil. Stir to loosen any bits stuck to the bottom of the pan.

5. **The braise:** Reduce the heat to a gentle simmer, and return the mushrooms and their juices to the pan. Stir to combine. Tuck the steaks into the onion-mushroom mixture, adding any juices that have seeped from the meat. Spoon some of the mushrooms and onions over the steaks so that they are "smothered." Reduce the heat to low, cover tightly (use foil if you don't have a proper tight-fitting lid), and simmer gently until the steaks are fork-tender, 1 ¼ to 1 ½ hours. (Because the steaks are covered with mushrooms and onions, they will braise evenly and don't need to be turned over.) Check the heat periodically to see if the liquid is bubbling too vigorously, and lower the heat or set the pan on a heat diffuser if necessary to maintain a gentle simmer.

6. **The finish:** Transfer the steaks to a serving platter, leaving the mushrooms and onions in the pan. Increase the heat to a boil, add the cream, and boil until the sauce is the consistency of thick cream soup, 3 to 5 minutes. Stir in the remaining 4 teaspoons sherry, a generous squeeze of lemon, and half the chopped parsley. Taste for salt and pepper. Spoon the sauce over the steaks. Sprinkle with the remaining parsley and serve.

Shopping for Top Blade Steaks

Top blade steaks come from the chuck portion of the steer, but what few people realize is that these little beauties are surprisingly tender. Indeed, meat scientists rate top blade steaks as one of the five most tender cuts of beef. Top blade steaks do have one drawback—each steak has a thick line of gristle running down the center. When grilling or sautéing, you need to carve out this gristle either before or after cooking. When the steaks are braised, however, this tough part softens into a savory bit that enhances the flavor of the steak and doesn't distract at all from its tenderness.

Perhaps the greatest advantage of top blade steaks is their price—they go for a fraction of what we pay for fancy steaks like New York strip, rib-eye, and tenderloin. Sold boneless and sometimes labeled "flat-iron" steaks, because they resemble an old-fashioned clothes iron, they are available in most meat cases. Look for ones that are at least 3/4 inch thick. And choice- or prime-graded beef is always best.

Top Blade Steaks

Shopping for and Handling Cremini and Portobello Mushrooms

Cremini, button, and portobello mushrooms are all more or less the same variety of mushroom (*agaricus bisporus*), with variations in size and color. Cremini are basically the same as white button mushrooms, with darker nut-brown caps and a slightly meatier, denser texture. According to Elizabeth Schneider, in her authoritative reference work *Vegetables from Amaranth to Zucchini*, cremini were common in the United States up until the advent of the now-more-familiar white button mushroom in the 1920s. The portobello (also spelled portobella) is simply a mature cremini, possessing the same dense, meaty texture and pronounced mushroom taste. The latest addition to this family, marketed as "baby bellas," are mid-sized cremini.

When shopping for mushrooms, it's easiest to judge their quality if they are loose, not packed in plastic. Avoid any mushrooms with signs of softness or dampness. Look for dry, smooth caps with no signs of shriveling or peeling. The caps should feel firm and smooth when you run your finger over them. Don't be concerned about bits of dirt; these are easily brushed off. Cremini and button mushrooms should be closed on the underside of the cap, with little or no exposed gills (the slat-like ribs on the underside of the cap). Portobellos have exposed gills: check to see that they are dry and intact. Flattened or deteriorated gills indicate that the mushrooms are past their prime. Never buy presliced mushrooms. They have no flavor.

When preparing cremini, button, or portobello mushrooms, first trim away the base of each stem. (Portobello stems typically come with a lot of earth and need to be trimmed more radically than the other two types.) Then wipe the cap and remaining stem with a soft brush or slightly damp paper towel. If the dirt is especially tenacious, give the mushrooms a quick rinse, but not until just before you are ready to cook. Once rinsed, mushrooms should be cooked immediately, or they will begin to deteriorate.

The stems of cremini, button, and portobello mushrooms, once trimmed and cleaned, are very bit as good as the caps. Be sure to slice them up and include them in your recipes.

Bisteces Rancheros ✈

Shoulder Steaks Braised with Tomatoes, Potatoes & Poblano Peppers

I tend to pass by thin-cut steaks when shopping for good beefsteak, but there are a few instances where these less expensive half-inch steaks are just the thing. Layering thin-cut steaks, preferably from the chuck, in a casserole with tomatoes, onions, potatoes, and roasted poblano peppers creates a hearty braise full of flavor. Unlike many steak recipes, where the beef takes center stage with the other ingredients playing supporting roles, here all the ingredients work in concert to a deeply satisfying end.

The inspiration for this dish comes from Diana Kennedy, a leading authority on Mexican cooking. In her book *The Essential Cuisines of Mexico*, Kennedy cites these country-style steaks as a prime example of the rustic cooking of Sonora, a state in northwestern Mexico on the Gulf of California. If you own a large *cazuela*, a shallow terra-cotta baking dish, this is the time to bring it out. If not, a gratin or baking dish works just as well—as long as you're happy to put it on the dinner table and serve directly from it, family-style.

This dish is a meal unto itself and needs no accompaniment. If you crave something crisp and fresh, follow with a salad of Boston lettuce, chopped scallions, and sliced radishes.

wine notes

This dish cries out for Argentine Malbec—one of the best beef wines in the world. Chilean Cabernet or Carmenere would also work well.

These steaks taste just as good when braised a day or two ahead. After braising, let the dish cool to room temperature, cover, and refrigerate. To serve, heat, covered, on the middle rack of a 325-degree oven for about 20 minutes.

Serves 4 to 6 | *Braising Time: about 1 1/2 hours*

2 medium poblano peppers (about 8 ounces total)

2 pounds thin-cut (1/2-inch) boneless chuck or shoulder steaks, cut into 8 or 10 individual steaks

Coarse salt and freshly ground black pepper

4 tablespoons extra-virgin olive oil

1 very large or 2 medium white onions (about 12 ounces total), thinly sliced

2 large garlic cloves, minced

1 tablespoon cumin seeds, toasted and ground

1 tablespoon coriander seeds, toasted and ground

One 28-ounce can whole peeled tomatoes, with their juice

1 pound small red or white potatoes, scrubbed

2 tablespoons red wine vinegar

1. **Heat the oven to 325 degrees.**
2. **Roasting the peppers:** Set the poblano peppers directly on a gas burner and turn the flame to high. Roast, turning with tongs as each side chars, until all sides are blistered and charred, about 8 minutes total. (If you don't have a gas burner, roast the peppers on a hot grill or under the broiler, turning with tongs until completely blistered and charred.) Transfer the peppers to a medium bowl, cover with plastic wrap, and set aside until cool enough to handle.
3. **Peeling the peppers:** When the peppers are cool, slip off the charred skin with your fingers. Avoid the temptation to rinse the peppers under the faucet—doing so would wash away much of their flavor. Instead, if the job is too messy, hold the pepper in one hand over the sink near the running faucet, wet your other hand under the running water, and slip off the skin with your wet hand; rinse your hand under the water as necessary and continue. Slice the peeled peppers open, cut away the stems, and remove all the seeds. Cut the peppers into 1/4-inch-wide strips and set aside.
4. **Browning the steaks:** Season the steaks all over with salt and pepper. Heat 2 tablespoons of the oil in a large skillet (12-inch) over medium-high heat until it shimmers. Add half the steaks and cook, turning once with tongs, until they develop a ruddy brown exterior, about 3 minutes per side. Transfer the steaks to a large *cazuela* or other shallow baking

dish (3-quart) and brown the second batch. Add another tablespoon of oil to the pan and heat it until it shimmers before adding the steaks.

5. **The aromatics and braising liquid:** When all the steaks are browned, pour the oil out of the pan. If the skillet is blackened, clean it before continuing, but if there is just a chocolate-brown crust of drippings, continue with the skillet as is. Add the remaining 1 tablespoon oil and heat over medium-high heat. When the oil is hot, add the onions, season with salt and pepper, stir, and sauté until limp and beginning to brown in spots, about 6 minutes. Add the garlic, cumin, and coriander and cook for another minute. Pour the juice from the tomato can into the skillet. Then break up the whole tomatoes one at a time with one hand, holding your other hand over them to keep the juice from spraying all over the kitchen as you squeeze, and drop them into the skillet. Season with salt and pepper, stir, and simmer the juices to thicken them a bit, about 4 minutes. Taste for salt and pepper, and remove from the heat.

6. **The braise:** Slice the potatoes into ⅛-inch-thick rounds, and layer them over the steaks. Stir the vinegar into the tomato sauce and spoon it over the potatoes. Top with the strips of peppers. Cover the dish tightly with heavy-duty foil and slide it onto the middle oven rack. Braise until the steaks and potatoes are fork-tender but not falling apart, about 1 hour.

7. **The finish:** Remove the foil, increase the oven temperature to 375 degrees, and braise until the tomato sauce is brown and crusty around the edges, another 20 to 25 minutes.

8. **Serving:** Carry the dish to the table with thick pot holders, and use a large serving spoon to serve.

VARIATION: FLANK STEAK *BISTECES RANCHEROS*

For a beefier-tasting dish, substitute flank steak for the chuck or shoulder steaks. Flank has more fat, but it won't produce quite the same fork-tender results. Buy a 2-pound flank steak and lay it out flat on a large cutting surface. With a large knife, cut the steak crosswise into 8 or 10 thin slices, holding the knife at a very steep angle so you are cutting more horizontally than downward. The steaks should be about ¼ inch thick, 3 inches wide, and as long as the flank steak was wide (about 6 inches). Proceed with the recipe as directed. The steaks are done when they are tender enough to be easily pierced with a sharp paring knife, about 1 hour.

Grillades & Grits ✈

The word *grillades* translates from the French as something either grilled or broiled, but in Creole parlance, it has another meaning. Throughout Louisiana, grillades are thinly sliced beef (or sometimes veal) braised in a roux-thickened stock and presented over a heaping mound of buttered grits. I like to use bacon drippings for the roux to give the dish a slightly salty, bacony undercurrent, but regular peanut or vegetable oil will do fine if you don't save your bacon drippings. The aromatics are what's known in Louisiana as the "holy trinity"— celery, green peppers, and onions. Even if you're not a fan of green peppers (which I'm not), you'll be pleased with the sweet, almost grassy flavor that this mix lends to an otherwise dark and meaty dish. Although they are traditionally eaten for brunch, I find grillades warming and filling enough for supper.

Top round is what Louisiana cooks choose for grillades, but my first choice is boneless chuck, with its fattier, juicier taste and unquestionably more tender texture.

wine notes

A lush, fruity Australian Shiraz or California Syrah, or a young Zinfandel.

Serves 6 | *Braising Time: about 1 hour*

2 pounds boneless beef steaks (chuck or
top round), about 1/2 inch thick
Coarse salt and freshly ground black
pepper
6 tablespoons bacon drippings or peanut
or vegetable oil
3 tablespoons all-purpose flour
1 large yellow onion (about 8 ounces),
chopped into 3/8-inch pieces
1 large green bell pepper, cored, seeded,
and chopped into 3/8-inch pieces

2 celery stalks, chopped into 3/8-inch
pieces
2 garlic cloves, minced
2 teaspoons chopped fresh thyme
2 tablespoons tomato paste
1/2 teaspoon sweet Hungarian paprika
1/4 teaspoon cayenne, or to taste
1 cup beef, veal, or chicken stock,
homemade (page 450, 451, or 448) or
store-bought

Buttered Grits (recipe follows)

1. **Pounding the steaks:** Slice the steaks crosswise into 2-inch-wide strips. Season all over
with salt and pepper. Using a meat mallet or the bottom of a small heavy saucepan, pound
the strips to a 1/4-inch thickness.

2. **Browning the steaks:** Heat 3 tablespoons of the bacon drippings or oil in a large deep
heavy skillet (12-inch) or a Dutch oven (5- to 6-quart) over medium-high heat. Lift a strip of
steak with tongs and lower just the tip into the hot fat—if it doesn't sizzle immediately,
wait another 20 to 30 seconds before trying again. Once the fat is hot, add only as many
strips of steak as will fit without crowding and sear them, flipping once, until mahogany
colored in spots and around the edges, 2 to 3 minutes per side. Set aside on a large plate,
without stacking, and continue searing the remaining steaks.

3. **The roux:** Once all the steak strips are browned, reduce the heat to medium-low and
add the remaining 3 tablespoons drippings or oil to the skillet. Add the flour and stir with
a wooden spoon to make a smooth paste, what is known as a roux. Expect to see black
specks in the roux left from browning the meat; the roux itself will be dirty beige.
Continue to stir gently but continuously until the roux begins to glisten, about 5 minutes.

4. **The aromatics:** Stir in the onion, green pepper, and celery until evenly coated with the
roux. Cook, still over medium-low, stirring often, until the vegetables begin to become
limp and fragrant (you'll smell the bell pepper most), about 20 minutes. The roux will
darken from a dirty beige color to more like caramel, and the moisture released from the
vegetables will help keep it from scorching. Don't stray far from the stove, though, when
the roux and vegetables are cooking. You have to be vigilant about stirring every few minutes so that nothing sticks or scorches.

5. **The braising liquid:** Stir in the garlic, thyme, tomato paste, paprika, cayenne, and a

healthy sprinkling of salt and pepper. Cook, stirring once or twice, for another 3 minutes. Slowly pour in the stock, stirring until smooth. Increase the heat to medium and boil for a minute or two, stirring once or twice, until the sauce thickens to the consistency of gravy.

6. **The braise:** Adjust the heat to low and wait for the sauce to slow to a quiet simmer. Return the steak to the skillet, along with any juices that have pooled on the plate, stir to combine the meat with the sauce and the vegetables, and cover tightly. After about 5 minutes, check to see that the sauce is only simmering sluggishly—if it is too close to a boil, you'll wind up with tough steak. If necessary, lower the heat or place a heat diffuser beneath the the pan. Continue to braise, lifting the lid every 25 minutes or so to stir, until the steaks are fork-tender and the sauce is quite thick, about 1 hour.

7. **Meanwhile, make the grits:** During the last hour, if using stone-ground grits, or half hour for plain grits, prepare the grits.

8. **The finish:** Remove the grillades from the heat and taste for salt, pepper, and cayenne. The sauce should be piquant. Serve over the grits.

BUTTERED GRITS

There are two distinct schools on cooking grits. Purists swear by simmering them only in water. The other camp insists on cooking them in milk or milk and water. And there are those who add heavy cream to the milk as well. I favor the simmer-in-water approach because you get so much more of the natural taste of the ground corn this way.

Be sure to buy plain grits, not instant. Instant grits have been parcooked and dried, and they don't have the appealing grainy texture or real corn flavor of plain grits. If you are lucky enough to find stone-ground "country grits," they will cook up to the most satisfying texture and fullest flavor of all. (To mail-order stone-ground grits, see Sources, page 456.) Use up any stone-ground grits quickly or store them in the freezer, since, like any whole grain, they will spoil if left too long on the shelf.

Serves 4 to 6

4 cups cold water

1 teaspoon coarse salt

2 to 3 tablespoons unsalted butter

1 cup grits (not instant)

1. Combine the water, salt, and 1 tablespoon of the butter in a heavy-based 3-quart saucepan and heat over high heat. When the butter has melted and the water is boiling furiously, gradually pour in the grits in a steady stream, whisking continuously with a large whisk. Bring back to a boil and continue to boil, whisking constantly, until the grits just begin to thicken up, about 3 minutes.

2. Turn the heat down to low, cover partially, and leave the grits to simmer slowly: big, slow bubbles should rise gently to the surface without splattering. Continue to simmer, stirring frequently and scraping the bottom of the pan with the wooden spoon, until the grits take on the texture of a thick, creamy porridge and are tender when you taste them, 20 to

30 minutes. (If you are cooking stone-ground "country grits," expect them to take closer to an hour.) If the grits become difficult to stir and thicker than porridge or begin to stick to the bottom of the pan before they become tender, add a few tablespoons of water. Once they are tender, stir in the remaining 1 to 2 tablespoons butter and additional salt to taste. Serve immediately.

Beef Birds →→

Birds is a somewhat outdated term for individual rolls of thinly sliced meat wrapped around a stuffing and braised. The name comes from the French, who call these small packets *alouettes sans tête* (headless birds). If you think about their appearance—little barrel-shaped things—this graphic but whimsical name makes sense. Nowadays you're more apt to come across the term *paupiette* or *roulade* in a cookbook or on a restaurant menu, but I ate my first *bird* when I studied cooking in France in the early 1980s, and the name stuck.

The formula for beef birds is endlessly variable, and you can alter the stuffing or braising medium according to your mood, the market, and your pantry. Here I've moved celery from its usual spot behind the scenes and given it a starring role. I like the way its light, herbaceous flavor pairs with the herbed-pork stuffing. Don't be put off by the amount of dill in the recipe: it doesn't come close to overwhelming the other flavors. Indeed, it's a perfect partner for the celery and tomato. One friend who has adopted this recipe loves to crumble feta over the top just before serving the birds alongside steamed rice. I'm happy with a more classic side dish, such as mashed potatoes or a creamy potato gratin.

The recipe can be easily doubled to serve a crowd.

wine notes

Medium-bodied red with herbal flavors and moderate oak, such as Merlot from California, Chile, or Australia; or Bordeaux from the appellations of St.-Emilion, Fronsac, and Cannon Froncac.

Makes 8 rolls; serves 4 | *Braising Time: 1 to 1 ¹/4 hours*

THE FILLING

3/4 pound ground pork, preferably not too
    lean

1 large egg

2 garlic cloves, minced

2 tablespoons chopped flat-leaf parsley

2 tablespoons chopped fresh dill

1 tablespoon chopped fresh thyme or
    oregano or 1 teaspoon dried

1/2 teaspoon coarse salt

1/4 teaspoon freshly ground black pepper

1/4 teaspoon freshly grated nutmeg

8 slices beef cut from the flank or top
    round (about 1 3/4 pounds total), each
    about 4 by 5 inches and 1/4 inch thick

(see "Making Stuffed Beef Rolls,"
    page 233)

THE AROMATICS AND BRAISING LIQUID

1 to 2 tablespoons unsalted butter

1 tablespoon extra-virgin olive oil

1 large yellow onion (about 8 ounces),
    cut into 1/4-inch dice

1 carrot, halved lengthwise and cut into
    1/4-inch slices

6 celery stalks, cut into 1/4-inch slices
    (3 1/2 to 4 cups)

Coarse salt and freshly ground black
    pepper

1 cup beef, veal, or chicken stock,
    homemade (page 450, 451, or 448) or
    store-bought

1 cup canned whole peeled tomatoes,
    drained and coarsely chopped

1 bay leaf

FINISH

2 tablespoons chopped flat-leaf parsley

2 tablespoons chopped fresh dill

2 tablespoons freshly squeezed lemon
    juice, or to taste

1. **The filling:** Place the ground pork in a medium bowl. Add the egg, garlic, parsley, dill, thyme or oregano, salt, pepper, and nutmeg. Mix gently with your hands to incorporate all the ingredients, but leave the filling loose and do not compact it: overworking a meat filling can make it tough.

2. **Shaping the rolls:** Lay 2 slices of the beef on a cutting board, cover with plastic wrap, and pound with a meat mallet or the bottom of a small heavy saucepan until the slices are about 1/8 inch thick. Set the slices aside on a plate and repeat with the remaining beef. Then place 1 slice of beef on the cutting board with a short end near you. Top with one eighth of the stuffing (about 1/4 cup), placing it across the lower third of the meat slice. Starting at the short end near you, fold the meat up over the stuffing and then roll the beef up around the stuffing to form a little sausage, open on each end. Secure the roll by

tying it snugly with kitchen string in two places, but don't pull the string too tight, or you will squeeze out the filling. Snip off the ends of the string close to the knots, and place the roll on a large plate. Repeat with the remaining beef slices and stuffing, arranging the rolls in a single layer on the plate. If the birds feel at all moist to the touch, pat them dry with paper towels (wet meat will stick to the pan during the browning process).

3. **Heat the oven to 325 degrees.**

4. **Browning the meat:** Heat 1 tablespoon butter and the oil in a large lidded ovenproof skillet or shallow braising pan (12-inch) over medium-high heat. When the butter and oil are sizzling hot, add the beef rolls and cook them, turning with tongs, until they develop a spotted brown crust on all four sides, 10 to 12 minutes total. Transfer the rolls back to the plate, without stacking. If the pan looks dry, add the additional tablespoon of butter.

5. **The aromatics and braising liquid:** Add the onion, carrot, and celery to the skillet, still over medium-high heat, and toss to coat the vegetables with the butter and oil. Season with salt and pepper. Sauté, stirring once or twice, until the vegetables are browned in spots, about 5 minutes. Raise the heat to high, add the stock, tomatoes, and bay leaf, and bring to a boil. Tuck the beef rolls into the vegetables, adding any juices that have accumulated on the plate. Return the liquid to a simmer, cover with parchment paper, pressing down on the paper so that it nearly touches the rolls and the edges hang over the sides of the skillet by an inch. Set the lid in place.

6. **The braise:** Slide the pan into the lower third of the oven and braise the rolls at a gentle simmer, turning once with tongs, until the meat is fork-tender, 1 to 1 ¼ hours. Check the rolls after the first 10 minutes to see that the liquid is not simmering too energetically. If it is, lower the oven temperature 10 or 15 degrees.

7. **The finish:** Transfer the beef rolls to a platter and cover with foil to keep warm. Place the skillet over high heat and bring to a boil. Evaluate the braising juices: if they appear greasy, skim off the surface fat with a wide spoon. With a large spoon, mash any bits of stuffing that have fallen out of the birds during braising—this will add body to the finished sauce. Boil to thicken a bit and concentrate the flavors, 3 to 5 minutes. (There will be enough to generously spoon over each serving.) Remove and discard the bay leaf, if you care to. Stir in the chopped parsley and dill and lemon juice. Taste for salt, pepper, and lemon.

8. **Serving:** Snip the strings from the birds. Spoon the juices and vegetables over them and serve.

Making Stuffed Beef Rolls

Whether you call them *birds*, *braciole*, *involtini*, *paupiettes*, *roulades*, or *rouladen*, they are all thin slices of meat wrapped around a filling and braised. For making beef rolls, choose either flank steak or top round, both cuts that possess the even-grained texture and tough fiber needed to enclose a filling and hold up to a long braise. Flank generally costs more than the round and you have to be comfortable enough with a carving knife to slice this rectangular-shaped steak into eight thin slices on a sharp angled. On the upside, flank contains a bit more fat than the round, which bastes the filling during braising and produces a more succulent roll. The round, on the other hand, often comes already sliced into thin steaks (sometimes labeled "*braciole* round steaks"). If not, a single chunk of top round has no bones, seams, or weird contours, so it's as easy to carve as slicing a loaf of bread.

To cut 8 slices from a flank steak: Hold a large knife (be sure it's sharp) so it's almost parallel with your cutting board. Cut the steak at a long shallow angle to create individual pieces that are about 4 inches wide and close to 1/4 inch thick. If you think of the way presliced smoked salmon comes, this is the type of overlapping angling you're after—albeit not as exaggerated and not as thinly sliced as smoked salmon. Each slice should weigh in the 3- to 4-ounce range. If you have a scale, weigh each slice before carving off the next. That way, you can make small adjustments so you don't end up with a big chunk left over at the end. Don't be too concerned if the slices are not all evenly 1/4 inch thick. You can rectify any unevenness when you pound them out.

To cut 8 slices from a piece of top round: Shop for an evenly shaped piece of top round—the squarer the better. Set the meat upright on your cutting board so that you will carve off slices from the wider face. Imagine the top round as a compact loaf of bread, and cut off slices the way you would make slices of bread—more square than long and narrow. Aim for slices that weigh 3 to 4 ounces each, and weigh each slice before carving off another just to be sure you're in the right ballpark.

Nonna's *Braciole* ⤻
Stuffed Beef Rolls with Tomato Sauce

I learned to make *braciole* years ago from the Italian grandmother of Anthony DePalma, a student of mine at New England Culinary Institute in Essex Junction, Vermont, where I taught for nearly seven years. Anthony had kindly invited a select group of chefs and students to spend a Sunday at his family home with his *nonna*, cooking and eating. It was a day of feasting like no other, and in the seemingly unending succession of dishes, the *braciole* stood out as the one I just couldn't stop thinking about long after that remarkable visit. Anthony's *nonna* made her filling with a generous amount of dried mint, and its sweet flavor captivated me. Because fresh mint is occasionally easier to come by than dried, I've sometimes substituted fresh, which provides a brighter, slightly more pronounced mint flavor, and been very pleased with the results.

Italians serve *braciole* in two courses: as *primi* and *secondi*, starting with pasta sauced with the tomato-based braising juices, followed by the beef rolls as a main course. I admit that I don't always adhere to tradition, especially when I'm not up for a copious multicourse meal. Instead, I serve the meaty tomato braising juices directly on the *braciole*. But if you want to go all out, prepare Nonna's Feast (see the variation that follows). Anthony's *nonna* would be proud.

wine notes

Italian Sangiovese is a perfect match. In particular, look for Chianti Classico Riserva, Rosso di Montalcino, or Carmignano from Tuscany.

Makes 8 rolls; serves 4 | *Braising Time: 1 to 1 ¹/₄ hours*

¹/₄ cup golden raisins

¹/₄ cup pine nuts

1 cup fresh bread crumbs made from day-
old rustic white bread

¹/₄ pound thinly sliced prosciutto, minced
(don't trim off the fat)

¹/₄ cup freshly grated Parmigiano-
Reggiano

2 tablespoons chopped flat-leaf parsley

1 tablespoon dried mint (or 1 to 2
tablespoons finely chopped fresh)

Freshly grated nutmeg

Coarse salt and freshly ground black
pepper

8 slices beef cut from the top round or
flank (about 1 ³/₄ pounds total), each
about 4 by 5 inches and ¹/₄ inch thick

(see "Making Stuffed Beef Rolls,"
page 233)

THE AROMATICS AND BRAISING LIQUID

2 tablespoons extra-virgin olive oil

1 medium yellow onion (about 6 ounces),
coarsely chopped

1 carrot, coarsely chopped

1 teaspoon chopped fresh thyme or ¹/₂
teaspoon dried

1 small bay leaf

Coarse salt and freshly ground black
pepper

¹/₂ cup dry red wine

One 28-ounce can whole peeled tomatoes,
drained and chopped (about 2 cups)

2 tablespoons chopped flat-leaf parsley

1. **Soaking the raisins:** If the raisins are at all dry or leathery, place them in a small bowl, cover with boiling water, and soak for 10 minutes. Drain. If they are moist and plump already, omit this step.

2. **Toasting the pine nuts:** Toast the pine nuts in a small dry skillet over medium heat until lightly golden. Set aside to cool. (Toasting may not be traditional, but it gives the pine nuts a more pronounced flavor.)

3. **The filling:** Place the bread crumbs in a medium bowl. Add the raisins, pine nuts, prosciutto, Parmigiano-Reggiano, parsley, mint, a hefty pinch of nutmeg, and salt and pepper to taste. Stir the ingredients with a fork until they are evenly mixed and you've broken up any clumps of prosciutto. Set aside.

4. **Shaping the rolls:** Lay 2 slices of beef on a cutting board and pound with a meat mallet or the bottom of a small heavy saucepan until about ¹/₈ inch thick. Transfer the slices to a plate and repeat with the remaining beef. Place one slice of beef on the cutting board with a short end near you. Divide the reserved stuffing into 8 portions (about ¹/₄ cup each),

and place one portion on top of the meat slice. Spread the stuffing with your fingers to ¼ inch from the edges, and press it evenly into the meat. Starting at the short end near you, roll the slice into a little sausage, open on each end. Tie securely with kitchen string in two places, but don't pull the string too tight, or the filling will come out. Repeat with remaining beef slices and stuffing. If the rolls are at all damp, pat dry with paper towels. (Wet meat tends to stick to the pan when browning.) Arrange the rolls in a single layer on a large plate, without crowding them.

5. **Heat the oven to 325 degrees.**

6. **Browning the meat:** Heat the oil in a large lidded ovenproof skillet or shallow braising pan (12-inch) over medium-high heat. Add the rolls and sauté until browned evenly on all four sides, 10 to 12 minutes total. Transfer the rolls to the large plate, arranging them in a single layer.

7. **The aromatics and braising liquid:** Add the onion, carrot, thyme, and bay leaf to the skillet. Season with salt and pepper, toss to coat the vegetables with the oil, and sauté, stirring once or twice, until the vegetables are browned in spots, about 5 minutes. Raise the heat to high, add the red wine, and bring to a boil. Boil for 1 to 2 minutes to reduce the wine a bit. Stir in the tomatoes and return the beef rolls to the skillet, nestling them into the vegetables. Bring to a simmer, cover tightly with parchment paper, pressing down so the paper nearly touches the beef and the edges of the paper hang over the sides of the skillet by an inch. Set the lid in place.

8. **The braise:** Place the skillet in the lower third of the oven and braise at a gentle simmer, turning once, until the meat is fork-tender, 1 to 1 ¼ hours. Check the rolls after the first 10 minutes or so to see that the liquid is not simmering too vigorously. If it is, lower the oven temperature 10 or 15 degrees.

9. **The finish:** Transfer the rolls to a platter and cover with foil to keep warm. If the sauce is thin, bring to a strong simmer over medium-high heat and reduce until the consistency of a loose tomato sauce, about 3 minutes. Taste for salt and pepper. Snip the strings from the rolls. Spoon the juices over, sprinkle with the chopped parsley, and serve.

VARIATION: NONNA'S FEAST

Follow the recipe up through Step 8. During the last 20 minutes of braising, bring a large pot of salted water to a boil. When the *braciole* are done, transfer the rolls to an oven-proof platter or baking dish, and spoon over some sauce to keep the meat moist. Reduce the oven temperature to 250 degrees, cover the braciole with foil, and keep warm in the oven. Drop 1 pound of short tube-shaped pasta (such as rigatoni, cavatelli, or penne rigate) into the boiling water, stir once or twice so it doesn't stick, and boil until al dente.

While the pasta cooks, work the sauce through the coarse blade of a food mill into a deep skillet. Skim any surface grease from the sauce and season to taste with salt and pepper. Drain the pasta, reserving about 1 cup of the pasta cooking water. Toss the pasta with the tomato sauce, adding some of the reserved cooking water as necessary to thin the sauce so that it coats the pasta.

Serve the pasta in warm bowls with freshly grated Parmigiano-Reggiano on top. Follow the pasta course with the *braciole*, serving them by themselves or accompanied with Peppery Braised Broccoli Rabe with Arugula (page 51) or sautéed spinach.

Making Sense of the Terminology: Braciole *versus* Involtini

After several circuitous discussions with a few other cooks, editors, and writers about whether beef rolls should be called *braciole* or *involtini*, I consulted Nancy Harmon Jenkins, a preeminent authority on Italian cooking. Here's the real answer: In Italy, *braciole* are meat chops, such as pork or veal, and *involtini* are little stuffed rolls (or *roulades*). When Italian immigrants came to America and began making *involtini*, they made them using the meat from a boneless chop, or *braciole*. Thus Italian Americans began referring to *involtini* as *braciole*. So what's known as *involtini* in Italy became *braciole* in America.

Farsumagru →→
Rolled Flank Steak with Meat & Cheese Stuffing

Farsumagru appears in many guises all over Sicily, and thanks to the variances of the Sicilian and Italian languages, in many spellings: *falsomagro, falsumagru,* and *farsumagru.* But no matter how you spell it, the word translates literally as "false-lean," indicating a lean cut of meat filled with a fatty stuffing. As the meat braises, the rich ground meat stuffing, studded with aged cheese and cured ham, bastes it with savory juices, and the surrounding braising liquid captures the whole exchange. In the end, you've got a perfectly seasoned meat roll with its own delicious sauce.

If you're a fan of tomato sauce on meat, you can heat up a cup or so of your favorite marinara and add it to the braising liquid just before serving. A heartier dish but equally appealing.

Some cooks roll *farsumagru* around the stuffing like a jelly roll, while others fold the meat over the stuffing and sew it shut like a big wallet. I find the roll method makes the stuffed meat easier to maneuver during browning, braising, and serving.

Braised Potatoes with Garlic & Bay Leaves (page 39) and sautéed spinach would be lovely alongside.

wine notes

Youthful Grenache blend from the southern Rhone Valley (Cotes-du-Rhone Villages or Lirac), or Primitivo and Salice Salentino from southern Italy.

Serves 4 to 5 | *Braising Time: 1 1/4 to 1 1/2 hours*

1/2 cup small torn bread pieces (day-old
     rustic country bread, without crust,
     torn into 1/4-inch bits)
2 tablespoons whole milk
One 1 1/4-pound flank steak
Coarse salt and freshly ground black pepper
1/4 pound ground veal, not too lean
2 heaping tablespoons freshly grated
     Pecorino Romano
1/4 cup 1/8-inch dice provolone (about
     1 ounce), preferably sharp or aged
     over 6 months

1/4 cup minced prosciutto (1 ounce or
     2 thin slices; don't trim off the fat)
4 tablespoons chopped flat-leaf parsley
1 tablespoon capers, rinsed, drained, and
     minced
1 large egg
Freshly grated nutmeg
2 tablespoons extra-virgin olive oil
1 small yellow onion (about 4 ounces),
     thinly sliced
2 garlic cloves, peeled and smashed
2/3 cup dry white wine or dry white vermouth

1. **The bread crumbs:** In a small bowl, combine the bread pieces and the milk. Stir with a spoon or your fingers, pushing the bread down into the milk so it can soak up all the liquid. Set aside.

2. **Heat the oven to 300 degrees.**

3. **Butterflying the steak:** Lay the flank steak on a cutting board with one of the shorter sides facing you: the grain of the meat should run up and down. Trim off any large bits of fat, but don't attempt to remove every speck (some fat is essential to baste the meat as it braises). Holding a long thin sharp knife parallel to the cutting board, begin slicing into one of the long sides of the steak to open it up like a book. (If you are right-handed, begin on the right side of the steak; left side if you are a lefty.) It helps to hold your hand flat on top of the steak and to move the knife with long, sweeping slices to cut the steak almost in half (like cutting a cake into layers). Stop slicing when you get to within an inch of the other side. Fold back the top half of the steak—it should open like a book. Evaluate the two halves of the steak: if one is noticeably thicker than the other (which is often the case), repeat the butterflying technique, reversing the direction of the knife and this time working away from the centerfold out to butterfly the thicker side so that the steak opens in three leaves. (Depending on whether you're slicing into the right or left side of the "book," you may need to first rotate the steak 180 degrees.) Once again, stop within an inch of the edge. This second butterfly will be trickier, as the thinner the steak, the harder it is to avoid cutting through. If you don't feel that your knife skills are up to it, just leave the steak in two somewhat uneven leaves; it will be fine. Using a meat mallet or the bottom of a small heavy saucepan, pound the steak to even out the thickness. Concentrate the pounding on the center seam(s), where you opened the steak. Season the cut side with salt and pepper and set aside.

4. **The filling:** In a medium bowl, combine the ground veal, Pecorino Romano, provolone,

prosciutto, parsley, capers, and egg. Break up the milk-soaked bread with your fingers, and add it, with any remaining milk, to the meat. Season with salt, pepper, and a healthy pinch of nutmeg. Work the stuffing gently with your fingertips to combine all the ingredients without pulverizing the meat; overworking the stuffing will make it tough.

5. **Shaping the roll:** With your hands, spread the stuffing out over the meat in an even layer, leaving clear about 1 inch along one of the short sides of the meat and 1/2 inch along the two long sides. (Leaving these three borders clear helps prevent the stuffing from squeezing out as you roll up the steak.) Wash and dry your hands, and, starting at the short end with the stuffing all the way up to the edge, roll up the steak to enclose the stuffing. You should have a neat, cylindrical roast. Using kitchen string, tie the roll with secure loops every 2 inches. Be sure that the loops of string are snug but not so tight as to squeeze out the filling. Then finish with one long loop that goes from end to end and weaves in and out of the crosswise loops. (For more detail, see "Tying a Roast Before Braising," page 258.) Dry the outside of the roll with paper towels, and season all over with salt and pepper.

6. **Browning the meat:** Heat the oil in a large Dutch oven or other braising pot (a 10- to 12-inch-long oval pot works best) over medium heat. When the oil is shimmering, lower in the rolled flank steak. Sear on all sides, turning with tongs, until a burnished chestnut brown, about 15 minutes total. When you turn the roll to brown the last side, add the onion and garlic cloves so they sizzle in the oil for a few minutes but do not brown.

7. **The braise:** Pour in the wine and let it come to a simmer. Cover the pot with parchment paper, pressing down so that the paper almost touches the beef and the edges of the paper hang over the sides. Secure the lid, and slide the pot into the lower third of the oven. Braise at a gentle simmer, turning once after 35 minutes, until the meat is fork-tender, 1 1/4 to 1 1/2 hours. Check the pot after about the first 10 minutes to make sure that the liquid is not simmering too vigorously. If it is, lower the oven temperature 10 to 15 degrees.

8. **The finish:** Lift the roll from the braising liquid with tongs, supporting it carefully with a long spatula, and set on a shallow platter to catch the juices. Cover with foil to keep warm. Skim any surface fat from the braising liquid, and taste. If the liquid tastes a bit thin or weak, boil it over medium-high heat for about 5 minutes to concentrate the flavor. With a wooden spoon, smash the garlic cloves so they disintegrate into the liquid. Taste again for salt and pepper. Pour any juices that have seeped from the roll back into the pot.

9. **Serving:** Snip the strings from the meat. Carve into 1/2-inch slices, spoon the braising liquid over the top, and serve.

Red Wine–Braised Short Ribs with Rosemary & Porcini

Red wine, tomatoes, and mushrooms are a classic trio for braising beef, and there's no cut more suited to this treatment than beefy short ribs. If you're not already a short-rib fanatic, this would be a good place to begin. Even though I don't usually subscribe to long marinades (I find them less effective than spice rubs at adding flavor), this is one instance where the marinade makes a real flavor contribution. There's something wonderfully satisfying about the way the spice-infused red wine permeates the beefy ribs and provides a backdrop for thc earthy porcini mushrooms and fresh piney taste of rosemary.

I first made these ribs with a lush Barolo wine and, not surprisingly, the results were exquisite. I'm not, however, always feeling up to pouring a full bottle of high-priced wine into the braising pot, but, fortunately, I've since had excellent results with several lesser wines. Look for a big red that can hold its own but without too much tannin or bitterness. Good choices are Syrah, Shiraz, Zinfandel, and a Rhone blend.

Polenta or mashed potatoes flecked with fresh chopped parsley would be a fine accompaniment.

wine notes

Red wine with intense fruit, savory herb flavors, and bright acidity—Italian Barbera or Nebbiolo-based wine from the Piedmontese appellations of Gattinara, Ghemme, and Barbaresco.

Working Ahead

The ribs need to marinate for 12 to 24 hours, so be sure to allow time for this (Steps 1 and 2). In addition, the flavor of short ribs improves if they are braised 1 to 2 days before you serve them. Complete the recipe through Step 6, and after braising, let the ribs cool to room temperature in their braising liquid. Once they are cool, transfer the ribs and sauce to a glass or other nonreactive container, cover tightly, and refrigerate. To serve, scrape almost all of the solidified fat from the surface of the sauce. Arrange the ribs in a shallow baking dish, along with the sauce; discard the spice sack. Cover the ribs with foil and bake in the center of a 375-degree oven for 15 minutes. Remove the foil, taste the sauce for salt and pepper, and baste the ribs with the sauce. Place back in the oven, uncovered, to heat for another 10 minutes before serving.

Serves 6 | Braising Time: 2 ¹/₂ to 3 hours

THE MARINADE

2 bay leaves

¹/₄ teaspoon allspice berries, coarsely crushed in a mortar or with the side of a large knife

8 to 10 black peppercorns

3 to 4 whole cloves

2 tablespoons extra-virgin olive oil

1 large yellow onion (about 8 ounces), coarsely chopped

1 celery stalk, coarsely chopped

1 carrot, coarsely chopped

2 garlic cloves, peeled and smashed

1 ¹/₂ teaspoons coarse salt

1 bottle robust dry red wine

3 ¹/₂ to 4 pounds meaty beef short ribs (see "Shopping for Beef Short Ribs," page 245)

Coarse salt and freshly ground black pepper

THE AROMATICS AND BRAISING LIQUID

¹/₂ ounce dried porcini mushrooms

³/₄ cup warm water

3 tablespoons extra-virgin olive oil

Coarse salt and freshly ground black pepper

1 large yellow onion (about 8 ounces), thinly sliced

2 garlic cloves, minced

One 14 ¹/₂-ounce can whole peeled tomatoes, seeded and chopped, juice reserved, or 1 pound ripe plum tomatoes, peeled, seeded, and chopped, with their juice

Two 3- to 4-inch leafy fresh rosemary sprigs

1. **Preparing the marinade—12 to 24 hours before braising:** Cut a small square of cheesecloth (about 5 by 5 inches). Place the bay leaves, allspice, peppercorns, and cloves in the center of the square, bring the corners up, and tie the cheesecloth with kitchen string to make a small sack. Set aside.

Heat the oil in a large skillet (12-inch) over medium heat. Add the onion, celery, carrot, and garlic and sauté, stirring once or twice, until beginning to soften but not brown, about 7 minutes. Pour in the wine, add the spice sack, and bring to a boil. Reduce the heat and simmer for 10 minutes to draw the flavors of the aromatics and vegetables into the wine. Set aside to cool to room temperature.

2. **Trimming and marinating the short ribs:** Trim away any thick layers of surface fat from the short ribs, but don't remove the silverskin or tough-looking tissue that hold the ribs together. (There's plenty of fat marbled into the beef to baste the ribs as they cook.) Place the ribs in a large wide bowl or baking dish, season with the salt, and pour over the cooled marinade. Rearrange the ribs if necessary so that the marinade covers them. Cover with plastic wrap and refrigerate for 12 to 24 hours, turning the ribs once or twice so they marinate evenly.

3. **Just before the plan to braise, soak the mushrooms:** Place the dried mushrooms in a small bowl and pour over the warm water. Set aside to soak for 20 to 30 minutes.

4. **Browning the short ribs:** Remove the ribs from the marinade and pat them dry with paper towels. Strain the marinade into a bowl. Reserve the wine and spice sachet and discard the vegetables. The ribs will have absorbed a good deal of the wine, so don't be surprised if there's not much more than 1 cup of the marinade.

Pour 2 tablespoons of the oil into a Dutch oven or other heavy braising pot (4- to 6-quart) wide enough to accommodate the short ribs in a crowded single layer and heat over medium heat. Make sure the ribs are completely dry, and season them all over with salt and pepper. Add only as many ribs as will fit without crowding and sear them, turning with tongs, until deeply browned on all sides, 4 to 5 minutes per side. Set aside on a large plate or tray, without stacking, and finish browning the remaining ribs. Set the pot aside. (The ribs may also be browned under the broiler. See directions on page 244.)

5. **Heat the oven to 325 degrees.**

6. **Draining the mushrooms:** Lift the softened mushrooms from the soaking liquid with your hands and, holding the mushrooms above the soaking liquid, squeeze gently to wring out any excess moisture. Set the mushrooms on a cutting board, and reserve the soaking liquid. Coarsely chop the mushrooms, and set aside. Strain the soaking liquid though a triple layer of cheesecloth or a coffee filter to catch any sand or grit. Reserve the liquid.

7. **The aromatics and braising liquid:** Pour off and discard any remaining fat from the braising pot. If there are lots of charred bits on the bottom, wipe these out with a damp paper towel, leaving behind any unburnt drippings. If there is a rich browned crust, leave it. The brown drippings and crust will contribute enormous flavor to the sauce. Add the remaining tablespoon of oil and heat over medium heat. Add the sliced onion and sauté, stirring, until browned and softened, 8 to 10 minutes. Add the garlic, tomatoes with their juice, and the chopped mushrooms and sauté for a few minutes, stirring once or

twice. Pour in the reserved mushroom soaking liquid and wine and bring to a boil. Let the liquid boil until it is reduced by about half, 2 to 3 minutes.

8. **The braise:** Return the short ribs to the pot, along with any juices. Tuck the reserved spice sack and the rosemary sprigs in between the ribs. Cover the pot with parchment paper, pressing down on the paper so it nearly touches the ribs and so the paper hangs over the sides by an inch. Set the lid in place, then slide the pot onto a rack in the lower third of the oven. Braise gently, turning the ribs with tongs so as not to tear up the meat every 40 to 45 minutes, until the meat is fork-tender and falling away from the bones, 2 1/2 to 3 hours. After the first 20 minutes, remove the lid and check to see that the liquid isn't simmering too furiously. If it is, lower the oven heat 10 or 15 degrees.

9. **The finish:** Transfer the ribs to a serving platter and loosely cover with foil to keep warm. Discard the spice sack. To degrease the braising liquid, either pour it into a gravy separator and then pour the liquid into a medium saucepan, leaving the fat behind, or simply tilt the braising pan and skim the fat off with a large spoon. The liquid should be the consistency of a thick vinaigrette. Heat the sauce to a simmer over medium-high heat, and taste for salt and pepper.

10. Serving: Transfer the ribs to dinner plates—the number depends on the size of the ribs and the size of your guests' appetites. Spoon the sauce over and serve immediately.

BROWNING THE SHORT RIBS UNDER A BROILER

Another way to sear the ribs is to brown them under the broiler. This avoids the splatter of grease onto the top of the stove, the walls, and the floor that you get when searing on the top of the stove.

In place of Step 4, preheat the broiler on high and adjust the oven rack so that it sits about 6 inches from the flames or heating element. Arrange the ribs 1 to 2 inches apart on a rimmed baking sheet (a half sheet pan) or broiler pan, and slide them under the broiler. Broil, turning with tongs as each side browns, until sizzling and chestnut brown on all sides, about 5 minutes per side. Transfer the ribs to a platter, without stacking them. Pour off and discard the grease left in the pan, and deglaze to capture any precious caramelized beef drippings: Set the pan over medium-high heat, add about 1/4 cup of red wine, stock, or water, and bring to a boil, stirring with a wooden spoon to scrape up and dissolve the drippings. Reserve this liquid.

Proceed with Step 5, chopping the mushrooms and straining their liquid. Then heat 1 tablespoon of the oil (you will only need 2 tablespoons oil, not the 3 specified, if using this method) in a large Dutch oven or other heavy braising pot (5- to 6-quart) over medium heat. Add the sliced onion and sauté as directed in Step 7. Then continue with Step 7, adding the deglazing liquid from the broiler pan along with the short ribs, and proceed with the recipe.

Shopping for Beef Short Ribs

Beef short ribs make a superb choice for braising because their high ratio of connective tissue to well-marbled beef translates into exquisitely tender meat with a velvety sauce. The compact size of short ribs also makes them easy to maneuver while cooking and very handy to serve.

Short ribs are sawed-off segments of meaty rib ends from the hard-working chest and front shoulders of the steer. Understanding exactly what cut short ribs represent can be confusing, because they can come from a number of places (plate, chuck, or rib), and many meat departments don't bother to differentiate. Some short-rib enthusiasts claim

**English-Style
Short Ribs**

**Flanken-Style
Short Ribs**

(continued on next page)

noticeable differences between the three types, asserting that short ribs from the plate have the most gristle and fat, those from the rib are too tender and not tasty enough, and those from the chuck have the best combination of taste and tenderness. Personally, I'm happy with most short ribs, but if given a choice, I would choose those from the chuck (also referred to as the arm), because they have the best ratio of meat to bone. All you really need to know is that they are tasty and ideal for braising.

Beef short ribs are generally a good value, although I have noticed lately that as more and more cooks discover their goodness, the price has risen some. When shopping for short ribs, look for ribs with the most meat and least surface fat. While you'll never find a completely lean short rib—nor would you want to—you'll get a better yield with leaner ribs. In my experience, boneless short ribs are inferior to bone-in, for the simple reason that meat cooked on the bone tastes best. In addition, with boneless short ribs you lose much of the connective tissue that holds the meat to the bone and contributes body to the sauce. Short ribs are cut two ways: individual lengths (in the range of 2 1/2 to 4 inches long) of meaty rib bones, called English-style, or strips that connect a number of shorter segments of rib bone, called flanken-style. Where I shop in Vermont, English-style are all that's available, so that's what I use. But given the chance, I'm just as happy with the longer strips of flanken-style ribs.

Beef short ribs should not be confused with back ribs or beef spareribs. These two cuts (one from the back and one from the belly) are what are referred to in the trade as *scalped* ribs, meaning nearly all the meat has been stripped from the bone and there's little left to eat.

Short Ribs Braised in Porter Ale with Maple-Rosemary Glaze ⇥

Ale-braised short ribs are thoroughly satisfying on their own, but finishing them with a rosemary-infused maple glaze makes them special enough for even your best company. To make things easy, they can be made ahead and briefly reheated and glazed under the broiler just before serving. Their flavor actually improves as they sit for a day or two in the refrigerator.

For the braise, I use a local porter ale from Otter Creek Brewery in Middlebury, Vermont, because it's robust and smooth but not too strong or too bitter. Select an ale with some body and a smoky taste—all the better if you can find one that's brewed locally. Stout will be too strong. The bit of horseradish in the maple glaze adds piquancy to balance the other elements in the dish.

Roasted beets would be a good choice with these ribs. If you can find golden beets, they look especially stunning next to the glistening ribs (see photograph, between pages 306 and 307).

beer and wine notes

Rich dark beer, such as Anchor Steam Porter or Guiness Stout; or try an intensely flavored red wine, such as an old-vine Zinfandel from Sonoma County or a concentrated Australian Shiraz.

Working Ahead

If you have the time and forethought, beef short ribs benefit greatly from advance salting (see Step 2). This mini-cure will tighten the meat a bit, improving its texture, help it to brown more readily in the first step of the braise, and deepen its hearty taste. If there's no time for advance salting, simply skip Step 2 below, seasoning with a bit of salt along with the black pepper as directed.

If you braise the short ribs ahead of time (from a few hours to a full two days) and then glaze them just before serving, the dish will taste even better. The flavors meld and develop as the ribs sit. Simply complete the recipe through Step 9 up to 2 days before you plan to serve them. Pour the strained and reduced braising liquid over the ribs, let cool, cover, and refrigerate. To serve, reheat, covered with foil, in a 350-degree oven until just heated through, about 25 minutes. Remove from the oven, and heat the broiler. Brush on the glaze and proceed as directed in Step 10.

Serves 6 | Braising Time: 2 1/2 to 3 hours

3 1/2 to 4 pounds meaty bone-in short ribs (see "Shopping for Beef Short Ribs," page 245)

Coarse salt

Freshly ground black pepper

2 tablespoons extra-virgin olive oil

2 large yellow onions (about 1 pound total), sliced about 1/2 inch thick

1 carrot, chopped into 1/2-inch pieces

1 1/2 cups porter ale, or more if needed

3/4 cup beef, veal, or chicken stock, homemade (page 450, 451, or 448) or store-bought, or water

One 3- to 4-inch leafy fresh rosemary sprig

1 large or 2 small bay leaves

THE GLAZE

3 tablespoons pure maple syrup

Two 3- to 4-inch leafy fresh rosemary sprigs

1 tablespoon prepared horseradish

1. **Trimming the ribs:** Trim any excess fat from the short ribs, but don't take off any of the silverskin or tough-looking bits that hold the ribs together.

2. **Salting the ribs—1 or 2 days before braising (optional):** Arrange the short ribs in a loose layer on a tray or in a nonreactive dish. Sprinkle them all over with 1 1/2 to 2 teaspoons salt (there's no need to rub the salt into the meat) and cover loosely with waxed paper or plastic wrap. Refrigerate for 1 to 2 days.

3. **Heat the oven to 300 degrees:** Pat the ribs dry with a paper towel, but don't try to rub off the salt. Season with pepper. (If you didn't salt the ribs in advance, season them with both salt and pepper.)

4. **Browning the ribs:** Pour the oil into a Dutch oven or other heavy braising pot (4- to 6-quart) wide enough to accommodate the short ribs in a crowded single layer and heat over medium heat. Add only as many ribs as will fit without touching, and brown them, turning with tongs, until chestnut-brown on all sides, about 4 minutes per side. Transfer

the seared ribs to a platter, without stacking, and continue until all the ribs are browned. (*Alternatively, you may want to brown the ribs under the broiler to avoid some of the spatter, although this will mean dirtying another pan. See directions on page 250.*)

5.   **The aromatics:** Pour off and discard all but about a tablespoon of fat from the pot. If there are any charred bits in the pot, wipe them out with a damp paper towel, being careful not to remove the precious caramelized drippings. Return the pot to medium-high heat and add the onions and carrot. Season with salt and pepper and sauté, stirring a few times, until the vegetables start to brown and soften, about 5 minutes.

6.   **The braising liquid:** Add the ale and bring to a full boil. Boil for 2 minutes, scraping the bottom of the pot with a wooden spoon to dislodge and dissolve any tasty bits cooked onto it. Pour in the stock, bring again to a boil, and reduce the heat to a simmer. Return the ribs to the pot, along with any juices released as they sat. Tuck the rosemary sprig and bay leaves in between the ribs. The ribs should be partially submerged in the liquid. If necessary, add a bit more ale or water.

7.   **The braise:** Cover with a sheet of parchment paper, pressing down so that it nearly touches the ribs and hangs over the edges of the pot by about an inch. Set the lid securely in place. Slide the pot into the oven and braise at a gentle simmer, turning the ribs with tongs so as not to tear up the meat, every 40 to 45 minutes, until fork-tender, about 2 1/2 hours. Check under the lid after the first 10 minutes to see that the liquid isn't simmering too aggressively; if it is, lower the oven temperature 10 or 15 degrees.

8.   **Meanwhile, prepare the glaze:** While the ribs are braising, combine the maple syrup with the rosemary sprigs in a small saucepan. Heat to a gentle boil over medium heat. Turn off the heat, cover, and set aside to infuse for 1 hour. (*The glaze can be made up to a few days ahead and refrigerated.*)

9.   **Removing the ribs from the braising liquid:** When the ribs are tender and the meat is pulling away from the bones, use tongs or a slotted spoon to carefully transfer them to a flameproof gratin dish or shallow baking dish that is large enough to accommodate them in a single layer. Try your best to keep the ribs on the bones and intact, but don't worry if some bones slip out. (Discard these clean bones, or save them for the dog.) Scoop out the vegetables with a slotted spoon and arrange them around the ribs. Cover loosely with foil to keep warm.

10. **Finishing the braising liquid:** Tilt the braising pot to collect the juices in one end and skim off as much surface fat as you can with a large spoon. If there is more fat than you care to skim off a spoonful at a time, transfer the braising liquid to a gravy separator and then pour the liquid into a medium saucepan leaving the fat behind. If the braising liquid exceeds 1/2 cup, bring it to a vigorous simmer over medium-high heat and cook it down to

close to ½ cup, 10 to 15 minutes; it should have a syrupy consistency. Taste and season with salt and pepper. Keep warm.

11. Glazing the short ribs: Heat the broiler on high. If the glaze has been refrigerated, warm it slightly so that it's pourable. Remove the rosemary sprigs, lightly running your fingers down the length of the sprigs so you save every drop of glaze. Put the horseradish in a small strainer (a tea strainer works great) or in the palm of your hand and press or squeeze over the sink to eliminate as much liquid as possible, then stir the horseradish into the glaze. Brush the glaze on the tops of the short ribs. Pour the reduced braising liquid around the ribs—*don't pour it over the ribs, or you'll wash off the glaze.* Slide the ribs under the broiler and broil until the surface of the ribs develops a shiny, almost caramelized glaze and you can hear them sizzle, about 4 minutes.

12. Serving: Transfer the ribs to serving plates—the number per serving depends on the size of the ribs. Spoon the braising liquid around, not over, the ribs, and serve immediately.

BROWNING THE SHORT RIBS UNDER A BROILER

You can also sear the ribs under the broiler, not in the braising pan on top of the stove. In place of Step 4, preheat the broiler on high and adjust the oven rack so that it sits about 6 inches from the flames or heating element. Arrange the ribs 1 to 2 inches apart on a rimmed baking sheet (a half sheet pan) or broiler pan, and slide them under the broiler. Broil, turning with tongs as each side browns, until sizzling and chestnut brown on all sides, about 5 minutes per side. Transfer the ribs to a platter, without stacking. Pour off and discard the grease remaining in the pan, and deglaze to capture any precious caramelized beef drippings: Set the pan over medium-high heat, add a small amount of ale, stock, or water, and bring to a boil, stirring with a wooden spoon to scrape up and dissolve the drippings. Reserve this liquid.

Heat 1 tablespoon oil (you will only need 1 tablespoon in all if using this method) in a medium Dutch oven or other heavy braising pot (4-quart) over medium-high heat. Add the onion and carrot to the pot and continue with Step 5 as directed above. In Step 6, add the deglazing liquid from the broiler pan, along with any meat juices, when you add the short ribs.

Yankee Pot Roast Redux ✈

In James Beard's definitive *American Cookery*, he explains that Yankee pot roast came into our repertoire by way of the French settlers in Maine and New Hampshire. Modeled after the succulent slow-cooked *daube* and *boeuf à la mode* of French regional kitchens, pot roast was an economical and sensible way to make tough cuts of beef taste good. Yet despite this rather promising pedigree, Yankee pot roast too often calls up dreary images of dried-out slices of overcooked beef and a tasteless wash of vegetables—the sort of home-style cooking that may be nourishing but is certainly not pleasurable.

Having settled in New England myself in the 1980s, I set about to re-create the original Yankee pot roast, as tender and moist as any good braise. The first step is to buy the right cut of beef (see "Shopping for Pot Roast," page 254), preferably from the chuck. Then it's a matter of braising gently and slowly and not letting the meat cook longer than it takes to become fork-tender. And adding the vegetables only during the last hour and a half of braising to ensure that they will not become mushy. This two-step technique also means that you can get the pot roast into the oven rather quickly, then work on peeling and trimming the vegetables as the meat braises—something an efficient-minded Yankee would applaud. The final result is the ultimate one-dish meal, with tempting meat and vegetables all in one pot.

Since pot roast is best appreciated as a cold-weather meal, I choose a mix of available winter root vegetables, such as turnips, carrots, and small potatoes. Other hearty members of this tribe, such as parsnips, celery root, rutabaga, or small onions, would also be good. If you want to nudge this dish toward springtime, include a few tender spring vegetables like peas or green beans. Just be sure not to add them until the last twenty minutes of braising so that they don't overcook.

I use hard cider to deglaze the braising pan after browning the meat because I like the sharp brace of acidity and touch of fruit it imparts to the sauce. Plus it's such a classic New England ingredient that it just feels right. Unfortunately, hard cider can be hard to find in other parts of the country. In that case, substitute a crisp white wine with acidity and fruit, such as a Sauvignon Blanc. The pot roast will still be incredibly good.

The final touch here of passing *fleur de sel* or coarse sea salt to sprinkle on the braised beef at the table reaches back to the French origins of the dish. Coarse sea salt traditionally accompanies pot-au-feu (the classic French boiled beef), not pot roast, but I've found that the salt has a magical way of sparking the flavor of most any mildly seasoned and gently cooked meat.

wine notes

Cabernet Sauvignon from California, Chile, or Australia is a sure bet with pot roast, especially a bottle with a few years of age.

Serves 6 | Braising Time: about 3 hours

One 3 1/2- to 4-pound boneless beef chuck roast or 4- to 4 1/2 bone-in beef chuck roast (see "Shopping for Pot Roast," page 254)

Coarse salt and freshly ground black pepper

1 bay leaf

1 medium yellow onion (about 6 ounces), peeled

3 whole cloves

1/4 cup hard cider or dry white wine

1 cup beef, veal, or chicken stock, homemade (page 450, 451, or 448) or store-bought, or water

1 1/2 teaspoons chopped fresh thyme or 1/2 teaspoon dried

1/2 pound small turnips, peeled and quartered

1/2 pound small white or red potatoes, peeled and, if larger than 1 1/2 inches, cut into halves or quarters

2 large carrots, peeled and cut into 1 1/2-inch lengths

Fleur de sel or coarse sea salt for serving (optional)

1. **Tying the meat:** Tie the roast with kitchen string so that it is snug and neat (for instructions, see "Tying a Roast Before Braising," page 258). Season all over with salt and plenty of pepper and place in a shallow baking pan (2- to 3-quart).

2. **Browning the meat:** Heat the broiler to high. Slide the roast under the broiler so that the surface is about 6 inches away from the element. Broil until the fat begins to sizzle and the surface begins to caramelize but not char, about 5 minutes. Turn with tongs and broil on the other side (or sides , depending on the shape of the roast) for another 5 minutes (each). Remove the roast from the broiler, and heat the oven to 300 degrees. (Alternatively, you can brown the roast in the braising pan according to the instructions on page 254.)

With tongs, transfer the seared roast to a Dutch oven or other heavy lidded braising pan (4-quart capacity). Tack the bay leaf to the onion using the cloves and tuck it into the pot alongside the beef.

3. **The braising liquid:** Pour off any excess fat from the pan you used to brown the beef and set over medium-high heat. Add the cider or wine and bring to a boil, scraping the bottom with a wooden spoon to dissolve any precious bits of caramelized beef juices that have stuck there. Continue to boil until the liquid is reduced by half, 3 to 4 minutes. Add the stock and let it come to a boil. Pour the boiling liquid over the beef and sprinkle with the thyme.

4. **The braise:** Cover the roast with parchment paper, pressing down so that the paper almost touches the meat and the edges extend about an inch over the sides of the pot. Then set the lid in place and slide the pot into the lower third of the oven to braise. Check to see that the liquid isn't simmering too fiercely after the first 10 to 15 minutes. If it is, lower the oven temperature 10 or 15 degrees. After 45 minutes, turn the roast with tongs. Continue braising at a gentle simmer for another 45 minutes.

Turn the roast again, and add the turnips, potatoes, and carrots to the pot, spooning some of the braising liquid over the meat before returning the parchment paper and lid. Continue braising until the meat is fork-tender and the vegetables are easily pierced with the tip of a knife, another 1 1/2 hours or so (for a total of about 3 hours).

5. **The finish:** Transfer the roast to a carving board or serving platter. With a slotted spoon, remove the vegetables and arrange them around the meat (discard the clove-studded onion). Cover loosely with foil to keep warm. Set the Dutch oven over medium heat, and skim the surface fat from the braising liquid as it comes to a simmer. Evaluate the braising liquid: if it appears too thin or watery, boil the liquid to reduce the volume and thicken up slightly, about 10 minutes. It should be the consistency of a slightly thickened vinaigrette.

6. **Serving:** Cut the strings from the roast and slice into 1/2-inch-thick slices. Serve slices of the pot roast alongside a mix of vegetables, with the braising liquid ladled on top. Pass *fleur de sel* or coarse salt at the table, if desired.

BROWNING THE POT ROAST DIRECTLY IN THE BRAISING PAN

Using the broiler to brown the meat leaves less of a greasy splatter mess in your kitchen, but it does mean another pan to clean. To brown the meat directly in the braising pan, in place of Step 2, heat 2 tablespoons of bacon drippings or peanut oil in a Dutch oven or other heavy braising pan (4-quart) over medium heat. Add the beef and brown it on all sides, turning it with tongs, about 15 minutes total. Remove the beef and set it aside on a plate or dish that will capture any juices. Pour off any fat, return the pot to medium-high heat, and continue as directed in Step 3, the only difference being that instead of pouring the braising liquid over the roast in the braising pan, you will lower the roast into the liquid.

Shopping for Pot Roast

The homey term *pot roast* has become so firmly planted in our culinary lexicon that it even earns itself a definition in *Webster's*: "a cut of beef that is browned and then cooked until tender, often with vegetables, in a covered pot." For many of us growing up (and I am no exception), pot roast appeared regularly in the family meal cycle. If we were lucky, this meant a happy occasion with tender, succulent meat and flavor-drenched vegetables. If unlucky, we were sitting down to sad plates of tough, dried-out beef and mushy, tasteless vegetables. While we may all know more or less what a pot roast is, or should be, what is perhaps less obvious is what a superlative one tastes like.

The first step toward making a great pot roast is buying the right cut of beef. Unfortunately, many markets slap the label "pot roast" on most any cheap cut without discriminating, so *caveat emptor*. But if you go shopping armed with a little knowledge, you will know what cuts work well and which ones don't.

CHUCK

In my experience, there's no contest for the best source for pot roast. If you're not familiar with where things come from on a steer, think of the chuck as the massive front shoulder. Because the chuck is both hardworking and fatty, it possesses just the right combination of flavor and richness. Within the chuck, there are many muscle groups and more than a few options. The exact cuts (and their names) vary from market to market.

While anything labeled chuck will be a smart choice for braising, look in particular for the following.

Top blade roast (boneless): The most elegant pot roast. A top blade roast is a neat cylindrical-shaped cut with great beefy flavor and superlative fork-tender texture, with no hint of the ropy dryness too often associated with pot roast. Other names for this splendid cut are *top chuck roast*, *flat-iron roast*, *lifter roast*, and the rather generic-sounding *chuck shoulder pot roast*. If you're not sure about the name, inspect the meat to see whether or not it is indeed a stout cylindrical shape comprised of only two long muscles with the coarse-grained texture common to the chuck. Don't mistakenly grab the similar looking *eye of the round roast*. Despite the resemblances in shape, the eye of the round won't deliver anywhere near the same tenderness or flavor.

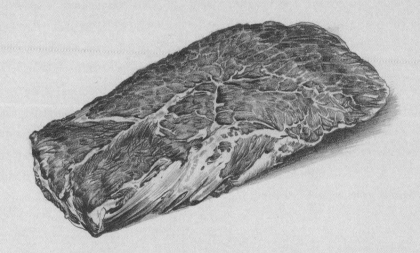

Top Blade Roast

Other boneless chuck roasts: Any boneless chuck roast is a sure bet for braising, and your selection will depend on what your market offers and what size roast you need. Other possibilities include *chuck arm roast*, *chuck eye roast*, and just plain old *chuck roast*. There are both rounded loaf-shaped pot roasts and flatter, boxier ones. When buying flat pot roast, make sure that they are at least 2 1/2 inches thick. Even so, expect flatter roasts to take less time to braise than thicker, plumper ones, so check for doneness about 30 minutes early if cooking one of these. All boneless chuck pot roasts will need to be tied with kitchen string to hold them in a neat, snug shape. (See page 258 for instructions on tying a roast.)

(continued on next page)

Chuck Pot Roast

Bone-in chuck roasts: Some markets also sell bone-in chuck pot roasts. Of these, I recommend the *7-Bone roast* for terrific flavor and fall-apart tender texture after braising. The roast earns its odd name from the shape of the blade bone in each roast—it somewhat resembles the number 7. Another good choice is the *cross rib roast*, sometimes called an *English cut pot roast*. Although cross rib roasts can be more awkward to carve than other pot roasts because of the flat rib bones attached to the meat, they do provide the same satisfying meatiness of short ribs. As with all pot roasts, tie bone-in pot roasts before braising so that they don't fall apart. (See page 258 for instructions on tying a roast.) Depending on the size and amount of the bones, most bone-in roasts braise in about the same time as boneless roasts, or perhaps just a bit longer. Judge doneness by when the meat pulls away from the bone.

BRISKET

The brisket is the top part of the breast of the steer, just below the shoulder. A whole brisket is shaped something like a lopsided briefcase and weighs close to 10 pounds. Since this is more than most people choose to cook at one time, butchers generally cut whole briskets crosswise in half. The two halves, each weighing in the 4- to 6-pound range, differ slightly. The flatter one, referred to as *flat half, thin cut,* or *first cut brisket,* is, as its name implies, flatter and more regular in shape. It is also leaner and can be a bit more expensive. The more compact, thicker half, known as *point cut, thick cut,* or *front cut brisket,* has more layering of fat and meat, and for this reason offers more juiciness and superior flavor. Both are grand, however, and you should not pass on brisket if all you can find is a flat half. Like a flatter chuck roast, the flat half of a brisket will braise a little more quickly than the point cut.

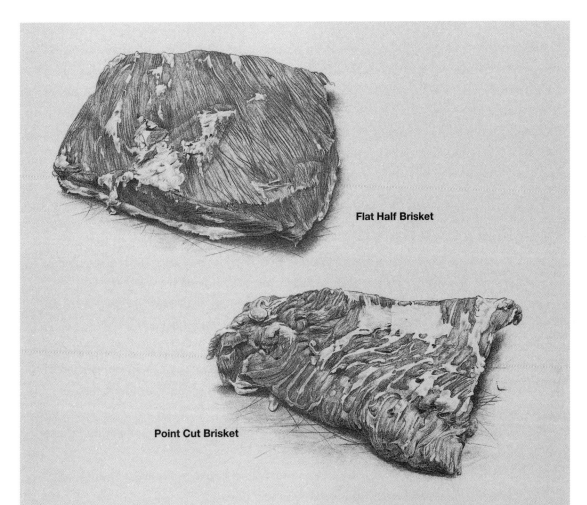

Flat Half Brisket

Point Cut Brisket

In some parts of the country, the only brisket available is already brined into corned beef—not what you should use for these recipes. Fortunately, fresh brisket is available through mail-order (see Sources, page 455).

ROUND

After years of being told that cuts from the round make good pot roast, and being perpetually disappointed, I have pretty much stopped trying—with one notable exception. The round sits just below or behind the sirloin on a steer; in other words, it's the bottom part of the rump and the upper hind leg. These hard-working muscles are much leaner than the chuck and, without the added benefit of intramuscular fat to baste the meat as it braises, cuts from the round tend to dry out during braising.

The one exception where I do find the round a good choice for braising is beef rolls (pages 230 and 234). For beef rolls (or birds or *braciole*), thin cutlets of *top round* are

(continued on next page)

pounded out and then rolled up around a flavorful and fatty stuffing. The round works well here because its lean fine-grained texture means it rolls easily; the chuck is too loose and too rugged. Fortunately, the fat in the filling adds the missing richness and bastes the meat as it braises.

Tying a Roast Before Braising

In many instances, you'll need to tie meat before braising to ensure that it doesn't fall apart in the long, slow simmer of the braising pot. As meat braises and becomes tender, its fibers give way and the meat shrinks, falls from the bone (if present), and generally collapses. Since this can make carving and serving difficult, your best approach is to tie the meat into a snug, compact package before braising. Tying also helps meat to cook more evenly, since it prevents any odd flap or thin bit from hanging out and cooking more quickly than the rest. Whether it's a thick bone-in chuck roast or a boneless leg of lamb that's been rolled around a filling, the principles of tying meat are the same:

- Use 16-ply all-cotton kitchen string. Thinner string will cut into the meat and cause more harm than good.
- Trim the meat before tying. Don't be too fastidious about trimming the fat. A bit of fat on the meat will baste it as it cooks and add flavor.
- Set the roast on a cutting board and shape it into the form you want with your hands. For instance, if it's a boneless lamb shoulder that you've stuffed, you'll want to compress and lengthen and smooth the roll into a stout evenly shaped cylinder, tucking in any loose pieces as you go. For a flat-shaped pot roast, there's little shaping to be done. You simply want to adjust and position the meat so it's not stretched or distorted.
- Most roasts have a long somewhat cylindrical or rectangular shape. These should be tied with loops of string secured at intervals along the roast. You will then finish with one or two lengths of string that run from end to end. In the rare instance where you have a rounder, more ball-shaped roast, loop the string around in both directions to secure the meat.
- Begin with a length of kitchen string about 6 inches longer than the circumference of the meat. Slide the string under the meat about 1 inch from one end, and bring

the ends up across each other to form a loop. Wrap one end of the string under the other twice and tug the ends to secure the loop against the meat. This step resembles the first half of a square knot with an extra wrap. The double wrap prevents the first half of the knot from slipping and avoids the need for someone to put a finger on the knot to hold it. Once the string is snug, but not so tight as to cut into the meat, wrap the ends back over each other (just once), tug, and secure the knot.

- Continue knotting loops of string at 1 ½- to 2-inch intervals down the length of the roast. The looser and more ragged the roast, the closer the strings should be. When all the loops are in place, snip the loose ends of the string.

- Now take a length of string three times as long as the roast. Starting at one end, weave the string in and out of the crosswise loops, wrapping it once around each loop, and keeping the string taut. When you reach the end, bring the string over the end, turn the roast, and continue down through the loops on the other side. Finish with a simple knot, and trim the loose ends. If the roast is very wide, make two lengthwise loops, about 2 inches apart.

- Many butchers use the half-hitch method, which involves a single length of string that is looped and hitched and looped again down the roast. However, this method is a little tricky to learn and can also result in lopsided results.

- Finally, boneless roasts often come from the market wrapped in a sort of elastic netting. The idea of anything synthetic in my braising pot bothers me, so I always cut this off, rinse and trim the meat, and retie it with my own all-cotton string.

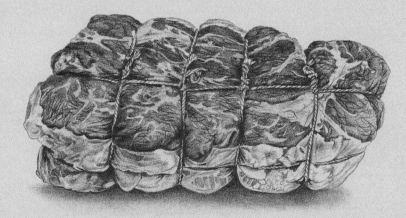

Pot Roast Tied Before Braising

Stracotto with Garlic & Pancetta ✈

Italian Red Wine Pot Roast

The best stracotto I ever tasted was years ago on a blustery, wet October evening in Venice. I was there helping to run a series of week-long cooking classes with Anne Willan, founder of La Varenne Cooking School, at the Hotel Cipriani. The program included a few outside visits, and on this particular night, we were all guests at the home of Count Carlo Maria Rocco, across the Giudecca Canal. The count's home was lovely and welcoming, but I had taken a serious chill on the boat ride over, and the weather seemed to seep through the walls. I was beginning to think I'd catch my death sitting there through dinner until the stracotto—Italian-style beef pot roast marinated in strong red wine and braised simply with onions and a few seasonings—arrived at the table. The meat and accompanying sauce had a depth of flavor that warmed me to the core. I have taken some liberties with the original recipe, adding a few more aromatics and some pancetta, but the idea remains the same.

Stracotto translates literally from Italian as "overcooked," but the term has come to refer to beef stews and braises—especially in the north of Italy. Perhaps a more appealing translation would be "long-cooked."

The best thing to round out this succulent dish is a steaming pot of soft polenta.

wine notes

Big, robust Sangiovese-based red from Tuscany, such as Rosso di Montalcino or Brunello di Montalcino; or one of the "Super Tuscan" blends of Sangiovese, Cabernet Sauvignon, and/or Merlot.

Stracotto needs to marinate for 24 to 36 hours before braising (Steps 1 & 2), so plan accordingly. In addition, stracotto tastes better the day after it's made, and better still the day after that. If you'd like to braise it ahead, follow the recipe up through Step 6. When the beef is tender, remove it from the braising liquid and place it in a glass bowl or other nonreactive storage container (not plastic). Strain the braising liquid over the beef. Retrieve the garlic and pancetta from the other spent aromatics, and put them with the beef. (The garlic usually holds together, but if it has separated into cloves, do your best to find them.) Discard the remaining aromatics. Cover the beef and refrigerate until an hour or so before serving.

To serve, scrape the cold fat from the surface of the sauce. Gently remove the garlic, pancetta, and beef from the sauce. Transfer the sauce to a saucepan and bring it to a simmer. Proceed to make the garlic paste and shred the pancetta as described in Step 8. To reheat the meat, remove the string and carve the roast. Lay the slices in a baking dish and spoon over the warm sauce. Cover and heat in a 300-degree oven until warmed through, about 20 minutes.

Serves 6 | *Braising Time: about 3 hours*

THE MARINADE

2 tablespoons extra-virgin olive oil

2 celery stalks, coarsely chopped

2 medium yellow onions (about 12 ounces total), coarsely chopped

1 medium carrot, coarsely chopped

1 head garlic, cut crosswise in half

2 bay leaves

Two 3-inch leafy fresh rosemary sprigs

1/2 teaspoon black peppercorns

One 750-ml bottle fruity dry red wine, such as Valpolicella, Chianti, or Montepulciano

One 3 1/2- to 4-pound boneless beef chuck roast or 4- to 4 1/2-pound bone-in beef chuck roast (see "Shopping for Pot Roast," page 254)

Coarse salt

THE AROMATICS AND BRAISING LIQUID

2 tablespoons extra-virgin olive oil

1/4 cup grappa or brandy

1 cup beef or veal stock, homemade (page 450 or 451) or store-bought

1/2 pound pancetta in one piece (about 1 inch thick)

Freshly ground black pepper

1. **For the marinade—24 to 36 hours in advance:** Heat the oil in a large saucepan over medium-high heat until shimmering. Add the celery, onions, and carrot and sauté, stirring intermittently, until the vegetables are tinged with brown, about 8 minutes. Add the garlic, bay leaves, rosemary, and peppercorns. Pour in the wine and bring to a boil. Simmer for 5 minutes to infuse the wine with the essence of the vegetables. Set aside to cool to room temperature.

2. **Tying the meat:** Using kitchen string, tie the beef into a neat, snug shape, according to the instructions on page 258. Season the meat all over with 1 teaspoon salt. Slide the meat into a gallon zip-lock bag or set it in a deep baking dish. Pour the cooled marinade over the beef and refrigerate for 24 to 36 hours. Turn the meat once or twice as it marinates.

3. **Heat the oven to 300 degrees.**

4. **Browning the meat:** Remove the meat from the marinade, reserving the marinade, and put it on a rack set over a platter to drain. Pour any drips from the meat back into the marinade and set the marinade aside. Wipe the meat thoroughly dry with paper towels. (If left damp, the meat won't brown well.)

    Heat the oil in a large skillet over medium heat. When shimmering, add the meat and sear it on all sides, using tongs to turn it, until mahogany colored, 15 to 20 minutes total. Because of the wine, the seared beef will take on a darker color than unmarinated meat, so don't be surprised by the depth of brown. Transfer the meat to a 3- to 4-quart Dutch oven or heavy lidded casserole.

5. **The aromatics and braising liquid:** Pour most of the fat from the skillet and discard. Wipe out the pan with a damp paper towel if it appears at all blackened, but if there are tasty-looking browned bits that aren't burnt, be careful to leave these behind—they will add tremendous flavor. Return the skillet to medium-high heat and carefully pour in the grappa or brandy—it may ignite, so stand back. Bring to a boil, and scrape the bottom of the skillet with a wooden spoon to dislodge the tasty seared-on bits. Continue to boil until the liquid is reduced to about 2 tablespoons, 3 to 4 minutes. Strain the marinade into the skillet, reserving all the vegetables, and bring to a boil. Boil the marinade until reduced to about 1 cup, about 15 minutes. Add the stock and boil again to reduce down by half, another 15 minutes. Remove from the heat.

6. **The braise:** Tuck the chunk of pancetta under or alongside the roast. Scatter over the reserved vegetables and seasonings, and reach in and push some vegetables under the roast as well. Pour over the reduced braising liquid, and cover the pot with a sheet of parchment paper, pressing down so the paper nearly touches the meat and the edges extend about an inch over the sides of the pot. Cover tightly with a lid, and slide the pot into the lower third of the oven. After the first 10 to 15 minutes, check to see that the liquid isn't simmering too furiously. If it is, lower the oven heat 10 to 15 degrees. Continue

to braise gently until the roast is fork-tender, 2 ½ to 3 hours, turning it once halfway though braising.

7. **The finish:** Lift the beef from the braising liquid, using a slotted spatula to support it so it doesn't fall apart, and transfer it to a shallow platter to catch the juices. Strain the braising liquid into a saucepan, reserving the pancetta and garlic (don't worry if the garlic head has lost some of its cloves), and discard the remaining spent aromatics. With a wide spoon, skim as much fat as possible from the braising liquid, and bring to a boil. Evaluate the sauce for consistency and flavor: typically it will need to be simmered vigorously over medium-high heat for about 10 minutes to give it body and to concentrate the flavor. Taste for salt and pepper.

8. **Meanwhile, make the garlic paste and shred the pancetta:** Squeeze the garlic from the cloves into a small bowl. Smash to a paste using the tines of a table fork. With your hands, pull apart the pancetta. Personally, I wouldn't dream of discarding the flavorful fatty parts, but some people disagree—keep or discard the fat according to your taste, but be sure to save every last bit of meat. Tear it into small shreds and add to the simmering sauce.

9. **Serving:** Snip the strings from the roast. Carve on an angle into ½-inch-thick slices. Spoon some sauce over each serving and top with a small spoonful of garlic paste.

Zinfandel Pot Roast with Glazed Carrots & Fresh Sage ➤➤

I think of this as dinner-party pot roast. While the basic technique is the same as a regular Sunday night pot roast, the herb-flecked carrot garnish makes it dressy enough for company. Instead of braising along with the beef, the carrots are glazed on top of the stove in a bit of the Zinfandel braising liquid just before serving, so that they remain bright and crisp-tender—a fresh contrast to the gorgeously tender beef. If you like, use half parsnips and half carrots. The parsnips will cook in the same amount of time.

My first choice for this recipe is always top blade roast because its neat shape makes it easy and elegant to carve for your guests. You can certainly select other pot roast cuts (see "Shopping for Pot Roast," page 254).

Serve with buttery mashed potatoes, soft polenta, or savory bread pudding, and a light salad of Bibb lettuce tossed with a creamy vinagrette.

wine notes

Zinfandel—especially the same wine used in the braise. Look for old-vine Zinfandels from the Sonoma, Mendocino, and Napa counties. Southern Rhone Grenache blends, such as Chateauneuf-du-Pape would also do well.

Serves 6 | *Braising Time: about 3 hours*

THE BRAISE

One 3 1/2- to 4-pound boneless beef chuck
  roast, preferably top blade roast (see
  "Shopping for Pot Roast," page 254)
Coarse salt and freshly ground black
  pepper
2 tablespoons extra-virgin olive oil
1 large yellow onion (about 8 ounces),
  coarsely chopped
1 carrot, coarsely chopped
1 celery stalk, coarsely chopped
2 garlic cloves, peeled and smashed

1 cup Zinfandel or other robust dry red
  wine
1 cup beef, veal, or chicken stock,
  homemade (page 450, 451, or 448) or
  store-bought
Three large 3- to 4-inch leafy fresh sage
  sprigs
Two to three 6- to 8-inch leafy flat-leaf
  parsley sprigs
8 to 10 black peppercorns

THE GARNISH

1 1/2 pounds small to medium carrots,
  peeled, or 3/4 pound each carrots and
  parsnips, peeled
1 tablespoon extra-virgin olive oil
1 tablespoon unsalted butter
Coarse salt and freshly ground black
  pepper

1 tablespoon red wine vinegar
Pinch of sugar
2 tablespoons chopped fresh sage
2 tablespoons chopped flat-leaf parsley

1. **Heat the oven to 300 degrees.**

2. **Tying the meat:** Using kitchen string, tie the beef into a neat, snug shape according to the directions on page 258.

3. **Browning the meat:** Season the beef all over with salt and pepper. Heat the oil in a large Dutch oven or other braising pot (5-quart works well) over medium heat. Add the beef and brown it on all sides, turning it with tongs as you go, about 18 minutes total. Remove the beef and set it aside on a large plate or dish that will collect any juices that the meat releases. If there are any charred bits in the pot, remove them with a damp paper towel, but leave behind any tasty-looking drippings.

4. **The aromatics and braising liquid:** Return the pot to medium-high heat and add the onion, carrot, celery, and garlic. Season lightly with salt and pepper. Cook, stirring often, until just starting to brown, about 5 minutes. Pour in the wine, scrape the bottom with a wooden spoon to loosen any of the cherished cooked-on bits of caramelized beef juices, and boil to reduce the wine by about half, about 6 minutes. Add the stock, return to a boil, and boil to reduce by just about one third, another 5 minutes. Return the meat to the pot,

and add the sage, parsley, and peppercorns. Cover with a piece of parchment paper, pressing down so that it nearly touches the meat and the edges of the paper overhang the pot by about an inch. Set the lid in place.

5.   **The braise:** Transfer the pot to the lower third of the oven and braise at a gentle simmer, turning the roast once halfway through braising, until fork-tender, about 3 hours. Peek under the lid after the first 10 to 15 minutes to check that the liquid isn't simmering too vigorously; if it is, lower the oven heat by 10 or 15 degrees.

6.   **The garnish:** While the beef braises, cut the carrots into sticks by cutting them crosswise in half, then cutting the halves lengthwise into sticks about 3 inches by 1/2 inch. This typically means cutting the thicker tops into quarters and the skinnier tips in half. (If using parsnips, remove any woody core before cutting them into sticks. See "Shopping for Parsnips," page 153.) (You can chop the sage and parsley for the garnish now as well.) Set aside.

7.   **The finish:** Remove the pot from the oven. Lift the beef out with tongs or a sturdy spatula, set on a carving platter to catch the juices, and cover loosely with foil to keep warm. Strain the cooking liquid, pressing down on the solids to extract as much liquid as possible. Discard the spent aromatics, and pour the liquid into a medium saucepan. Let the braising liquid settle, then spoon off and discard as much fat as you easily can with a wide spoon. Measure out 1/2 cup of the juices for glazing the carrots and set the rest aside in a warm spot.

8.   **Glazing the carrots:** Heat the oil and butter in a large skillet (12- or 13-inch) over medium-high heat. When quite hot, add the carrots (and parsnips, if using), season with salt and pepper, and cook briskly, shaking or stirring them, until lightly glazed and browned in spots, about 8 minutes. Add the 1/2 cup braising liquid, cover partway, reduce the heat to medium, and simmer until tender but not at all mushy, 6 to 8 minutes. Uncover, raise the heat, and bring back to a boil. Add the vinegar, sugar, sage, and parsley and cook until the liquid is reduced to a glaze, about 1 minute. Taste for salt and pepper.

9.   **The finish:** Heat the remaining reserved cooking juices over medium-high heat, and boil for 1 or 2 minutes to concentrate their flavor. Taste. You may not need to add any salt or pepper, but do so if the juices are lacking in flavor.

10.   **Serving:** Remove the strings from the roast. For a platter presentation, arrange the carrots (and parsnips, if using) around the pot roast. Alternatively, slice the roast into 1/2-inch thick slices and arrange the slices on dinner plates along with the carrots (and parsnips, if using). Spoon a bit of sauce over the meat and serve immediately. Pass any remaining sauce at the table.

Pot-Roasted Brisket with Rhubarb & Honey →→

Jewish cooks have long known the real secret to superior pot roast—brisket.
The wonder of this cut is that, like the chuck, it is both fatty and muscular but,
unlike the chuck, with all its different muscles and bones, brisket holds
together in one piece, needs no tying, and slices up as neatly as a loaf of bread.
When braised, brisket delivers that ideal pull-apart tenderness that we seek in
a braise, and there's no shortage of flavor. If you've only come across brisket in
its more popular form as corned beef, you owe it to yourself to try it fresh.

Every time I make this dish, I am swept away by the perfection of the
combination of the rhubarb and the spice-rubbed beef. The rub (allspice,
coriander, black pepper, and salt) adds an exotic flavor note, and it also creates
a gorgeous ruddy crust on the outside of the brisket. During braising, the
rhubarb collapses into the meaty braising liquid, mingles with the meat juices,
and becomes a spicy-tart-sweet fruit compote-like sauce. Removing the
fibrous strings from the rhubarb stalks before braising ensures that the sauce
will be smooth, not stringy. The rhubarb is added in two stages (some at the
very beginning and the rest toward the end) so that you get a combination of
soft puree with some pieces that retain a bit more bite.

Make this in the early spring (April and May) when fresh local rhubarb
is at its peak. I've also had good results with late-season "forced" rhubarb (a
second crop that some gardeners grow in the summer months). If you've
missed rhubarb season altogether, tart apples are a fine substitute (see the
variation that follows).

wine notes

The spicy-tart-sweet components call for a wine with similar characteristics—a deeply flavored Shiraz
from Australia, Syrah from California, or a rich Zinfandel.

You need to rub the brisket with the spice mixture 12 to 36 hours before braising (Step 1), so plan accordingly. Otherwise you won't get the full impact of its flavor on the beef.

Braised brisket is wonderful served soon after braising, but it really tastes extraordinary when left to sit for 1 or 2 days in the refrigerator. If you'd like to do so, after braising the meat, transfer it to a glass baking dish or other storage container and pour the braising liquid over it. Let cool to room temperature, then cover tightly and refrigerate.

To serve, scrape off and discard the fat that has solidified on the surface of the jelled cooking liquid, and remove the meat, scraping any rhubarb and sauce off it. Carve the brisket diagonally across the grain into 1/2-inch-thick slices. If you stored the brisket in a baking dish, return it to the dish. Otherwise, transfer the sliced meat and the jelled liquid to a baking dish. Cover with foil and heat in a 350-degree oven until heated through, 25 to 30 minutes; remove the foil after the first 20 minutes.

Serves 6 to 8 | Braising Time: 3 to 3 1/2 hours

THE SPICE RUB

2 teaspoons coriander seeds

1 teaspoon black peppercorns

1/2 teaspoon allspice berries

1 1/2 teaspoons coarse salt

One 4- to 5-pound beef brisket (see "Shopping for Pot Roast," page 254), trimmed of some but not all excess fat

1 pound rhubarb

THE AROMATICS AND BRAISING LIQUID

2 tablespoons extra-virgin olive oil or bacon drippings

1 medium yellow onion (about 6 ounces), chopped into 1/2-inch pieces

Coarse salt and freshly ground black pepper

2 tablespoons minced fresh ginger

1/3 cup golden raisins

3/4 cup dry white wine or dry white vermouth

1 cup beef, veal, or chicken stock, homemade (page 450, 451, or 448) or store-bought

2 strips orange zest, removed with a vegetable peeler (each about 3 inches by 3/4 inch)

Two 3-inch leafy fresh marjoram or sage sprigs

1 bay leaf

1 tablespoon honey, plus more if needed

1. **For the spice rub—12 to 36 hours in advance:** Combine the coriander, peppercorns, and allspice in a small dry skillet over medium heat, and heat, shaking the pan frequently, until the spices are fragrant and lightly toasted, 1 to 2 minutes. Let cool for a minute, then grind the toasted spices to a coarse powder in a small mortar or a spice grinder. Add the salt and grind to combine.

    Wipe down the brisket with paper towels, and spread the spice rub all over both sides of the meat, rubbing lightly so the spices adhere. Lay the brisket on a rimmed baking sheet (half sheet pan) or broiler pan, cover loosely, and refrigerate for 12 to 36 hours.

2. **Browning the meat:** Heat the broiler on high. Slide the brisket under the broiler so the meat is 4 to 5 inches from the heat. Broil, rotating the pan as necessary, until the surface is beautifully browned and crusty but not charred, then turn and brown the other side, 2 to 6 minutes per side, depending on the intensity of your broiler. Watch the brisket carefully, and don't walk away: it can brown very quickly. Remove the brisket from the broiler, and set it aside on the pan. Turn the oven down to 300 degrees.

3. **Trimming the rhubarb:** Trim both the ends of the stalks of rhubarb, being sure to cut away any evidence of leaves or leaf stems from the top (rhubarb leaves are toxic). With a paring knife or vegetable peeler, strip the stingy outer layer from the rhubarb. Chop the stalks into 1/2-inch pieces. You should have about 4 cups.

4. **The aromatics:** In a large Dutch oven or other braising pot (7- to 9-quart), heat the oil or drippings over medium-high heat. Add the onion and sauté until softened and beginning to color, 5 to 7 minutes. Season with salt and pepper, add the ginger and raisins, and sauté for another minute, until the ginger releases its fragrance.

5. **The braising liquid:** Add the wine, bring to a boil, and boil until reduced by about three quarters, 5 minutes. Add the stock, 2 cups of the rhubarb, the orange zest, herb sprigs, bay leaf, and 1 tablespoon honey. Bring the liquid to a boil and boil for a few minutes, stirring once or twice, to dissolve the honey and meld the flavors. Lower the brisket into the pot. If it feels a bit squeezed, don't worry: the meat will shrink by almost one third as it braises.

6. **Deglazing the pan:** Pour off and discard the fat from the pan used to brown the brisket. Set the pan over one or two burners turned to medium-high. When the pan is hot, add 1/4 cup water, bring to a boil, and stir and scrape with a wooden spoon to dislodge and dissolve the cooked-on juices from the brisket. (You'll be making a sort of meat "tea," which will add tremendous flavor to the finished dish.) When the bottom of the pan is clean and the liquid is simmering, pour it into the pot with the brisket.

7. **The braise:** Cover the pot with parchment paper, pressing down so that the paper nearly touches the meat and the edges hang about an inch over the sides. Then set a heavy lid in place. Slide into the lower third of the oven to braise. After 10 to 15 minutes, check

to see that the liquid isn't simmering too fiercely. If it is, lower the oven temperature 10 or 15 degrees. Then continue to braise at a gentle simmer. Turn the brisket with tongs after another 30 minutes, Then, after another 1 1/2 hours, turn the brisket again and add the remaining 2 cups of rhubarb. Continue braising for another hour or so, until the meat is fork-tender, a total of 3 to 3 1/2 hours.

8. **The finish:** Remove the brisket from the pot using a spatula or tongs (handle the brisket gingerly, as it tends to pull apart), and set it on a carving board with a moat to collect any juices. Cover loosely with foil to keep warm. The rhubarb will have mostly collapsed into the braising liquid, adding body and some texture. Skim any clear surface fat from the liquid, and remove the spent herb sprigs, orange zest, and bay leaf. Taste, and stir to smooth out the rhubarb. If the sauce tastes too sharp, add a drizzle more of honey. Go easy, though, as a small amount of honey can overpower the other flavors. If the sauce seems thin or dull, boil over medium-high heat to reduce and concentrate it for about 5 minutes. Season with salt and pepper.

9. **Serving:** If serving right away, carve the brisket diagonally across the grain into 1/2-inch-thick slices. Ladle the rhubarb sauce over, and serve. If making ahead, see the note at the beginning of the recipe.

VARIATION: POT-ROASTED BRISKET WITH APPLES

If rhubarb is out of season, substitute the same amount of any good-tasting tart apples, such as Pippin, Gravenstein, or Granny Smith. Take a good bite of one apple first—it must be tart, crisp, and juicy. Peel, core, and chop the apples into 1/2-inch pieces. Use only 1 teaspoon of honey (even tart apples are much sweeter than rhubarb), and follow the recipe as directed. The timing will be the same.

Ideas for Leftover Pot Roast

Most pot roast recipes make enough to serve 4 to 6 people, but I don't let that stop me from making pot roast when I'm serving fewer people. In fact, I love to braise a pot roast on a Sunday afternoon even if I'll be alone for dinner—it's a perfect low-stress kitchen activity for a day when you want to do nothing more than read the paper and maybe sneak in a nap. By dinnertime, the house is filled with the intoxicating aromas of slow-cooked meat, and aside from a little skimming and slicing, there's little to do but set the table. Then, in addition to having a perfectly delicious Sunday dinner, you'll have some promising leftovers to start the work week. Besides, like most braises, pot roast tastes better the next day, and the day after, and the day after that. Here are a few of my favorite uses for leftover pot roast.

- **Pot roast sandwiches with fresh cheese and arugula**: Tuck thin slices of cold pot roast into a crusty roll or split baguette. Smear the meat with some of the jellied braising juices (they gel when refrigerated). Spread on a bit of fresh whole-milk ricotta cheese or other soft cheese, such as fresh goat cheese or a ripe camembert. Top with a few leaves of arugula, watercress, or spinach.

- **Pot roast sandwiches with sweet onions**: Slather slices of white sandwich bread with mayonnaise. Arrange a few thin slices of pot roast on the bread. Season with salt and pepper. Top with paper-thin slices of sweet onion (such as Walla Walla or Vidalia, but red onion will do) and another slice of mayonnaise-slathered bread.

- **Instant ragù**: Shred leftover pot roast and add it to a pot of your favorite marinara sauce. Although homemade marinara is great, this is also a great way to improve a decent-quality store-bought sauce—just heat the sauce and meat gently in a sauce-pan. Ladle the sauce over most any shape al dente pasta (I like spaghetti, tagliatelle, and rigatoni), add some grated Parmigiano-Reggiano, and call it dinner.

- **Baked pasta with leftover pot roast**: Boil any short tubular or squiggly-shaped pasta (penne, ziti, or fusilli are my favorites; I also like medium shells) in well-salted water until al dente. Figure about 3 to 4 ounces of dried pasta per serving. Drain, saving 1 cup of the pasta cooking water, and toss the pasta with leftover pot roast chopped into ½-inch bits, along with any accompanying vegetables. (The amount of meat you add depends on how much you have left over and whether you're in the mood for something very meaty or something less so.) Spread the pasta in an oiled casse-role or gratin dish. Pour over enough reheated braising liquid to moisten the pasta

(continued on next page)

(if you don't have enough braising liquid, add as much of the pasta cooking water or stock as you need). Season the top with freshly ground black pepper, and sprinkle with a generous amount of freshly grated Parmigiano-Reggiano. Bake at 400 degrees until heated through and the cheese is melted but not browned, about 10 minutes. Serve warm.

This variation begs for improvisation. When tossing the pasta with the leftover meat, feel free to add other enhancements—blanched spinach or chard, fresh herbs, chopped ripe tomatoes, caramelized onions, sautéed mushrooms, pitted olives, and so forth. I even made this once with sliced black truffles, but that was a very special occasion.

- **Hash**: Combine shredded leftover pot roast and diced cooked potatoes or other left-over vegetables. Season well with salt and plenty of black pepper, and add a few tablespoons of heavy cream (the cream will enrich the hash and promote the forma-tion of the delicious brown crust you're after). Sauté some chopped onion in bacon drippings, unsalted butter, or extra-virgin olive oil in a cast-iron skillet over medium heat. Once the onion is softened, add the pot roast mixture and stir to combine. Cook the hash over medium heat, pressing down with a spatula to compress the top, until a dark brown crust forms on the bottom. Flip the hash with the spatula, break-ing up the crust, and flatten the hash back into the skillet. Again let a good crust form on the bottom, and then repeat the turning and breaking up one more time. Cooking hash this way ensures that every bite has some good crunchy bits. Serve with poached eggs on top.

Cannelloni Stuffed with Leftover Pot Roast, Spinach & Ricotta ✈

Leftover pot roast is never a dilemma, because it reheats beautifully for a quick supper and makes excellent cold sandwiches (turn to page 271, "Ideas for Leftover Pot Roast," for more suggestions). The only problem with leftover pot roast is that there never seems to be enough—especially once you've discovered this cannelloni recipe. In fact, I often braise an entire pot roast just to be able to make cannelloni later in the week. They are that good. And, unfortunately, there's no cheating here by using store-bought roast beef or anything like that, since you really need the pot roast with its juices and vegetables to make this right.

Making your own pasta (*pasta fatta in casa*) for the cannelloni does take some time, but the results are entirely worth the effort. (If making pasta is out of the question, however, there are a few alternatives in the note below.) After that, it's a simple matter of making a white sauce (what the Italians call *besciamella*) and tossing together the filling. I especially like to make cannelloni with leftover Zinfandel Pot Roast with Glazed Carrots & Fresh Sage (page 264) because the tender, sweet carrots are delicious in the filling. But any tasty, soft-cooked vegetables will do—onions, shallots, celery, and the like. The fresh spinach adds a touch of welcome green, but other leafy greens, such as chard or beet greens, are also good here. Because this is a dish for using up leftovers, go ahead and play with the formula to suit what you have on hand. Just be sure to always use a light hand when mixing and filling the cannelloni. Adding too much filling or too much white sauce will make a dish that is heavy and unappealing.

If you are serving these as a starter course or as a light meal, one per person will do. For a more serious entrée, serve two.

Italian red with vibrant fruit and bright acidity—Chianti Classico, Vino Nobile di Montepulciano, or Rosso di Montalcino.

Working Ahead

Making the cannelloni takes a bit of time. If you'd like to break up the tasks, here's how: Make the pasta dough through Step 2 (shaping it into a ball) and the white sauce (Step 5) a day or two ahead. Keep both tightly covered and refrigerated. You can also blanch the spinach (Step 6) ahead and keep it covered and refrigerated for 2 days. To finish, roll out the pasta, make the filling, and assemble the cannelloni as directed.

Serves 4 to 8

THE PASTA

1 ¹/₃ cups all-purpose flour, plus more for kneading and rolling (preferably a hard wheat brand, such as King Arthur or Hecker's)

¹/₂ teaspoon coarse salt
2 large eggs
2 tablespoons extra-virgin olive oil

THE WHITE SAUCE (BESCIAMELLA)

3 tablespoons unsalted butter
3 tablespoons all-purpose flour
1 ¹/₂ cups whole milk

Coarse salt and freshly ground black pepper
Freshly grated nutmeg

THE FILLING

10 ounces spinach, tough stems removed
2 ¹/₂ to 3 cups shredded or chopped leftover beef pot roast and accompanying vegetables
¹/₄ cup chopped flat-leaf parsley
1 cup whole-milk ricotta (see "Shopping for Ricotta Cheese," page 334)

Coarse salt and freshly ground black pepper
³/₄ to 1 cup leftover pot roast braising liquid or sauce
¹/₃ cup freshly grated Parmigiano-Reggiano

1. **Making the pasta:** Pile the flour onto a clean work surface, shape it into a mound, and make a well in the center (you can also start the dough in a large bowl, turning it out when it comes time to knead it). Sprinkle the salt on the flour. Crack the eggs into the well and add 1 tablespoon of the oil to them. With a fork, beat the eggs without breaking down the wall of flour, then use your free hand to reinforce the wall of flour as you slowly draw flour into the egg mix little by little. Continue until you get a dough that's too stiff to mix with the fork. There will still be a good deal of unincorporated flour. Put the fork aside and begin mixing the dough with your fingers and palms, much like kneading bread, incorporating only as much of the remaining flour as you need to make a soft dough that hangs together. As soon as you sense that the dough is no longer picking up flour, put the ball of dough to the side. Scrape the work surface to get rid of the excess flour and hard bits of half-mixed dough. Discard these. Wash and dry your hands. Lightly flour the work surface and your hands and knead the dough until it is very soft and smooth—like an earlobe— about 6 minutes.

2. **Letting the pasta rest:** Wrap the dough in plastic and set aside to rest for 20 to 40 minutes. (*You can refrigerate the dough at this point for a day or two: let it stand at room temperature for 30 minutes before continuing.*)

3. **Kneading the pasta:** Cut the ball of dough into quarters. Set 3 pieces aside, loosely covered with plastic. Flatten the fourth piece with your palms into a rough oval or rounded rectangle, and dust it lightly with flour. Set the pasta machine at the widest setting, and roll the pasta through. Fold the sheet in half or in thirds, as you would a letter, and, positioning it so it goes into the rollers perpendicular to the first roll, roll it through again. Repeat this 3 or 4 more times, dusting the pasta or rollers lightly with flour if necessary to prevent sticking and changing the direction each time, until you have a smooth, pliable pasta sheet. Lay the sheet on a lightly floured board or countertop, and continue with the other 3 pieces.

4. **Rolling the pasta into thin sheets:** Set the rollers down one notch and roll one sheet through. As you proceed, lightly dust the pasta with flour if it feels as though it might stick. Adjust the setting down one notch at a time and continue rolling the pasta through only once at each setting. (If you're not adept at rolling pasta, it may help to have a second pair of hands to help you feed the sheet into the machine and then catch it as it emerges.) Stop when the sheet is very thin but not translucent—this should be at the third- or second-to-last setting on the machine. When you finish, lay the pasta sheet on a lightly floured board or tray covered with a clean dish towel. Repeat with the other 3 sheets, setting the pasta machine back at its second-widest setting and rolling the pasta into thin sheets one at a time. With a large knife, cut each sheet into 2 rectangles that measure about 6 by 9 inches. Ideally, you want to fill and shape the cannelloni when the pasta

sheets are fresh and pliable. If you must take a break, lay the pasta rectangles on lightly floured half sheet pans (rimmed baking sheets) and cover tightly with plastic. The pasta will stay pliable for a couple of hours.

5. **Making the white sauce:** In a small saucepan, melt the butter over medium heat. Whisk in the flour and cook, whisking, for a few minutes to make a smooth paste, or roux. Slowly pour in the milk and whisk until smooth, being careful to get any bits of the roux in the corners of the pot. (A long narrow whisk or a special flat roux whisk works best here.) Bring to a gentle boil and simmer, stirring occasionally, until the sauce is the consistency of a thick cream soup, 5 to 7 minutes. The sauce should be ivory colored—do not let it brown at all. Season with salt, pepper, and a pinch of nutmeg. Taste (it should be boldly seasoned), and set aside.

6. **Blanching the spinach:** Bring a large pot of salted water to a boil. Drop in the spinach a few large handfuls at a time, and let the water return to a boil. As soon as all the spinach is in the pot and the water has returned to a boil, count about 30 seconds, then drain. (If the leaves are very large and tough, boil for a full minute.) Rinse the spinach under cold water, and drain again. Squeeze the spinach dry, a little at a time, in your hands, making a tight fist to get rid of as much water as possible. Roughly chop the spinach and put it in a large bowl.

7. **Making the filling:** Add the leftover pot roast and vegetables and the parsley to the bowl. Using a large rubber spatula, gently fold in ½ cup of the white sauce and the ricotta. (If you've made the white sauce in advance, it will have firmed up. Warm it briefly over low heat to loosen it up.) Fold just enough to incorporate the ingredients, and avoid overworking the filling. Season to taste with salt and pepper. You should have about 4 cups of filling.

8. **Boiling the pasta:** Bring a large pot of water to a boil. Add a handful of salt (about 2 tablespoons) and the remaining 1 tablespoon oil to the pot to prevent the sheets from sticking. (In most cases, adding oil to pasta water makes no difference, but when making flat sheets for cannelloni, I find that it does help.) Once the water boils, drop in 4 pasta sheets and cook for about 1 minute after the water returns to a boil. Using a large skimmer, lift out the pasta and lay the sheets out on clean dish towels to dry. Be sure to separate the cooked pasta sheets or they will stick together. If you need to stack them, separate the stacks with clean linen dish towels. Repeat with the remaining sheets.

9. **Assembling the cannelloni:** Heat the oven to 350 degrees. Warm the leftover braising juices so they are pourable (a microwave is handy for this), and pour all but about 3 tablespoons of the juices into the bottom of a baking dish that will hold the cannelloni, such as a 9- by-13-inch dish. Lay out one pasta sheet and spoon about ½ cup of filling along the edge of one of the short ends. With a rubber spatula, spread the filling so it covers one

third of the pasta. Roll the pasta up jelly-roll fashion to enclose the filling, and tuck the cannelloni seam side down into the baking dish. Continue with the remaining sheets of pasta and filling.

10. **Baking the cannelloni:** Pour the remaining white sauce over the top of the cannelloni and spread it evenly. Pour over the reserved few tablespoons of braising juices. Dust the top with the Parmigiano and cover with foil. Bake for 30 minutes, then remove the foil. Bake until the cannelloni are heated through, the sauce is bubbling around the edges, and the cheese is beginning to brown, another 20 to 30 minutes. Serve hot or warm.

Blanching Spinach

If you have one of those slotted pasta cooking inserts that fits inside a large pasta pot, you can use it to cook the spinach in the water you plan to use for boiling the pasta. This saves you the time and hassle of boiling two large pots of water. Just use the pasta cooking insert for cooking the spinach and lift it out to drain the spinach, without dumping the boiling water. Don't forget to add the oil to the water after cooking the spinach. I don't use the insert for the actual pasta sheets because they are so delicate; I find it safer to lift them out one by one with a skimmer.

If you decide to use frozen spinach in place of fresh, figure 3/4 cup cooked, squeezed dry, and chopped spinach (about three quarters of a 10-ounce package).

Alternatives to Making Your Own Pasta for Cannelloni

In place of making your own pasta, there are three alternatives. The first is to make or buy crepes and use them instead. The second is to buy fresh lasagne sheets. These tend to be thicker than homemade, so cut the rectangles a bit shorter, 6 by 6 inches, so there won't be as much overlap. Or you can buy cannelloni or manicotti shells. Cook the shells according to the package directions, and use a pastry bag or long ice tea spoon to fill them.

Neapolitan Beef Ragù →→

For the longest time, the only ragù I recognized was a meaty pasta sauce known as ragù bolognese (well, that and the not-very-good supermarket stuff in a jar). But then in the mid-90s, I discovered a recipe by the exquisitely talented California chef Paul Bertolli of Oliveto restaurant in Oakland, and I was smitten. It's a dish I make again and again and never tire of. Instead of the hand-chopped (or sometimes ground) meat in a typical bolognese sauce, Bertolli uses a whole pot roast, which he sears slowly and then braises in a tomato-based sauce. The remarkable layering of flavors comes from browning the meat gently over low heat (rather than the usual medium-high) and then adding pancetta and dried porcini mushrooms to the braise. If you can get your hands on a few ounces of pork rind to add to the pot as well, the sauce will have the most seductive texture you've ever experienced. If you can't manage the pork rind, the ragù will still be wonderful.

Beyond its flavor, what I really love about this recipe is serving it according to the Italian tradition of two courses, the same way you serve the braciole for Nonna's Feast (page 236). The tomato-based braising liquid sauces rigatoni for a first course (or *primo*). Then for the main course (or *secondo*), you have delectable thick slices of tender pot roast. A side dish of braised greens would be lovely with it on the plate.

wine notes

Rich, earthy European red, like a Grenache-based wine from Priorato in southern Spain, or Rosso di Montalcino and Brunello di Montalcino from Italy, or Mourvedré-based Bandols from Provence.

If you want to make two meals out of this, you can refrigerate either the sauce or the meat for another day. Reheat the sauce in a medium saucepan while you boil the pasta. Or reheat the meat, covered, in a 325-degree oven until heated through, about 30 minutes.

Serves 6 to 8 | *Braising Time: 2 1/2 to 3 hours*

1/4 pound fresh pork rind (see "Meaty
    Enrichments," page 31; optional)

1/2 ounce dried porcini mushrooms

2 cups warm water

2 tablespoons extra-virgin olive oil

Coarse salt and freshly ground black
    pepper

One 3 1/2- to 4-pound boneless beef chuck
    roast (see "Shopping for Pot Roast,"
    page 254)

3 ounces thickly sliced pancetta or 3 slices
    thick-cut bacon

1 large yellow onion (about 8 ounces),
    chopped into 1/2-inch pieces

1 carrot, chopped into 1/2-inch pieces

1 celery stalk, chopped into 1/2-inch pieces

3 garlic cloves, coarsely chopped

1/3 cup tomato paste

One 28-ounce can whole peeled tomatoes,
    with their juice

1 1/2 pounds dried tube-shaped pasta,
    such as rigatoni or penne rigate

Freshly grated Parmigiano-Reggiano for
    serving

1. **Blanching the pork rind:** If you are using the pork rind, cut it into 2 or 3 strips, place them in a small saucepan, and fill the pan with cold water. Bring to a boil over high heat, reduce to a gentle boil, and blanch the rind for 5 minutes. (This removes some of the fat and mellows the porky character.) Drain and set aside.

2. **Soaking the porcini mushrooms:** Soak the mushrooms in the warm water for 20 to 30 minutes, until softened.

3. **Tying and browning the meat:** Using kitchen string, tie the beef into a neat, snug shape according to the instructions on page 258. Heat the oil in a Dutch oven or heavy lidded braising pot (7-quart capacity works well) over medium-low heat. Pat the beef dry with paper towels and season all over with salt and pepper. Lower the beef into the pot (your hands probably work best since you don't have to worry about the oil being so hot that it spits). Listen for a gentle sizzling. If there is no sound after a minute or two, raise the heat in small increments. If, on the other hand, the meat seems to be sizzling loudly, nudge the heat down. Ideally, you should hear a consistent, quiet seething and see juices bubbling around the edges of the beef. After 10 to 12 minutes, turn the meat, lifting it with heavy tongs and supporting the roast with a wooden spoon as you maneuver it onto its other side. Continue browning the beef gently, turning every 8 to 10 minutes, until all sides have a chestnut-brown crust and the bottom of the pan has bits of brown but nothing even remotely burnt, 30 to 40 minutes. Transfer the meat to a tray or large plate.

4. **The aromatics:** Add the pancetta or bacon and pork rind, if using, to the pot. Sauté over medium heat, stirring occasionally, until the pancetta (or bacon) has rendered some of its fat and both pancetta (or bacon) and rind are browning in spots but not at all crisp, 8 to 10 minutes. If there appears to be more than a couple of tablespoons of fat in the pot, pour or spoon off all but 2 tablespoons, and return the pot to the heat. Add the onion, carrot, and celery and sauté, stirring occasionally, until the vegetables are beginning to soften and take on a burnished appearance, about 10 minutes.

   While the vegetables cook, lift the mushrooms out of the water, reserving the soaking liquid. Chop the mushrooms, and add them to the vegetables. Strain the soaking liquid though a triple layer of cheesecloth or a coffee filter to catch any sand or grit. Reserve.

5. **Heat the oven to 300 degrees.**

6. **The braising liquid:** Stir the garlic and tomato paste into the pot and sauté, stirring almost constantly, until the tomato paste is smeared evenly into the other ingredients. Pour half of the mushroom soaking liquid into the pot and stir with a wooden spoon, scraping the bottom to dislodge and dissolve all the tasty caramelized bits that have formed there. Increase the heat to medium-high and let the liquid boil until it reduces almost to a syrup that barely covers the bottom of the pot, about 8 minutes. Pour in the remaining mushroom soaking liquid, taking care to leave any sediment behind, and boil down until it's reduced by about half, 4 minutes. Add the tomatoes, pouring in the juices first and then, holding your hand over the pot, squeeze one tomato at a time to crush it, letting the juices fall into the pot, then add the tomato. Let the sauce come to a simmer.

7. **The braise:** Return the meat to the pot (a strong set of tongs will probably work best) and add any juices that have escaped from the meat as it sat. Cover with parchment paper, pressing so that the paper nearly touches the meat and the edges hang over the sides of the pot by about an inch. Then cover with the lid, and slide onto a rack in the lower third of the oven to braise at a gentle simmer. Check after 10 or 15 minutes to see that the sauce isn't simmering ferociously. If necessary, reduce the oven temperature by 10 or 15 degrees. After an hour of braising, turn the meat (because of the bulk of the roast, this can be tricky, but a pair of tongs and a flat wooden spoon will do the job well). Continue to braise quietly for another hour, then remove the lid and parchment paper (letting the beef braise uncovered for the last 30 to 60 minutes concentrates the sauce some and adds a richness to the flavor). Continue braising until the meat is absolutely fork-tender, a total of 2 ½ to 3 hours.

   Meanwhile, during the last 20 minutes of braising, set a large pot of water on to boil for the pasta.

8. **Degreasing the sauce:** When the beef is done, lift it from the sauce, using your tongs and spoon, and set it on a heatproof platter or large plate. Remove the strings. Don't worry if the meat pulls apart some; just piece it together as best you can. Spoon off as much clear fat from the surface of the sauce as you can without being too fastidious. Some fat is good and enriches the flavor enormously. Ladle out 1/2 to 3/4 cup of the braising liquid and pour it over the meat. Cover with foil and set in a very low oven, about 225 degrees.

9. **Finishing the sauce:** Lift out and discard the pork rind, if you used it. Set up a food mill with a coarse or medium blade over a medium bowl. Work the braising liquid through the food mill energetically until you've pureed it as best you can. You should have about 4 cups of sauce. Transfer the sauce to a medium saucepan and bring to a simmer. If you had less than 1 quart of sauce, simmer the sauce gently and don't let it reduce. Otherwise, simmer the sauce rapidly, stirring occasionally, until it reduces by about one quarter, 10 to 12 minutes. The sauce is ready when the bubbles rising to the top become thick and sluggish, almost syrupy. Taste for salt and pepper, but the sauce is unlikely to need any adjustment.

10. **Boiling and serving the pasta:** When the pasta water boils, add a handful of salt (about 2 tablespoons) and the pasta, stir one or twice to prevent sticking, and boil vigorously until it's al dente. Drain, reserving about 1 cup of the pasta cooking water. Toss the pasta with the sauce, adding a bit of the cooking water if the sauce seems too thick. Serve the pasta in warm pasta bowls sprinkled with Parmigiano.

11. **Serving the beef:** After the pasta course, slice the meat into thick chunks and serve.

Sauerbraten ➻

Sauerbraten is indigenous to every region of Germany, but, as with most traditional home-style dishes, regional differences abound and no two recipes are alike. At its most basic, sauerbraten is pot roast marinated in spiced vinegar and served with a pungent sweet-and-sour gravy. The gravy, made from the braising liquid, is the real defining characteristic of a good sauerbraten, and most German cooks believe that it should titillate the nostrils and practically bring tears to the eyes. Many cooks, myself included, add crumbled gingersnaps to the gravy to thicken it and to contribute a sweet-spicy note. Others crumble up honey cake, or lebkuchen. I've also heard of some who add raisins to the gravy. The best version I've tasted so far comes from a German friend of a friend. She swears by the use of sour cream to finish the gravy, and I'd have to agree. The rich tang strikes just the right balance with all the other flavors.

Sauerbraten is traditionally served with potato dumplings or boiled potatoes and red cabbage. I'd also recommend potato pancakes for a little crunch, or buttered egg noodles.

wine notes

Dry to off-dry Riesling from Germany or Austria.

Working Ahead

The pungent flavor of sauerbraten relies on a 2- to 3-day marinade. Be sure to allow time (and space in your refrigerator) for this.

Serves 6 to 8 | *Braising Time: about 3 hours*

1 teaspoon black peppercorns

4 juniper berries

8 allspice berries

2 bay leaves

2 whole cloves

$^1/_2$ teaspoon coarse salt

1 $^1/_2$ cups red wine vinegar

1 $^1/_2$ cups dry red wine

1 large yellow onion (about 8 ounces),
    sliced

One 4- to 5-pound boneless beef
    chuck roast (see "Shopping for Pot
    Roast," page 254)

THE AROMATICS AND BRAISING LIQUID

Coarse salt

1 tablespoon unsalted butter

1 tablespoon extra-virgin olive oil or
    vegetable oil

Reserved marinade

THE FINISH

6 thin store-bought gingersnap cookies,
    broken into coarse crumbs ($^1/_3$ to $^1/_2$
    cup crumbs)

1 tablespoon sugar

1 cup sour cream

1. **The marinade—48 to 72 hours in advance:** Place the peppercorns, juniper, and allspice in a mortar or small plastic bag, or fold up in a piece of waxed paper. Crush with the pestle if using the mortar or a rolling pin or hammer if using the bag or paper. Transfer the crushed spices to a small saucepan. Add the bay leaves, cloves, salt, vinegar, wine, and onion slices and bring to a boil. Transfer the marinade to a large bowl and let cool to room temperature. (I prefer a glass or stainless steel bowl. Whatever you use, don't use plastic: the acidic marinade will absorb flavors from plastic.)

2. **Tying and marinating the meat:** Using kitchen string, tie the beef into a neat, compact shape according to the directions on page 258. As soon as the marinade is cool, add the beef to the bowl and roll in the marinade to coat all sides. Cover, refrigerate, and marinate for 2 to 3 days, turning the meat once or twice a day. (There is no special timing here for turning the beef in the marinade. You just want to make sure that over the course of 48 or 72 hours, the meat is turned 3 or 4 times so it marinates evenly.)

3. **Heat the oven to 300 degrees**.

4. **Browning the meat:** With tongs, lift the meat out of the marinade, scraping any onion slices or spices that stick to the meat back into the marinade, and transfer it to a plate.

Reserve the marinade. Pat the meat thoroughly dry all over with paper towels. Heat the butter and oil in a large Dutch oven or other braising pot (6- to 7-quart) over medium heat. Add the meat to the pot and brown well on all sides, 20 to 25 minutes total. (You may need two implements to turn the meat: try tongs and a large metal spatula—lift the meat from the pan with the spatula, grab with the tongs, and turn.) Transfer the meat back to the plate. Pour off all the fat from the pan, and deglaze the pan with the reserved marinade, scraping any browned bits to loosen. Bring the marinade to a simmer and add the meat. Cover with parchment paper, pressing down so it nearly touches the meat and the edges of the paper hang over the sides of the pot by about an inch. Set the lid firmly in place, and transfer to the lower third of the oven.

5. **The braise:** Braise the meat at a gentle simmer for 1 1/2 hours. Check after about the first 10 minutes to see that the liquid is not simmering too energetically; if it is, lower the oven by 10 or 15 degrees. After 1 1/2 hours, turn the meat over, using the tongs and metal spatula, and continue braising gently for another 1 1/2 hours, or until fork-tender.

6. **The finish:** With the tongs and metal spatula, transfer the meat to a cutting board with a moat and cover loosely with foil to keep warm. Strain the cooking juices into a saucepan and let sit for a minute. Gently tilt the pan and skim off the fat with a large spoon. Whisk in the gingersnap crumbs and sugar, place the pan over medium-high heat, and bring to a boil. Gently boil the sauce for 5 minutes, whisking often, to reduce and thicken it slightly. Lower the heat to low and whisk in the sour cream until smooth. Heat through, but do not let the sauce boil, or the sour cream will curdle. Taste the sauce for salt.

7. **Serving:** Remove the strings from the meat, and pour any accumulated juices into the sauce. Carve the beef into thick slices. If the slices crumble, which they sometimes will, just cut into irregular pieces and arrange on a platter. Spoon the sauce over the beef and serve.

Christmas *Estouffade* ➳

A grand dish for a grand occasion, the king of all pot roasts. The term *estouffade* comes from Provence, borrowed from the Italian *stufato*, the word for stew, and refers to a slow-cooked braise or stew. Cooks farther to the west in Languedoc say *estouffat*. I learned to make Christmas *estouffade*—an elaborate version of the original—from a self-taught French home cook when I was traveling around France. She taught me to marinate the beef for a full day in red wine and Cognac, and then, after searing it slowly in bacon drippings, to braise it for hours with herbs, vegetables, slab bacon, and a pig's foot. The pig's foot may be the surprise ingredient here, but it lends incomparable body and a velvety texture to the sauce. And it provides succulent little bits of pork to serve with the beef. Of course, you can make *estouffade* without the pig's foot, but if you can manage it, I urge you to include it.

To serve this magnificent dish, I toss fresh pasta with the concentrated braising liquid, the braised bacon, and the shredded meat from the pig's foot, and then I arrange slices of the tender beef on top of the dressed pasta. Yes, *estouffade* takes some time to prepare, but the steps can easily be spread out over the few days before the holiday.

In Provence, the beef is traditionally set to simmer early on Christmas Eve. Then, following midnight Mass, everyone sits down to a grand dinner of seductively tender beef suffused with flavor. For a less opulent meal, serve the dressed pasta by itself, and save the beef for another day.

wine notes

This calls for special occasion wines from the cellar—fine, aged bottles of classified-growth Bordeaux, Cote-Rotie, Chateauneuf-du-Pape, California Cabernet, or Australian Shiraz.

The various steps to this remarkable dish take some planning. For starters, be sure to marinate the beef for at least 24 hours before you plan to braise (Steps 1 through 3). After braising, the *estouffade* needs to cool before you can prepare it for serving. I often find it most convenient to let it cool overnight. When you're ready for the grand feast, it's a matter of slicing the beef, straining the sauce, shredding the pork from the pig's foot, and heating the various components. There's also the matter of making the fresh pasta, which can be done anywhere from several hours to a day before serving. You can also skip that step and use a good-quality dried pasta instead, such as Martelli or Rustichella brand.

Serves 6 to 8 | *Braising Time: about 3 hours*

1 pig's foot, split lengthwise in half (see "Shopping for Pig's Foot," page 288)

One 4- to 5-pound boneless chuck roast, preferably an oblong top blade roast (see "Shopping for Pot Roast," page 254)

2 large carrots, coarsely chopped

1 large yellow onion (about 8 ounces), coarsely chopped

1 celery stalk, coarsely chopped

3 to 4 garlic cloves, peeled and smashed

3 strips orange zest, removed with a vegetable peeler (each about 3 inches by 3/4 inch)

2 bay leaves

4 leafy flat-leaf parsley springs

Four 4-inch leafy fresh thyme sprigs

2 teaspoons coarse salt

1 teaspoon black peppercorns, cracked

One 750-ml bottle robust dry red wine, such as Côtes de Provence, Cahors, Bandol, or Rhone

1/2 cup Cognac

1/2 pound slab bacon (see "Slab Bacon," page 395)

1 tablespoon extra-virgin olive oil

Freshly ground black pepper

Fresh Maltagliati (recipe follows) or fresh pappardelle or tagliatelle (or substitute good-quality dried tagliatelle or farfalle)

1. **Blanching the pig's foot—24 to 36 hours in advance:** Place the pig's foot in a medium (2-quart) saucepan and pour in enough cold water to cover by 2 inches. Bring to a strong simmer over medium-high heat. Lower the heat and simmer gently for 10 to 12 minutes; drain. Rinse the pig's foot with cool water and place it in a large nonreactive container.
2. **Tying and marinating the meat:** Using kitchen string, tie the beef into a neat, snug shape according to the instructions on page 258. Place the beef in the container with the pig's foot. Add the carrots, onion, celery, garlic, orange zest, bay leaves, parsley, thyme,

salt, and peppercorns. Pour over the wine and Cognac. Cover and refrigerate for 24 to 36 hours, turning the meat and pig's foot every 6 to 8 hours to distribute the marinade evenly.

3. **Heat the oven to 300 degrees.**

4. **Browning the bacon:** Cut the bacon lengthwise into ½-inch-wide strips (you'll get 3 or 4 strips). Then cut each strip into 2-inch lengths. Heat the oil in a large Dutch oven or other braising pot (7- to 9-quart) over medium heat. Add the bacon and fry, turning once with tongs, until the bacon is browned on both sides but not crisp, about 15 minutes total. Remove the bacon with tongs, and set aside on a small bowl or plate. Remove the pot from the heat.

5. **Browning the meat:** Lift the beef from the marinade and set it on a plate to drain, then thoroughly dry the beef with paper towels, rolling it over as you work and using more paper towels as needed. Return the pot with the olive oil and bacon drippings to medium heat. (These two fats will add great flavor to the exterior of the pot roast.) Lower the beef into the pot and brown, turning with tongs, until all sides have a ruddy brown crust, about 20 minutes total. Using tongs and a meat fork, lift the beef from the pot and set it back on the plate. Pour off as much excess fat as you can from the braising pot, without losing any of those precious meat drippings.

6. **The braising liquid:** Set a strainer over the braising pot and strain the marinade into the pot. Reserve the marinade vegetables and seasonings. Bring the marinade to a vigorous simmer over medium heat, and simmer until reduced by two thirds, about 15 minutes. There should be about 1 to 1 ½ inches of slightly thickened liquid in the pot.

7. **The braise:** Return the beef to the pot, along with any juices that have accumulated on the plate. Tuck the two pig's foot halves into the pot on either side of the beef. Scatter the strained marinade vegetables and seasonings over the beef. Cover the pot with parchment paper, pressing down so that it nearly touches the meat and the edges extend about an inch over the sides. Set a secure lid in place, and slide onto a rack in the lower third of the oven. Check after the first 15 minutes or so, and if the liquid seems to be simmering too intensely, lower the oven heat by 10 or 15 degrees. Then continue to braise gently, turning the beef and pig's foot with tongs after about 1 ¼ hours. Continue braising until the beef is fork-tender and the meat on the pig's foot is pulling away from the bone, about 3 hours total. Remove the pot from the oven and set aside until cool enough that you can lift out the pig's foot, about an hour. (*The* estouffade *can be made ahead up to this point and kept refrigerated, well covered, for 2 to 3 days.*)

8. **Heat the oven to 275 degrees.**

9. **The finish:** Set a large pot of water on to boil for the pasta. Lift the beef from the pot, using the strings and supporting it with a spatula, and transfer it to a cutting board with a moat to catch the juices. Remove the strings and slice the beef into ½-inch slices. Arrange the slices in a baking dish and pour over any juices that collected on the cutting board. Set aside.

Transfer the pig's foot to the cutting board. Using your fingers, pull the meat and skin from the bones. Discard the bones and any unappealing bits. With a large chef's knife, coarsely chop the skin and meat, and put in a small baking dish. With tongs or a slotted spoon, lift the bacon from the braising pot and set it aside with the chopped pork.

10. **The sauce:** Strain the braising liquid into a saucepan, pushing lightly on the vegetables to extract the maximum liquid without forcing them through the sieve; discard the vegetables. (If you've chilled the *estouffade,* scrape off the fat and then warm the braising liquid over medium heat until it's thin enough to strain.) Skim the surface fat from the liquid. Spoon about 1/2 cup of the braising liquid over the sliced beef and the chopped pig's foot and bacon to keep them moist. Cover both with foil and slide into the oven to heat through.

Set the remaining braising liquid over medium-high heat and simmer to concentrate the flavor and reduce in volume by about half, about 12 minutes. Taste for salt and pepper. It rarely needs any seasoning. Set aside in a warm place.

11. **Serving:** When the meats are heated through and the water for the pasta has come to a boil, add a handful (about 2 tablespoons) of salt to the pot and drop in the pasta. Boil until just al dente, as little as 1 minute for fresh pasta, closer to 10 for dried. Drain, shaking to get rid of any excess water, and transfer the pasta to a large shallow serving platter. Pour over the reduced braising liquid, scatter the chopped pork and bacon over the top, and toss lightly. Arrange the slices of beef over the top and serve.

Shopping for Pig's Foot

Depending on where you live, pig's feet (also called trotters) may or may not be easy to find. Where I live in Vermont, I can regularly find pig's feet, fresh ham hocks, salt pork, slab bacon, and so on, in most any supermarket. In other parts of the country, you may have to look a little harder. If pig's feet aren't standard fare in your supermarket, your best bet is an ethnic market. Asian markets that carry fresh meat will typically carry pig's feet. I've also had good luck at Polish meat stores that specialize in sausages and hams. If you still have no luck, most butchers can order pig's feet. Wherever you shop, be sure you're getting a fresh pig's foot, not a pickled one—a specialty in many regions. Most markets sell pig's feet already split. If not, ask them to split it in half lengthwise—a simple matter for a butcher with a band saw. Store pig's feet as you would any fresh meat, wrapped in plastic and refrigerated for no more than 2 or 3 days. They also freeze well.

Maltagliati translates literally as "badly cut," indicating the irregular shape of the noodles. I like making maltagliati because the random shapes are easy and fun to cut. More important, I like the way the silky flat sheets soak up the concentrated braising sauce of the *estouffade.*

2 cups all-purpose flour, plus more for dusting (preferably a hard wheat brand, such as King Arthur or Hecker's)

1/2 teaspoon coarse salt
3 large eggs
1 1/2 tablespoons olive oil

1. **Making the pasta:** Pile the flour onto a clean work surface, shape it into a mound, and make a well in the center (you can also start the dough in a large bowl, turning it out when it comes time to knead it). Sprinkle the salt on the flour. Crack the eggs into the well and pour the oil onto them. With a fork, lightly beat the eggs without breaking down the wall of the flour, then use your free hand to reinforce the wall of flour as you slowly draw flour into the egg mix little by little. Continue until you get a dough that's too stiff to mix with the fork. There will still be a good deal of loose flour. Put the fork aside and begin mixing the dough with your fingers and palms, much like kneading bread, incorporating only as much of the remaining flour as you need to make a soft dough that holds together. As soon as you sense that the dough is no longer absorbing flour, put the ball of dough to the side. With a pastry scraper or large knife, scrape the work surface clean of the excess flour and hard bits of half-mixed dough. Wash and dry your hands. Lightly flour the work surface and your hands and knead the dough until it is very soft and smooth—like an earlobe—about 6 minutes.

2. **Letting the pasta rest:** Wrap the dough in plastic and set aside to rest for 20 to 40 minutes. (*You can refrigerate the dough at this point for a day or two; let it stand at room temperature for 30 minutes before continuing.*)

3. **Kneading the pasta:** Cut the dough into 4 even pieces. Set 3 pieces aside, loosely covered with plastic. Flatten the fourth piece with your palms into a rough oval or rounded

rectangle, and dust it lightly with flour. Set the pasta rolling machine at the widest setting, and roll the pasta through. Fold the dough in half and, positioning it so it goes through the rollers perpendicular to the first roll, roll it through again. Repeat this 3 or 4 more times, dusting the pasta lightly with flour if necessary to prevent sticking and changing the direction each time, until you have a smooth, pliable pasta sheet. Lay the sheet on a lightly floured board or countertop, and continue with the other 3 pieces.

4. **Rolling out the pasta:** Set up some kind of pasta drying rack in an out-of-the-way place, away from any sort of steam or draft. I typically set a broom handle over two chair backs, but any sort of thin horizontal pole will do. Set the rollers of the pasta machine down one notch and roll one sheet of pasta through. As you proceed, lightly dust the pasta with flour if it feels as though it might stick. Adjust the setting down one notch at a time and continue rolling the pasta through only once at each setting. Stop when the sheet is thin but not translucent—this should be the second-to-last notch on the machine. Drape the pasta sheet over the drying rack, and continue with the remaining pasta sheets. Let the sheets dry until they are dry to the touch, somewhat like parchment, but still pliable, not brittle, about 20 minutes.

5. **Cutting the pasta into maltagliati:** With a large knife, cut the long strips crosswise into roughly 1 ½-inch-wide strips. Don't obsess getting the cuts straight or regular: the charm of maltagliati is its irregular shape. Then cut these smaller strips crosswise 3 or 4 times at random angles to shape rectangles, triangles, and other shapes. Place the maltagliati on a dish towel–lined baking sheet or tray. Shuffle the noodles gently with your hand to check that they are not at all moist or sticking. If they are dry (as they should be), it's okay to pile the noodles three or four layers deep. Set aside. (*If you are making the pasta more than a few hours in advance, cover loosely with plastic wrap. It can be set aside in a dry spot for up to 24 hours.*)

Beef Rendang ✈

Malaysian Beef Braised in Coconut Milk

Rendang is an exceptional Southeast Asian dish that reverses the ordinary braising sequence so that the meat is first simmered to tenderness and then browned. Beef chunks (or sometimes chicken) are seasoned with ginger, garlic, lemongrass, chiles, and a few other exotic flavorings and simmered uncovered in coconut milk. Then, in the most remarkable transition, just when the beef becomes perfectly tender, the coconut milk evaporates, leaving behind only the enriched spice paste and the coconut oil. In the final stage of braising, the supple beef cubes fry in the coconut oil. Because there is almost no braising liquid remaining in the end, the technique is described as a dry braise. This particular version is said to have originated in Sumatra, where water buffalo meat would have been used. Today rendang is found throughout Malaysia and Indonesia.

Traditional rendang requires a few hard-to-find ingredients (fresh galangal, fresh turmeric, kaffir lime leaves, and assam). If you have access to these, by all means include them, but I've made this without these less familiar ingredients and have never been disappointed by its deep and haunting flavor. The number of chiles used may appear daunting, but the coconut milk manages to tame their heat nicely. Since rendang is very rich, serve small amounts atop bowls of steamed white rice.

beer notes

Beer with fruity elements and a touch of spice—Bass Ale or Sierra Nevada Pale Ale.

Since beef rendang is equally good warm or at room temperature, it can be made a day or two in advance and refrigerated. To serve, let it come to room temperature or warm slightly in a skillet over medium heat.

Serves 6 | Braising Time: about 3 1/2 hours

THE SPICE PASTE

4 to 6 dried red chiles, such as chile de árbol

2 lemongrass stalks, woody tops, root ends, and outer layers removed, fragrant 4-inch cores coarsely chopped

4 small shallots, coarsely chopped (scant 1/2 cup)

2 to 3 garlic cloves, peeled

One 2 1/2-inch piece fresh ginger, peeled and coarsely chopped

One 2-inch piece fresh turmeric, peeled and coarsely chopped, or 1/2 teaspoon ground

One 2-inch piece fresh galangal, peeled and coarsely chopped (optional)

Pinch of coarse salt

THE BRAISE

2 tablespoons peanut oil

3 whole star anise

5 cardamon pods

Two 3-inch cinnamon sticks

2 1/2 pounds boneless beef chuck or brisket, cut into 1 1/2- to 2-inch cubes

1 1/2 teaspoons sugar

Coarse salt

2 1/2 to 3 cups unsweetened coconut milk, or as needed

4 fresh kaffir lime leaves (optional)

1. **Make the spice paste:** Combine the chiles, lemongrass, shallots, garlic, ginger, turmeric, and galangal, if using, in a blender, small food processor, or mortar and pestle. Season with the salt. Grind the spices to a coarse paste, adding 3 to 4 tablespoons of water as necessary if the flavorings are too dry to grind. Be sure to grind thoroughly; too many fibers or chunks will be unpleasant in the finished dish.

2. **Frying the spice paste:** Heat the oil in a wok or large deep skillet (12- to 13-inch) over medium-low heat. Add the spice paste and fry, stirring frequently with a wooden spoon, until the paste appears a bit glossy as the oil begins to separate out of it, 3 to 8 minutes. (If you added water to grind the paste, this will take the longer amount of time.) Add the star anise, cardamom, and cinnamon and stir to combine. Add the beef and stir to coat the meat evenly with the paste. Season with the sugar and a healthy pinch of salt.

3. **The braise:** Pour in enough coconut milk to just cover the beef and stir to blend the paste into the milk. Bring to a gentle simmer, and braise, uncovered, until the meat is almost tender, about 2 ½ hours. Stir the beef every 20 to 25 minutes, and check that the simmer remains quiet—there should be occasional bubbles but certainly not a torrent. If necessary, lower the heat or place the pan on a heat diffuser. The color of the coconut milk will darken to a light milk chocolate color as it absorbs the beef juices.

4. **The dry braise:** As the liquid reduces to a thick paste, stir in the lime leaves, if using, and continue braising, monitoring the pan more closely. Eventually a clear oil will separate out from the paste. When this happens, stir more frequently, and then fry the beef in the oil until it becomes mahogany brown, another 45 to 60 minutes. During this last stage, you may want to retrieve the whole spices when you spy them (star anise, cardamom, and cinnamon), since you may not want to bite down on them unknowingly—though I sometimes like to encounter them in a finished dish. (If you do remove the whole spices, collect them in a small bowl, then splash over a few teaspoonfuls of water to rinse them and return this flavored water to the pan.)

5. **Finishing the sauce and serving:** If you've used chuck, there will be as much as ⅓ cup clear oil in the pan when the rendang is done; brisket will give off less. Either way, spoon off and discard as much oil as you care to. Don't be afraid to leave a bit for flavor. Stir and taste for salt. Serve warm or at room temperature.

The Distinction Between a Braise and a Stew

From a purely semantic perspective, braising and stewing are closely related, but braising has a specific definition (cooking food in a closed vessel with very little liquid at a low temperature and for a long time; see page 3), and stewing does not. Stewing is a broader term that means, quite simply, to cook food by simmering it in liquid—any amount of liquid, with or without a lid. This being the case, braising remains a more precise technique.

From a practical standpoint, however, cooks make a distinction between the two terms that depends on three things: the amount of liquid used, the size of the foods being cooked, and the use of a lid.

- *Braising uses less liquid than stewing.* A primary objective of braising is to develop a rich and concentrated sauce. To achieve this, the liquid at the start rarely reaches more than one-third of the way up the sides of the foods being braised. In stewing, the ingredients are often completely covered by liquid.
- *Stews are made with smaller chunks of meat.* Braising primarily refers to cooking larger cuts, such as pot roast, leg of lamb, or whole leeks. Stews are more often made with chunks or smaller pieces in a soupy mixture of liquid and seasoning.
- *Most braises are cooked under a lid.* The theory of braising relies on concentrating a small amount of liquid into a rich sauce through a cycle of evaporation and condensation. This can only be accomplished by enclosing the ingredients and liquid in a tightly sealed pot. When stewing, however, the process begins with a more generous amount of liquid, so evaporation is less of a concern. Many stews are left uncovered or partially covered as they simmer; just as many are covered. There's no overriding principle with stewing.

Oxtails Braised in Red Wine →→

It perplexes me that oxtail is categorized under the euphemistic title "variety meats" along with the odder bits like tongues, hearts, and livers. The only thing even remotely odd about oxtail might be its appearance. From a pure taste standpoint, oxtail is as beefy a cut of beef as you'll ever taste. If you're a first-timer, you may want to pull the meat from the bones before serving, as working around the knobby bones at the dinner table can feel clumsy until you do it a few times. But one taste of the exquisitely tender meat with its honest beef flavor, and you'll become a convert.

Although I usually cook wine to tame its flavor some before using it as a marinade, here I like the more rugged character of raw wine. Its aggressive character works well with the bold taste of oxtail. After marinating, the wine is substantially reduced down to become the base for a very concentrated braising liquid. In the end, the aromatic vegetables and the braising liquid collapse into a savory compote that is perfect with the tender meat. Buttered egg noodles or polenta would be good with this.

wine notes

Sangiovese-based reds from Italy used in the braise would be perfect. Look for Chianti Classico, Carmignano, or Brunello di Montalcino.

Working Ahead

The oxtails need to marinate for 1 to 2 days before braising (Step 1).

Braised oxtails taste delicious as soon as they are ready. And they taste even better if you refrigerate them for a day or two in their braising liquid—either on the bone or off. To serve, heat the oxtails in the braising liquid in a covered baking dish in a 350-degree oven for about 30 minutes.

**About 5 pounds oxtails, cut into 1 ¹/₂-
 to 2-inch pieces (see "Shopping for
 Oxtails," page 299)**

THE MARINADE

1 teaspoon black peppercorns

¹/₂ teaspoon allspice berries

4 whole cloves

**Three 5-inch leafy fresh rosemary sprigs,
 broken into 1-inch pieces**

2 bay leaves, broken in half

1 teaspoon coarse salt

**One 750-ml bottle dry red wine,
 preferably Sangiovese or Chianti**

THE AROMATICS AND BRAISING LIQUID

¹/₂ ounce dried porcini mushrooms

³/₄ cup warm water

2 tablespoons extra-virgin olive oil

**¹/₄ pound pancetta in one thick slice, cut
 into ¹/₂-inch dice**

**1 large yellow onion (about 8 ounces),
 coarsely chopped**

1 large carrot, coarsely chopped

1 celery stalk, coarsely chopped

**Coarse salt and freshly ground black
 pepper**

2 garlic cloves, coarsely chopped

2 tablespoons tomato paste

2 tablespoons grappa or brandy

**1 ¹/₂ cups beef, veal, or chicken stock,
 homemade (page 450, 451, or 448) or
 store-bought, or more as needed**

1. **Trimming and marinating the oxtails—1 to 2 days in advance:** Trim any excess fat from the oxtails, but don't trim off any of the silver membrane that attaches the meat to the bone.

Lay a 6-inch square of cheesecloth on a work surface. Put the peppercorns, allspice, cloves, rosemary, and bay leaves in the center of the cheesecloth, bring up the corners, and tie with kitchen string to form a little bundle. Place the oxtails in a bowl (not plastic) or a gallon-size heavy-duty zip-lock bag. Tuck the spice bundle in with the oxtails. Sprinkle over the salt, and pour over the entire bottle of wine. Cover the bowl or close the bag and refrigerate, turning the oxtails every 12 hours or so, for 1 to 2 days.

2. **Soaking the porcini mushrooms:** Soak the mushrooms in the warm water for 20 to 30 minutes to soften.

3. **Browning the oxtails:** Heat the broiler on high. Remove the oxtails from the marinade, reserving the wine and spice bundle. Dry the oxtails with paper towels and arrange them on a rimmed baking sheet or broiler tray. Broil the oxtails about 4 inches from the broiling element, turning with tongs to brown all sides, until they are a beautiful dark brown but not charred, about 25 minutes total. Keep close by while the oxtails are browning, as they can go from perfectly browned to badly charred very quickly if ignored. Set aside, and lower the oven temperature to 300 degrees.

4. **The aromatics:** Heat the oil in a Dutch oven or other braising pot (6- to 7-quart) over medium-high heat. Add the pancetta, onion, carrot, and celery and season lightly with salt and pepper. Sauté, stirring with a wooden spoon, until the pancetta renders some of its fat and the vegetables brown in spots, 10 to 12 minutes. A deep brown crust will form on the bottom of the pot. Add the garlic, then stir in the tomato paste so that it coats the vegetables and pancetta. Sauté for another minute or so. By now the bottom of the pot should be quite dark but not at all burnt.

   Lift the porcini mushrooms from the soaking liquid, reserving the liquid. Coarsely chop the mushrooms and stir them into the pot. Strain the mushroom soaking liquid though a triple layer of cheesecloth or a coffee filter to catch any sand or grit. Set aside.

5. **The braising liquid:** Pour the grappa or brandy into the pot, and scrape the bottom with a wooden spoon to loosen the crust as best you can. Bring to a boil. Pour in about half the reserved marinade, bring to a boil, and boil until reduced by about half, about 6 minutes. Pour in the remaining wine, add the spice bundle, and boil again until reduced by about half, another 6 minutes or so. Add the reserved mushroom soaking liquid and the stock and boil until the liquid is reduced by half, about 15 minutes. The bubbles will begin to appear more sluggish as the liquid thickens somewhat. By reducing the liquids in stages like this, you are building a more complex layering of flavors than you would if you added them all at once.

6. **The braise:** Arrange the oxtails in the pot, tucking them in as close together as possible. Cover with parchment paper, pressing it down so that it nearly touches the oxtails and the edges hang over the sides of the pot by about an inch. Set the lid in place and slide the pot into the lower third of the oven to braise gently until the meat is completely tender and pulling away from the bone, about 4 hours. After the first 10 or 20 minutes, check to see that the liquid is not simmering rapidly. If necessary, lower the oven temperature by 10 or 15 degrees. Turn the oxtails with tongs about halfway through cooking, and check that there is enough liquid in the pot. If it appears to be drying out at any time, add 1/2 cup of water.

7. **The finish:** Transfer the oxtails to a platter or dish and cover loosely with foil to keep

warm. Remove the spice bundle, squeeze it gently with tongs or press it against the side of the pot with a wooden spoon to extract as much liquid as you can, and discard. The braising liquid and vegetables will have cooked down to a rather thick, jam-like mix. Tilt the pot, and skim off most of the surface fat with a wide spoon. Don't be too fastidious—a bit of fat adds tremendous flavor. Taste and evaluate the braising liquid. It should be deeply caramelized and concentrated, a sort of savory compote. If you would like it more deeply concentrated, boil over medium-high heat to reduce. If, on the other hand, the braising liquid is too thick for your taste, add ¼ cup water or stock to loosen it up. Taste for salt and pepper, and keep warm over low heat.

8.   **Serving:** If you're serving the oxtails on the bone, place them on a small bed of the braising vegetables and juices on each plate. If you prefer the meat off the bone, use a small knife to cut and tear the meat from the bones, discarding the bones and leaving the meat in chunks. Return the meat to the pot to heat through. Serve the boned meat with the cooked-down braising juices and vegetables ladled over the top.

Shopping for Oxtails

Although oxtail was once an inexpensive cut, its scarcity has made it rather dear. Depending on where you live, oxtails may or may not be hard to find. In the Northeast, for instance, they appear in the regular meat case, but only during the winter. A whole oxtail typically weighs around 2 1/2 pounds, so you'll need 2 for this recipe. Because of its high ratio of bone to meat, figure 3/4 to 1 pound per person. If the oxtails are sold whole, ask the butcher to cut them into 1 1/2- to 2-inch pieces. If they are already cut up, be sure to get a good number of meaty pieces along with a few not-so-meaty pieces. The smaller pieces are from the tip of the oxtail, and while they don't provide much meat, they should be included because they contribute essential body to the braise. Some oxtails come already trimmed, others come with an outer layer of fat that must be cut away. Good oxtails are available through mail-order (see Sources, page 455).

VEAL

Sausage-&-Pistachio–Stuffed Veal Marsala ✦✦

Unlike most braises, which begin with a rugged cut of tough meat, this recipe calls for the tender and rather pricey thin-cut veal scallops. The general thinking behind cooking delicate veal scallops is to sauté them briskly over high heat and to serve them with little more than a quick pan sauce or a squirt of lemon. (Think veal marsala or veal piccata.) So, why fuss with a braise? Simple. Rolling veal scallops around a pistachio-studded sausage filling and braising them creates a fullness of flavor and juiciness impossible to achieve with a fast sauté. The filling bastes the veal as it braises, so it remains tender and moist, and the meat juices meld with the Marsala-based braising liquid to create a perfectly integrated, complex sauce.

Dry Marsala wine, with its smoky, almost nutty flavor, is a classic complement to the sweet taste of veal. I also add a splash of Cognac to enrich the filling, but if there's no bottle in the cupboard, don't go out and buy one just for this. More Marsala will work just as well.

Braised Leeks with Bacon & Thyme (page 86) and risotto and would be good on the plate with these.

wine notes

Medium-bodied red with tart fruit and bright acidity—Dolcetto or Barbera from northwestern Italy.

Makes 8 rolls; serves 4 | Braising Time: about 1 1/2 hours

THE FILLING

1/2 pound sweet Italian sausage,
   preferably without fennel seeds,
   casings removed

1/4 cup coarsely chopped unsalted
   pistachios

2 tablespoons chopped flat-leaf parsley

1/2 cup fresh bread crumbs made from
   day-old rustic white bread

1 tablespoon Cognac or dry Marsala wine

1 large egg yolk

Coarse salt and freshly ground black
   pepper

Pinch of freshly grated nutmeg

Eight 1/4-inch-thick veal scallops (about
   1 3/4 pounds), preferably from the leg
   (see "Shopping for Veal Scallops,"
   page 306)

Coarse salt and freshly ground black
   pepper

All-purpose flour for dredging (about
   1/2 cup)

THE AROMATICS AND BRAISING LIQUID

1 tablespoon unsalted butter

1 tablespoon extra-virgin olive oil

1 carrot, chopped into 1/2-inch dice

1 small yellow onion (about 4 ounces),
   chopped into 1/2-inch dice

1 celery stalk, chopped into 1/2-inch dice

1/3 cup dry Marsala wine

3/4 cup veal or chicken stock, homemade
   (page 451 or 448) or store-bought

Coarse salt and freshly ground black
   pepper

1. **The filling:** In a medium bowl, combine the sausage, pistachios, parsley, bread crumbs, Cognac or Marsala, and egg yolk. Season with salt and pepper and the nutmeg. Work the mixture gently with your hands to blend all the ingredients evenly without working the sausage too much; overworking the filling can make it tough.

2. **Pounding the veal scallops (if the slices of veal are less than 1/4 inch thick, omit this step):** Lay 1 or 2 scallops on a cutting board. Cover with plastic wrap, and pound with a meat mallet or the bottom of a small heavy saucepan until the slices are just under 1/4 inch thick. It's best to pound with angled, glancing blows, so that you come across the meat rather than directly down on top of it. Remember that veal is tender to begin with—if you pound too aggressively, you may destroy the texture of the meat. Set the slices aside on a plate and repeat with the remaining veal.

3. **Shaping the rolls:** Place 1 veal scallop on the cutting board with a short end near you. Top with one eighth of the stuffing (about 2 tablespoons). Spread the filling across the lower third of the meat, leaving a 1/4-inch border along the sides and spreading it right up

to the bottom edge. Starting at the short end near you, fold the meat up over the stuffing and then roll the beef up around the stuffing to form a little sausage, open on each end. Set the roll aside on a plate, and repeat with remaining veal slices and stuffing. (Veal rolls usually hold together neatly without tying. If, however, this worries you, or they seem to want to unfurl, just tie a loop of kitchen string around each one to secure.) If the veal feels at all moist to the touch, pat it dry with paper towels. (Wet meat will stick to the pan when browning.)

4. **Dredging the rolls:** Season the veal rolls on all sides with salt and pepper. Put the flour into a shallow dish (a pie plate works well) and dredge the rolls one at a time, rolling in the flour to coat all sides, then lifting and patting gently to knock off any excess. Discard the remaining flour.

5. **Browning the rolls:** Heat the butter and oil in a large deep lidded skillet (12-inch) over medium-high heat. When the butter stops foaming, use tongs to add as many veal rolls, seam side down, as will fit without crowding. Cook, turning only after each side is browned, until all sides are a true chestnut color, about 10 minutes total. Set aside on a plate, and repeat with any remaining rolls.

6. **The aromatics and braising liquid:** Add the carrot, onion, and celery to the fat remaining in the pan, and sauté, stirring occasionally, until the vegetables become tinged with brown, about 5 minutes. Add the Marsala, bring to a boil, and stir with a wooden spoon to scrape up the browned bits from the bottom of the pan. Continue to boil until the Marsala is reduced to a few tablespoons, 1 to 2 minutes. Pour in the stock, and bring to a boil.

7. **The braise:** Return the veal rolls to the pan, tucking them in as best you can to make a single layer. Cover tightly and reduce the heat to low. After 5 minutes, check to see that the liquid has settled down to a relaxed simmer. If it is boiling, reduce the heat or place a heat diffuser on the burner to keep the heat low enough. Continue to braise at a gentle simmer, checking every 20 minutes and turning the rolls once about halfway through, until the meat is fork-tender, 1 1/4 to 1 1/2 hours.

8. **The finish:** Transfer the rolls to a carving board or platter (depending on which way you will serve them), and cover loosely to keep warm. Taste the sauce for salt and pepper. (If you tied the rolls, remove the strings.) Serve the rolls one of two ways: whole on the platter or sliced into 1/4-inch slices and arranged on individual dinner plates. Either way, spoon some of the sauce over, and pass the rest at the table.

Shopping for Veal Scallops

Veal scallops, sometimes sold as cutlets or scaloppine, are 3/8- to 1/8-inch-thick slices of veal. Traditionally veal scallops are cut from the leg. Veal connoisseurs may talk about differences in scallops cut from the top round, bottom round, and eye of the round (all parts of the leg), but in my experience, few markets offer you the luxury of choosing among these—and they are all good and all comparable in taste and texture. When making veal rolls, however, avoid scallops from the eye of the round, which are simply too small to wrap around the filling. Look for scallops that are about 5 inches across (eye of the round scallops will be smaller, closer to 3 inches). Look also for scallops that are 1/4 inch thick. Too thin, and they won't hold up to the long braise.

In many markets, you may find veal scallops cut from the shoulder, typically labeled as such. Shoulder scallops should be less expensive than leg scallops, and while a bit less tender for quick cooking, they are fine for braising. My only complaint with shoulder scallops is that they are often irregularly shaped and therefore more difficult to shape into neat rolls. If shoulder scallops are all you can find, the dish will still taste delicious but may perhaps not be as pretty to look at.

You may also find veal labeled "Plume de Veau" or "Provimi" in some markets. These are brand names of companies producing good-quality veal. Plume de Veau and Provimi often cost more than regular supermarket-label veal, but you are guaranteed tender, mild meat.

Coq au Vin, page 157

Caribbean Pork Shoulder, page 354, with World's Best Braised Green Cabbage, page 59

Pot-Roasted Brisket with Rhubarb &
Honey, page 267

Fresh raw pork belly, page 384

Red-Cooked Pork Belly with Bok Choy, page 385, and rice

Braised Cauliflower with Capers &
Toasted Bread Crumbs, page 84

Osso Buco alla Milanese, page 321

Herb-Stuffed Leg of Lamb Braised
in Red Wine, page 419

Veal Pot Roast with Almonds, Raisins & Sweet Marsala ✈

Boneless veal shoulder studded with garlic and almonds and then braised with golden raisins, sweet Marsala wine, and more almonds is almost too elegant to call pot roast. With its tender meat, creamy sauce, and subtle sweet balance of flavor, this dish is good enough to serve at your fanciest dinner parties. It's also easy enough to make for family—especially if you braise it on a Sunday and then serve it on Monday or Tuesday.

As the veal braises, the juices mingle with the nutty Marsala wine and the almonds lose their crunch and turn milky-soft. Then, when the meat is tender, the braising liquid is pureed to create a thick, creamy sauce made without a speck of cream. Expect to have a generous amount of sauce, but that's by design. It's so good that you'll want extra to spoon over mashed potatoes or rice pilaf.

wine notes

Something with a touch of sweetness or very ripe fruit—Amarone from the Veneto region of Italy or old-vine Shiraz from Australia.

Working Ahead

The day before you plan to braise the veal, stud it with almonds and garlic and rub the surface with the seasonings (Steps 1 and 2).

Once braised, the veal may be held for up to 2 days before serving. Complete the recipe through Step 7. To serve, carve the cold roast into 1/2-inch-thick slices, and arrange in a shallow baking dish. Coat the slices with sauce, cover with foil, and warm in a 325-degree oven until heated through, about 25 minutes.

Serves 6 | Braising Time: about 2 hours

1/2 cup slivered almonds

One 3 1/2- to 4-pound boneless veal
    shoulder roast (see "Shopping for Veal
    Shoulder," page 312)

2 large garlic cloves, cut into slivers

1 tablespoon coarsely chopped fresh
    rosemary

Coarse salt and freshly ground black
    pepper

Pinch of crushed red pepper flakes

3 tablespoons extra-virgin olive oil

1 medium yellow onion (about 6 ounces),
    thinly sliced

2 garlic cloves, minced

2 tablespoons loosely packed golden
    raisins

1/3 cup sweet Marsala wine

1/2 cup chicken stock, homemade (page
    448) or store-bought

1/2 lemon if needed

Chopped flat-leaf parsley for garnish
    (optional)

1. **Toasting the almonds:** In a medium skillet, toast the almonds over medium heat, stirring or shaking them frequently, until fragrant and evenly and lightly toasted, 8 to 9 minutes. Set aside to cool.

2. **Studding the veal:** Using kitchen twine, tie the roast into a neat, compact shape (see "Tying a Roast Before Braising," page 258). With a small knife, make 3/4-inch-deep incisions all over the roast, about 1 1/2 inches apart. Stuff a sliver each of garlic and almond into each incision until you've used up all the garlic. Reserve the remaining almonds.

3. **The spice rub:** In a small bowl, combine the rosemary, 3/4 teaspoon salt, a good pinch of pepper, and red pepper flakes. Rub this mix all over the veal roast. Set the roast in a baking dish or on a large plate, cover loosely with plastic, and refrigerate overnight.

4. **Heat the oven to 300 degrees.**

5. **Browning the meat:** Pat the veal roast dry with paper towels, trying not to wipe off much of the spice rub. Reserve any that falls off. Heat 2 tablespoon of the oil in a deep braising pot (5-quart) over medium heat. Add the veal roast and sear, turning with tongs as you go, until the meat has developed an appetizing brown crust on all sides, 15 to 20 minutes total. Lift the roast from the pot and return it to the baking dish or plate.

6. **The aromatics and braising liquid:** Pour off the oil from the pot and wipe out any burned bits with a damp paper towel, being careful not to remove any precious caramelized meat drippings. Add the remaining 1 tablespoon oil, and return the pot to medium heat. Add the onion and sauté, stirring occasionally, until softened, about 6 minutes. Add the minced garlic and sauté until fragrant, about 30 seconds. Add any seasonings that fell off the roast before browning, then add the raisins and Marsala, bring to a simmer, and simmer until the wine is reduced by three quarters, about 5 minutes. Scrape the bottom of the pot with a wooden spoon as the wine simmers to release and dissolve any

tasty drippings left from browning the meat. Pour in the stock, bring to a simmer, and simmer until reduced by half, another 4 minutes.

7. **The braise:** Add the reserved almonds, then set the roast back in the pot, along with any juices that have accumulated under the meat. Cover with parchment paper, pressing down so that the paper nearly touches the meat and the edges hang over the rim of the pot by about an inch. Set the lid in place, and slide into the lower third of the oven. Braise at a gentle simmer, turning the roast with tongs after 1 hour, until the veal is fork-tender, about 2 hours. During the first 30 minutes, lift the lid of the braising pan to check that the liquid isn't simmering too energetically. If it is, lower the oven temperature 10 or 15 degrees.

8. **The finish:** Using tongs or a sturdy spatula, lift the veal from the pot and transfer to a carving board or large platter. Cover loosely with foil to keep warm. Skim as much surface fat as you care to from the surface of the braising liquid, without losing patience. Scrape the braising liquid into a blender, filling it no more than two-thirds full. (There will be close to 2 cups of sauce, so if you have a small blender, do this in batches.) Being sure to leave the lid open a crack so it doesn't pop off (see "Pureeing Hot Liquids in a Blender," below), puree the liquid until creamy. The almonds will thicken the sauce, but don't expect it to be entirely smooth. Pour the almond sauce into a medium saucepan. Taste for salt and pepper. If, after seasoning the sauce, it tastes a little flat, add a few drops of lemon juice. This will make all the flavorings sing. Taste again and bring to a gentle simmer.

9. **Serving:** Remove the strings from the veal and slice into 1/2-inch-thick slices. Serve with a generous coating of sauce, sprinkled with parsley, if desired, for a bit of color.

Pureeing Hot Liquids in a Blender

If you've ever had a blenderful of hot sauce or soup explode all over your kitchen, you know what can happen. The hot liquid carries with it a great deal of steam, and the minute you hit the on button, that steam can force the contents up and the lid off in a sudden scalding surge. Sure, clamping down on the lid with an oven mitt or kitchen towel can solve the problem, but it's risky. The best, and safest, solution is to fill the blender no more than two-thirds full and, most important, to vent the blender cap by leaving the cap open a bit to allow steam to escape. If the blender lid has a removable center (ostensibly for adding liquids during blending), remove it. If not, nudge up one corner of the lid so there is not a tight seal. Then drape a kitchen towel over the blender. It may still spit up a bit where the lid is open, but there will be no powerful explosion.

Veal Shoulder Braised with Figs & Sherry ✈

Every time I make this dish, I fall in love again with its enchanting combination of flavors and textures. The actual list of ingredients contains nothing too remarkable—veal, leeks, garlic, coriander seed, sherry, stock, and dried figs. It's the transformation of these ingredients as they simmer together beneath the lid of the braising pot that gets to me. The veal becomes silky-tender and infused with the concentrated sweetness of the figs and sherry. The figs and leeks cook down into a thick compote-like sauce rich with the savor of the veal. This is an ideal braise to make in the fall, when the air is cooler but you're not quite ready for the heartier, deep winter braises.

I use a medium-dry amontillado sherry here. I like the way its nutty flavor plays against the figs. A drier fino would be good, too, making the sauce just a bit lighter tasting. Oloroso, or cream sherry, is too sweet and too heavy for the veal.

Serve with a side of butternut squash puree or Risotto Milanese (page 325).

wine notes

Earthy red with spicy red fruits and not too much tannin—Rioja Reserva or Navarra from Spain.

Serves 3 to 4 | Braising Time: about 1 1/2 hours

One 2- to 2 1/2-pound bone-in veal shoulder blade roast, about 2 inches thick (see "Shopping For Veal Shoulder," page 312)

Coarse salt and freshly ground black pepper
2 tablespoons unsalted butter
1 cup thinly sliced leeks, white and pale green part only (2 medium)

2 garlic cloves, thinly sliced

1/2 teaspoon coriander seeds, toasted and
   lightly crushed

1/2 cup medium-dry amontillado or dry
   fino sherry

1/2 cup veal or chicken stock, homemade
   (page 451 or 448) or store-bought

3 ounces dried figs, preferably Black
   Mission, hard stems removed and
   quartered (about 1/2 cup)

1.   **Heat the oven to 300 degrees.**

2.   **Tying the meat:** Tie the veal with kitchen string so that it is a snug roast and won't fall apart during braising (see "Tying a Roast Before Braising," page 258). Dry the roast thoroughly with paper towels and season all over with salt and pepper.

3.   **Browning the meat:** Heat the butter in a Dutch oven or other heavy lidded braising pot large enough to hold the veal (12-inch) over medium heat. When the butter stops foaming, lower the veal into the pot using tongs. Brown the first side of the roast, without disturbing it, until you can see that the butter is beginning to brown, about 5 minutes. Lift the side of the veal with tongs to check that the bottom surface has browned. Using tongs, turn and brown the second side, another 5 minutes or so.

4.   **The aromatics and braising liquid:** Transfer the veal to a large plate or tray. Wipe out any burnt bits of butter with a damp paper towel, being careful to leave behind the caramelized juices. Add the leeks and garlic to the pot and stir to coat with the butter. Add the coriander and a pinch each of salt and pepper. Sauté over medium heat until the leeks begin to soften and turn a gentle gold color on the edges, about 5 minutes; do not let them crisp. Add the sherry, bring to a simmer, and simmer until reduced by about half, 3 to 4 minutes. Add the stock and bring to a simmer.

5.   **The braise:** Return the veal to the pot, pouring in any juices that have seeped from the meat. Cover with parchment paper, pressing down so the paper nearly touches the meat and the edges extend about an inch over the sides of the pot. Then set the lid in place and slide into the lower third of the oven to braise at a gentle simmer.

   After 30 minutes, add the figs to the pot and, using tongs, turn the veal. If the liquid is simmering too energetically, lower the oven temperature by 10 or 15 degrees. Continue braising at a quiet simmer until the meat is fork-tender and pulling away from the bone, another 50 to 60 minutes.

6.   **The finish:** Carefully transfer the veal to a serving platter or carving board, using a spatula to support the meat so it doesn't fall off the bone. Cover loosely with foil to keep warm. Set the braising pot on a burner set at medium and evaluate the sauce: if there's much surface fat (veal is so lean there rarely is), skim it with a wide spoon. The sauce should be the consistency of a classic vinaigrette, chunky with bits of figs. Usually when I

make this, the sauce tastes perfect as is, but if you desire a thicker or more concentrated sauce, boil to reduce for 3 to 4 minutes. Taste for salt and pepper.

7. **Serving:** Snip the strings, pull the veal from the bone using a carving fork and knife, and cut into chunks. Transfer to plates or a platter, and spoon the sauce over the top.

VARIATION: BONELESS VEAL SHOULDER BRAISED WITH FIGS & SHERRY

Follow the recipe above using a 1 3/4-pound boneless shoulder roast, rolled and tied (see "Tying a Roast before Braising," page 00). Since this roast is a bit more compact than the bone-in roast, use a 9- to 10-inch Dutch oven or other heavy lidded braising pot in place of the larger one. The braising time will be the same. Snip the strings before serving and slice into 1/2-inch-thick slices.

Shopping for Veal Shoulder

Veal shoulder is a smart choice for the braising pot because it is so high in collagen that you are guaranteed a gorgeous sauce. Plus, the mild flavor of veal marries so well with a broad range of aromatics and liquids. Veal shoulder is basically the front portion of veal with the shank (leg) and breast removed. It corresponds directly to the chuck of beef, but it is quite a bit smaller. The shoulder consists of a number of different muscle groups, and it is the connective tissue between these muscles that contains the collagen that melts to create such a richly bodied sauce during braising.

Cuts from the veal shoulder are sold bone-in and boneless. Bone-in cuts are the *veal shoulder blade roast* (or *steak*) and *veal shoulder arm roast* (or *steak*). (The only difference between the roasts and the steaks is that the roasts are thicker and better suited for a long braise.) The complicated bone structure of a bone-in veal shoulder roast can make carving awkward, which is another good reason to braise it. The meat becomes so tender that it pulls away from the bone without the need for carving.

Boneless cuts from the veal shoulder, which are usually rolled and tied into a cylindrical shape, can come from either the arm or the blade portion of the shoulder. Both are ideal for the braising pot. Some markets simplify things by labeling any veal shoulder roast (bone-in or boneless) as *veal pot roast*.

Breast of Veal Braised with Garlic, Parsley & Lemon ✈

Shopping the meat case at my local supermarket one day, an older woman saw me reach for a bone-in breast of veal and asked me how I was going to cook it. Her mother used to cook this economical cut, she said, yet she had never bothered to learn how. I started in about removing the bones and stuffing it or rolling it, but she stopped me and said, "No, no, nothing so complicated." After some talking, we deduced that her mother would just cover the meat with garlic, parsley, salt, and pepper and cook it to tenderness. Sounded good to me. We both dropped a packaged breast of veal in our carts and headed off to the produce department for the garlic and parsley. I thought lemon sounded like a good addition so I grabbed a few of them as well.

If you have never cooked or tasted a breast of veal, this is the place to start. The simple directness of the recipe brings out all the goodness this inexpensive cut has to offer. Breast of veal is not dissimilar to bacon, meaning it has its fair share of fat, but the combination of pale, tender meat bathed in succulent juices is deeply satisfying. I serve relatively small portions, since breast of veal is so rich, and accompany it with something soft and comforting, like risotto or polenta. To serve a crowd, buy a whole breast of veal (about 6 pounds), double the other ingredients, and use a roasting pan, covered tightly with heavy-duty foil, as a braising dish. Ideal party fare.

wine notes

Sangiovese always pairs well with veal. Try Chianti Classico Riserva, Carmignano, or Rosso di Montalcino.

Serves 4 to 6 | Braising Time: about 2 1/2 hours

2 tablespoons extra-virgin olive oil

One 3- to 4-pound bone-in breast of veal
    (see "Shopping for Breast of Veal,"
    page 316)

8 garlic cloves, peeled

Coarse salt

1/4 cup finely chopped flat-leaf parsley

Grated zest of 1 lemon

Freshly ground black pepper

1 cup dry white wine or dry white
    vermouth

1 cup veal or chicken stock, homemade
    (page 451 or 448) or store-bought

1.   **Heat the oven to 300 degrees.**

2.   **Browning the meat:** Be warned that the veal will splatter a fair amount, so wear an apron or old shirt and stand back as best you can. Heat the oil in a heavy skillet large enough to hold the veal comfortably (12- to 13-inch) over medium heat until it shimmers. Pat the veal dry with paper towels, and lower it into the skillet with tongs. Cook, turning once, until the meat has a deep roasted appearance on both sides, about 8 minutes per side. If there is a thick blunt end on the breast, use the tongs to stand it up on end and brown this as well. Transfer the veal to a large plate or platter to collect any juices that seep out, and let cool slightly. Discard the fat from the skillet and wipe out any charred bits with a damp paper towel, being careful not to dislodge the precious caramelized drippings. Set the skillet aside.

3.   **Making the garlic paste:** Drop the garlic cloves into a mortar, sprinkle with 1 teaspoon salt (the salt crystals will act as an abrasive and help break the garlic down into a puree), and smash and grind to a paste. You should have about 2 tablespoons. Scrape the garlic paste into a small bowl. (If you don't have a mortar and pestle, see "Making Garlic Paste," page 315.) Stir in the parsley, lemon zest, and a few grinds of black pepper.

4.   **Seasoning the meat:** When the veal is cool enough to handle, use your fingers to smear the garlic-parsley mixture all over it. Push the seasoning into any folds and crevices of the veal: do not tear the meat apart, but push the seasoning paste into the meat as deep as you can. Set the veal in a Dutch oven or other heavy lidded casserole (3- to 4-quart) that holds it snugly. Pour over any juices that seeped from the veal as it cooled. Set aside.

5.   **The braising liquid:** Return the skillet to high heat and add the wine. Bring to a boil, scraping the bottom with a wooden spoon to dislodge any flavorful bits stuck there, and reduce down to about 1/4 cup, about 8 minutes. Add the stock, bring to a boil, and boil for another 2 to 3 minutes. Pour this liquid around the breast of veal; don't pour it directly over the meat, or you will wash off the parsley-garlic paste. Cover with parchment paper, pressing down so the paper nearly touches the veal and the edges hang about an inch over the sides of the pot. Set the lid in place.

6.   **The braise:** Slide the pot into the lower part of the oven to braise at a gentle simmer. After 15 minutes or so, check to see that the liquid is not simmering too vigorously. If it is,

reduce the oven by 10 or 15 degrees. Continue to braise gently for 15 minutes more, then, using tongs, turn the veal over. After 2 hours, turn the veal again, more carefully this time as the meat may be starting to fall off the bone—use a spatula or wooden spoon along with the tongs to make this maneuver more manageable. Then continue to braise, uncovered, so that the surface can caramelize, until the veal is completely tender, about 30 minutes more (2 ½ hours total). If at any point there's so little liquid in the pot that it looks as if it might dry up, add about ⅓ cup of water.

7. **Boning the veal breast:** Remove the veal from the pot and set it on a platter or cutting board with a moat to catch the juices. Let it sit for 20 to 30 minutes, until cool enough to handle. Set the pot aside. Turn the oven up to 325 degrees.

With your hands, tug on the rib bones extending from the meat until they come loose: they will slide out neatly with no meat attached. Discard. Feel around the veal for any flat bits of cartilage that may be present. These take a bit more wrangling to remove, but just work at the meat with your hands, wriggling and tugging until they come free. You may have to pull the meat apart in a few places, but not to worry.

8. **Serving:** Degrease the pan juices as best you can, and taste for salt and pepper. There are two options for serving: you can carve the breast of veal in the kitchen and then warm the pieces, or warm the whole glorious thing (breast and juices together), present it at the dining table, and make a ceremony out of carving. Whichever you choose, it's best to cut the breast into rustic hunks rather than neat slices. Set the veal (whole or sliced) into a shallow baking or ovenproof serving dish and pour over the degreased pan juices. Heat until warmed though, 15 to 25 minutes.

Spoon some pan juices over each serving.

Making Garlic Paste

If you don't have a mortar and pestle, here's how to make the garlic paste: Set the garlic cloves on a cutting board and, one by one, smash each clove with the flat side of a large knife. Then mince the garlic as fine as possible. Once the garlic is well minced, sprinkle over a healthy pinch of coarse salt (the salt crystals will act as an abrasive and help break down the garlic into a puree) and continue mincing the garlic. Every 10 or 15 seconds, scrape the blade of the knife clean and pile up all the minced garlic, then press down on the pile with the flat side of the knife (sharp edge facing away) and drag the knife toward you, applying pressure to flatten and smash the garlic. Continue to mince and smash until you have a smooth, moist paste.

Shopping for Breast of Veal

Breast of veal is one of the best buys of meat in the market. But few home cooks seem to know what tremendous eating you can get for so little money. You can keep your veal rib chops and give me the breast any day.

Breast of veal corresponds to the brisket section of beef or belly section of pork, and it boasts the same combination of flavorful meat and juicy fat. A whole breast of veal will weigh more than 6 pounds and sometimes as much as 12 pounds. Keep in mind, however, when we're referring to four-legged animals, the carcass is first split down the middle, so that a "whole" breast is actually only one side, (that is, each veal carcass will offer two "whole" breasts of veal, unlike chicken, where the whole breast refers to both sides). Most markets sell smaller breast of veal, closer to 3 or 4 pounds. These more manageably sized cuts are convenient for feeding 4 to 6 people. For bone-in breast of veal, I count about 12 ounces per person. Although this isn't a lot of meat after you've braised it and removed the bones, it will satisfy most appetites. If you're feeding extra-hearty eaters, figure 14 or 15 ounces per person.

Boning a breast of veal is a rather complicated operation and best left to the pros. Depending on where you shop, you may need to call ahead to request a boneless breast of veal. If you are making Breast of Veal Stuffed with Sausage & Red Peppers (page 317), be sure to specify that you need a boneless breast of veal with a pocket for stuffing: on occasion, I've bought a boneless breast of veal without specifying the need for a pocket and ended up with a thin butterflied stretch of meat with no opening for the stuffing. If this does happen to you, lay the veal out flat on a cutting board and spread the stuffing over it as you would for *Farsumagru* (page 238).

Breast of Veal Stuffed with Sausage & Red Peppers ⇥

Make this for a big sit-down dinner party or a holiday buffet. Not only is a whole boneless breast of veal an impressive dish to behold, but it's also entirely more satisfying and original than the standard baked ham or roast beef. I like to make a stuffing of sweet Italian sausage and stewed red bell peppers, but there's plenty of room for improvisation. Try ground veal in place of the sausage, sautéed Swiss chard in place of the bell peppers, maybe a bit of chopped ham or a handful of pine nuts—you get the idea.

Before you set out to make this dish, I should tell you that the recipe has quite a few steps: first you stuff the veal, then you roast it in a hot oven for an hour to caramelize the surface, then you braise it for 2 hours, and finally you work the braising liquid through a food mill to make a meaty, tomatoey sauce. But I should also tell you that, in the end, this grand dish is worth every minute of your time. Serve with a loaf of crusty, artisanal bread so that your guests can sop up the delectable sauce. Any leftover sauce can be tossed onto pasta on another day.

Boneless breast of veal is not an everyday item in most markets. Call ahead and be sure to specify a whole breast of veal, boned and with a pocket for stuffing. You'll need a heavy-duty needle and kitchen string to sew up the pocket.

wine notes

Full-bodied red, such as a rich Australian Shiraz or California Zinfandel, to match the intensity of the sausage-and-pepper stuffing.

Working Ahead

Stuffed breast of veal tastes even better when made a day or two in advance. Braise the veal as directed through Step 8, and leave to cool in the braising liquid. Once cooled to room temperature, cover, and refrigerate for 1 to 2 days. To serve, remove the veal and surface fat from the braising liquid. Proceed to make the sauce as described in Step 9, and ladle about 1 cup of the sauce into the bottom of a baking dish. Carve the cold veal into ½-inch-thick slices and layer them on top of the sauce. Ladle a bit more sauce over the top, cover with foil, and reheat in a 350-degree oven for 20 to 30 minutes. Remove the foil during the last 5 minutes.

Warm the remaining sauce in a saucepan, and serve the veal, passing the extra sauce at the table.

Serves 6 | Braising Time: about 2 hours, plus 1 hour of roasting

THE STUFFING

2 tablespoons plus 2 teaspoons extra-virgin olive oil

1 small yellow onion (about 4 ounces), finely chopped

1 red bell pepper (about 6 ounces), cored, seeded, and cut into ½-inch dice

Coarse salt and freshly ground black pepper

3 garlic cloves, minced

One 4-pound boneless breast of veal with a pocket for stuffing (see "Shopping for Breast of Veal," page 316)

⅓ cup coarsely chopped flat-leaf parsley

1 pound sweet Italian sausage (with or without fennel), casings removed

½ cup fresh bread crumbs made from day-old rustic white bread

1 large egg

¼ cup freshly grated Pecorino Romano or Parmigiano-Reggiano

⅛ teaspoon ground allspice

Coarse salt and freshly ground black pepper

THE AROMATICS AND BRAISING LIQUID

1 large yellow onion (about 8 ounces), coarsely chopped

2 carrots, coarsely chopped

1 celery stalk, coarsely chopped

5 garlic cloves, thinly sliced

One 14 ½-ounce can whole peeled tomatoes, with their juice

2 teaspoons chopped fresh thyme or ¾ teaspoon dried

Coarse salt and freshly ground black pepper

1 cup dry white wine or dry white vermouth

2 cups veal or chicken stock, homemade (page 451 or 448) or store-bought

Finely chopped flat-leaf parsley for garnish

1. **Heat the oven to 400 degrees.**

2. **The stuffing:** Heat the 2 tablespoons oil in a medium skillet over medium-low heat. Add the onion and bell pepper, season with salt and pepper, and sauté, stirring frequently, until the onion is translucent and the pepper is soft, about 15 minutes. Do not let the vegetables brown. Add the garlic and parsley and sauté just until fragrant, another minute or so. Set aside to cool.

    In a large bowl, combine the sausage, bread crumbs, egg, cheese, allspice, 1/2 teaspoon salt, and a few grinds of black pepper. Add the cooled onion-pepper mixture, scraping the skillet with a spatula to capture all the juices. With your hands, gently work the meat to blend in all the ingredients, stopping as soon as everything is evenly distributed. Avoid overworking the stuffing. At this point, it's good practice to cook up a bit of stuffing to taste. Pull off a small knob of stuffing, shape it into a little (1-inch) patty, and panfry it in the 2 teaspoons oil. Taste and correct the seasoning accordingly with salt and pepper.

3. **Stuffing the veal:** Lay the breast of veal on a cutting board with the fat side up and the opening facing you. Trim off any thick layers of fat, but don't go overboard, and don't cut away any fat that holds the breast of veal together. You need to leave some fat to baste the meat as it braises. Season inside and out with salt and pepper. Scoop the stuffing into the pocket, flattening it with your hands to distribute it evenly. Close the pocket and sew it shut, using kitchen string and a heavy-duty large-eyed needle to make 5 or 6 whip-stitches: Start by tying a thick knot at the end of the string, then push the needle through the bottom side of the veal about 1/2 inch from the edge, push the needle out through the top side, and tug so that the pocket is closed. Then bring the needle down and repeat this same stitch, pushing the needle back up through the bottom side about 1 1/2 inches from the first stitch. Don't pull the string too tight, you just need to secure the opening.

4. **The aromatics:** Scatter the onion, carrots, celery, and garlic in a deep roasting pan or shallow braising dish large enough to accommodate the veal (9-by-13-inch). Using your hands, break up the tomatoes over the vegetables, letting all their juices fall into the pan, and then pour over the juice from the can. Season with the thyme and salt and pepper. Set the stuffed veal on top of the vegetables.

5. **Browning the meat:** Slide the pan into the center of the oven and roast, uncovered, until the bits of fat are sizzling and the veal has developed an attractive deep brown appearance, about 1 hour. This initial roasting is a somewhat unusual way to brown meat before braising, but it works well for this unwieldy cut, a good way to give the finished dish an appealing caramelized flavor and color.

6. **The braising liquid:** While the veal browns, bring the wine to a boil in a small saucepan over medium-high heat. Boil until reduced by about three quarters, about 6 minutes. Add the stock and boil until reduced by half, another 8 minutes or so. Remove from the heat.

7. **The braise:** Pour the wine-stock mixture over the veal, and cover the pan tightly with heavy-duty foil. Reduce the oven temperature to 300 degrees. Braise at a quiet simmer, turning the veal with sturdy tongs after an hour, until it is fork-tender, about 2 hours (for a total of about 3 hours in the oven). Expect the veal to shrink quite a bit.

    With the same sturdy tongs, transfer the veal to an ovenproof dish. Ladle some of the cooking liquid over the veal to moisten it, leaving the vegetables behind. Cover the veal with foil and set in a very low oven, about 225 degrees, to keep warm.

8. **The finish:** Spoon off as much clear fat from the surface of the braising liquid as you can without losing patience. Set up a food mill with a coarse or medium blade over a medium saucepan. Work the braising liquid through the food mill, churning vigorously to push through the solids as best you can. Bring the sauce to a simmer. You should have 1 1/2 to 2 cups of sauce. If the sauce appears thin, bring it to a rapid simmer over medium-low heat, stirring occasionally. The sauce should be the consistency of marinara sauce; simmer until it reduces and thickens, usually about 10 minutes. The sauce is ready when the bubbles rising to the top become thicker and move more slowly. Taste for salt and pepper.

9. **Serving:** Remove the veal from the oven, and carve into thick slices. Serve with a generous ladle of sauce over the top, and garnish with chopped parsley.

Osso Buco alla Milanese →→

Veal Shanks Braised with Tomato & White Wine

Classic osso buco alla Milanese is probably the dish that inspired me to write an entire book on braising in the first place. I don't remember where or when I first tasted a veal shank slow-cooked with tomato and white wine, but I know that for years afterward I couldn't go to a restaurant where it was on the menu without ordering it. Fortunately, I finally taught myself to make it—the recipe is surprisingly straightforward considering the complexity of flavor it delivers—and I still haven't lost my appetite for the dish. I add a bit of chopped fresh fennel to the traditional aromatic mix of onions, celery, and carrots, and I also add orange zest to enliven the braising liquid, but otherwise, this is pretty much the classic recipe I first tasted.

Veal shanks are ideally suited for braising because they're so high in collagen, the connective tissue that breaks down in the moist, low heat of a braise and enriches the sauce like nothing else. Shanks also have a remarkably fine meat texture, which is what makes them so luxurious when braised.

Some cooks forgo the gremolata, the pungent mixture of garlic, parsley, and lemon zest added to the osso buco during the last minutes of the braise, but I wouldn't dream of it. The bright, fresh flavors of the gremolata are released as soon as it comes in contact with the warm veal, giving the whole dish a divine lift. In fact, I like the effect of the gremolata so much that I sometimes add a double dose. That is entirely up to you.

Risotto Milanese (the recipe follows) is the classic accompaniment, and with good reason. Its creamy texture and saffron-laced flavor go perfectly with the tender shanks. If you're not in the mood for risotto, plain rice or mashed potatoes are fine alternatives.

This classic calls for one of Italy's best red wines: Barolo, Barbaresco, or Brunello di Montalcino.

Serves 4 to 6 | *Braising Time: about 2 hours*

All-purpose flour for dredging (about
   1/2 cup)
4 meaty veal shanks, each 2 to 2 1/2 inches
   thick (3 to 3 1/2 pounds total; see
   "Shopping for Veal Shanks,"
   page 330)
Coarse salt and freshly ground black
   pepper
2 tablespoons extra-virgin olive oil
3 tablespoons unsalted butter
1 medium yellow onion (about 6 ounces),
   chopped into 1/2-inch pieces
1 medium carrot, chopped into 1/2-inch
   pieces
1 celery stalk with leaves, chopped into
   1/2-inch pieces

1 small fennel bulb (about 12 ounces),
   trimmed, cored, and chopped into
   1/2-inch pieces
3 garlic cloves, minced
2 strips orange zest, removed with a
   vegetable peeler (each about 3 inches
   by 3/4 inch)
1 1/2 teaspoons chopped fresh marjoram
   or 1/2 teaspoon dried
1 bay leaf
1 cup dry white wine or dry white
   vermouth
1/2 cup veal or chicken stock, homemade
   (page 451 or 448) or store-bought
1 cup chopped peeled tomatoes, fresh or
   canned, with their juice

THE GREMOLATA
2 tablespoons chopped flat-leaf parsley
1 teaspoon minced garlic

1 teaspoon grated lemon zest

Risotto Milanese (recipe follows; optional)

1. **Heat the oven to 300 degrees.**
2. **Dredging the shanks:** Pour the flour into a shallow dish (a pie plate works nicely). Season the veal shanks on all sides with salt and pepper. One at a time, roll the shanks around in the flour to coat, and shake and pat the shank to remove any excess flour. Discard the remaining flour.
3. **Browning the shanks:** Put the oil and 1 tablespoon of the butter in a wide Dutch oven or heavy braising pot (6- to 7-quart) and heat over medium-high heat. When the butter has

melted and the oil is shimmering, lower the shanks into the pot, flat side down; if the shanks won't fit without touching one another, do this in batches. Brown the shanks, turning once with tongs, until both flat sides are well caramelized, about 5 minutes per side. If the butter-oil mixture starts to burn, lower the heat just a bit. Transfer the shanks to a large platter or tray and set aside.

4. **The aromatics:** Pour off and discard the fat from the pot. Wipe out any burnt bits with a damp paper towel, being careful not to remove any delicious little caramelized bits. Add the remaining 2 tablespoons butter to the pot and melt it over medium heat. When the butter has stopped foaming, add the onion, carrot, celery, and fennel. Season with salt and pepper, stir, and cook the vegetables until they begin to soften but do not brown, about 6 minutes. Stir in the garlic, orange zest, marjoram, and bay leaf, and stew for another minute or two.

5. **The braising liquid:** Add the wine, increase the heat to high, and bring to a boil. Boil, stirring occasionally, to reduce the wine by about half, 5 minutes. Add the stock and tomatoes, with their juice, and boil again to reduce the liquid to about 1 cup total, about 10 minutes.

6. **The braise:** Place the shanks in the pot so that they are sitting with the exposed bone facing up, and pour over any juices that accumulated as they sat. Cover with parchment paper, pressing down so the parchment nearly touches the veal and the edges hang over the sides of the pot by about an inch. Cover tightly with the lid, and slide into the lower part of the oven to braise at a gentle simmer. Check the pot after the first 15 minutes, and if the liquid is simmering too aggressively, lower the oven heat by 10 or 15 degrees. Continue braising, turning the shanks and spooning some pan juices over the top after the first 40 minutes, until the meat is completely tender and pulling away from the bone, about 2 hours.

7. **The gremolata:** While the shanks are braising, stir together the garlic, parsley, and lemon zest in a small bowl. Cover with plastic wrap and set aside in a cool place (or the refrigerator, if your kitchen is very warm).

8. **The finish:** When the veal is fork-tender and falling away from the bone, remove the lid and sprinkle over half of the gremolata. Return the veal to the oven, uncovered, for another 15 minutes to caramelize it some.

Using a slotted spatula or spoon, carefully lift the shanks from the braising liquid, doing your best to keep them intact. The shanks will be very tender and threatening to fall into pieces, and the marrow will be wobbly inside the bones, so this can be a bit tricky. But if they do break apart, don't worry, the flavor won't suffer at all. Arrange the shanks on a serving platter or other large plate, without stacking, and cover with foil to keep warm.

9. **Finishing the sauce:** Set the braising pot on top of the stove and evaluate the sauce: if

there is a visible layer of fat floating on the surface, use a large spoon to skim it off and discard it. Taste the sauce for concentration of flavor. If it tastes a bit weak or flat, bring it to a boil over high heat, and boil to reduce the volume and intensify the flavor for 5 to 10 minutes. Taste again for salt and pepper. If the sauce wants more zip, stir in a teaspoon or two of the remaining gremolata.

10. Portioning the veal shanks: If the shanks are reasonably sized, serve one per person. If the shanks are gargantuan or you're dealing with modest appetites, pull apart the larger shanks, separating them at their natural seams, and serve smaller amounts. Be sure to give the marrow bones to whomever prizes them most.

11. Serving: Arrange the veal shanks on warm dinner plates accompanied by the risotto, if serving. Just before carrying the plates to the table, sprinkle on the remaining gremolata and then spoon over a generous amount of sauce—the contact with the hot liquid will aromatize the gremolata and perk up everyone's appetite with the wiff of garlic and lemon.

RISOTTO MILANESE

I like to start the risotto when I uncover the veal shanks during the last 15 minutes of braising. This way, I'm standing at the stove finishing the risotto and the shanks at the same time. If you're not comfortable multi-tasking at the stove, prepare the osso buco up through Step 11, and set the veal, covered, in a low oven until you make the risotto. The shanks won't suffer at all if kept waiting for a half hour. The risotto, on the other hand, is best served as soon as it's made.

Serves 6

4 cups chicken stock, homemade (page 448) or store-bought

Heaping 1/2 teaspoon coarse salt, or more to taste

2 tablespoons unsalted butter or extra-virgin olive oil

1 large shallot or small onion, minced

Large pinch of saffron threads

1 cup medium-grain risotto rice, such as Arborio or Carnaroli

1/2 cup dry white wine or dry white vermouth

1/3 cup freshly grated Parmigiano-Reggiano

1.   Heat the stock in a medium saucepan over medium-low heat to just below a simmer. Season with the salt.

2.   Heat the butter or oil in a heavy-based deep skillet or wide saucepan over medium heat. Add the shallot or onion and cook, stirring occasionally, until translucent, about 6 minutes. Crumble the saffron into the pan, stir, and cook for another minute. Add the rice and stir until the grains are well coated with butter or oil. Pour in the wine, stir with a wooden spoon, and cook until the wine is mostly evaporated and the pan is almost dry, 3 to 4 minutes.

3.   Ladle about 1 1/2 cups of the hot broth into the rice, and stir the rice. Simmer, stirring occasionally, until the broth is absorbed. Continue adding stock in 1/2-cup increments, stirring and simmering until it is absorbed each time, at intervals of about 3 to 5 minutes.

After about 18 minutes, check to see if the rice is tender by biting into a grain. It probably won't be quite done, but you want a sense of how much longer the rice needs so you know how much more stock to add; as the rice gets closer and closer to being done, you want to add less and less stock. The rice should have a slight resistance to it, al dente, and, when you cut open a grain, there should be just a tiny speck of bright white. Continue simmering, adding only a few tablespoons of stock at a time and stirring, until the rice is creamy and perfectly al dente, 20 to 25 minutes total time.

4. Remove from the heat, and fold in the Parmigiano-Reggiano. Taste for salt. Serve immediately.

Veal Shanks Braised with Honey & Rosemary ✈

Veal has an inherent sweetness that really comes to the fore when it is braised with a bit of honey. If you're a honey fiend, as I am, and stock up on different varieties, then you'll want to choose one that's got more going for it than just sweet. I especially like the delicate complexity of herb honeys, such as rosemary, lavender, thyme, or sage. (Herb honey is not infused with herbs, but rather made by bees that suck the nectar from herbs in blossom—an important distinction). Orange blossom honey is another good choice, because it picks up the orange in this braise.

This recipe comes from my dear friend Randall Price, a profoundly talented chef living and working in Burgundy, France. Randall's been working on a series of honey-based recipes for his brother, a beekeeper, and he was kind enough to share this one with me. As we all know, food shopping in France can be quite a different experience than shopping here. Randall is able to purchase whole veal shanks at his butcher, and that's what he uses: one enormous three- to four-pound shank. Much like a leg of lamb or standing rack of anything, an entire shank makes a grand centerpiece. They can be special-ordered in some markets here, and can be great fun to prepare and serve. The braising time will be about the same.

wine notes

Chateauneuf-du-Pape is the first choice; otherwise, a deeply flavored Grenache-blend from the southern Rhone Valley, California, or Australia.

Serves 4 to 6 | Braising Time: about 2 hours

4 meaty veal shanks, each 2 to 2 1/2 inches
    thick (3 to 3 1/2 pounds total; see
    "Shopping for Veal Shanks,"
    page 330)

Coarse salt and freshly ground black
    pepper

2 tablespoons extra-virgin olive oil

1 large yellow onion (about 8 ounces),
    coarsely chopped

1 cup dry white wine or dry white
    vermouth

2 cups veal or chicken stock, homemade
    (page 451 or 458) or store-bought

2 tablespoons honey (rosemary or
    lavender honey if possible)

Zest and juice of 1 orange, zest removed
    in strips with a vegetable peeler

Zest of 1 lemon, removed in strips with a
    vegetable peeler

Two 6-inch leafy fresh rosemary branches

2 tablespoons balsamic vinegar

THE CARROT AND SHALLOT GARNISH

1 tablespoon unsalted butter, plus more to
    finish if desired

1 tablespoon extra-virgin olive oil

12 to 18 small to medium shallots, peeled
    (about 10 ounces)

12 to 18 small carrots, peeled, or 4 larger
    carrots, cut into 3-by-3/4-inch sticks
    (about 12 ounces)

Coarse salt and freshly ground black
    pepper

Two 6-inch leafy fresh rosemary branches

1. **Heat the oven to 300 degrees.**

2. **Browning the shanks:** Season the veal shanks on all sides with salt and pepper. Heat the oil in a wide Dutch oven or heavy braising pot (6- to 7-quart) over medium-high heat. When the oil is quite hot, add as many shanks as will fit without crowding. (If necessary, sear the shanks in batches.) Sear the shanks, turning once with tongs, until both flat sides have an attractive bronze color, about 5 minutes per side. Transfer to a large plate or tray, without stacking.

3. **The aromatics and braising liquid:** Add the onion to the pot, stir, and sauté, still over medium-high, until it softens and begins to brown, 3 to 4 minutes. The bottom of the pot should be developing a caramelized crust. Pour in the wine, stir to dissolve the brown crust on the bottom of the pot, and boil until the wine is reduced by half, about 10 minutes.

4. **The braise:** Add the stock, honey, orange zest and juice, lemon zest, rosemary, and balsamic vinegar to the pot. Return the shanks to the pot, arranging them in a snug single layer, and pour over any juices that accumulated as they sat. Bring to a simmer and cover with parchment paper, pressing down so the paper nearly touches the shanks and the edges hang over the sides of the pot by about an inch. Then secure the lid in place and

slide into the lower third of the oven to braise at a gentle simmer for 1 hour. After the first 10 or 15 minutes, check that the liquid is not boiling too energetically; if it is lower the oven heat by 10 or 15 degrees and continue to braise.

5.   **Meanwhile, prepare the garnish:** Heat the butter and oil in a large skillet (12-inch) over medium-high heat. When the butter has melted and the oil is quite hot, add the shallots and carrots, season with salt and pepper, and sauté, stirring and shaking the pan frequently, until tinged with brown all over, about 8 minutes. Add the rosemary branches and sauté for another minute.

After the veal has braised for 1 hour, add the shallots, carrots, and rosemary to the pot. Turn the shanks with tongs when you add the vegetable garnish and continue to braise gently until the veal is fork-tender and pulling away from the bone, about 2 hours total. Remove the pot from the oven.

6.   **Finishing the sauce:** With a slotted spoon, lift the shanks, along with the shallots and carrots, onto a platter, without stacking. Handle the veal carefully at this point, as it will tend to fall apart. Cover loosely with foil to keep warm. Strain the braising liquid into a saucepan, pushing down on the vegetables, zest, and spent herbs to extract all the juices, and discard the solids. Skim the surface fat from the strained liquid, and bring to a simmer over medium-high heat. Simmer, skimming a few more times, until reduced enough to lightly coat the back of a spoon, about 15 minutes. Season with salt and pepper, and keep at a low simmer.

7.   **Portioning the veal shanks:** If the shanks are reasonably sized, serve one shank per person. If the shanks are enormous, pull apart the larger shanks, separating them at their natural seams, and serve smaller amounts. Be sure to offer the marrow bones as well.

8.   **Serving:** For a luxurious sauce, whisk a walnut-sized knob of butter into the barely simmering sauce. Once you've added the butter, avoid prolonged boiling. Serve the shanks accompanied by the carrots and shallots, and spoon the sauce over the top.

Shopping for Veal Shanks

Veal shanks, the front and hind legs, represent the quintessential cut for braising because they contain more collagen than any other cut of meat available—even more than other shanks, such as lamb shanks. This means that the cook is guaranteed moist, tender meat in an ultra-silky sauce. In most retail markets, veal shanks are sliced cross-wise into thick rounds, easily recognizable by the round marrow bone staring out from the center of each. (The name *osso buco* translates literally as "bone hole," referring to the round marrow-filled bones.)

There's been a fair amount said (and written) on which is best, the hind shank or the foreshank. I like both, for different reasons. The hind shanks are bigger and meatier—more magnificent when presented on a plate. Foreshanks are more modest in size, but, and here's what most cooks don't know, they are the more flavorful of the two. I also find that hind shanks, which can weigh close to 1 pound, can be too much for one appetite. If I am given a choice, I will choose extra-thick (close to 2 1/2 inches) fore-shanks—but I would never complain about being served, or sold, hind shanks. Whichever you buy, look for shanks that are no less than 1 1/2 inches thick; 2 inches is best. If they're too thin, they'll braise too quickly and therefore won't release enough collagen to make the sauce as exquisite as it should be. As for how many shanks or how many pounds of shanks to buy, it's neater if you can serve one per person, but if your market only sells enormous hind shanks, figure about 10 ounces per person, and follow the directions in the second to last step of the recipes on portioning shanks.

Restaurant chefs sometimes buy and serve whole veal shanks for a large table. These are enormous pieces of meat, weighing 3 to 4 pounds each, and they are best presented like a leg of lamb, whole and carved at the table. Whole veal shank is not appropriate for osso buco, since the marrow bones are part of the experience, but if you get your hands on one, a whole shank is an outstanding choice for the Veal Shanks Braised with Honey & Rosemary (page 327).

Polpettone Braised in Tomato Sauce ⇥

Giant Veal & Ricotta Meatballs Braised in Tomato Sauce

Polpettone isn't the easiest dish to define. The word itself translates directly from the Italian as meat loaf or meat roll, but that's not what these are. The best description would have to be giant meatballs, close to three inches in diameter—almost more like individual meat loaves. These are definitely not the kind of meatballs you serve on spaghetti. Instead, polpettone stand up on their own as a gorgeous main course, accompanied perhaps by braised broccoli rabe (page 51) or sautéed potatoes. Or serve them unaccompanied for lunch, with nothing more than a crusty piece of bread for mopping up the sauce. I even delight in snitching leftovers for breakfast—warm or cold.

What pleases me most about polpettone is that they are gently braised, not fried, so they come out remarkably tender throughout and infused with the sweet flavor of the tomato sauce.

Be forewarned: when you serve polpettone, people will demand the recipe. One friend made them the very day after she ate them at my house. She used the traditional meat loaf mix of pork, beef, and veal instead of all veal, and still called to say that they were "beyond divine." Personally, I prefer the pure taste of all veal.

wine notes

Sangiovese-based red, such as Chianti Classico, Carmignano, or Rosso di Montalcino.

Working Ahead

The polpettone may be braised ahead and kept in their sauce at room temperature for an hour or so. To serve, warm them in the sauce over low heat for about 10 minutes. If cooked further in advance, refrigerate the meatballs in the tomato sauce. To serve, spoon the meatballs into a baking dish, spoon over the sauce, cover with foil, and warm in a 300-degree oven for about 20 minutes. Polpettone are also very good cold—better than meat loaf for making a sandwich.

Makes 12 very large meatballs; serves 6 | *Braising Time: 35 to 45 minutes*

THE BRAISING SAUCE

3 tablespoons unsalted butter

1 large yellow onion (about 8 ounces), finely chopped

1 celery stalk with leaves, finely chopped

2 garlic cloves, minced

Coarse salt and freshly ground black pepper

1 bay leaf

2 cups tomato juice

2 cups chicken stock, homemade (page 448) or store-bought

THE MEATBALLS

1 cup fresh bread crumbs made from day-old rustic white bread

1/2 cup buttermilk (whole milk may be substituted)

3/4 cup whole-milk ricotta (see "Shopping for Ricotta Cheese," page 334)

1/4 cup freshly grated Parmigiano-Reggiano

1/4 cup chopped flat-leaf parsley

1 large egg, lightly beaten

1 teaspoon coarse salt

Freshly ground black pepper to taste

1 1/2 pounds ground veal

1. **The braising sauce:** Heat the butter in a large deep skillet over medium heat (a 13-inch skillet with 3-inch sides is ideal, or use any wide skillet with a 4- to 5-quart capacity). When the butter is melted, add the onion, celery, and garlic and cook, stirring occasionally, until soft and barely translucent but not at all browned, about 10 minutes. Season lightly with salt and pepper, keeping in mind that canned tomato juice can be salty.

    Add the bay leaf, tomato juice, and stock. Bring to a simmer, stirring once or twice, and simmer for 15 to 20 minutes to meld and concentrate the flavors. Taste for salt and pepper.

2. **While the sauce is simmering, make the meatballs:** Combine the bread crumbs and buttermilk in a small bowl. Stir the bread crumbs around with a small spoon or your hands to moisten them. Let sit from 5 to 10 minutes.

    In a medium bowl, combine the ricotta, Parmigiano, parsley, egg, salt, and pepper. Add the soaked bread crumbs and buttermilk and stir the whole lot with a wooden spoon or your hands until well mixed. Break off hunks of the ground veal and drop them into the bowl. Then gently knead the meat to work in all the other ingredients. The goal is to blend everything evenly without overworking the meat—if you overmix, the meatballs can become tough and heavy.

3. **Shaping the meatballs:** Using a ⅓-cup measure, scoop out a heaping portion of the veal mixture for each meatball and shape it into a round ball. Again, take care not to squeeze or overmanipulate the mixture. Arrange the balls on a large platter or tray without touching one another.

4. **The braise:** When the sauce is ready, reduce the heat to medium-low and, one by one, lower the meatballs into the skillet. (I use a large spoon to avoid mauling the meatballs or burning my fingers.) Once all the meatballs are in the pan, spoon a little sauce over the top of each one and cover the pan. Adjust the burner so that the sauce stays at a low simmer with bubbles lazily rising to the surface. If it simmers too fast, the meatballs will toughen and the full exchange of flavor between sauce and meat won't occur.

After 20 minutes, carefully turn the meatballs with a large spoon. They're fragile, so work slowly. Spoon sauce over the tops again, cover, and continue to simmer until the meatballs feel firm to the touch, indicating that they are cooked all the way through, 35 to 45 minutes.

5. **Serving:** Let the meatballs sit in the sauce for about 5 minutes off the heat. To serve, place 2 meatballs on each plate and spoon some sauce over the top.

Leftover Braising Liquid

There may be leftover braising liquid. I like to use it to make rice pilaf (recipe follows). It's also good as a base for soup.

Shopping for Ricotta Cheese

If you are fortunate enough to live near an Italian market that sells fresh ricotta, that's what you should use. It's better tasting, fresher, and less watery than supermarket brands. I have also had good luck with an organic brand made in Connecticut, Calabro. If the only ricotta available to you is the ordinary supermarket stuff, you can greatly improve its quality (and the quality of your recipes) by draining it first. To do so, line a mesh strainer with a double layer of cheesecloth or sturdy paper towels and set the strainer over a deep bowl to catch the drips. Spoon the ricotta into the strainer and leave it overnight in the refrigerator to drain. If the flavor of the ricotta is flat and bland, here's a tip I learned from my friend Roy Finamore, a very talented and resourceful cook: stir in a tablespoon of fresh goat cheese for every $1/2$ cup of drained ricotta. This will make it taste closer to the real thing.

Tomatoey Rice Pilaf →→

Made with the leftover tomato-based braising liquid from the polpettone (page 331), this is a near-instant pilaf. Because the sauce already contains onions and celery, there's no peeling or chopping required. But, more important, you get all the great flavor that the polpettone lent to the sauce.

Serves 4

About 1 cup leftover braising liquid from
    the polpettone (page 331)
1 cup chicken stock, homemade (page 448)
    or store-bought, or water, or as
    needed

Coarse salt and freshly ground black
    pepper
2 tablespoons unsalted butter
1 cup long-grain white rice

1. Heat the oven to 350 degrees. Measure the leftover braising liquid and add enough stock or water to equal 2 cups. Taste for salt and pepper. The seasoning should be mild but apparent.
2. Melt the butter in an ovenproof, medium deep skillet or wide saucepan (2-quart) over medium heat. Add the rice, stir, and sauté until the grains are coated with butter and you hear a faint crackling sound, 2 to 3 minutes.
3. Pour in the braising liquid mixture and bring to a simmer. Cover tightly and slide into the oven to bake until the rice is tender and has absorbed all the liquid, 30 to 35 minutes.
4. Let the rice sit, covered, for 5 minutes, then stir with a fork before serving.

PORK

Braised Pork Chops & Creamy Cabbage ⇢⇢

Nothing fancy here: ordinary green cabbage, thick pork chops, a bouillon cube in place of stock, and a bit of cream. The bouillon cube may surprise you, but Italian home cooks have long appreciated the value and convenience of these little cubes (sold in Italy as *dadi*). While I would never unilaterally forgo real stock in place of bouillon, it does have its place, adding a meaty, savory edge to quick braised dishes. Crushing the cube with the side of a knife or in a mortar ensures that it will dissolve readily into the dish.

The creamy, sweet cabbage laced with a hint of caraway gets braised along with the chops and then spooned over them for serving. This is meal enough for most appetites, but if you're serving voracious eaters, or just want more, a side of mashed potatoes would be just the thing.

wine notes

Youthful fruity red with medium tannins—a lighter-style Zinfandel, Cotes-du-Rhone, or Australian Shiraz.

Serves 4 | *Braising Time: 30 minutes*

Four 1-inch-thick bone-in loin pork chops
  (about 2 1/2 pounds total)
Coarse salt and freshly ground black
  pepper
All-purpose flour for dredging (about
  1/2 cup)
3 tablespoons extra-virgin olive oil
2 tablespoons unsalted butter
1 teaspoon caraway seeds
1 teaspoon yellow mustard seeds

2 medium shallots, thinly sliced
1/2 small head green cabbage (about
  1 pound), cored and thinly shredded
1/2 cup dry white wine or dry white
  vermouth
2/3 cup water
1 tablespoon cider vinegar
1 small (1/8-ounce) chicken bouillon cube,
  crushed
1/4 cup heavy cream or crème fraîche

1. **Dredge the chops:** Wipe the chops thoroughly dry with paper towels. Season on both sides with salt and pepper. Put the flour in a shallow dish (a pie plate works well) and dredge the chops one at a time: place each one in the flour, turn to coat both sides, then lift it out, pat lightly to shake off any excess, and set on a plate. Discard the remaining flour.

2. **Browning the chops:** Heat the oil in a large (10- to 12-inch) heavy skillet or shallow braising pan over medium-high heat. When the oil slides across the pan, add as many chops as will fit without touching, and let them cook, without turning or moving them, until russet brown on the first side, about 4 minutes. Turn with tongs and repeat on the second side, another 3 to 4 minutes. You're not trying to cook the chops through, just to form a tasty brown crust. Transfer to a large plate. If you're browning in batches, repeat with the second batch. Set aside while you wilt the cabbage.

3. **Wilting the cabbage:** Melt the butter in a Dutch oven (4 1/2- to 6-quart) or large deep skillet or shallow braising pan (12-inch) over medium heat. Add the caraway and mustard seeds and cook, stirring with a wooden spoon, until you can smell their fragrance and the mustard seeds begin to pop—they will literally begin to jump around the pan—about 1 minute. Add the shallots, stir, and sauté for another 2 minutes, until they just begin to soften. Add the cabbage, season with salt and pepper, and reduce the heat to medium-low. Cook, stirring so the cabbage wilts evenly but doesn't brown, until all the shreds begin to turn limp, about 10 minutes.

4. **The braise:** Once the cabbage has become limp but not entirely tender, add the wine and let simmer for 1 to 2 minutes. Add the water, vinegar, and bouillon cube, stir with a wooden spoon to dissolve the bouillon cube, and bring to a gentle simmer. Transfer the chops to the cabbage, nestling them in it and overlapping them as necessary. Cover tightly, reduce the heat to low, and simmer gently. Check to see that the liquid settles down to a lazy simmer, not a lively one, after about 3 minutes. If necessary, lower the heat a bit or set a heat diffuser beneath the pan. Continue braising, turning the chops once halfway through, until the pork is tender and measures 150 degrees on a meat thermometer, about 20 minutes.

5. **The finish:** Transfer the pork chops to your serving dish or individual dinner plates. Increase the heat under the cabbage to medium-high and bring to a boil. Stir in the cream or crème fraiche, and boil gently to thicken just so that the cabbage is moist but not soupy, about 5 minutes. Taste for salt and pepper. Spoon the creamy cabbage over the chops and serve.

Today's Pork

In the late 1970s, American pigs were put on a stringent diet. Until then, farmers had aimed to raise fat pigs, which meant they produced juicy, well-marbled pork. In addition to rich-tasting pork chops, succulent roasts, and tender hams, the producers sold lard (rendered pork fat), fatback, salt pork, and other by-products of plump pigs. But in the late 1970s and early '80s, Americans started looking for ways to cut fat from their diets. Motivated by a concern over the negative health effects of a high-fat diet, they began to reject fatty pork in favor of leaner meats, primarily chicken. They also cut way back on fatty pork by-products, such as lard and fatback. Responding to this shift in consumer taste, pork producers developed ways to produce leaner pigs. Through changes in genetics and animal husbandry, commercially raised pork went from containing 4 to 10 percent fat to as little as 1 percent—a dramatic transformation. And because these leaner pigs were sent to market smaller and younger, the meat didn't have the chance to develop the flavor it once had. By eliminating all of that fat, the producers also lost much of pork's good flavor. The color of the meat changed from a deep rosy hue to a very pale pink, and the campaign for the "other white meat" was launched.

In the kitchen, this new breed of leaner pork poses a new set of challenges. Back in the 1970s, a medium-well or well-done pork chop would still be juicy and moist because the fat would have basted the meat and protected it from drying out. With the leaner pork, cooking it even the slightest bit past medium (with a trace of pink in the center) renders it dry and unpleasant. This problem is compounded by an almost universal tendency to overcook pork, a vestige from the days when trichinosis was a concern. (The fear of trichinosis derives from the time when pigs were raised on kitchen scraps, not on commercial-grade animal feed. The parasite is no longer a problem in commercially raised pigs, but many people cannot get used to eating medium-cooked pork.)

After experimenting with various cooking methods for modern-day lean pork, I've discovered two reliable solutions for keeping it juicy. Not surprisingly, the first is braising. The gentle, slow heat of the braising pot prevents the pork from drying out. It also provides the benefit of a flavorful sauce made from the braising liquid to further moisten the meat. The second method is one I use when grilling or roasting pork. It requires an overnight soak in a brine of water, salt, and sometimes a bit of sugar. The salt in the brine causes the meat to absorb enough water to keep it juicy and succulent even when exposed to the high, dry heat of the grill or the oven.

(continued on next page)

"Extra Tender" Supermarket Pork

Aware that consumers were overcooking the new-style pork, pork producers and packagers responded with an additional strategy. They would continue to produce lean pork, but they would inject it with a chemical solution prior to packaging it for retail sale so that the meat would retain more moisture. The scientific explanation is this: When fresh meat is treated with sodium phosphate and water, the muscle proteins begin to uncoil and soak up the added water, somewhat like a sponge. When you cook this treated pork, much of the added water remains in the meat so it is juicy even when overcooked. Unfortunately, the pork still has no real flavor: it won't taste deliciously porky even though it will be moist. In addition, this chemically treated pork has an unnatural bouncy texture and a distinct saline taste. And finally, the juice that are released from "pumped-up" pork during braising are dilute—and taste similar to canned broth—not nice. I avoid it if at all possible.

The technology for adding moisture to meat is nothing new. The poultry industry has been using it for years, as in the Butterball turkey. As general as the practice is, however, not all treated meats are the same. Producers and packagers use different amounts of the sodium phosphate solution, depending on the product. For instance, many hams contain as much as 35 percent water solution by weight. Fresh pork can contain as much as 30 percent by law, but most supermarket brands of pork contain only 7 or 10 percent. Besides the sodium solution, producers also enhance pork by adding flavorings and seasonings. If you've ever come across a teriyaki or lemon-pepper pork tenderloin vacuum-sealed in plastic, it's been pumped with sodium phosphate along with any number of seasonings. In my experience, these taste horrible.

All this technology provides another benefit to producers, packagers, and supermarkets. Treated pork has a longer shelf life than natural fresh pork. But while this benefits the people selling the pork, as a consumer, I prefer fresh products to be just that—fresh, and not injected with preservatives.

Shopping for Pork

When shopping for pork, you'll need to read the label closely to know what you're getting. In the past few years, the amount of treated pork in the supermarket has grown from a small specialty caseful to as much as the entire stock in some markets. Fortunately, the USDA requires that treated pork bear an ingredient label listing the amount of added solution. (The print tends to be very small, however, so you may have to look carefully to find it.) Good hints that you're looking at treated pork are the words "guaranteed tender," "extra tender," "basted," or "marinated" on the package. And any pork vacuum-sealed in a thick plastic pouch (known as Cryovac) will invariably have been treated. A puddle of liquid (referred to in the industry as purge) in the package is also a sign that the pork has been treated.

As much as I encourage you to eschew treated pork, there may be times when that's all that is available. In that instance, look for brands that have the least amount of added solution—typically in the 8 to 10 percent range. As you get into higher amounts, the meat becomes spongy and increasingly unpleasant tasting. Better yet, if your supermarket only carries treated pork, talk to the meat manager. Hopefully he or she will want to hear your opinion.

The good news is that there's been a renewed interest by a growing number of farmers in producing the old-fashioned kind of pork with great flavor and plenty of fat. Today the best-tasting pork comes from smaller, nonindustrial farms, where the animals are treated as livestock, not as a commodity. Whether the farmer produces organic meat or not, seek out pork that has been raised naturally on healthy feed, without growth hormones or antibiotics. Because the term *organic* can be used only by farmers who meet very strict criteria, there are in fact many farms producing excellent-quality meat without the organic label. To find natural, unadulterated pork, look to specialty markets, health food stores, farmers' markets, or mail-order businesses (see Sources, page 455). I've found the best assurance of quality is to learn the story behind the label. If it's a local farmer, ask how he or she raises the pigs. If it's a mail-order source, such as Niman Ranch, look on their website to read about their commitment to carefully and naturally raised top-quality meats.

And finally, forget all that "other white meat" nonsense. The best-tasting pork, especially those cuts from the shoulder and sirloin, has a deep rose color.

Sirloin Pork Chops Braised with Hot Cherry Peppers ⇥

A lively weeknight braise that takes much of its character from plain old pickled peppers. If you don't keep pickled hot cherry peppers in your refrigerator, use this as an excuse to buy a jar. But don't go looking in the gourmet section of your market for them. They are typically right there with all the other jars of nonrefrigerated pickles, relishes, and condiments. Once opened, a jar seems to last forever, and their vinegary heat makes a piquant addition to everything from egg salad to pasta sauces. The peppers do vary in heat and size, so add 1 to 3 according to your daring and the size of the peppers. The vinegary brine from the jar also carries a ton of flavor, so don't be timid about including a few drops of it as well.

Boneless sirloin pork chops, sometimes labeled as cutlets, are standard supermarket fare. These meaty chops come from the bottom end of the loin, or the hip section of a pig, and cost less than the pale center cut rib and loin chops. Serve with rice or polenta.

wine notes

Fruity, slightly sweet white—German Riesling from the Rheingau and Pfalz regions.

Serves 6 | Braising Time: about 40 minutes

2 tablespoons extra-virgin olive oil

1/4 pound spicy cured sausage, such as chorizo, andouille, or soppressata, cut into 1/4-inch dice

1 medium yellow onion (about 6 ounces), chopped into 1/2-inch pieces

Coarse salt and freshly ground pepper

3 garlic cloves, minced

1/2 cup dry white wine or dry white vermouth

2 tablespoons white wine vinegar

3/4 cup chicken stock, homemade (page 448) or store-bought

| 2 ½ pounds boneless pork sirloin chops (½ inch thick) | 1 to 3 small pickled hot cherry peppers, with juice to taste |

1. **Frying the sausage:** Heat 1 tablespoon of the oil in a large deep skillet or shallow braising pan (12-inch) over medium heat. Add the sausage and fry, stirring often, until browned on most sides, 6 to 8 minutes. With a slotted spoon, transfer the sausage to a paper towel–lined plate to drain.

2. **The aromatics and braising liquid:** Pour off and discard the fat from the pan. Add the remaining tablespoon of oil, and heat over medium heat. Add the onion, season with salt and pepper, and sauté, stirring, until the onion begins to soften and brown on the edges, 4 to 5 minutes. Add the garlic, stir, and sauté for another minute, until fragrant. Add the white wine, stir and scrape the bottom of the pan with a wooden spoon, and boil until the wine is reduced by about half, about 4 minutes. Add the vinegar, stir, and boil for a minute or two. Add the stock and bring to a simmer.

3. **The braise:** Season the pork all over with salt and pepper. Add the chops to the skillet, and immediately reduce the heat to a gentle simmer. One by one, tear the peppers into small pieces, discarding the seeds and stems, and adding the pieces to the skillet. (I like to hold them over the skillet while I tear them so that the juices fall directly into the pan. The only trouble with this approach is that a few errant seeds will fall in too, making the dish spicier still. If you'd prefer to minimize the peppers' heat, tear them over a cutting board so that any juices drip onto the board, then scrape every last seed to the side, and add the peppers and as much of the juices as you like to the skillet.) Cover the skillet and braise the pork quietly, checking after 5 minutes to see that the liquid is not simmering too furiously. If it is, lower the heat or set a heat diffuser beneath the pan. After 20 minutes, turn the pork with tongs. Continue to braise at a gentle simmer until the pork is fork-tender, about 40 minutes total.

4. **The finish:** Transfer the chops to a platter or plates and cover loosely with foil to keep warm. Bring the cooking juices to a boil over medium-high heat. Skim any surface fat with a large spoon. Boil until the juices are tasty and slightly thickened, 8 to 10 minutes. Lower the heat to a simmer, add the sausage to the sauce, and simmer for about 3 minutes to heat through. Taste for salt and pepper. Spoon over the pork and serve.

VARIATION: CREAMY PORK CHOPS BRAISED WITH HOT CHERRY PEPPERS

Add 2 tablespoons heavy cream to the sauce when it is boiling in Step 4. The cream contributes an elegant roundness to the flavor and tempers the heat of the peppers as well.

Pork Loin Braised in Milk ⇥

Marcella Hazan popularized this ancient and somewhat magical dish in *The Classic Italian Cookbook*. Hazan's Bolognese-style recipe is exquisitely simple—nothing more than pork simmered in milk until the meat is tender and the milk reduced to a caramelized sauce of soft custardy curds. The technique is genius and the results are a revelation, as the milk both tenderizes the pork and transforms into a uniquely concentrated sauce.

In digging around further, I've discovered other versions of *maiale al latte*, pork in milk. Cooks in the Veneto marinate the pork overnight in white wine and vinegar, those in other regions rub it with herbs and spices, and some American chefs enrich the milk with heavy cream—but I return again and again to the original idea. I do add a bit of seasoning in the form of garlic, fennel seed, and rubbed sage, because these flavors have such an affinity for pork. I also braise the meat in the oven, not, as Hazan does, on top of the stove, because I can better maintain the low heat needed to properly cook today's leaner pork (see "Today's Pork," page 341).

Unlike most pork braises, which use the darker, fattier shoulder and arm cuts, this dish has a certain delicacy and elegance best suited to the finer-grained meat from the rib section—either the blade end (sometimes called a 7-rib or 5-rib roast) or loin. For my money, I prefer the blade roast over the loin, because it remains just a bit juicier, but both are guaranteed to give you a superlative meal. Fennel Braised with Thyme & Black Olives (page 67) makes a great side dish. The pork is equally delicious served hot or cold.

wine notes

Youthful red with bright acidity, such as Italian Barbera, Dolcetto, or non-Chianti Sangiovese.

The pork is studded with sage, fennel, and garlic before braising; if time allows, season the pork (Step 1) up to 12 hours ahead of time, and refrigerate until you're ready to braise. This gives the seasonings a chance to permeate the meat.

Serves 6 | *Braising Time: about 1 1/2 hours*

One 2 1/2- to 3-pound boneless pork blade or loin roast

4 garlic cloves, peeled

1 tablespoon fresh sage, finely chopped, or 1 teaspoon dried sage

1/2 teaspoon fennel seeds, lightly crushed

Coarse salt and freshly ground black pepper

2 tablespoons extra-virgin olive oil

1 tablespoon unsalted butter

1 1/4 cups whole milk

1/2 lemon

1.   **Seasoning the pork—up to 12 hours ahead:** If the pork has a thick layer of fat on the surface, trim some, but not all, of it away. It's always a good idea to leave some fat to baste the pork as it braises. Tie the pork with kitchen string so it is in a neat log shape (see "Tying a Roast Before Braising," page 258).

Cut 3 of the garlic cloves into slivers. Smash the fourth, and set it aside. Put the garlic slivers in a small bowl, add the sage, fennel, 1/2 teaspoon salt, and 1/4 teaspoon black pepper, and toss the garlic to coat in the seasonings. With a small knife, poke 1-inch-deep incisions all over the pork, about 1 1/2 inches apart. Stuff each hole with a seasoned garlic sliver, and rub any leftover seasoning over the surface of the pork. (*The pork may be seasoned up to 12 hours ahead. Cover and refrigerate until ready to braise.*)

2.   **Browning the pork:** Heat the oven to 275 degrees. Choose a heavy Dutch oven that will hold the pork without too much extra space (an oval 3- to 4-quart pot works well), add the oil and butter, and heat over medium-high heat. When the butter stops foaming, add the pork and brown it, turning with tongs to color all four sides, 12 to 16 minutes total. If at any time the butter shows signs of burning and black specks appear, lower the heat a little. Transfer the pork to a plate.

3.   **The braise:** Depending on the pork, there may be an excess of fat in the pan: pour off all but about 1 to 2 tablespoons. Return the pot to medium-high heat and add the smashed garlic clove. Stir and heat until fragrant and just beginning to brown, about 40 seconds. Gradually pour in the milk, taking care that it doesn't foam up and spill over. Bring to a boil, lower to a simmer, and stir once or twice with a wooden spoon to scrape up any browned bits from the bottom of the pot. Return the pork to the pot, along with any

juices that have pooled on the plate. Cover with the lid, and slide into the lower third of the oven to braise gently. Ten to 15 minutes into the braise, lift the lid to check that the liquid is not boiling too vigorously. If it is, lower the oven temperature 10 to 15 degrees.

After 45 minutes, turn the pork with tongs. The milk will have separated and begun to take on an ivory color. Set the lid slightly ajar to allow steam to escape, so that the milk will begin reducing to a concentrated sauce as the pork continues braising. Continue braising at a gentle simmer with the lid ajar, basting the pork occasionally with a soupspoon, until it reaches an internal temperature of 150 degrees, 35 to 45 more minutes, depending on the thickness of the pork. Transfer to a carving board with a channel that will catch the juices and cover loosely with foil to keep warm.

4. **The finish:** While the meat rests, tilt the pot and spoon off the better part of the clear fat that sits on the surface of the curdled milk sauce. Don't worry about getting every last bit—you don't want the sauce to be too lean, or it will lack flavor. Turn the heat to high and boil the sauce to reduce it and concentrate the flavor. Stir with a wooden spoon, scraping up any bits stuck to the sides and bottom of the pot. If the liquid in the pan is thin and watery, you may need to boil it for 10 to 12 minutes. When the sauce is ready, it will be a light caramel color and resemble a loose broken custard. If, however, after only a few minutes, there's very little liquid and mostly milk curds, stir in a few tablespoons of cold water and return just to a simmer. Taste for salt and pepper—the sauce should be on the salty side—and add one or two drops of lemon juice to taste.

5. **Serving:** Remove the strings from the pork. Pour any juices from the meat into the sauce and stir in. Slice the pork into slices about 1/4 inch thick and serve with sauce spooned on top. Pass any extra sauce at the table.

VARIATION: MILK-BRAISED PORK WITH A CREAMY FINISH

As delicious as this sauce is, some people are put off by its curdled appearance. If you want a creamy-smooth sauce, just before serving, put the finished sauce in a blender with a few drops of heavy cream. Whir until completely smooth (see "Pureeing Hot Liquids in a Blender," page 309), then spoon over the pork. The sauce will be beautifully creamy smooth and a lovely fawn color.

VARIATION: MILK-BRAISED PORK WITH SAGE & LEMON

As an alternative to the garlic-studded pork, here's a version I like when I have fresh sage on hand.

The day before or early in the morning before you plan to braise the pork, mix together in a small bowl: 2 tablespoons chopped fresh sage, 1 1/2 tablespoons grated lemon zest, 1 1/2 tablespoons minced garlic, 2 tablespoons extra-virgin olive oil, and 1 teaspoon coarse salt. Rub the mixture over the entire surface of the trimmed and tied pork. Cover loosely and refrigerate.

When you are ready to braise, gather together two 2 1/2-by-3/4-inch strips of lemon zest, a small sage sprig (or 1 very large sage leaf), and a bay leaf, and tie them into a neat bundle with kitchen string. Remove the pork from the refrigerator and scrape off as much of the seasoning as you can. Proceed with the recipe above, starting with Step 2, and adding the herb bundle to the milk in Step 3. After braising, discard the herb bundle before finishing the sauce.

Pork Pot Roast with Apricots, Cardamom & Ginger ✈

Americans bear a longstanding affection for pork with fruit, whether it's the pineapple rings we arrange on the holiday ham or the applesauce we spoon over pork chops. No doubt it's the pleasure of that sweet-tart-savory combination and the way that the meat juices mingle with the fruit that keep us coming back for more.

In this version, I use dried apricots because I love the way their pale orange flesh collapses into the sauce (and they're available all year). The sauce comes out every bit as pretty as it is tasty. The cardamom lends the whole dish its exotic perfume, and it's backed up by a gang of other compatible flavors — ginger, turmeric, cayenne, garlic, and orange. Make this when company's coming, for an impressive and delicious meal. Serve couscous or wild rice on the side.

wine notes

Fruity white with a touch of sweetness—off-dry Riesling from Germany or Austria, or a Pinot Gris from Alsace.

Serves 6 to 8 | *Braising Time: 2 hours*

One 4 1/2- to 5-pound boneless pork
  shoulder roast, preferably Boston butt
  (see "Shopping for Pork Shoulder,"
  page 353)
Coarse salt and freshly ground black
  pepper
2 tablespoons extra-virgin olive oil

1 medium leek, white and pale green part
  only, coarsely chopped (about 1 cup)
2 carrots, coarsely chopped
1 medium yellow onion (about 6 ounces),
  coarsely chopped
6 cardamom pods, husks split and
  discarded, seeds lightly crushed
1/2 teaspoon ground turmeric

1/4 teaspoon cayenne

1 tablespoon minced or grated fresh
   ginger

2 large garlic cloves, peeled and bruised

3 strips orange zest, removed with a
   vegetable peeler (each about 3 inches
   by 3/4 inch)

1 bay leaf

2 tablespoons apricot brandy or Cognac

1/2 cup dry white wine or dry white
   vermouth

2 cups chicken stock, homemade (page
   448) or store-bought

1 cup dried apricots (about 6 1/2 ounces)

1. **Heat the oven to 325 degrees.**

2. **Trimming and tying the pork:** Trim any especially thick bits of fat from the surface of the pork, but don't be too scrupulous. Leaving some fat will improve the flavor of the braise. Roll and tie the pork into a neat, compact shape according to the instructions on page 258.

3. **Browning the pork:** Pat the surface of the pork dry with paper towels. Season all over with salt and plenty of pepper. Pour the oil into a Dutch oven or other deep lidded pot that will hold the pork snugly (4- to 5-quart works well), and heat over medium heat. Lower the pork into the pot and sear it on all sides, using tongs to turn the meat as it cooks, until deeply browned but not at all burnt, 15 to 20 minutes total. Transfer the pork to a plate.

4. **The aromatics:** Pour off and discard all but 1 tablespoon of the fat, and return the pot to medium heat. Add the leek, carrots, and onions, stir in the crushed cardamom, turmeric, and cayenne, and cook, stirring once or twice, until the vegetables begin to soften but do not take on much color, about 5 minutes. Add the ginger, garlic, orange zest, and bay leaf and cook until the spices are quite fragrant, another 2 minutes.

5. **The braising liquid:** Pour the brandy into the pot. Bring to a boil and boil, stirring and scraping the bottom of the pot with a wooden spoon to release any caramelized bits, until reduced by about half, about 1 minute. Add the wine and let it boil for 4 minutes, scraping the sides and bottom of the pot with the spoon. Pour in the stock and bring to a boil. Add the apricots and boil for another 2 minutes.

6. **The braise:** Lift the pork with the tongs and set it on top of the vegetables and fruit. Pour in any accumulated juices from the plate. Bring the liquid to an easy simmer, and spoon some over the pork. Cover the meat with a sheet of parchment paper, pressing down so that it almost touches the meat and the edges extend over the sides of the pot by about an inch. Set the lid in place, and slide the pot onto a shelf in the lower third of the oven to braise. Every 30 minutes, lift the lid to check that the liquid is simmering gently, and give the pork a turn. If the liquid is simmering too aggressively, lower the oven heat 10 or 15 degrees. Continue to braise gently until the pork is fork-tender, about 2 hours in all.

7. **The finish:** Remove the pork from the pot with a large meat fork or tongs and set it on a carving board or platter to catch the juices. Cover loosely with foil, and let rest for 10 minutes.

Return the pot to the top of the stove and skim off as much surface fat as you can with a wide spoon. With tongs or a large fork, remove the zests and bay leaf if you like—I often don't bother. If the sauce is very thin, reduce it by boiling over medium-high heat for about 5 minutes. It should be the consistency of a thick vinaigrette. Taste for salt and pepper. Pour any juices that have accumulated under the pork into the sauce, and stir.

8. **Serving:** Remove the strings from the pork, and carve into 1/2-inch-thick slices. Serve with the sauce and apricots.

Shopping for Pork Shoulder

Pork shoulder is ideal for braising, but shopping for it can be confusing. There are actually two cuts of pork that bear the name *shoulder:* the *Boston butt* (or *Boston shoulder*) and the *picnic shoulder.* The best way to sort this out is to imagine the whole pork shoulder, the area from the back of the shoulder blade forward and down to the shank. In other words, the entire front quarters of a pig (trotters, neck, and head excluded). If you picture the whole shoulder cut horizontally in half into a top and a lower portion, you will have the two shoulder sections.

The uppermost half is the Boston butt. It contains the shoulder blade bone, the uppermost rib bones, neck bones, and backbone. The meat is hugely flavorful and fatty, and it takes well to any sort of slow cooking. Boston butt is the cut of choice for the best pulled pork barbecue, and Chinese chefs use it exclusively for pork braises and stews. A whole Boston butt will weigh 6 to 7 pounds and is often sold skin on. Boston butt can also be sold in smaller portion, both bone-in and boneless. Boneless portions need to be tied into a neat shape before braising. The *blade roast* and *blade steaks* are both smaller bone-in cuts from the Boston butt.

The picnic shoulder is the lower part of the shoulder, sometimes called an *arm roast.* Picnic shoulder is often sold whole, bone-in and with some skin attached. A bone-in picnic shoulder has a higher ratio of bone to meat than a Boston butt, so if given the choice, choose the meatier Boston butt. You can also find boneless picnic shoulder, but because of its complicated bone structure, it requires a great amount of tying to hold it together. *Pork arm steaks* come from the picnic shoulder. When a picnic shoulder is cured, as it often is, this smaller ham is known as a *picnic ham* or *daisy ham.*

For braising, choose either the Boston butt or picnic shoulder. Oftentimes a market will carry one or the other, not both. Fortunately, both work beautifully for a braise. But given the choice, my preference is always for the Boston butt.

Caribbean Pork Shoulder ✈

This recipe was inspired by a meal of jerked pork cooked over an open fire at someone's birthday party years ago. The meat was slow-cooked till luscious and infused with spice. I've long since forgotten who the party was for, but I've never lost my appetite for that pork. So I came up with a way to get that same succulence and deep flavor without having to dig a fire pit. The finishing step of browning the pork under the broiler delivers just enough taste of smoke-charred meat to recall the original.

Allspice, called pimiento or Jamaican pepper in the Caribbean, gives jerked meats a sweet, warm backdrop flavor to balance the spicier accents of chiles and garlic. The seasonings are rubbed into a pork shoulder (Boston butt) and left overnight to work their way into the meat. Leaving the skin on the pork has two important benefits: the layer of fat under the skin bastes the meat as it cooks and then, right before serving, the skin browns and crisps under the broiler to create just enough cracklings to go around. If you can't find a Boston butt with the skin, this is still a great recipe (see the variation below).

Serve with World's Best Braised Green Cabbage (page 59), fried plantains, and rice.

beer notes

Cold beer with fruity notes and not too much bitterness—Red Stripe from Jamaica, or Corona and Pacifico from Mexico.

Working Ahead

Be sure to leave time—12 to 24 hours—to let the pork sit after rubbing it with spices (Steps 1 and 2). These steps allow the flavors to penetrate the meat—don't skip them.

One 4- to 5-pound boneless Boston butt, preferably with skin on (see "Shopping for Pork Shoulder," page 353)

4 garlic cloves, minced

1/2 teaspoon allspice berries, toasted and coarsely ground

1 teaspoon coriander seeds, toasted and coarsely ground

1 tablespoon chopped fresh thyme or 1 teaspoon dried

1 teaspoon pimentón (Spanish smoked paprika) or Hungarian paprika (sweet or hot) (see "Hungarian Paprika and Pimentón," page 357)

Generous pinch of cayenne

1/3 cup freshly squeezed orange juice

1/4 cup freshly squeezed lime juice

1 teaspoon coarse salt

1/4 cup water

1.   **Scoring the pork skin—12 to 24 hours ahead:** Score a 1-inch-deep crosshatch pattern into the pork skin to expose the fat beneath. Using kitchen string, tie the pork roast into a neat, compact shape according to the instructions on page 258. Place the pork in a deep glass or ceramic bowl or on a flat dish.

2.   **The spice rub:** In a small bowl, combine the garlic, allspice, coriander, thyme, pimentón or paprika, cayenne, orange and lime juices, and salt. Rub this mixture all over the pork, being sure to rub the seasonings into all the crevices and folds. Cover with plastic wrap and refrigerate for 12 hours to 24 hours. Turn the pork 2 or 3 times as it marinates to redistribute the seasonings.

3.   **Heat the oven to 300 degrees.** Let the pork sit at room temperature while you wait for the oven to heat.

4.   **The braise:** Transfer the pork skin side up to a large Dutch oven (5- to 6-quart). Pour over any remaining marinade, and add 1/4 cup water. Cover the pot with parchment paper, pressing down so it nearly touches the pork and the edges extend about an inch over the sides of the pot. Set the lid in place, slide onto a shelf in the lower third of the oven, and braise at a gentle simmer, turning every hour, until the meat is falling from the bone, 3 1/2 to 4 hours. (A flat wooden spoon and a spatula make a good pair of tools for turning the pork.) Check after the first 15 minutes or so, and if the liquid is simmering ferociously, lower the oven heat by 10 or 15 degrees.

5.   **When the pork is done:** Carefully transfer the pork to a rimmed baking sheet or shallow baking dish to capture any juices. (Lift with a large spatula or wooden spoon to help keep the pork from falling apart.) Cover loosely with foil to keep warm.

6.   **Degreasing the sauce:** Heat the broiler on high. Skim the clear layer of fat from the surface of the braising liquid with a wide spoon. You can also use a gravy separator here if you like. It's a quicker but it means dirtying another dish. Expect to collect as much as 1/2 cup of clear fat. Taste the sauce for salt, and keep warm on a low burner (or reheat just before serving).

7.   **Browning the pork:** When the broiler is very hot, slide the pork under it so the top of the roast is 6 to 8 inches from the heat. Broil, standing close by and rotating as necessary so the skin browns evenly, until crisped, sizzling, and nicely browned, 8 to 10 minutes total. Remove from the oven. (Alternatively, if the pork won't fit under your broiler, heat the oven to 475 degrees and roast the braised pork until the skin is crispy and sizzling, 12 to 15 minutes.)

8.   **Serving:** Using a large knife or tongs, pull the skin off the pork. Chop the skin into bite-sized crackling bits and set aside. Slice the pork into 1/2-inch slices or shred it into chunks with tongs and a meat fork. Arrange the pork on a serving platter or individual plates. Spoon the warm braising liquid over the meat and scatter the cracklings over the top.

VARIATION: CARIBBEAN-STYLE PORK POT ROAST

I frequently use this same recipe to braise a smaller (3- to 3 1/2-pound) boneless pork butt or shoulder roast, without skin, rolled and tied (see "Tying a Roast Before Braising," page 00). These smaller roasts typically come without the skin, so you won't have the cracklings, but you'll have a superb dinner anyway. Follow the recipe as directed, skipping Step 1, but going ahead with the spice rub 12 to 24 hours in advance. Braise the meat until fork-tender, about 3 hours. Skip Step 7 (browning the meat). Skim the braising liquid and remove the strings from the pork before slicing and serving. *Serves 4 to 6*

Hungarian Paprika and Pimentón

Many cooks disdain paprika as nothing more than a tasteless sprinkle useful in adding a dash of color to deviled eggs or potato salads. This couldn't be further from the truth. Real paprika is a vibrant, complex spice that exists in many varieties and takes a central role in many cuisines, most notably those of Eastern Europe and Spain.

The word *paprika* comes from the Latin *piper* (pepper), and the powder is derived from drying and grinding small chile peppers, known as paprika peppers. If you've never tasted extraordinary paprika, treat yourself to a small canister of Hungarian paprika. It's some of the best produced in the world. Hungarian paprika can range from sweet and earthy to fiery and sharp, with several grades in between. The degree of heat is a function of the ripeness of the peppers when they are picked—the riper the fruit, the hotter the flavor. Try Hungarian paprika in spice rubs, stews, roast chicken, and eggs. Look for *Pride of Szeged* brand Hungarian paprika. It comes in a bright red tin with a map of Hungary on the front, and its quality is first rate.

Spanish paprika, known as *pimentón*, is distinguishable from other paprika in that it's been smoked-dried before being ground. The high humidity in the chile-growing region of Spain means that the paprika peppers will not dry in the sun the way they do in Hungary and other parts of the world. To solve this, growers pack the ripe peppers into sacks and dry them slowly over smoldering fires. The resulting spice possesses a remarkable smoky, rich flavor. Available in hot and sweet varieties, the best smoked Spanish paprika comes from La Vera valley. Indeed, pimentón de la Vera is so prized that it has been granted a *Denominación de Origen,* or controlled name status. Try it in spice rubs, tomato sauces, eggs, and most any type of pork dish.

As with all ground spices, paprika and pimentón should be purchased in small amounts, stored in a cool dark place, and used within a few months. For mail-order information, see Sources, page 456.

Cochinita Pibil ⇥

Pork Braised in Banana Leaves Yucatan-Style

If you want to put on a grand fiesta, make this the centerpiece. This is a home version of the traditional Mexican pig roast in which cooks rub a whole suckling pig (*cochinita*) with spices, wrap it in banana leaves, and then bury it with wet burlap or gunny sacks in a wood-fired stone-lined pit (or *pib*) to slow-cook. The pork slowly braises to absolute tenderness in the moist environment of the pit while the party gets underway.

Wrapping the pork in large banana leaves does more than protect the pork from the heat; it contributes a floral scent and pleasing sweet straw-like quality to its flavor. Depending on where you shop, these large tropical leaves may or may not be easy to find. (See "Using Banana Leaves," page 362, for more on these exotic wrappers.)

The traditional marinade for a Yucatan pork is based on annatto seeds, small, chalky red seeds, also called achiote, used in Mexican, Caribbean, and South American cooking. Annatto seeds, however, can be difficult to find and nearly impossible to grind at home, and when I have found them, they have often been terribly stale and more musty than aromatic. Fortunately, there's an easier to find and more convenient alternative—achiote paste. This commercially ground paste provides the characteristic brick-red color and slightly bitter, earthy flavor you're after. If there's not a Latin market near you that carries achiote paste, consider mail-order (see Sources, page 456). You can also do without: the pork will still be delicious.

The fresh tomato salsa provides a refreshing counterpoint to the tender meat, but you can add any number of other side dishes as you like. Stewed black beans, white rice, and a simple salad are all good choices. Whatever you do, don't forget to serve warm corn tortillas.

Either a slightly sweet blush wine, such as White Zinfandel, or a lighter-style ale with spice notes, such as Sierra Nevada Pale Ale.

Working Ahead

The flavor of the pork depends a great deal on the spice rub and the direct contact with the banana leaves. For this reason, you want to be sure to allow enough time—12 to 24 hours—for the pork to sit after being rubbed with spices and wrapped before braising (Steps 1 through 3).

Serves 10 to 12 | *Braising Time: 5 1/2 to 6 1/2 hours*

THE SPICE PASTE

4 large garlic cloves, peeled and smashed

1 tablespoon coarse salt

2 tablespoons cumin seeds, toasted and ground

1 tablespoon dried oregano

2 dried red chiles, crushed, or 1 1/2 teaspoons crushed red pepper flakes

2 tablespoons achiote paste (optional)

2 to 3 tablespoons cider vinegar

THE BRAISE

2 to 3 large fresh or thawed frozen banana leaves (see "Using Banana Leaves," page 362), rinsed and dried

One 7- to 9-pound bone-in Boston butt or picnic shoulder, skin on or off (see "Shopping for Pork Shoulder," page 353)

THE SALSA

1 small white onion (4 ounces), finely chopped (about 1 cup)

2 jalapeños, seeded or not as you like, finely chopped

1 cup chopped loosely packed cilantro leaves and tender stems

1 pound ripe tomatoes, cored and chopped into 1/2-inch pieces

3 to 4 tablespoons freshly squeezed lime juice

Coarse salt

Warm corn tortillas for serving

1. **Making the spice paste—12 to 24 hours ahead:** Put the garlic cloves in a mortar, add the salt, and work it into a paste with the pestle. (If you don't have a mortar, pour the salt over the garlic on a cutting board and, using a combination of a chopping motion and smearing with the side of the blade, reduce the garlic to a paste. See "Making Garlic Paste," page 315.) Place the garlic paste in a small bowl. Add the cumin, oregano, chiles, and achiote paste, if using. Stir in enough vinegar to make a thick paste. Set aside.

2. **Searing the banana leaves:** Unfold the banana leaves. With scissors, trim off the fibrous center rib that usually runs down the length of one side of the leaves. (Try to cut the rib off in one piece, and save it to tie up the pork once it's wrapped in the leaves.) If you have gas burners on your stove, set one to high and, holding each banana leaf about 2 inches above the burner, pass it slowly across the flame until the leaf appears a darker green and almost wet looking. This will make the leaves more flexible and easier to roll. If you have electric burners, skip this step; the leaves will be a bit less flexible, but they'll work fine. Lay the leaves out on a work surface, duller side up.

3. **Rubbing the pork with the spice paste and wrapping it in the banana leaves:** If the pork has skin, score a 1-inch-deep crosshatch pattern into it to expose the fat beneath. Rub the spice paste all over the entire pork shoulder—top and bottom. Place the pork on one length of banana leaf and fold the leaf snugly around the pork. Lift the wrapped pork onto another leaf and wrap it around perpendicular to the first one so that you encase the pork. Keep wrapping until you have a neat package without gaps or openings and at least three layers of leaves, depending on the shape and size of your leaves. Tie off the package with several loops of the reserved center ribs or kitchen string. Set the pork in a baking dish or on a tray and refrigerate for 12 to 24 hours.

4. **Heat the oven to 300 degrees.** Let the pork sit at room temperature while you wait for the oven to heat.

5. **The braise:** Place a rack or a crosshatch of chopsticks in the bottom of a very large Dutch oven (8- to 9-quart) or a deep roasting pan. (The rack or sticks will keep the pork off the bottom of the pot and better imitate the environment of a fire pit.) Add 1 to 1 ½ cups water to the pot—just enough to come about ½ inch up the sides, enough to create a bit of steam. Place the wrapped pork on the rack or chopsticks. Cover the pot tightly with a lid or heavy-duty aluminum foil and slide it onto a rack in the lower third of the oven to braise.

    After 3 hours, open the pot and carefully turn the pork: Since the roast is so large and unwieldy, this can be a tricky maneuver. I find it easiest to use a pair of thick pot holders or folded dishtowels and to lift the pork with my hands. It might also help to have someone stand by to hold the pot to make sure you don't get off balance and drop the whole thing. Return the pork to the oven and continue to braise gently for another 2 ½ to 3 ½ hours.

You will know the pork is getting close when the house fills with an exotic sweet aroma. To check for doneness, press on the sides of the pork. It should feel soft and tender, and it will have shrunk some inside the package too.

6. **Meanwhile, make the salsa:** Soak the chopped onion in cold water for 5 minutes to take away some of its bite. Drain, place in a clean dish towel, and squeeze dry. In a medium bowl, combine the onion, jalapeños, cilantro, tomatoes, lime juice, and salt to taste. The salsa should taste sharp to balance the rich taste of the pork.

7. **Serving:** Lift the pork from the braising pan by the strings, if they feel secure, or by grasping it with two pot holders or dish towels and set it on a large platter or tray. Tear a few big pieces of banana leaves from the pork and line a platter with them, then unwrap the pork. With two dinner forks, shred the pork into big chunks and pile them onto the banana-leaf–lined platter; the pork will be very hot, so be content to pull off large pieces. If you braised a skin-on pork butt, the skin will have softened and melded with the fat layer underneath. A taste of these two together will make any true pork lover weak in the knees. I like to shred this fatty meat into smaller bits and toss it in with the leaner meat; you can also set it aside in reserve for those who really love the richest bits. Spoon some of the warm pan juices over the pork. Serve with the salsa and warm corn tortillas.

   Or for a casual, hands-on *Cochinita Pibil* party: After braising, set the whole still-wrapped pork butt on a big serving platter, snip off the ties, tear open the package, and peel back the leaves. Put out a few good-sized dinner forks and small sharp knives and let your guests tear off their own portions. Not only is the roast a magnificent sight, but we all know how satisfying it is to pick at an impressive hunk of succulent meat. Don't forget the tortillas and salsa.

VARIATION: *COCHINITA PIBIL* FOR A SMALLER CROWD

A pig roast is food for a big gathering or party, which is why I make this with a whole pork Boston butt or picnic shoulder. For a smaller party, scale things back and follow the same recipe with a smaller pork shoulder roast (4 1/2 to 5 pounds)—just be sure it's bone-in for the best flavor. Braise the smaller roast for 4 to 4 1/2 hours.

Using Banana Leaves

Banana leaves are exactly that, the leaves of a banana tree, and they are huge—several feet long and up to a foot wide. Most packaged banana leaves are actually half leaves, already cut lengthwise through the central spine. Outside of tropical climates, banana leaves are most commonly sold frozen, and they keep frozen for months. To use, thaw the leaves in the refrigerator until flexible. Rinse and dry each leaf to remove any residue. Use scissors to trim off the tough, fibrous spine that runs down one side of each leaf half. Finally, sear the leaves one by one as directed in Step 2 of the *Cochinita Pibil* recipe (page 360).

Shop for banana leaves at Latin markets or through mail-order (see Sources, page 456).

Country-Style Pork Ribs Braised with Mango, Lime & Coconut ⇥

The arresting scent of ripe mangoes in the market on a cold February day gave me the idea for this recipe. With mangoes as the starting point, the tropical flavors of lime, chiles, ginger, and coconut seemed only natural. I even added a dash of rum to amplify the sunny island mood of this dish. The end result is something fragrant and spicy and quite pretty. As the mango cooks, it gives itself up entirely to the sauce, thickening it and contributing a lovely pale orange color.

Serve the ribs with plain white rice and a crunchy slaw.

beer notes

Slightly fruity beer that's not too bitter—Red Stripe from Jamaica or Corona from Mexico.

Serves 4 | Braising Time: about 1 ¹/₄ hours

2 ¹/₂ pounds bone-in country-style pork ribs (see "Shopping for Country-Style Pork Ribs," page 365)

Coarse salt and freshly ground black pepper

2 tablespoons extra-virgin olive oil or peanut oil

2 cardamom pods

1 ripe mango (about 1 pound)

1 medium yellow onion (about 6 ounces), thinly sliced

2 garlic cloves, minced

2 teaspoons minced fresh ginger

1 serrano chile, minced

One 2- to 3-inch cinnamon stick

1 teaspoon grated lime zest

2 tablespoons golden or amber rum (not dark), such as Mount Gay

¹/₂ cup unsweetened coconut milk

¹/₄ cup freshly squeezed lime juice

Lime wedges for serving

1.   **Browning the pork:** Pat the pork dry with paper towels. Season all over with salt and pepper. Heat the oil in a large deep heavy lidded skillet (a 12-inch skillet with 3-inch sides works well) over medium-high heat until it shimmers. Add the pork ribs, in batches so they aren't crowded, and cook, turning once with tongs, until they are lightly browned and the fat is starting to crisp up, about 4 minutes per side. Transfer the pork to a platter and return the skillet to medium heat.

2.   **Preparing the cardamom and mango:** With your fingers or the side of a large knife, split open the cardamom husks. Remove the dark, grain-like seeds and discard the husks. In a mortar or spice grinder, crush the seeds to a fine powder. Set aside.

   Peel the mango (see "Shopping for Mangoes," page 365) with a vegetable peeler or sharp paring knife. Then, using a larger chef's knife, slice the flesh away from the large, flat pit. Chop the flesh into a 1/2-inch dice and set aside.

3.   **The aromatics and braising liquid:** Add the onion and sauté, stirring, until soft, about 4 minutes. Add the garlic, ginger, serrano, cardamom, cinnamon, and lime zest, stir to distribute them evenly, and sauté until fragrant, another minute or so. Pour in the rum, stir to loosen any tasty browned bits left from browning the pork, and simmer until there is almost no liquid left, about 1 minute. Add the coconut milk, lime juice, and mango, and stir.

4.   **The braise:** Settle the pork ribs into the sauce, adding any juices that seeped out from the meat. Bring to a simmer, cover tightly, and reduce the heat to low. Simmer quietly, turning the ribs once halfway through, until the meat is fork-tender, about 1 hour and 15 minutes. Check after 5 to 10 minutes, and if the sauce seems to be simmering too vigorously, lower the heat or place a heat diffuser beneath the pan. If, when you turn the ribs, you notice that the sauce is beginning to stick to the bottom of the pan, add 1/4 cup water (sometimes the sugar in the mango will cause the sauce to stick). By the time the pork is ready, the sauce will have cooked down some and be beginning to caramelize around the edges of the skillet. It may appear slightly broken, but it will come together when you stir it.

5.   **The finish:** Transfer the ribs to a serving platter or plates and cover loosely with foil to keep warm. Discard the cinnamon stick, and skim the surface of the sauce to remove as much fat as you can. Usually there won't be much, but remove what you do see. Stir with a large wooden spoon so that the mango collapses and thickens the sauce. Taste for salt and pepper. Spoon the sauce over the ribs and serve.

Shopping for Country-Style Pork Ribs

Country-style pork ribs are a relative newcomer to the meat case, having first appeared in the 1970s as a way to market the shoulder-blade section of the pork loin, where the chops aren't as neat and lean as the pricier rib chops. The idea was that the narrow, meaty ribs would be ideal on a grill or under the broiler. In reality, because country-style ribs have the tougher, fattier character of pork shoulder, they are best when cooked slowly in any sort of braise or traditional covered barbecue. For my money, there really is no better cut of pork for relatively quick braising.

Shopping for country-style ribs can be confusing, since they appear in a variety of shapes. For one thing, they can come from the top end of the loin or bottom end of the shoulder (the loin version being the meatier of the two). Both braise beautifully, but if given the choice, I would choose the shoulder. Also, because of the way country-style ribs are cut, some have a long rib bone, some have a portion of the blade bone, and others contain a piece of backbone. Since it's all but impossible to find symmetrical country-style ribs, look for an even mix. In some markets in the Northeast, country-style ribs may bear the label "Southern-style ribs"—perhaps this is because it was a Kentucky butcher who spawned the idea.

Some markets sell boneless country-style ribs, but I have never had much luck with these. They seem to dry out no matter what I do.

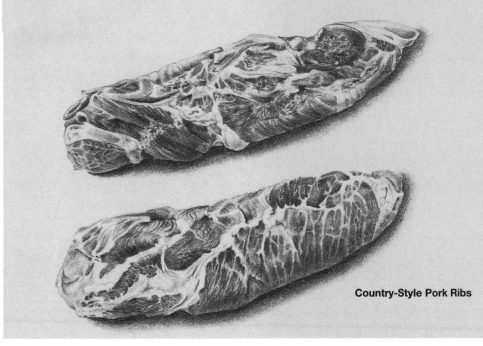

Country-Style Pork Ribs

Shopping for Mangoes

For those of us who begin to crave fresh fruit long before summer produce comes in, mangoes can be a godsend. The season for mangoes begins in January and runs through the summer, and the height of the season is late spring. Most of the mangoes we see are imported from Mexico and the Caribbean. Unlike many fruits, mangoes are good travelers, and their quality doesn't suffer when picked underripe. Mangoes ripen perfectly well at room temperature both in the market and at home on your counter. Occasionally, however, a mango will not ripen but will soften and blacken. The best way to avoid this is to buy mangoes that are partly or all the way ripe. In selecting ripe or almost-ripe mangoes, aroma is the best indicator. A ripe mango should have an intense sweet, floral aroma at the stem end and yield slightly when pressed—like a ripe peach. Don't press too hard, or you may bruise the fruit. The color of mango skin ranges from green to red to yellow. Most mangoes redden or lighten as they ripen, but color is not a reliable indicator since not all varieties follow the same pattern. A truly ripe mango should be stored in the refrigerator for no longer than a few days.

Country-Style Pork Ribs Braised with
Chipotle, Roasted Tomatoes & Red Peppers ⇥

Here's a recipe for early fall, when the first threats of frost awaken an appetite for slow-cooked braises but the markets are still glutted with local summer produce. If the tomatoes are fully ripe and sweet, they'll be perfect. If not, add the teaspoon of sugar to give the sauce the little sweetness it needs.

     This braise uses a gratin dish covered with foil instead of a deeper Dutch oven. The foil is removed during the last half hour so that the sauce will caramelize and deepen its already earthy, roasty flavor. Serve with rice and warm corn tortillas.

wine notes

Youthful red with moderate tannins—a fruity Zinfandel or a lighter Australian Shiraz-Grenache blend.

Serves 4 | Braising Time: about 1 1/4 hours

3/4 pound ripe tomatoes

1 large red bell pepper

3 garlic cloves, unpeeled

2 or 3 canned chipotle peppers, along with 1 tablespoon of the sauce from the can (see "Chipotle Peppers," page 370)

1 teaspoon dried oregano

1 teaspoon cumin seeds, lightly toasted and ground

1/4 teaspoon ground cloves

1 1/2 tablespoons cider vinegar

Coarse salt

1 teaspoon sugar, or as needed

1/4 cup water

2 1/2 pounds bone-in country-style pork ribs (see "Shopping for Country-Style Pork Ribs," page 365)

2 tablespoons extra-virgin olive oil

1 large white onion (about 6 ounces), finely chopped

Cilantro leaves for garnish (optional)

1. **Roasting the tomatoes, red pepper, and garlic:** Heat the broiler to high. Line a small baking sheet with foil and brush it generously with oil. Arrange the tomatoes, bell pepper, and garlic cloves on the baking sheet and slide it under the broiler, about 4 1/2 inches from the heat. When the skins of the vegetables darken and begin to split, about 5 minutes, turn with tongs and broil on the second side. Transfer the tomatoes to a bowl to cool. If the garlic skins have darkened and cracked and the cloves are somewhat softened, set aside with the tomatoes. If the garlic cloves are still as hard as before broiling, return them to the broiler for another few minutes. The bell pepper will take a bit longer, another 5 to 7 minutes; turn to broil all sides. Transfer the pepper to another bowl, cover tightly with plastic wrap, and let cool. Lower the oven temperature to 300 degrees.

2. **Making the chipotle-tomato puree:** Once the tomatoes are cool enough to handle, remove the cores, slip off their skins, and drop them into a food processor. Peel the garlic and add it to the work bowl. Add the chipotle peppers and adobo sauce, the oregano, cumin, cloves, vinegar, 1/2 teaspoon salt, and the sugar, if using. (The sugar helps if the tomatoes are not super-ripe.) Peel the bell pepper over a bowl to collect the juices. Remove the seeds and core, and add the pepper and collected juices to the food processor. Run the processor until you have a rough puree. Add the 1/4 cup water and pulse a few times to loosen the puree. Taste. It should be quite piquant but not bitter. Add a pinch of sugar if needed.

3. **Browning the ribs:** Lightly oil a large gratin dish or other baking dish that will just accommodate the ribs in a single layer. Pat the meat dry with paper towels, and season all over with salt and pepper. Heat the oil in a large heavy skillet (10- to 12-inch) over medium-high heat. Sear the ribs, in batches, since they won't all fit in the skillet with plenty of space in between, until nicely browned on all sides, 6 to 7 minutes per side. Set the ribs in the gratin dish.

4. **The aromatics and braising liquid:** Lower the heat under the skillet to medium and add the onion. Cook, stirring occasionally, until the onion has softened and turned a light brown, about 10 minutes. Add the chipotle-tomato puree and simmer until the sauce turns a dark rust color and reduces a bit, 8 to 10 minutes. Spoon the sauce over the ribs.

5. **The braise:** Cover the baking dish with parchment paper and then cover tightly with aluminum foil (the parchment protects the aluminum from the acidic tomato-based sauce, and the foil makes a tight seal). Slide onto the middle rack in the oven and braise gently, turning the ribs once with tongs halfway through, until the meat is fork-tender, about 1 hour and 15 minutes. Peek under the foil after the first 10 or 15 minutes. If the sauce is simmering too ferociously, lower the oven heat 10 or 15 degrees.

6. **Roasting the ribs:** Remove the foil and parchment paper from the dish, and increase the oven temperature to 350 degrees. Carefully turn the ribs over (tongs will prevent tear-

ing the tender meat from the bone) and spoon some of the sauce and onions on top of each rib. Roast for about another 30 minutes so that the sauce and any exposed bits of meat caramelize and become sweet and tasty. The sauce will cook down some too, which will concentrate its flavor nicely.

7.   **Serving:** Using tongs or a slotted spatula to handle the ribs gently, or they will risk falling apart, transfer the ribs to a platter. Cover loosely with foil to keep warm. Tilt the gratin dish and skim off any clear fat that floats to the surface. Taste for salt. Serve the ribs, spooning a generous ladleful of sauce over each one. Sprinkle with cilantro, if desired.

VARIATION: PORK TACOS WITH CHIPOTLE, ROASTED TOMATOES & RED PEPPERS

To turn the ribs into a taco filling, braise and roast the ribs as directed. After removing the ribs from the sauce in Step 7, let them cool enough so you can handle them; pour the sauce into a saucepan. Tear the meat from the bones, and then shred it into bite-sized pieces. (You can cut the pork up with a knife, but somehow it tastes better when shredded.) Return the meat to the sauce and simmer gently to reheat. Serve in warm corn tortillas, with a little fresh salsa, if desired.

Chipotle Peppers

Chipotle peppers are, by definition, smoked and dried jalapeños, yet they are quite a bit spicier than most fresh jalapeños. These small chiles contribute a smoky warmth to dishes and are especially good paired with tomatoes. Chile aficionados will explain that there are two types of chipotle—the smaller reddish-black one known as *chile mora* or *chipotle colorado*, and the slightly larger, paler brown chile known as *chipotle meco*—but few markets are sophisticated enough to distinguish between them. The varieties can be used interchangeably.

Chipotles are available dried and canned. The dried are typically toasted and then rehydrated in warm water before being used. Canned chipotles are packed in a vinegary paste or sauce known as *adobo*. When using canned chipotles, I don't wipe them clean of the adobo. I like the way the adobo sauce underscores the chile's flavor, so much so that I usually add a tablespoonful or so of the sauce to the dish as well. Once you open a can of chipotles in adobo, transfer the contents to a glass or other nonreactive container and refrigerate. They will keep for months. A little bit of sauce and/or pureed chipotle adds a warming touch to vinaigrettes, salsas, guacamole, and other dips.

Chengdu Braised Pork with Daikon Radish ✈

My friend Steve Bogart is an inspired cooking teacher and talented chef who runs a superb Chinese restaurant in Vermont. I learned from him that the Chinese were masters at braising, and knowing that Steve had lived and trained in China, I asked him to describe his favorite braised dishes. Of all the recipes Steve provided, this one put the biggest smile on his face, and I could see why. Chunks of pork shoulder and daikon radish are braised together, uncovered, in an authentic combination of ground Sichuan peppercorns, garlic, soy, sherry, hot bean paste, and stock. The pork and radish emerge fork-tender, imbued with an exciting combination of sweet, spicy, sharp flavors. To serve, ladle the pork and sauce over a bowl of Chinese egg noodles.

You will need an electric spice grinder with sharp blades to grind the Sichuan peppercorns for this braise. I've tried to grind them to a fine enough powder using a mortar and pestle but have never fully succeeded. And when the peppercorns aren't fully ground, they leave a trace of sand-like grit in the sauce that can ruin an otherwise fabulous meal.

wine notes

Fruity, off-dry white or blush wine—domestic Chenin Blanc, German Riesling, or White Zinfandel.

Working Ahead

To fully appreciate the flavor and tenderness of this braise, wait at least a day after braising to serve it. Trust me. There's an almost miraculous transfer of flavor that occurs as the pork sits overnight in the fragrant braising liquid. I like to make this on a Wednesday or Thursday, then cover and refrigerate it for a day or two. When Friday comes, I can invite a few guests over and have nothing to do but heat the braise and boil the noodles.

It's also worth noting that toasting, grinding, and sifting the Sichuan peppercorns does take a bit of time, but it is a task that can easily be done up to a week ahead.

Serves 4 to 6 | *Braising Time: about 1 3/4 hours*

THE BRAISE

3 tablespoons Sichuan peppercorns (see "Sichuan Peppercorns," page 375)

2 1/2 to 3 pounds boneless pork Boston shoulder, cut into 2-inch cubes (see "Shopping for Boneless Chunks of Pork Shoulder," page 374)

3 tablespoons peanut oil

1 1/2 cups chicken stock, homemade (page 448) or store-bought

1 bunch scallions, white and green parts, cut into 1/2-inch pieces (about 1 cup)

1/2 cup dry sherry

1/4 cup hot bean paste (see "Hot Bean Paste," page 374)

2 ounces Chinese rock sugar (see "Chinese Rock Sugar," page 374), smashed into small rocks with a hammer, or 1/4 cup packed dark brown sugar

1 tablespoon soy sauce (not "lite")

6 garlic cloves, peeled and smashed

3/4 pound daikon radish, peeled and cut into 3/4-inch cubes (purple-top turnips may be substituted)

1 pound dried Chinese egg noodles or rice noodles

3 tablespoons finely chopped scallions for garnish

1. **Toasting, grinding, and sifting the peppercorns (up to a week in advance):** Heat the peppercorns in a small dry skillet (6-inch) over medium heat until you can smell their piney fragrance and small wisps of smoke appear, about 4 minutes. Pour the peppercorns onto a plate to cool for a minute, then transfer them to a spice grinder. Grind the peppercorns to an ultrafine powder, pulsing again and again until the powder is almost as fine as cornstarch. Sift the powder through a fine-mesh sieve, working it through the sieve with a pestle or the end of a knife handle. The resulting powder should be light and fluffy. (*This may be kept in an airtight jar for up to 1 week.*)

2. **Browning the meat—1 to 2 days in advance:** Pat all the surfaces of the pork dry with paper towels. Heat the oil in a wok or wide (13-inch) skillet over medium-high heat until it shimmers. Add only as many pieces of pork as will fit without crowding and sear, leaving the pieces undisturbed so a crust can form, for 2 to 3 minutes. Turn with tongs, and con-

tinue turning the pork only when each side browns, until the pork forms a ruddy brown crust on all sides, about 10 minutes total. Transfer to a large plate to catch the drips while you sear the remaining pork.

3. **Braising liquid:** Pour off all the fat from the pan, but be sure not to pour off any loose drippings. There will be a lovely caramelized crust on the bottom of the pan that will add enormous flavor to the sauce. Return the pan to medium heat and pour in the stock. Bring to a boil, stirring with a wooden spoon to dislodge the crust on the bottom of the pan. Add the scallions, sherry, bean paste, sugar, soy sauce, garlic, and ground Sichuan peppercorns, stir, and simmer, stirring, until the sugar is dissolved and the ingredients are well blended, about 10 minutes.

4. **The braise:** Return the pork to the sauce, along with any juices that have accumulated on the plate. Bring to a simmer, reduce the heat to low, and simmer gently, uncovered, turning the pieces of pork with tongs once or twice, for 45 minutes. If you experience difficulty maintaining a quiet simmer, place the pan over a heat diffuser. Add the daikon, stir, and continue to braise uncovered, turning once or twice more, until the pork is fork-tender, another 50 to 60 minutes.

5. **Straining the sauce:** Using tongs, lift out the chunks of pork and daikon and transfer to a shallow baking dish or medium bowl. Strain the braising liquid though a fine-mesh sieve onto the pork and daikon, pressing on the vegetables and seasonings to extract all the liquid. Let cool to room temperature, then cover and refrigerate for at least several hours, preferably 1 to 2 days.

6. **The finish:** Heat the oven to 350 degrees. Remove the solid layer of fat from the surface of the chilled braising liquid. Cover the baking dish with foil and bake, stirring once or twice, until heated through, 20 to 30 minutes.

    While the pork warms, cook the noodles according to the package directions until soft; drain and keep warm.

7. **Serving:** Serve the pork and radishes over the noodles, ladling over some of the braising liquid, and garnish with chopped scallions.

Shopping for Boneless Chunks of Pork Shoulder

When a recipe calls for boneless chunks of meat, it's always best to cut the meat into large chunks yourself rather than buy what the market sells as "stew meat." Too often, supermarkets cut the meat too small or into unevenly sized pieces. If you have trouble finding a 2 ½- to 3-pound piece of pork Boston shoulder, look for country-style ribs and chop them up with a cleaver or heavy knife. Leaving the bone attached to the chunks of meat will add even more to the flavor of the sauce. When using bone-in chunks of pork in place of boneless, figure 2 to 3 ounces more per person.

Special Ingredients for Chengdu Pork

CHINESE ROCK SUGAR

If you ate rock candy as a child, you'll recognize these sharp-edged chunks of crystallized sugar. Made from a combination of refined and unrefined sugar, Chinese rock sugar is available in either cloudy white or dark amber lumps. The darker sugar tastes more like honey, while the white tastes very much like ordinary white sugar. Rock sugar adds the characteristic sweet taste to Chinese red-cooked dishes (such as Red-Cooked Pork Belly with Bok Choy, page 385), and it imparts an attractive glossy sheen to the sauce. Rock sugar is available at Asian markets and through mail-order (see Sources, page 456). You can substitute regular light or dark brown or white sugar in its place. I prefer brown sugar because I like its more complex, caramelized flavor, but either is fine. The sauce will still possess the captivating sweet taste. It will, however, lack a bit of sheen.

HOT BEAN PASTE

An essential ingredient in Sichuan cooking, hot bean paste is made from fermented beans and hot chile peppers. The spicy, salty paste ranges from red to dark purple and from chunky to smooth. According to Chinese cooking expert and author Fuschia Dunlop, the best are made from fava beans (also called broad beans), not soybeans. I've also found that the better pastes contain nothing other than beans, salt, and chiles, and so I try to avoid those with ingredients such as sesame oil, sugar, and garlic. Read the label (if it's in English!) to determine what's in the jar. I buy different brands depending on what's available, and as long as I stick to those with the fewest ingredients, I've been pleased. The best place to shop for bean paste is at an Asian market, or through mail-order (see Sources, page 456). Once opened, the paste will last indefinitely in the refrigerator, tightly covered.

SICHUAN PEPPERCORNS

These rough-textured little red berries are about the size of a black peppercorn and they do possess a little peppery bite, but the two spices are not at all related. Sichuan peppercorns, sometimes called *fagara*, come from China, and they have been a staple in Chinese cooking for centuries. Added to braises, soups, stocks, and stews, the peppercorns contribute an enchanting woodsy, somewhat resinous taste that is hard to replicate.

Sichuan peppercorns are sold in Asian markets and through mail-order (see Sources, page 456). The peppercorn itself is actually the empty outer husk of a berry. Inside is a shiny little black seed that has no flavor but adds an unwelcome gritty texture to dishes. The best-quality Sichuan peppercorns come well sorted, so that you only get the knobby red husks, not the black seeds or any woody stems. Unfortunately, I've yet to find a source here that sells anything but a mix of husks and seeds. To solve this, I simply sift the peppercorns after grinding them to remove any of the little black seeds or stems that don't grind up easily.

A Final Note about Sichuan Peppercorns: As of this writing, the USDA has imposed a ban on the importation of whole Sichuan peppercorns because they may harbor a citrus canker that could endanger domestic groves. This is not the first ban on these exotic berries, but it is impossible to determine how long it will last. Technically it is still legal to sell Sichuan peppercorns as long as the retailer can prove that they were imported before the ban. In developing and testing recipes for this book, I was able to find the peppercorns from several retailers (see Sources, page 456), but there's no knowing how long this will be the case. The one bit of good news is that roasted and ground Sichuan peppercorns that test negative for the citrus canker can be imported. At present, however, I haven't found a source for the ground spice, but I'll keep looking. If you do find roasted, ground Sichuan peppercorns, use a heaping 2 tablespoons in place of the 3 tablespoons called for in the Chengdu Braised Pork (page 371). The difference accounts for the amount you lose in sifting the spice when you grind and sift it yourself.

Honey-Glazed Five-Spice Baby Back Ribs →→

Mysteriously spicy, sweet, addictive, and a real crowd pleaser. Even with the glaze, these ribs are nowhere near as messy to eat as most ribs, which makes them ideal as an unexpected hors d'oeuvre at the most chichi cocktail party. I confess that I also like to serve these at big rowdy gatherings (a Super Bowl party, for instance) right along with pretzels and chips. Fortunately, the recipe is easily doubled, tripled, or even quadrupled. And, best of all, the ribs can be braised several hours ahead and then quickly glazed before serving—something that always simplifies the life of a host.

beer and wine notes

Medium-weight ale, such as Anchor Steam's Liberty Ale, or deeply fruity red wine, like old-vine Zinfandel or a rich Australian Shiraz.

Working Ahead

Much of the ribs' flavor comes from rubbing them with a dry spice rub at least 12 hours before braising (Step 1). Be sure to allow time for this.

Serves 4 as an hors d'oeuvre | *Braising Time: 1 1/2 hours*

THE SPICE RUB

2 tablespoons five-spice powder (see "Five-Spice Powder," page 377)

1 1/2 teaspoons coarse salt

1 1/2 teaspoons brown sugar (light or dark)

1 slab baby back ribs (1 3/4 to 2 pounds)

THE BRAISE

1 cup lager beer

1 tablespoon molasses (dark or light)

3 tablespoons honey

1 tablespoon ketchup

1/2 teaspoon Asian fish sauce (soy sauce
may be substituted)

1. **The spice rub—12 to 24 hours in advance:** A day before (or early the morning before) you plan to serve the ribs, combine the five-spice powder, salt, and brown sugar in a small bowl. Rub this mixture over the entire surface of the ribs, turning and rubbing until it adheres; this may take a few turns. Place the ribs on a tray or baking dish, cover loosely, and refrigerate for 12 to 24 hours.

2. **Heat the oven to 325 degrees.**

3. **The braise:** Place the ribs bone side down in a deep roasting pan or baking dish large enough to accommodate the slab (9-by-13-inch works well). Measure the beer in a large glass measuring cup and stir in the molasses. Pour this mixture around, not over, the pork. Cover tightly with foil and braise, basting every 30 minutes or so, until the ribs are tender enough that you can easily slide a knife between the meat and bone, about 1 1/2 hours. Remove from the oven. (*The ribs may be made ahead to this point and held at room temperature for a few hours.*)

4. **The glaze:** Heat the broiler on high. Whisk together the honey, ketchup, and fish sauce. Separate the ribs by cutting down between the bones with a sharp knife. Discard the braising liquid. Place the ribs on a broiling pan or baking sheet and paint them on all sides with the glaze. Broil about 4 inches from the heating element, turning once, until glazed and blackened in spots, about 7 minutes total. Serve hot or warm.

Five-Spice Powder

Five-spice powder, often referred to as Chinese five-spice powder, is a combination of warm and fragrant spices used widely in the Chinese kitchen. Sold both whole and ground, five-spice typically contains star anise, cassia (a cinnamon-like spice), fennel seed, and Sichuan peppercorns. Some blends include cloves and/or dried ginger. Five-spice powder adds a warm-sweet-spicy character to marinades and braises. It can also be combined with salt for a dipping condiment. As with any ground spice, five-spice powder will lose its potency in a matter of months. Buy it in small quantities and store it in a tightly closed jar or container in a cool, dry place.

Pork Riblets Braised in Vietnamese Caramel Sauce ⇶

Traditional Vietnamese cooks make large batches of a tantalizing savory caramel sauce known as *nuoc duong thang* and use it in an array of dishes. Sometimes the sauce gets stirred into meat dishes after cooking to add a deep gloss. What appeals to me more is the technique of using this pungent sauce as a braising medium—especially for pork.

Tender and salty-sweet, these little riblets are perfect with a round of drinks to pique your guests' appetites before the main course. Unlike the many rib recipes that result in ribs drenched in a sticky, thick glaze, the braising liquid here becomes a thin (but intensely flavored) sauce that only serves to moisten the ribs. You'll want to have sturdy napkins on hand and a big bowl to collect the discarded bones.

wine and beer notes

A slightly sweet blush wine, such as White Zinfandel, or an ale with spice notes, such as Sierra Nevada Pale Ale.

Working Ahead

These ribs are excellent make-ahead party fare. Braise the riblets (through Step 3), then let them cool in the braising liquid. Cover and refrigerate for 1 to 3 days. To serve, remove and discard the solid layer of white fat from the surface of the braising liquid, and transfer the riblets and liquid to an ovenproof baking dish. Cover with foil and heat in a 350-degree oven until hot, about 20 minutes.

Serves 4 as an hors d'oeuvre | Braising Time: 1 ¹/₂ hours

1 cup sugar

1/2 cup water

1 tablespoon freshly squeezed lime or
   lemon juice

1/3 cup Asian fish sauce

1/3 cup sliced shallots

1 teaspoon cracked black pepper

1 slab baby back ribs (1 3/4 to 2 pounds),
   sawed lengthwise in half by the
   butcher (see "Shopping for Pork
   Riblets," page 380)

1.   **Making the caramel:** Spread the sugar in the bottom of a wide heavy-based skillet (12-to 13-inch). Pour over 1/4 cup of the water and the lime or lemon juice, and let it sit for a minute to soak in. (The citrus juice is not traditional, but its acid helps keep the sugar from crystallizing, something that can happen easily when caramelizing such a large amount of sugar.) Heat over medium heat until the sugar begins to liquefy. You can shake or swirl the pan or stir with a wooden spoon once or twice so the sugar melts evenly, but don't stir constantly, and stop shaking or stirring once the contents of the saucepan have liquefied entirely. If you stir too often, you risk crystallizing the sugar. Reduce the heat to medium-low, and let the caramel boil until it turns a deep reddish-brown, but not black, about 10 minutes. The caramel will smoke a bit around the edges and begin to smell toasted or burned, a sign that it is ready.

2.   **The caramel braising liquid:** Remove the caramel from the heat, and, standing back and pouring slowly so the caramel does not boil over, add the fish sauce and the remaining 1/4 cup water. Don't worry if the caramel hardens. Return the caramel to the heat, stir, and let boil until you have a smooth, thick sauce, about 4 minutes. Add the shallots and black pepper and simmer for another 2 minutes. Remove from the heat and set aside to cool to warm. (*The caramel sauce may be made ahead up to this point and kept refrigerated for a week.*)

3.   **The braise:** With a sharp knife, separate the pork ribs into individual riblets by cutting down between the bones. Add them to the caramel sauce, stir to coat, and bring to a simmer over low heat. Cover and braise, stirring and turning every 10 to 15 minutes with tongs so that the ribs remain evenly coated in the caramel sauce, for about 1 1/2 hours. If at any time the caramel sauce is simmering too hard (it will foam up when it boils), lower the heat or set a heat diffuser beneath the pan. The ribs are done when they have become tender enough to pull easily away from the bone and are a deep mahogany color.

4.   **Serving:** When the riblets are tender, transfer them to a serving platter or large plate. Skim as much of the clear fat from the surface of the sauce as you can without losing patience. The sauce is supposed to be quite thin. Pour some if the sauce over the riblets to moisten. Serve warm or at room temperature, with plenty of napkins.

Shopping for Pork Riblets

Riblets are simply mini spareribs, but unless you own a band saw (and one you would want to use on pork), you'll need some help from the butcher. I've found that most supermarkets sell wrapped slabs of spareribs in the meat case, which can be some distance from where the meat cutters are. What you need to do is this: grab a wrapped slab of spareribs, walk it over to the meat cutters, and ask them to please saw the slab in half lengthwise down the middle. Since even the least helpful of meat departments has to have a band saw, they should be happy to oblige. Many Asian markets that carry fresh meat also sell spareribs and will easily accommodate your request for riblets.

Braised Pork Belly with Glazed Turnips →→

There's so much to commend the virtues of braised pork belly that I hardly know where to begin. If you've had the pleasure, you know exactly what I'm talking about (and your mouth may water at the memory). If you've not yet been introduced to pork belly, this recipe is a good place to start. A spice rub of coriander, dill seed, and black peppercorns imparts a bright aromatic taste to the dish, and the white-wine-and-chicken-stock-based braising liquid keeps the flavors light. The finished dish is richly flavored without being at all heavy. One qualifying note: Pork belly is not for those who trim the fat from pro-sciutto or cook their bacon until completely crisp and dry. What makes pork belly so uniquely delicious are the streaky layers of fat and lean. The juicy fat is as much a part of the enjoyment of this dish as the succulent meat.

I like to pair pork belly with something sweet and earthy, and glazed turnips are just that. In the spring and fall, seek out baby turnips in the markets and don't bother peeling them. (Round white Japanese varieties are especially mild and good.) The rest of the year, the standard-issue purple-top turnips must be peeled. A salad of sharp greens such as arugula, watercress, baby mustard greens, and mizuna would be good either on the side or to follow.

wine notes

Full-bodied white with plenty of fruit and little or no oak—lighter-style Californian and Australian Chardonnay, or Pinot Gris and Pinot Blanc from Alsace.

Working Ahead

Make the spice rub and season the pork belly 1 to 2 days before braising (Step 1). This allows the spices to penetrate the meat and impart their full flavor.

THE SPICE RUB

1 teaspoon black peppercorns

1 teaspoon coriander seeds, toasted

¹/2 teaspoon dill seeds

1 ¹/2 teaspoons coarse salt

2 ¹/2 pounds bone-in, skin-on pork belly or
    1 ¹/2 to 2 pounds boneless pork belly,
    skin on or off (see "Shopping for Pork
    Belly," page 384)

THE AROMATICS AND BRAISING LIQUID

1 tablespoon extra-virgin olive oil

1 small yellow onion (about 4 ounces),
    coarsely chopped

1 carrot, coarsely chopped

1 celery stalk, coarsely chopped

4 garlic cloves, coarsely chopped

2 bay leaves

4 whole cloves

¹/2 cup dry white wine or dry white
    vermouth

1 cup chicken stock, homemade (page 448)
    or store-bought

THE TURNIPS

1 ¹/2 pound small turnips

1 tablespoon reserved pork fat or unsalted
    butter

¹/4 cup chicken stock, homemade (page
    448) or store-bought, or as needed

1 teaspoon sugar

Coarse salt and freshly ground black
    pepper

1. **The spice rub—1 to 2 days in advance:** Combine the peppercorns, coriander, and dill
seed in a small mortar or a spice grinder. Grind until cracked but not reduced to a powder.
Add the salt and grind briefly to combine.

    Dry the pork well with paper towels, and place it on a small baking sheet or large
plate. Rub the spice mixture all over the pork, turning and rubbing until all the spices
adhere; this may take a few turns. Cover with plastic and refrigerate for 1 to 2 days.

2. **Heat the oven to 325 degrees.**

3. **Browning the pork:** Pat the surface of the pork dry with paper towels. If some of the
spices come off, save these for later. Heat the oil in a large heavy skillet or shallow braising
dish (4- to 5-quart) over medium-high heat. Add the pork, skin side down, and sear until

the skin (or fat) sizzles and browns evenly, 8 to 10 minutes. Transfer the pork to a plate and pour off all but 2 tablespoons of fat from the pan.

4. **The aromatics:** Return the pan to medium-high heat, add the onion, carrot, and celery, and sauté until the vegetables are softening and beginning to brown, about 8 minutes. Add the garlic, bay leaves, and cloves. Stir and sauté for another minute or so.

5. **The braising liquid:** Add the white wine, bring to a simmer, and stir with a wooden spoon to dislodge any seared-on bits from the bottom of the pan. Simmer until the wine reduces down to a couple of tablespoons, about 3 minutes. Add the stock and bring to a simmer.

6. **The braise:** Return the pork, skin side up, to the pan. Scrape in any spices that have fallen off the pork. Cover with foil or a secure lid, and slide into the middle of the oven. Braise, checking every 45 minutes to baste and to make sure that the liquid isn't simmering too rapidly or evaporating, until the pork is completely tender, 2 1/4 to 3 hours. Turn down the oven 10 or 15 degrees if the liquid is simmering too briskly. And if the pan threatens to dry out, add some water, about 1/4 cup at a time. Remove the pork from the oven and let cool in the braising liquid.

7. **The finish:** When the pork is cool enough to handle, heat the oven to 425 degrees. Transfer the pork to a cutting board, and set the pan aside. If the pork is skin-on, run a long sharp knife blade just under the skin and remove it. If using bone-in pork, slide the pork off the bones. Score the exposed fat in a cross-hatch pattern, making shallow cuts about 1 inch apart, then cut the pork into 4 even portions.

8. **Browning the pork:** Strain the braising liquid into a large glass measuring cup, pressing down lightly on the vegetables to extract any liquid (don't press so hard as to mash the vegetables), and then discard the vegetables. With a large spoon, skim off the excess fat that floats on the surface of the strained liquid—reserve 1 tablespoon of the fat to sauté the turnips if you like (you can also use butter). Return the pork to the braising pan or another shallow baking dish. Reserve 1/4 cup of the braising liquid for the turnips, and pour the remaining braising liquid over the top of the pork. Slide the pork, uncovered, onto the middle oven rack until sizzling and browned and heated through, about 20 minutes.

9. **Meanwhile, glaze the turnips:** If using baby turnips, trim the stalks and scrub the turnips. For larger, purple-top turnips, peel and cut into 1-inch wedges. Choose a skillet just large enough to hold the turnips in a single layer (10-inch). Combine the turnips, the reserved pork fat or butter, sugar, and reserved 1/4 cup braising liquid in the skillet. Season with salt and pepper, and bring to a simmer over medium heat. Cover and simmer until the turnips are just tender when prodded with a small knife or thin skewer, 10 to 12 minutes. Remove the lid and cook, shaking and stirring, until the liquid has evaporated and the

turnips have a golden sheen, another 5 minutes or so. If the pork is not ready, set aside in a warm place.

10. Serving: Serve the pork and turnips on warm plates. Taste the braising liquid for salt and pepper, and spoon a bit over each serving.

Shopping for Pork Belly

Fresh pork belly (basically raw, uncured bacon) is a prime example of how the appetites of chefs and food cognoscenti can change our marketplace. As recently as ten years ago, the only place you could purchase fresh pork belly was in Chinatown or other small ethnic markets. Today pork belly can be easily procured at specialty markets and mail-order meat companies (see Sources, page 455).

Pork belly comes in a few forms, depending on where you shop and what you're after: skin-on and bone-in, skin-on and boneless, skinless and boneless. While all of these forms are fine for the recipes in this book, whole pork belly (with skin and bone) is always my first choice. The meat comes out with a slightly richer flavor when it is protected by the skin and bone during braising. Unfortunately, it can be hard to find pork belly this way in most markets. More typically, I am able to find fresh pork belly with skin-on but no bones, and this is more than fine. If all you can find is skinless, boneless pork belly (it will look exactly like raw bacon), that's okay too. The pork will still be delicious. Just be sure to check for doneness early, as the pork will braise a bit faster without skin and bone.

Red-Cooked Pork Belly with Bok Choy ↠

Red-cooking, the Chinese method of braising meat, poultry, seafood, and even tofu in an aromatic soy-based sauce, takes its name from the reddish-brown tint that it imparts to the food. Serious Chinese kitchens always have a simmering pot of this "master cooking sauce" (*lu*) that they use repeatedly for red-cooking different foods. After braising, the food is left to cool in the *lu*, then lifted out with only the cleanest utensils (to avoid contaminating the sauce). The *lu* is then refrigerated and saved for the next braise. Traditional Chinese cooks claim that the *lu* gets more complex and better tasting with each cooking. The only rules are to avoid lamb and seafood, both of which would overpower the other flavors, and to replenish the *lu* with fresh spices and additional liquid from time to time between braises. I know one Chinese chef who claims his *lu* is twelve years old—and he also insists that he's eaten food braised in ones that were more than one hundred years old!

Since I don't do enough red-cooking to merit a *lu*, I make a smaller version and start fresh each time. I especially love red-cooking pork belly, because the seasonings penetrate the fat-streaked meat in such a way as to make it firm and tender all at once, not at all wobbly or flabby. In place of pork belly, hefty cubes of pork shoulder (not trimmed of fat) are also good. Serve with bowls of steamed white rice.

wine notes

Young, fruity red with moderate tannins and little oak—lighter Syrah, Shiraz, or Zinfandel.

Serves 4 | *Braising Time: about 3 hours*

THE BRAISE

THE BRAISE

One 2-inch piece fresh ginger, sliced into
6 to 8 coins and smashed

3 scallions, white and green parts, cut into
1-inch pieces

One 3-inch cinnamon stick

2 ounces Chinese rock sugar (see "Chinese
Rock Sugar," page 374), smashed into
small rocks with a hammer, or 1/4 cup
packed brown sugar

2 whole star anise

1/4 cup dry sherry

1/4 cup soy sauce (not "lite")

1/4 cup dark mushroom soy sauce (see "Dark
Mushroom Soy Sauce," page 156)

5 cups chicken stock, homemade (page
448) or store-bought, or water

1 1/2 to 2 pounds pork belly, preferably
skin on (see "Shopping for Pork Belly,"
page 384), cut into 2-inch chunks

THE BOK CHOY

1 pound bok choy (1 medium head or
3 baby heads)

1 1/2 tablespoons peanut oil

Coarse salt and freshly ground black
pepper

1/4 cup water

1. **The braising liquid (lu):** In a well-seasoned carbon steel or stainless steel wok (or shallow 12- to 13-inch braising pan), combine the ginger, scallions, cinnamon stick, sugar, star anise, sherry, both soy sauces, and stock or water. Bring to a boil over medium-high heat, stirring to dissolve the sugar, and boil for 12 to 15 minutes to infuse the liquid with the spices.

2. **The braise:** Slide the pork into the wok and lower the heat to a gentle simmer. Braise, uncovered, turning the pork with tongs from time to time so that it braises evenly, until the meat is fork-tender, about 3 hours. Monitor the heat so the sauce simmers modestly, never vigorously. If necessary, lower the heat.

3. **Meanwhile, wash and trim the bok choy:** Rinse the bok choy thoroughly, paying close attention to the inside hollow at the base of each leaf, where dirt tends to gather. Drain. Cut the lower ribs crosswise into 1-inch pieces, and slice the leaves into slightly wider 1 1/2-inch strips. Set the stems and leaves aside in separate bowls.

4. **Simmering the bok choy:** When the pork is tender, turn off the heat and let it sit. Heat the oil in a large skillet over medium-high heat. Add the bok choy stems a handful at a time and cook, stirring, until the stems begin to throw off their water and soften some, 4 to 5 minutes. Immediately begin adding the leaves, stirring and tossing with tongs, and season lightly with salt and pepper. Add the water, cover, and lower the heat to medium. Simmer just until the bok-choy is crisp-tender, about 5 minutes more. Set aside in a warm spot.

5. **The finish:** With tongs, transfer the pork to a large platter, and cover loosely with foil to keep warm. Strain the braising liquid into a medium saucepan, and discard the solids. Skim some but not all of the clear fat from the surface—some fat is essential to the flavor, but the amount is up to you. Boil the braising liquid until it is reduced by one quarter to one half, about 8 minutes. Taste. It should be salty and intense.

6. **Serving:** Serve the pork and bok choy with a drizzle of the reduced braising liquid.

Ham Braised in Madeira with Rosemary & Green Peppercorns ⇥

There are certain occasions that call for a big ham—holidays, an open house, weekend house party—but that doesn't mean it has to be the same old ham. Here's a way to revive an ordinary supermarket ham by braising it in a mix of good Madeira wine and green peppercorns. I promise it will be one of the best hams you've ever served, or tasted. And if you want to go all out and buy a really good ham from an artisan producer, all the better. If it's a true country ham, however, you'll have to soak it for at least a day before braising.

Braised ham is good warm or cold. And don't forget the biscuits for divine ham sandwiches.

wine notes

Fruity, off-dry to slightly sweet white wine, such as Riesling from Germany or Austria, or Pinot Gris from Alsace.

Working Ahead

The ham keeps nicely, wrapped and refrigerated, for 2 to 3 days after braising. Let it stand at room temperature for an hour before carving. Warm the sauce as directed in Step 5.

Serves 10 to 12 | Braising Time: about 1 3/4 hours
for a fully cooked ham; about 2 1/2 hours for a partially cooked ham

2 tablespoons extra-virgin olive oil

2 carrots, coarsely chopped

2 medium yellow onions (12 ounces total),
    coarsely chopped

2 celery stalks, coarsely chopped

1 heaping tablespoon green peppercorns
    in brine, rinsed and drained

2 garlic cloves, peeled and smashed

Four 3-inch leafy fresh rosemary sprigs

2 small or 1 large bay leaf

1 cup dry Madeira, such as Sercial or
    Rainwater

1 cup chicken or veal stock, homemade
    (page 448 or 451) or store-bought

One 6- to 8-pound bone-in ham, fully or
    partially cooked, preferably shank or
    rump (see "Shopping for Cured Ham,"
    page 391)

1. **Heat the oven to 300 degrees.**

2. **The aromatics:** In a large Dutch oven or deep braising pan (7-quart) large enough to hold the ham, heat the oil over medium-high heat. When the oil is shimmering, add the carrots, onions, and celery. Sauté, stirring a few times, until the vegetables brown on the edges and begin to soften, about 10 minutes. Add the peppercorns, garlic, rosemary, and bay leaf, stir, and sauté for another 2 minutes.

3. **The braising liquid:** Pour in the Madeira and bring to a boil. Lower the heat to medium and simmer for 10 minutes to meld the flavors and reduce the liquid somewhat. Pour in the stock, bring to a simmer, and simmer for another 5 minutes.

4. **The braise:** Whether you bought a fully cooked or partially cooked (sometimes labeled "ready to cook") ham will affect the cooking time. Lower the ham into the pot, setting it either flat side down or on its side, whichever fits best. Cover tightly with the lid or heavy-duty foil, and slide the pot into the lower part of the oven. For a fully cooked ham, braise until fork-tender and heated all the way through, about 1 hour and 45 minutes. For a partially cooked ham, braise until the ham is fork-tender and an instant-read thermometer reads 155 degrees when inserted in the thickest part of the ham, closer to 2 ½ hours. (Be careful that the thermometer does not hit the bone, which will give you a falsely high reading.)

5. **The finish:** Transfer the ham to a platter and cover loosely with foil to keep warm. Strain the braising liquid, and discard the vegetables—they will be too salty. Skim as much fat from the surface of the braising liquid as you can without losing patience. Taste. If the liquid tastes a bit weak, pour it into a medium saucepan and simmer to reduce until it tastes like a mild broth, 10 or 15 minutes. If the liquid is already tasty as is, set it over a low burner to keep warm. The sauce will not need any salt—in fact, if you do reduce it, be careful not to go too far, as it can quickly become too salty.

6. **Serving:** Carve the ham into thin slices, and serve warm or at room temperature, with a bit of the warm sauce spooned over the top.

VARIATION: CREAMY MADEIRA SAUCE FOR BRAISED HAM

To dress up a braised ham even more, make this quick Madeira sauce. Melt 1 tablespoon unsalted butter in a small saucepan over medium heat. Add 1 large shallot, chopped, and sauté until the shallot is translucent, about 6 minutes. Add 1/4 cup of the same Madeira you used to braise the ham. Increase the heat to medium-high, and simmer until the Madeira is reduced to about 1 tablespoon, about 5 minutes. Add 1 tablespoon apricot or red current jelly and whisk until smooth. Add 1/2 cup heavy cream and simmer until the cream is quite thick, another 6 to 8 minutes. Add 3/4 to 1 cup of the strained braising liquid from the ham and bring to a simmer. Taste for salt and pepper. Spoon over slices of the braised ham.

Shopping for Cured Ham

Technically the word *ham* refers to the entire rear leg of a pig, fresh or cured. In today's marketplace, however, since few consumers are out shopping for such a large hunk of fresh pork, *ham* has come to refer solely to pork that has been cured. To avoid confusion, we now refer to the unprocessed, uncured hind leg as fresh ham.

Cured hams come in a variety of styles and shapes. The character and taste of a ham depends on whether it was cured by salting, brining, or injection. Once cured, many hams are smoked—some heavily, some lightly—to further dry the meat and impart a smoky flavor. The method and type of cure is largely what determines the final taste and character of a ham. For instance, the world-famous prosciutto di Parma hams from Italy have been salt-cured, not smoked, and then dried in cool mountain air to produce a superb-tasting, moist ham. The venerable Smithfield hams from Virginia, on the other hand, are also salt-cured, but then they are hickory-smoked and aged, producing an intensely flavored, drier ham. The best type of ham is largely a matter of personal taste and availability. Most regions of the country have their own styles and tastes.

Fully cooked hams are just that—cooked to an internal temperature of 148 degrees or higher and ready to eat. Even though these hams can be sliced and eaten directly from the package, they benefit from a reheat before serving. Partially cooked hams have been cured but not exposed to such high temperatures. They must be treated like fresh pork and baked to an internal temperature of 155 degrees before serving. Use either kind for the Ham Braised in Madeira with Rosemary & Green Peppercorns (page 388).

A whole ham is the entire hind leg of pork and weighs more than 10 pounds. Unless you have a need for something that grand, there are several smaller options. The leg is often divided into two smaller hams: the rump portion and the shank portion, each one half of the whole leg. The shank portion is easiest to carve and therefore present, but the rump will work just as well. Either way, look for one that is compact and plump in shape.

Another source for smaller hams is the front shoulder of pork (see "Shopping for Pork Shoulder," page 353). Here you find the smaller picnic ham (from the arm portion of the shoulder) and the Boston butt, also known as a daisy ham, or cottage ham (the upper part of the shoulder).

Spaghetti alla Carbonara with Braised Slab Bacon ➜➜

I had honestly never considered braising a slab of cured bacon until I hit upon
a recipe by San Francisco chef extraodinaire Judy Rodgers in her brilliant book
The Zuni Café Cookbook, and what a revelation it is. The slow braise tames the
salty-smoky character of the bacon, mellowing the flavor and giving it a
meatier, less floppy texture. Once braised, bacon enhances all sorts of dishes
and is especially good with eggs, salads, and pasta. My favorite thing to do with
braised bacon, however, is make spaghetti alla carbonara. It transforms this
familiar bacon-and-egg pasta dish into something altogether sublime.

You need to find a market that sells slab bacon to make this recipe—not
all do. You can also buy it through mail-order (see Sources, page 455), as long
as you plan ahead. But once you do find slab bacon, don't be shy about making
more than the recipe calls for. Braised bacon keeps well in the refrigerator, and
you'll have no trouble discovering other ways to serve it. Before adding the
bacon to anything, warm it in the braising liquid or sauté briefly in drippings
or olive oil. (For more on slab bacon, see page 395.)

wine notes

Youthful, tart red, such as Barbera or non-Chianti Sangiovese from Italy.

Serves 4 | Braising Time: 2 1/2 to 3 hours

THE BRAISE

3/4 pound slab bacon, rind removed (see "Slab Bacon," page 395)

1 small carrot, chopped into 1/2-inch pieces

1 small yellow onion (about 3 ounces), chopped into 1/2-inch pieces

2 garlic cloves, peeled and bruised

One 2- to 3-inch leafy fresh rosemary or thyme sprig

1 bay leaf

4 to 6 black peppercorns

3/4 cup chicken stock, homemade (page 448) or store-bought, or water

1/2 cup dry white wine or dry white vermouth

THE PASTA

3 tablespoons extra-virgin olive oil

2 garlic cloves, smashed

1/2 cup dry white wine or dry white vermouth

1 pound spaghetti, linguine, or bucatini

3 large eggs

Coarse salt

1/4 cup *each* freshly grated Parmigiano-Reggiano and Pecorino Romano, plus more for serving

1/4 cup chopped flat-leaf parsley

Freshly ground black pepper

1. **Heat the oven to 275 degrees.**

2. **Blanching the bacon:** Put the bacon into a medium saucepan (if you need to cut the bacon into two pieces to fit, do so) and cover with cold water. Bring to a boil over medium-high heat, reduce to a steady simmer, and cook for 5 to 7 minutes. Drain.

3. **The aromatics and braising liquid:** Choose a heavy tight-lidded flameproof pot that will accommodate the bacon snugly. Again, don't hesitate to cut the bacon into two or three pieces to fit—ultimately it will be cut into cubes. Put the carrot, onion, garlic, rosemary or thyme, bay leaf, and peppercorns in the pan. Set the bacon on top, fat side up, and pour in the stock (or water) and wine. The liquid should come about halfway up the sides of the meat; if not, add a bit more stock (or water). Bring the liquid to a steady simmer over medium-high heat. Lay a piece of parchment paper over the top, pressing down so it nearly touches the meat and the edges of the paper extend over the sides of the pot by about an inch, then cover with the lid.

4. **The braise:** Place the bacon in the middle of the oven and braise at a gentle simmer, basting and turning once or twice, until completely tender, 2 1/2 to 3 hours. You should be able to easily pierce the meat with a regular table fork. Remove from the oven, and turn the broiler on high.

5. **Browning the bacon:** As soon as the broiler is hot, slide the bacon under it so that it is about 4 inches away from the heating element. Broil, turning once with tongs, until you

hear sizzling and popping sounds and the surface is brown and crisp, 3 to 8 minutes per side, depending on the strength of your broiler. Remove from the broiler and let the bacon cool to room temperature in the braising liquid.

6. **Degreasing the braising liquid:** Transfer the bacon to a cutting board. Tilt the pot and skim off the fat on the surface—there may be as much as ½ cup. Strain the braising liquid, and discard the vegetables. If you are not making the pasta right away, return the bacon to the braising liquid, cover, and refrigerate until ready to use (up to 1 week). If you are making the pasta right away, taste the braising liquid. It should have a pleasant broth-like flavor, but occasionally, depending on the bacon, the braising liquid will have an over-powering smoky taste—in which case, discard it. But if you like the flavor, save the liquid for another use (such as cooking vegetables, adding to soups, or adding to another braise).

7. **Making the pasta sauce:** Bring a large pot of water to a boil. Cut the bacon into large dice (about ½-inch cubes). You should have a generous cup. Heat the oil in a medium skillet (9- to 10-inch) over medium heat. Add the bacon and garlic and sauté, shaking frequently, to crisp the bacon on all sides. As soon as the garlic cloves are golden, about 3 minutes, remove and discard them—this will probably happen before the bacon is ready, but continue sautéing the bacon until crisp, 10 to 12 minutes. Add the wine and simmer to reduce by about half, 10 to 12 minutes. Set aside in a warm corner of the stove.

8. **Cooking the pasta:** When the pasta water boils, add a handful of salt (about 2 table-spoons) and the pasta, stir once or twice, and boil vigorously until it's al dente. While the pasta boils, break the eggs into a small bowl, add a pinch of salt, and lightly beat them. Set aside. Drain the pasta, reserving ½ cup of the cooking water.

9. **The finish:** Transfer the pasta to a warm serving bowl. Gradually pour ¼ cup of the reserved pasta cooking water into the eggs, whisking constantly to prevent the eggs from curdling. Whisk in the cheese and parsley. Immediately pour the egg-cheese mixture over the pasta and toss with tongs or two large wooden spoons so that it thoroughly coats all the strands of pasta. Quickly rewarm the bacon and wine over high heat, and immediately pour it over the pasta. Toss. If the pasta seems dry, add some or all of the remaining pasta cooking water. Season with a few generous grinds of black pepper and serve right away. Pass more cheese at the table.

Slab Bacon

Slab bacon of good quality often comes with the skin (also referred to as rind) still on. To remove this, set the bacon rind side down on a cutting board. Steady the slab with the palm of one hand and, holding a sharp long knife in the other, slide its blade just above the rind, keeping the knife parallel to the work surface, and remove the rind in one piece. (If you've skinned a salmon fillet, the technique will be familiar.)

Once you've removed the rind, don't toss it out. It's loaded with collagen (the protein that melts from tough cuts of meat during braising and adds body to the surrounding liquid) and good bacony flavor. A few strips of bacon rind added to most any braised dish will enrich the taste and texture of the sauce. Slice the rind into strips about 2 inches wide. Sealed in a zip-lock bag, the bacon rind will keep for several months in the freezer. To use the rind, just tuck 1 or 2 strips under meat or poultry the next time you braise. If you want to minimize the smoky flavor of the bacon rind before adding it to a braise, blanch it first: place it in a small pot of cold water, bring to a boil, and boil for 5 minutes; drain.

Good slab bacon is essential to Spaghetti alla Carbonara (page 392), and there's no substituting pre-sliced bacon. If you can't find slab bacon at a local market, consider ordering it through mail-order (see Sources, page 455). For other recipes that call for slab bacon, such as Coq au Vin (page 157) or Spring Vegetable Braise (page 75), you can get away with using thick-cut bacon. Just be sure to shop for the thickest-cut, best-quality bacon you can find. Take note, however, that pre-cut bacon will throw off more fat when you cook it than slab bacon, so adjust the recipe accordingly by pouring off the drippings or adding less of the additional fat called for.

Sausages & Plums Braised in Red Wine →→

Each time I make this, I marvel at the interplay of flavors between the plump pork sausages, the sweet-tart fruit, and the lightly acidic wine. And because this is such an easy dish, requiring few ingredients and little time, I make it often, especially in the summer, when plums are at their peak. As you're cutting up the plums for this recipe, taste a piece. If the plums are on the sour side (as some early-season varieties are), add a pinch of sugar to the braise to bring out their sweetness. If plums aren't in season make the dish with grapes (see the variation that follows).

Since there's no stock in the braising liquid to round out the flavor of the wine, it's important here to use a wine that really tastes good to you. I particularly like using a lightly fruity but dry Beaujolais—a real Beaujolais, not the raw-tasting Nouveau Beaujolais that shows up every November.

Serve with polenta or sautéed potatoes and a baguette or other crusty bread to sop up every last bit of the gorgeous magenta-hued sauce. It's too good to leave any behind. Pass a simple tossed arugula or spinach salad at the table.

wine notes

Lighter-style Pinot Noir from California, or another fruity red, such as Beaujolais Villages.

Serves 4 to 6 | Braising Time: 25 to 30 minutes

1 pound ripe purple or red plums, such as
Santa Rosa or Italian

1 ³/₄ to 2 pounds sweet Italian sausages
(with or without fennel seed)

1 tablespoon extra-virgin olive oil

1 large shallot, minced (about 3 scant
tablespoons)

1 to 2 garlic cloves, minced

1 ¹/₂ teaspoons minced fresh sage or ¹/₂
teaspoon rubbed

Coarse salt and freshly ground black
pepper

Pinch of sugar, if needed

²/₃ cup light, fruity dry red wine, such as
Beaujolais, Dolcetto, or Pinot Noir

1.   **The plums:** Working over a bowl to collect the juices, cut the plums into ¹/₂-inch wedges, tasting a piece to judge their sweetness, and letting them drop into the bowl. If the plums are not freestone, you'll have to cut the flesh away from the pits with a knife. Set aside.

2.   **Browning the sausages:** If the sausages are linked together, separate the links with a sharp paring knife or a pair of scissors. Prick each link in several places with the tip of a sharp knife (this will prevent the sausages from exploding). Heat the oil in a large lidded skillet or shallow braising pan (12-inch is a good choice) over medium-high heat until the oil slides easily across the pan. Add the sausages and fry them, turning frequently with tongs, until a medium brown crust has formed on at least three sides, 10 to 12 minutes total. Using tongs, so as not to pierce the casings further, transfer the sausages to a large plate, without stacking.

3.   **The aromatics:** Depending on how fatty the sausages are, there may or may not be an excess of fat in the pan. Pour off all but 1 tablespoon, return the pan to medium heat, and add the shallot. Stir immediately with a wooden spoon, and sauté just until the shallot begins to brown, about 1 minute. Add the garlic and sage, stir again, and sauté until fragrant, another 30 seconds or so. Add the plums and all of their juices. Season with salt, pepper, and pinch of sugar if the plums tasted tart. Stir and sauté until the juices begin to sizzle, about 2 minutes.

4.   **The braising liquid:** Pour in the wine, increase the heat to medium-high, and stir with a wooden spoon, scraping the bottom of the pan to dislodge any precious cooked-on bits that will enrich the flavor of the braising liquid. Simmer for 3 to 4 minutes to meld the flavors some.

5.   **The braise:** Return the sausages to the pan, nestling them down so they are surrounded by the plums. Add any juices that may have accumulated on the plate. Cover the pan and reduce the heat to a very gentle simmer. Check after 5 minutes to make sure that the wine is not simmering too excitedly. If it is, lower the heat or put a heat diffuser beneath the pan. Continue braising gently, turning the sausages after 15 minutes, until the sausages are cooked all the way through, 25 to 30 minutes total. Check for doneness by

piercing a sausage with a skewer or meat fork to see if the juices run clear. If you are unsure, nick a sausage with a small knife and peer inside to see that there is no pink left.

6.   **The finish:** Transfer the sausages with tongs to a serving platter. Lift the plums from the pan with a slotted spoon and arrange them around the sausages. Cover loosely with foil to keep warm. Return the braising liquid to the stove. Taste and evaluate the sauce. Depending on how juicy the plums and sausages were, you may or may not need to reduce the sauce: it should be the consistency of a thick vinaigrette. If necessary, bring to a strong simmer over medium-high heat, and simmer for 2 to 4 minutes to thicken and concentrate the flavor. I don't bother skimming this sauce, since the fat from the sausages is integral in balancing the taste, but it never tastes oily or fatty. Taste for salt and pepper. The sauce is meant to be slightly sharp to offset the rich taste of the pork sausage. Pour the sauce over the sausages and plums, and serve.

VARIATION: SAUSAGES & GRAPES BRAISED IN RED WINE

Substitute whole seedless red or purple table grapes for the plums. Add them in place of the plums in Step 3. Most grapes are sweet enough on their own so as not to need the pinch of sugar. Taste and judge for yourself. (For more on table grapes, see page 198.)

Cabbage Rolls Stuffed with Pork & Sauerkraut →>-

Stuffed cabbage rolls are a staple in Eastern European cooking, and they come in a variety of shapes with an even greater variety of fillings. Traditionally the filling is wrapped up in fermented whole cabbage leaves. But since it's not easy to find whole pickled leaves here, I use fresh cabbage for the outer wrapping and sauerkraut in the filling. The idea of combining fresh and pickled cabbage may have come out of necessity, but it turned out to be more delicious than the recipe that inspired it.

If you've only ever had heavy cabbage rolls, these will be a revelation. They are light and brimming with bright flavors and plenty of refreshing crunch from the fresh vegetables. The rolls are filled with a well-seasoned mix of rice and ground pork and beef, then layered in a sauce composed of onions, tomatoes, celery, carrots, sauerkraut, and bacon. As the rolls braise, all the flavors mingle and marry to create a memorable main dish that needs little more than some dark bread as an accompaniment.

wine notes
_____

Dry, aromatic Muscat or Gewürztraminer from Alsace.

Working Ahead

These cabbage rolls do take a while to put together, but all the work can be done ahead, and they are well worth the effort. Complete the recipe through Step 11, cover with plastic, and refrigerate for 1 to 2 days. To serve, braise as directed.

Makes 12 rolls; serves 6 to 8 | *Braising Time: 1 ¹/₂ hours*

1 head green cabbage (about 2 pounds)

1 pound bagged sauerkraut (see
 "Shopping for Sauerkraut," page 403)

3 medium yellow onions (about
 18 ounces total)

1 tablespoon unsalted butter

1/2 cup long-grain white rice

3/4 cup chicken stock, homemade (page
 448) or store-bought

1 pound ground pork, preferably
 not too lean

1/2 pound ground beef, preferably
 not too lean

1 large egg, lightly beaten

1 tablespoon chopped fresh thyme or
 1 teaspoon dried

1 teaspoon coarse salt

Freshly ground black pepper

1/4 teaspoon freshly grated nutmeg

6 slices bacon (about 5 ounces)

3 celery stalks, cut into 1/4-inch slices
 (1 1/2 to 2 cups)

2 carrots, cut into 1/4-inch slices

One 28-ounce can whole peeled tomatoes,
 chopped, juice reserved

1. **Blanching the cabbage:** Bring a large deep pot of water to a boil over high heat. Remove any tough or bruised outer leaves from the cabbage and core the cabbage using a strong paring knife. Immerse the head of cabbage core side down in the boiling water, using two slotted spoons or metal spatulas, and bring back to a boil. Boil the cabbage for 5 minutes. You may need to hold the cabbage down with a slotted spoon since it tends to bob above the surface of the water. Remove the cabbage, leaving the pot on the stove, and set on a platter or baking sheet with sides. Gently remove the outer leaves of the cabbage using tongs, so as to avoid burning your fingers, and lay them out in one layer on another platter or baking sheet with sides. When you have removed 6 leaves, return the cabbage to the pot and boil for another 3 minutes. Remove the cabbage from the water again, and drain the water. Gently remove another 6 leaves and lay them out flat in one layer on another platter or baking sheet with sides. Place the remaining cabbage head in a bowl and set aside to cool.

2. **Rinsing the sauerkraut:** Place the sauerkraut in a colander and rinse well with plenty of cold running water. Toss the sauerkraut around in the colander to rinse all of its strands, then drain. Grab a handful of sauerkraut, squeeze to remove the excess water, and transfer to a small bowl. Continue squeezing handfuls of the sauerkraut until it is all dry. Set the bowl aside.

3. **The onions:** Chop 1 onion into 1/4-inch dice, and transfer to a small bowl or plate. Cut the remaining 2 onions into 1/4-inch slices, transfer to another bowl or plate, and set aside.

4. **Partially cooking the rice:** Melt the butter in a small heavy saucepan over medium heat. Add the chopped onion and toss with a wooden spoon to coat the onion with the

butter. Cook the onion, stirring once or twice, until translucent and softened, 5 to 7 minutes. Add the rice and toss well to coat each grain with butter. Cook, stirring once or twice, until the rice is hot when you touch it with the back of your fingers, 1 to 2 minutes. Raise the heat to high, add the stock, stir the rice, and bring to a boil. Lower the heat to simmer, cover the saucepan, and cook for 10 minutes. There will be some liquid remaining in the pan, and the rice will be crunchy and underdone; it will finish cooking in the oven. With the wooden spoon, transfer the rice and the liquid to a large bowl, and spread the rice over the bottom and up the sides of the bowl into a 1-inch layer, for quicker cooling. Set aside to cool.

5. **The cabbage for the filling:** When the remaining cabbage head has cooled, transfer to a cutting board and cut into thick slices. Coarsely chop the slices and set aside again.

6. **The filling:** When the rice has cooled, add the ground pork, beef, egg, thyme, salt, 1/2 teaspoon black pepper, and the nutmeg. Mix well with your hands to incorporate all the ingredients, and set aside.

7. **Frying the bacon:** Place the bacon in a large skillet, set over medium heat, and fry, turning once or twice with a large fork, until browned and crisped, 10 to 12 minutes. Transfer the bacon to a plate lined with paper towels to drain, and reserve the bacon fat in the skillet.

8. **The aromatics and braising liquid:** Add the reserved sliced onions, along with the celery and carrots, to the bacon fat in the skillet and toss well with a wooden spoon to coat the vegetables with the fat. Sauté the vegetables, stirring several times, until softened and lightly browned, about 15 minutes. Add the reserved chopped cabbage, mix well, and continue cooking for another 5 minutes, stirring once or twice. Add the sauerkraut and mix well with the large fork that you used for the bacon, separating the sauerkraut strands as you mix. Transfer the mixture to a large bowl and add the chopped tomatoes with their juice. Season with a generous grinding of black pepper, mix well, and set aside.

9. **Heat the oven to 325 degrees.**

10. **Shaping the cabbage rolls:** Divide the rice filling into 12 portions. Place 1 cabbage leaf on a work surface, hollow side up. Cut out the thickest part of the center rib, about 2 inches of rib. Arrange the cabbage leaf if necessary so that the core end of the leaf is near you, and overlap the leaf where the rib was removed. Place one portion of the filling in the center of the leaf. Fold the core end of the leaf up and over the filling, fold the right and left sides in over the filling, and roll up the leaf. (This is the same method used for folding a blintz or spring roll.) Repeat with the remaining 11 cabbage leaves.

11. **Assembling the braise:** Spread one third of the sauerkraut-vegetable mixture in a large 3-inch-deep baking dish or lasagne pan. Tuck 6 cabbage rolls into the vegetables,

seam side down. Crumble and scatter 3 slices of the bacon over the rolls. Top with another one third of the sauerkraut-vegetable mixture. Place the remaining 6 rolls in the dish, seam side down. Crumble and scatter the remaining bacon over the rolls, and finish with the remaining sauerkraut-vegetable mixture.

12. The braise: Cover the dish tightly with foil, place in the lower third of the oven, and braise undisturbed for 1 1/2 hours. Remove the dish from the oven, uncover, and let the rolls rest for 10 minutes. Serve from the dish, topping the rolls with plenty of the saucy sauerkraut-vegetable mixture.

VARIATION: HUNGARIAN-STYLE CABBAGE ROLLS

Add 2 teaspoons sweet Hungarian paprika to the filling in Step 6, and add another 1/2 teaspoon to the sautéed vegetables in Step 8. Serve with a spoonful of sour cream on each roll.

Shopping for Sauerkraut

Avoid the sauerkraut sold in cans: its texture is mushy and the flavor can be downright nasty. Instead, look for bags of "fresh" sauerkraut in the refrigerator section of the supermarket, typically near the other pickles or with the sausages and bacon. Bagged sauerkraut offers much higher quality in terms of both texture and flavor. I am also quite fond of the jars of Wellspring Farms organic sauerkraut sold at natural food stores throughout the Northeast. It's got the appealing crunch and flavor of freshly made pickles.

Braised Lamb Shanks Provençal ✈

Braising meaty lamb shanks in a piquant mix of sour lemons, black olives, and fresh tomatoes offsets their rich, gamy flavor. If you make this in early autumn when the first nips of cold air wake up your appetite for slow-cooked meats, look for the last of the local ripe plum tomatoes in the market. If good fresh tomatoes are unavailable, use canned. The dish will be every bit as satisfying. Serve with soft polenta or buttery mashed potatoes.

wine notes

A deep red wine with savory herb flavors from the southern Rhone or Provence, especially wines from Chateauneuf-du-Pape, Gigondas, and Bandol.

Serves 6 | Braising Time: about 2 1/2 hours

6 lamb shanks (about 1 pound each)

All-purpose flour for dredging (about 1 cup)

1 tablespoon plus 1/2 teaspoon sweet Hungarian paprika

Coarse salt and freshly ground black pepper

1 tablespoon extra-virgin olive oil

2 large yellow onions (about 1 pound total), chopped into 1/2-inch pieces

1 pound plum tomatoes, coarsely chopped (or one 14 1/2-ounce can whole peeled tomatoes, coarsely chopped, juice reserved)

4 garlic cloves, finely minced

1 cup dry white wine or dry white vermouth

1 cup chicken stock, homemade (page 448) or store-bought

2 lemons

3 small or 2 large bay leaves

1/2 cup pitted and coarsely chopped oil-cured black olives, such as Nyons or Moroccan

1/4 cup coarsely chopped flat-leaf parsley

1. **Heat the oven to 325 degrees.**

2. **Trimming the lamb shanks:** If the shanks are covered in a tough parchment-like outer layer (called the fell), trim this away by inserting a thin knife under it to loosen and peeling back this layer. Remove any excess fat as well, but don't fuss with trying to peel off any of the thin membrane—this holds the shank together and will melt down during braising.

3. **Dredging the lamb shanks:** Pour the flour into a shallow dish and stir in 1 tablespoon of the paprika. Season the shanks all over with salt and pepper. Roll half the shanks in the flour, lifting them out one by one and patting to remove any excess, and set them on a large plate or tray, without touching.

4. **Browning the lamb shanks:** Heat the oil in a large heavy-based braising pot (6- to 7-quart) over medium heat until it shimmers. Add the 3 flour-dredged shanks (you're searing in two batches so as not to crowd the pot). Cook, turning the shanks with tongs, until they are gently browned on all sides, about 10 minutes total. Transfer the shanks to a plate or tray, without stacking or crowding. Dredge the remaining shanks in flour, patting to remove any excess, and brown them. Set beside the already browned shanks, and discard the remaining flour.

5. **The aromatics and braising liquid:** Pour off all but 1 tablespoon of fat from the pot and return the pot to the heat. If the bottom of the pot is at all blackened, wipe it out with a damp paper towel, being careful to leave behind any tasty caramelized drippings. Add the onions, tomatoes with their juice, and the garlic and season with the remaining 1/2 teaspoon paprika and salt and pepper to taste. Sauté over medium heat, stirring occasionally, for 8 to 10 minutes, or until the onions are mostly tender. Pour in the wine and stir and scrape with a wooden spoon to dislodge any browned bits on the bottom of the pot that will contribute flavor to the liquid. Simmer for 3 minutes. Pour in the stock, stir and scrape the bottom again, and simmer for another 3 minutes.

6. **Meanwhile, zest the lemon:** Using a vegetable peeler, remove the zest from half of 1 lemon, being careful to remove only the outermost yellow zest, not the bitter-tasting white pith; reserve the lemon. Add the zest to the pot, along with the bay leaves.

7. **The braise:** Arrange the lamb shanks on top of the vegetables. The shanks should fit fairly snugly in the pot, but you may need to arrange them "head-to-toe" so they fit more evenly. Don't worry if they are stacked in two layers. Cover the pot with parchment paper, pressing down so that it nearly touches the lamb and the edges of the paper extend about an inch over the side of the pot. Set the lid in place, slide the pot into the lower part of the oven, and braise for about 2 1/2 hours. Check the shanks every 35 to 45 minutes, turning them with tongs and moving those on top to the bottom and vice versa, and making sure that there is still plenty of braising liquid. If the liquid seems to be simmering too aggressively at any point, lower the oven heat by 10 to 15 degrees. If the liquid threatens to dry

out, add ⅓ cup water. The shanks are done when the meat is entirely tender and they slide off a meat fork when you try to spear them.

8. **Segmenting the lemon:** While the shanks braise, use a thin-bladed knife (a boning knife works well) to carve the entire peel from the 2 lemons. The easiest way to do this is to first cut off the stem and blossom end of each one so the lemon is flat on the top and bottom. Then stand the lemon up and carve off the peel and white pith beneath it with arcing slices to expose the fruit. Trim away any bits of pith or membrane that you've left behind, until you have a whole naked lemon. Now, working over a small bowl to collect the juices, hold a lemon in one hand and cut out the individual segments, leaving as much of the membrane behind as you can. Drop the segments into the bowl, and pick out the seeds as you go. When you finish, you should be holding a random star-shaped membrane with very little fruit pulp attached. Give this a squeeze into the bowl and discard. Repeat with the second lemon.

9. **The finish:** Transfer the shanks to a tray to catch any juices, and cover with foil to keep warm. Using a wide spoon, skim as much surface fat from the cooking liquid as possible. Lamb shanks tend to throw off quite a bit of fat: continue skimming (tilting the pot to gather all the liquid in one corner makes it easier) until you are satisfied. Set the pot over medium heat and bring to a simmer. Stir in the lemon segments, olives, and parsley. Taste for salt and pepper. Return the shanks to the braising liquid to reheat for a minute or two. Serve with plenty of sauce spooned over each shank.

Lamb Shanks Braised with Lentils & Curry

Lamb and curry belong together, and here they are paired with the earthy taste of Le Puy lentils. Parcooking the lentils and only adding them to the braise during the last thirty minutes ensures both that they hold their shape and don't turn to mush and that they take on the aromatic flavor of the curried braising liquid. Serve this in shallow soup bowls, with a large spoonful of the fragrant, brothy lentils in the bottom and a falling-off-the-bone-tender lamb shank on top. I like to pass lemon wedges or a small cruet of good-quality red wine vinegar at the table. A few drops of either really spark the combination of flavors and makes them sing. Add a baguette or boule from an artisan bakery, and you've got a complete, and very comforting, meal.

wine notes

The intense berry-and-spice flavors of Syrah/Shiraz were tailor-made for the combination of lamb and curry. Look for wines from the northern Rhone Valley (Cote-Rotie and Crozes-Hermitage); or bolder-style Australian Shiraz, or Syrah from California or Washington State.

Serves 6 | Braising Time: 2 1/2 to 2 3/4 hours

2 tablespoons extra-virgin olive oil
6 lamb shanks (about 1 pound each)
Coarse salt and freshly ground black pepper
1 large red onion (about 8 ounces), coarsely chopped
2 carrots, coarsely chopped
1 celery stalk, coarsely chopped
4 garlic cloves, minced
1 1/2 tablespoons curry powder, preferably Madras
1 1/2 tablespoons chopped fresh thyme or 1 1/2 teaspoons dried
2 bay leaves
1 cup canned whole peeled tomatoes (about 6), drained and chopped

2 cups lamb, veal, or chicken stock,
   homemade (page 452, 451, or 448) or
   store-bought
1/2 pound Le Puy lentils (about 1 1/4 cups;
   see "Le Puy Lentils," page 412)

1/4 cup chopped flat-leaf parsley
Lemon wedges or red wine vinegar for
   serving (optional)

1. **Heat the oven to 325 degrees.**

2. **Trimming the lamb shanks:** If a tough white leathery outer layer (referred to as the fell) covers the shanks, trim this away by inserting a thin knife under it to loosen and peeling back the layer. Remove any excess fat as well, but don't fuss with trying to peel off any of the thin membrane—this holds the shank together and will melt down during braising.

3. **Browning the lamb shanks:** Heat the oil in a large Dutch oven or other heavy lidded braising pot (6- to 7-quart) over medium heat. Season the lamb shanks all over with salt and pepper. Brown them in two batches (so as not to crowd the pan), turning with tongs to sear all sides and form a ruddy reddish brown crust, a total of about 12 minutes per batch. Transfer the shanks to a platter, without stacking them.

4. **The aromatics:** Pour off all but 2 tablespoons of fat from the pot. Add the onion, carrots, and celery, toss to coat the vegetables with the fat, and cook, stirring occasionally, until browned in spots, about 8 minutes. Lower the heat to medium, add the garlic, and cook, stirring once or twice, for 2 minutes. Stir in the curry powder, 1 tablespoon of the fresh thyme (or 1 teaspoon if using dried), and 1 bay leaf and cook for 1 minute. Stir in the tomatoes and stock, raise the heat to high, and bring to a boil. Stir a few times, scraping the bottom of the pot with a wooden spoon to dislodge any tasty caramelized bits, and boil for 4 to 5 minutes to meld the flavors.

5. **The braise:** Return the lamb shanks to the pot, along with any accumulated juices on the platter: overlap the shanks as necessary so that they fit snugly. When the liquid returns to a simmer, cover with parchment paper, pressing down so that it almost touches the lamb and the edges extend about an inch over the sides of the pot. Set the lid in place, and place in the lower third of the oven to braise at a gentle simmer. Check the pot after the first 10 to 15 minutes. If the liquid appears to be simmering ferociously, lower the oven heat by 10 or 15 degrees. After 1 hour, turn the lamb shanks over, and if they are stacked on top of one another, move the shanks on the bottom to the top. Continue braising for 1 hour more.

6. **While the lamb braises, parcook the lentils:** Place the lentils in a saucepan with 6 cups of water, the remaining 1/2 tablespoon (or 1/2 teaspoon) thyme, the remaining bay leaf, and 1/2 teaspoon salt. Bring to a boil, lower the heat, and simmer for

10 minutes. Drain the lentils and transfer to a plate, leaving the bay leaf with the lentils. Spread them out to stop the cooking and to cool, and set aside.

7.   **Braising the lentils with the lamb:** When the lamb shanks have braised for 2 hours, transfer them to a platter. Skim the fat from the braising liquid with a wide spoon and discard. Stir in the lentils, and return the lamb shanks to the pot. Cover again with parchment and the lid, return the pot to the oven, and continue braising the lamb and lentils together at a gentle simmer for another 30 to 45 minutes, or until the lamb is fork-tender and the lentils are soft but with a slight bit of resistance remaining.

8.   **The finish:** Transfer the lamb shanks to a platter to catch any juices, and cover loosely with foil to keep warm. Taste the lentils and braising liquid for salt and pepper. Remove and discard the bay leaves. Spoon the lentils and liquid into a deep serving dish and nestle the lamb shanks in the lentils. Pour any juices that accumulated on the platter over the lamb, sprinkle the dish with the parsley, and serve. Pass lemon wedges or red wine vinegar at the table, if desired.

Le Puy Lentils

The small deep-colored Le Puy lentils grown in the volcanic soils near the town of Le Puy in the center of France are worth seeking out. These special lentils, which have a mottled dark sage–bluish hue, taste much better and more distinctive than the standard khaki-green lentils from the supermarket. Le Puy lentils also hold their shape when cooked, remaining pleasantly chewy and not at all mushy or muddy looking. Look for Le Puy lentils at gourmet or specialty food stores (or see Sources, page 456).

Mist Grill Minted Lamb Shanks →→

My friend Steve Schimoler is one of those big-guy rock-and-roll chefs who spends a lot of time trying to amp up the flavor of everything—and he typically succeeds. When these lamb shanks appeared on a spring menu at his restaurant, The Mist Grill, in Waterbury, Vermont, I couldn't for the life of me figure out how he got such a deep mint flavor into the meat. So I asked. He starts by making a brine with salt, sugar, and an enormous amount of fresh mint. As the shanks bob around in the brine for two days, they take on an intense mint flavor and become incredibly juicy. Once brined, the shanks are seared and then braised in a bit of the mint brine, some shallots, and dry white vermouth. In Steve's words, "These rock."

At his restaurant, Steve pulls the meat off the bone and arranges it in a chefy tower, layering in caramelized onions and fennel. At home, I prefer to present an individual shank on each plate leaned up against a mound of rustic smashed potatoes or a puree of fresh green peas.

wine notes

Cabernet Sauvignon from California, Australia, or Chile will complement the assertive mint flavor.

Working Ahead

To get the full flavor of the mint, the shanks need 2 days brining time (Steps 1 and 2).

Serves 4 | Braising Time: about 2 ¹/₂ hours

4 meaty lamb shanks (about 1 pound
   each)

$1/4$ cup sugar

$1/4$ cup coarse salt

2 leafy bunches fresh mint (6 to 7 ounces
   total), preferably peppermint

7 cups water

2 tablespoons extra-virgin olive oil

2 shallots, thinly sliced

1 cup dry white wine or dry white
   vermouth

1. **Trimming the lamb shanks—2 days ahead:** If the shanks are covered with a tough parchment-like outer layer (referred to as the fell), trim this away by inserting a thin knife under it to loosen and peeling back the layer. Remove any excess fat as well, but don't peel off any of the thin membrane—this holds the shank together and will melt down during braising. Put the shanks in a non-reactive bowl or deep dish.

2. **Brining the lamb shanks:** Pluck the mint leaves and tender stems from the bunches (discard the woody stems), and wash and drain them. You should have about 4 cups loosely packed. Select a small stack of the larger leaves to garnish the dish later on, wrap them in a damp paper towel, and refrigerate. Combine the remaining mint, the sugar, and salt in a food processor. Add $1/2$ cup water, and process to a coarse puree. Pour the mint puree over the lamb. Add the remaining 6 $1/2$ cups water to cover the shanks completely. Cover with plastic wrap and refrigerate for 2 days. Give the shanks a stir once during brining to ensure that they brine evenly.

3. **Heat the oven to 300 degrees.**

4. **Removing the lamb shanks from the brine:** Remove the shanks from the brine and pat dry on paper towels; never mind if there are bits of mint stuck to the lamb. Strain the brine, reserving the mint puree. Save 1 cup of the brine, discarding the remainder.

5. **Browning the lamb shanks:** Heat the oil in a Dutch oven or other large braising pot (I like to use an oval 6- to 7-quart pot) over medium-high heat. When the oil shimmers, add the lamb shanks and brown them on all sides, turning with tongs, about 8 minutes total. (If the pot won't hold the shanks without crowding, brown them in batches.) Once the shanks are browned, remove them from the pot and pour off the excess fat. Immediately return the shanks to the pot, scatter over the shallots, and let the shallots brown for a minute.

6. **The braise:** Pour in the wine, and let it boil to reduce by about half over medium-high heat, about 5 minutes. Add the reserved mint puree and 1 cup brine, stir as best you can to spread the mint around, and bring to a boil. Cover the pot with parchment paper, pressing down so the paper nearly touches the lamb and the edges of the paper extend about an inch over the sides of the pot. Set the lid in place, slide the pot onto a rack in the lower third of the oven, and braise at a gentle simmer. After the first 10 to 15 minutes, check that the liquid is simmering peacefully. If it's not, lower the oven temperature 10 to 15 degrees.

Turn the shanks with tongs after an hour, and continue braising until the shanks are fork-tender and pulling away from the bone, about 2 1/2 hours in all.

7.   **The finish:** Transfer the shanks to a platter or tray to catch their juices, and cover loosely with foil to keep warm. Strain the braising liquid through a fine-mesh sieve into a medium saucepan, without pushing down on the mint and shallots; discard the spent mint and shallots. You should have about 1 1/2 cups of liquid. Skim off the surface fat, and taste. If the sauce is not too salty, bring it to a boil over medium-high heat, and boil to reduce by about half, skimming occasionally, 10 to 12 minutes. If it's already plenty salty, set it over low heat to keep warm. The sauce should be salty and minty, but not too much so. (This is not a sauce you liberally spoon over the meat or pass at the table; a few spoonfuls to moisten the meat is all you want.)

8.   **Serving:** Meanwhile, retrieve the reserved mint leaves from the refrigerator and slice them crosswise into thin shreds. Sprinkle the mint on the shanks, spoon a bit of sauce on top, and serve.

Moroccan Spice-Rubbed Lamb Shoulder Chops ⇥

I've lived in Vermont long enough (on and off for twenty-five years) to know that we Vermonters eat more lamb than people in other parts of the country—a fact that I'm quite happy about. Our fondness for the sweet, musky taste of lamb stems back to a long tradition of sheep farming, but I like to think it persists simply because we appreciate lamb's goodness.

In eating a lot of lamb over the years, I've developed an undying fondness for lamb shoulder chops. Less expensive than rib or loin chops, shoulder chops provide a richness that the more delicate chops can't match. Shoulder chops also contain a high amount of collagen (the gnarly connective tissue that makes meat tough), which means that you need to slow-braise them in order to render them tender.

The seasonings here are borrowed from Moroccan cuisine, where lamb plays a central role and cooks know just how well this flavorful meat marries with a pungent blend of spices. The most famous Moroccan spice blend, called *ras el hanout,* can contain anywhere from ten or twenty to as many as fifty spices or more. I've come up with a manageable version using about a dozen of the most characteristic spices. When toasted, ground, and rubbed onto the lamb chops, this spice blend permeates the dish with a wonderful warming fragrance both exotic and familiar. If you're a fan of spice rubs, as I am, you might consider doubling or tripling the amounts in order to have leftovers for another day. It's fabulous on beef and chicken as well. A side dish of couscous would be perfect.

wine notes

Deeply flavored Grenache-Syrah blend from the southern Rhone Valley, California, or Australia.

In order to infuse the lamb with the full flavor of the spices, you need to prepare the spice mix and rub it on the chops 12 to 24 hours before braising.

Serves 4 | *Braising Time: about 1 1/4 hours*

THE SPICE RUB

1/2 teaspoon fennel seeds

1/4 teaspoon coriander seeds

1/4 teaspoon black peppercorns

1/4 teaspoon allspice berries

3/4 teaspoon coarse salt

1/2 teaspoon ground ginger

1/4 teaspoon freshly grated nutmeg

1/4 teaspoon ground cinnamon

1/4 teaspoon ground cloves

Pinch of ground turmeric

Pinch of cayenne

THE BRAISE

4 bone-in lamb shoulder chops (1 3/4 to 2 pounds total), at least 3/4 inch thick

2 tablespoons unsalted butter

1 large yellow onion (about 8 ounces), sliced 1/3 inch thick

Large pinch of saffron threads

Coarse salt

2 garlic cloves, minced

1 cup lamb, veal, or chicken stock, homemade (page 452, 451, or 448) or store-bought

Freshly ground black pepper

1. **The spice rub—12 to 24 hours in advance:** Combine the fennel, coriander, peppercorns, and allspice in a small skillet. Heat over medium heat, shaking the pan frequently, until the spices become mildly fragrant, 3 to 4 minutes. Let cool briefly. Transfer the spices to a mortar or spice grinder, and grind the toasted spices to a coarse powder. Add the salt, ginger, nutmeg, cinnamon, cloves, turmeric, and cayenne and grind briefly to combine.

   Dust the lamb chops on both sides with the spice rub, patting and rubbing them so that the spices adhere and cover them thoroughly. Lay the chops in a single layer on a plate or dish, cover loosely with waxed paper or plastic, and refrigerate for 12 to 24 hours.

2. **Heat the oven to 300 degrees.**

3. **Browning the lamb chops:** Melt 1 tablespoon of the butter in a large heavy-bottomed ovenproof skillet or other shallow braising pan (12-inch) over medium heat. Add the chops in one layer and brown well on both sides, turning once with tongs, about 5 minutes per side. Transfer to a large plate, without stacking, to catch any juices; set aside.

4. **The aromatics and braising liquid:** Lower the heat to medium-low, add the remain-

ing tablespoon of butter to the pan, and wait for it to melt. Add the onion and stir to coat with the butter. Crumble the saffron threads against the palm of one hand, letting the pieces fall into the onions. Season with a pinch of salt, and cook gently until the onions have taken on the color of saffron and softened but still have some bite, 8 to 10 minutes. Add the garlic and cook for another minute, until the garlic becomes fragrant. Add the stock, increase the heat to medium-high, and bring to a simmer. Stir and scrape the bottom of the pan with a wooden spoon to dislodge any precious cooked-on bits that will enhance the flavor of the braise. Simmer for 3 to 4 minutes to meld the flavors.

5. **The braise:** Return the lamb chops to the pan, and spoon some of the onions over the chops to partially smother them. Place a sheet of parchment paper over the pan, pressing down so that it nearly touches the lamb and the edges extend about an inch over the sides of the pan. Then cover tightly with a lid or heavy-duty foil and slide it onto a rack in the lower third of the oven. Check the pan after 10 minutes or so to see that the liquid is simmering gently. If it's not, lower the oven temperature 10 to 15 degrees. Continue to braise, turning the chops once with tongs after about 30 minutes, until the meat is fork-tender and falling away from the bone, 1 hour and 15 to 20 minutes.

6. **The finish:** Transfer the chops to a plate or tray to catch the juices, and cover loosely with foil to keep warm. Spoon off the surface fat from the braising liquid with a large spoon and discard. (Lamb can be quite fatty, so don't be surprised if there's quite a lot to skim. If you like to use a gravy separator, this is a good opportunity to do so.) Set the pan over medium-high heat and bring to a rapid simmer. (If you're using a skillet, drape a towel or pot holder over the handle to remind yourself that it's extremely hot.) Simmer the juices for 1 to 2 minutes to reduce and concentrate the flavor. Skim any remaining fat that coalesces on the surface of the sauce. Taste for salt and pepper. Arrange the chops on plates and spoon the onion sauce on top.

Herb-Stuffed Leg of Lamb Braised in Red Wine →→

Boneless leg of lamb makes a reliable main course for a sit-down dinner party.
It's elegant, it's not at all fussy to cook, and it carves as neatly as a loaf of bread.
But if all you've ever done is roasted leg, you owe it to yourself (and your guests)
to try braising it. As much as I adore rosy-pink roasted lamb, nothing matches
the succulence of a braised leg of lamb. I roll the boned lamb up around a simple stuffing of herbs, garlic, and shallots to add flavor and color to the meat.
And, the best part: the strained braising liquid turns instantly into a wonderful
meaty sauce that tastes as good as something you'd get in a fine restaurant.
(Plus, it gives you an excuse to dust off that old gravy boat.)

Most markets carry boned and rolled leg of lamb. In order to stuff the
lamb, you'll need to slip off the netting or untie the butcher twine that holds it
together. Then it's simply a matter of rolling it back into a cylinder and tying it
up with kitchen string after stuffing. If you have a butcher who does bone the
lamb for you, ask him to saw or chop the bones into 1-inch pieces so you can
add them to the braising pan. They will add flavor and body to the sauce.

Serve with a creamy potato gratin and buttered green beans.

wine notes

One of the classic Cabernet Sauvignon-dominated Bordeaux appellations, such as St.-Julien, Margaux,
or Pauillac; or a fine, aged Cabernet or Cabernet-blend from California, Washington State, or
Australia.

Working Ahead

The lamb can be seasoned, rolled, tied, covered, and refrigerated up to 18 hours before braising
(Steps 1 and 2).

Serves 6 to 8 | Braising Time: 2 to 2 1/2 hours

One 5-pound boneless leg of lamb (plus
reserved bones, sawed or chopped
into 1-inch pieces; optional)

Coarse salt and freshly ground black
pepper

THE STUFFING

1/2 cup chopped flat-leaf parsley, stems
reserved

2 tablespoons chopped fresh thyme, mint,
rosemary, and/or sage (in any
combination)

1 shallot, finely chopped

2 garlic cloves, minced

1/4 teaspoon ground allspice

THE BRAISE

2 tablespoons extra-virgin olive oil

1 large yellow onion (about 8 ounces),
coarsely chopped

2 large carrots, coarsely chopped

2 tablespoons tomato paste

1 teaspoon chopped fresh thyme, mint,
rosemary, and/or sage (the same
combination you used in the stuffing)

2 bay leaves

Reserved parsley stems from the stuffing,
torn into 4-inch lengths

1 cup dry red wine

2 cups lamb, veal, or chicken stock,
homemade (page 452, 451, or 448) or
store-bought

1. **Trimming the lamb:** Open the lamb out flat, fat side down, on your work surface. If there are any especially thick spots, make a lengthwise incision with a knife, without cutting through the meat, and lay it open like a book. You want to get the meat as even in thickness as possible while keeping it intact. Season the cut side generously with salt and pepper.

2. **The stuffing:** In a small bowl, combine the parsley, mixed herbs, shallot, garlic, and allspice. Stir until evenly mixed together.

3. **Stuffing and shaping the lamb:** Spread the stuffing over the cut side of the leg of lamb with a rubber spatula. Press the stuffing into the meat with your hands to make it adhere, and spread it around so that it covers the entire inside surface. Roll the lamb up into a cylinder, and tie it neatly and snugly with kitchen string (see "Tying a Roast Before Braising," page 258). Season the outside of the meat with salt and pepper. (*The lamb can be prepared to this point and refrigerated for up to 18 hours before braising. When you are ready to braise the lamb, remove it from the refrigerator, and let it sit at room temperature while you heat the oven.*)

4. **Heat the oven to 325 degrees.**

5.   **Browning the lamb:** Add the oil to a heavy lidded Dutch oven or braising pan just large enough to hold the lamb (5-quart), and heat it over medium-high heat until it shimmers. Lower the lamb into the pot with tongs, and brown it evenly, turning to brown all sides, until mahogany in spots but not at all burnt, 10 to 12 minutes total. Transfer the lamb to a platter. Add the bones to the pot if you have them, and brown them as best you can without charring, turning them every 4 minutes, for about 12 minutes. Set aside with the lamb. Pour off all but about 1 tablespoon of fat from the pot. If the bottom is at all blackened, wipe those bits out with a damp paper towel, doing your best to leave behind the caramelized juices.

6.   **The aromatics and braising liquid:** Return the pot to medium-high heat, add the onion and carrots, and sauté, stirring, until beginning to brown, about 4 minutes. Add the tomato paste and stir it in with a wooden spoon so it coats the carrots and onions. Add the teaspoon of herbs, the bay leaves, and parsley stems. Pour in the wine and bring to a boil, stirring and scraping with the spoon to dislodge all those wonderful caramelized bits stuck to the bottom of the pot from browning the lamb. Boil to reduce the wine by about half, about 2 minutes. Pour in the stock and bring to a boil. Continue to boil, stirring occasionally, for 4 minutes allowing the flavors to meld.

7.   **The braise:** Return the lamb to the pot, along with any juices that have seeped from the meat, and tuck the bones, if using, around the meat. Cover with a piece of parchment paper, pressing down so the paper nearly touches the meat and the edges extend over the sides of the pot by about an inch. Then put the lid in place, and slide the pot onto a rack in the lower third of the oven. After about 15 minutes, check to see that the liquid is simmering gently, not aggressively. If it's simmering too vigorously, lower the oven heat 10 or 15 degrees. Continue to braise, turning the lamb with tongs and basting once or twice, until the meat is fork-tender and cooked through, 2 to 2 1/2 hours.

8.   **The finish:** Transfer the lamb to a carving board with a moat or platter to catch the juices, and cover loosely with foil to keep warm. Strain the pan juices into a saucepan, and skim off and discard excess fat—there may be as much as 1/2 cup, so it's a good chance to use your gravy separator, if you have one. Bring the sauce to a boil and simmer for 5 minutes to concentrate the flavor and thicken it some. Taste: if it tastes too brothy, boil for another 3 or 4 minutes. Taste again for salt and pepper.

9.   **Serving:** Remove the string from the lamb, pour any juices that have accumulated on the carving board into the sauce, and carve the lamb into 1/2-inch slices. Arrange the slices on dinner plates or a serving platter, and pour over enough sauce to moisten. Pass the remaining sauce at the table.

Braised Lamb Shoulder Roll with Fennel, Ginger & Orange Compote ✈

The combination of lamb and fennel evokes images of the sunny Mediterranean, and I've always loved cooking the two together. The only problem is that fresh fennel doesn't have the fortitude to stand up to a long braise. If it is added to the pot with the other aromatics, its sweet flavor dissipates before the meat becomes tender. To solve this problem, I make a fennel compote with a bit of ginger and orange and roll it up inside the lamb. This protects the fennel from the braising liquid and allows its flavor to work its way into the meat as well. The lamb makes a great centerpiece for a sit-down dinner, redolent with the aroma of fennel, orange, and just a hint of ginger.

Not all markets carry boneless lamb shoulder, so you may have to call ahead. If so, ask the butcher to saw or chop the bones into 1-inch pieces so you can add them to the braising pan. They'll improve the flavor and body of the sauce.

wine notes

Chateauneuf-du-Pape, Gigondas, or Bandol, or other deeply flavored red from the southern Rhone Valley or Provence.

Working Ahead

To allow the flavor of the fennel compote to permeate the meat, make the compote and stuff the lamb 6 to 12 hours before you plan to braise it (Steps 1 through 3).

Serves 4 to 6 | *Braising Time: about 2 1/4 hours*

THE STUFFING

2 tablespoons extra-virgin olive oil

1 small fennel bulb (about 12 ounces), trimmed, cored, and finely chopped, branches reserved

Coarse salt and freshly ground black pepper

2 garlic cloves, finely chopped

1 teaspoon fennel seeds, lightly crushed

1 teaspoon grated orange zest

1 teaspoon grated fresh ginger

1/2 cup dry white wine or dry white vermouth

One 3 1/2-pound boneless lamb shoulder roast (plus reserved bones, sawed or chopped into 1-inch pieces; optional)

Coarse salt and freshly ground black pepper

THE BRAISE

2 tablespoons extra-virgin olive oil

1 heaping cup coarsely chopped reserved fennel branches

1 small yellow onion (about 4 ounces), coarsely chopped

1 celery stalk, coarsely chopped

3 garlic cloves, finely chopped

1-inch piece of ginger, finely chopped

2 strips orange zest, removed with a vegetable peeler (each about 3 inches by 3/4 inch)

1 cup hearty dry red wine, such as Syrah or a Rhone-style blend

1 cup lamb, veal, or chicken stock, homemade (page 452, 451, or 448) or storebought

Coarse salt and freshly ground black pepper

1. **Making the stuffing—6 to 12 hours in advance:** Heat the oil in a medium skillet over medium-high heat. Add the fennel, stir to coat with oil, and season with salt and pepper. Sauté, stirring frequently, until the fennel begins to seethe and sizzle a bit, about 4 minutes. Add the garlic, fennel seeds, orange zest, ginger, and wine, stir, cover, and reduce the heat to medium. Simmer until the fennel is tender, about 20 minutes. Check every 5 minutes to see that the pan isn't dry; if so, add 2 to 3 tablespoons water. Remove the lid, and continue to simmer until all the liquid has evaporated. Set aside to cool.

2. **Trimming and seasoning the lamb:** Unroll the lamb shoulder. Depending on the skill of your butcher, it may or may not hold together in one piece. Trim any large hunks of fat from the meat, but don't trim too radically: the fat will baste the lamb as it braises. Lay the lamb out flat, boned side up. Season the inside of the meat with salt and pepper. At this point, I roll the lamb into a compact cylinder, with no filling, just to get a sense of how it will roll up once I do add the stuffing. Since a boneless shoulder sometimes has holes from

where the bones were removed, this little dry run helps me envision how the cylinder will come together. Don't worry about the holes, the lamb will hold together just fine.

3. **Stuffing and rolling the lamb:** When the fennel has cooled to room temperature, scrape it into a food processor and puree it to a coarse paste. Taste for salt and pepper. Smear the fennel paste over the boned side of the lamb, then roll the meat up as neatly as you can. Secure the roll with kitchen string tied at 2-inch intervals. If the ends are flopping open, wrap another length of string lengthwise around the roll, weaving it up and under the crosswise ties and pulling it snug as well (see "Tying a Roast Before Braising," page 258). Scrape up any fennel puree that has squeezed out and rub it all over the surface of the roll. Set the lamb in a baking dish or on a plate, cover loosely with plastic, and refrigerate for at least 6 hours, or overnight.

4. **Browning the bones and meat:** Heat the broiler to high. If you have the lamb bones, arrange 3 or 4 pieces on a half sheet pan or in a broiler pan (this may leave you with a few leftover bones, which you can reserve for stock). Broil about 4 inches from the broiling element, turning with tongs, until the bones are brown and roasty looking in spots but not charred, about 15 minutes total. Remove from the baking sheet and set aside on a large plate.

    Place the lamb shoulder on the baking sheet or broiler pan and broil about 4 inches from the element until the surface is browned but not charred, about 6 minutes. Turn with tongs and brown the other side, another 6 minutes or so. Set the lamb aside while you prepare the aromatics and braising liquid. Reduce the oven temperature to 300 degrees.

5. **The aromatics and braising liquid:** Heat the oil in a Dutch oven or other braising pot (6-quart) over medium-high heat. Add the chopped fennel branches, onion, and celery and sauté until beginning to soften and take on some bronze color, 10 to 12 minutes. Add the garlic, ginger, and orange zest and sauté until fragrant, about 1 minute. Pour in the wine and simmer until reduced by almost three quarters, about 8 minutes. Add the stock and simmer to reduce by half, another 4 to 5 minutes. Add the browned bones to the pot if you have them, and then settle the lamb shoulder in the center. Depending on the shape and size of the pot, it's usually best to arrange the bones around the perimeter and nestle the meat in the center. Set the pan over low heat while you tend to the drippings on the baking sheet or broiler pan.

6. **Capturing the caramelized drippings:** Pour off and discard the fat from the baking sheet or broiler pan. If the drippings are charred, skip this step and move on to the braise. But if the drippings are caramelized and tasty looking and can be scraped off with a rubber spatula, do so, adding them to the braising pot. If the drippings are cooked on but still not blackened, set the pan over high heat, add ⅓ cup water, and, scraping with a wooden spoon, dissolve the drippings. Boil the liquid down to a few tablespoons and add to the pot.

7.   **The braise:** Cover the pot with parchment paper, pressing down so it nearly touches the lamb and the edges extend about an inch over the sides of the pot, then set the lid in place. Slide the pot onto a rack in the lower part of the oven and braise at a gentle simmer, turning the lamb once after 1 hour, until the meat is fork-tender, about 2 hours and 15 minutes. Check on the lamb after the first 15 minutes or so to see that the liquid is not simmering wildly. If it is, reduce the oven temperature by 10 or 15 degrees.

8.   **The finish:** Lift the lamb carefully from the braising liquid with tongs and a spatula or wooden spoon, and set it on a cutting board or platter to catch the juices. Cover loosely with foil to keep warm. Strain the braising liquid into a medium saucepan, pressing down on the aromatics (and bones) to extract as much liquid as you can, then discard them. Skim off as much surface grease from the braising liquid as you can with a wide spoon, and evaluate the sauce: if it tastes thin or needs more body, set the saucepan over medium-high heat and reduce the sauce for 5 to 10 minutes. Season with salt and pepper.

9.   **Serving:** Remove the strings from the lamb and carve into thick slices. Ladle some sauce over each serving and pass more sauce at the table.

Seven-Hour Leg of Lamb ⇥

Seven hours seems like a long time to cook anything, but in this instance the results are worth every minute. In France, where I first encountered this dish, they refer to it as *gigot à la cuillère*, "leg of lamb with a spoon," which is the only tool you need to "carve" the meat after braising. Fall-apart-tender doesn't even begin to describe the almost velvety texture of the meat, not to mention its tremendous flavor. The vegetables that braise alongside the lamb turn glossy and soft, yet miraculously retain their shape. I like the combination of small onions, turnips, and carrots, but you can add and subtract as you like. I sometimes add celery stalks cut into 4-inch lengths or fennel bulbs cut into fat wedges.

One of the best parts about this recipe is the way the aromas seep out of the oven rather subtly after a few hours and then build into a tantalizing crescendo by the time the lamb is ready. It's ideal for a feast, since it serves a crowd and all the work is done early. The braised lamb and flavor-soaked vegetables are certainly hearty enough to satisfy any appetite, but if it's a grandiose holiday gathering, you'll want to add your favorite seasonal side dishes. I like Sweet Braised Whole Scallions (page 92), buttered English peas with fresh mint, and a golden potato gratin. Soft dinner rolls to sop up the juices are a must.

wine notes

Bordeaux, or a big California Cabernet Sauvignon (or Merlot) with five or more years of age.

Serves 8 to 12 | *Braising Time: 6 to 7 hours*

One 6- to 8-pound bone-in leg of lamb
(see "Shopping for Bone-in Leg of
Lamb," page 428)
Coarse salt and freshly ground black
pepper
1 cup dry white wine or dry white
vermouth
2 cups lamb, beef, or chicken stock,
homemade (page 452, 450, or 448) or
store-bought
2 bay leaves

2 tablespoons chopped fresh thyme or
2 teaspoons dried
15 garlic cloves, peeled and smashed
1 cup chopped canned peeled tomatoes,
juice reserved
8 golf ball–sized yellow onions (about
2 pounds total), peeled
6 carrots, cut crosswise in half and then
halved lengthwise into fat sticks
6 medium turnips (about 1 1/2 pounds
total), peeled and halved

1. **Heat the broiler on high.**

2. **Trimming the lamb:** If there is a whitish dry parchment layer on the top side of the lamb (known as the fell), trim it off by inserting a thin knife under it to loosen and peeling back this layer. Trim any excessively thick layers of fat from the outside of the lamb, but don't be overly fastidious, and certainly don't cut into the meat. You want to leave a thin layer of fat to protect the meat as it braises. Season the lamb all over with salt and pepper, and place it in a large roasting pan.

3. **Browning the lamb:** Slide the lamb under the broiler and broil until the fat begins to sizzle and the surface of the lamb takes on a speckled brown appearance, 5 to 10 minutes. Turn the lamb by grabbing the shank end with a thick dish towel, and broil the other side, another 5 to 10 minutes. Remove the pan from the broiler and turn the oven down to 275 degrees.

4. **Deglazing the roasting pan and building the braising liquid:** Transfer the lamb to a baking sheet or tray, and pour off as much fat as you can from the roasting pan without pouring off any meaty brown bits of caramelized juices. Set the roasting pan over one or two burners set on high, add the wine, and bring it to a boil. Boil until the wine is reduced by about half, about 5 minutes. Add the stock, bay leaves, thyme, garlic, and tomatoes with their juice, and bring to a boil.

5. **The braise:** Return the lamb to the roasting pan, lower the heat to medium-high, and bring the liquid back to a simmer. Scatter the onions, carrots, and turnips around the meat. Cover the roasting pan tightly with heavy-duty foil and place on a rack in the lower third of the oven. Braise the lamb for 6 to 7 hours, gently turning it over every 2 hours (use tongs, two slotted spoons, or two metal spatulas), until the meat is butter-tender and falling off the bone. If you worry that your oven runs at all hot, lower the heat to 265 degrees after the first 2 hours. It's good assurance that the lamb won't cook too quickly.

6. **The finish:** Carefully transfer the lamb and vegetables to a platter with two slotted spoons. The shank bone may slip right out, and the lamb will no longer hold together well at this point, so don't worry if things seem to be coming apart. Cover the platter with foil to keep warm. Pour the pan juices into a wide saucepan and let sit for a minute, then skim off most of the fat with a large spoon. (Alternatively, pour the pan juices into a gravy separator. Once they settle, pour the juices into a wide saucepan, leaving the clear fat behind.) There may be as much as, or more than, 1/2 cup of fat to remove. Bring the juices to a simmer over medium heat, and skim a bit more as the remaining fat coalesces on the surface. Once the sauce is skimmed to your liking, taste it. Every time I make this, the first taste of sauce makes me nearly swoon—and it needs no seasoning at all. If you do find it lacking, by all means season with salt and pepper as needed.

7. **Serving:** Spoon some warm juices over the lamb and vegetables. You won't need to carve the lamb, because it will be collapsing. Instead, serve it with a meat fork and large spoon, putting a few vegetables on each plate and spooning over a bit more sauce.

Shopping for Bone-in Leg of Lamb

A whole leg of lamb consists of a series of connected bones: hip bone, thigh bone, and shank. More and more, I find that markets are selling lamb legs with the uppermost of the three bones, the hip bone, removed. This is advantageous to anyone roasting a leg of lamb, because carving around the convoluted hip bone can be a real challenge. With Seven-Hour Leg of Lamb, however, it makes no difference, since the meat falls from the bone during braising and makes carving a nonissue.

If the hip bone has been removed, some markets refer to the leg as "semiboneless." If you come across a lamb leg with the hip bone in place (there will be a wide blade-shaped bone at the wide end of the leg), go ahead and leave it in place and proceed as directed. A fully bone-in lamb leg will weigh closer to 7 or 8 pounds.